SOCIAL INEQUALITY IN AUSTRALIA

DISCOURSES, REALITIES AND FUTURES

○

SECOND
EDITION

○

DAPHNE HABIBIS
MAGGIE WALTER

OXFORD
UNIVERSITY PRESS
AUSTRALIA & NEW ZEALAND

OXFORD
UNIVERSITY PRESS

Oxford University Press is a department of the University of Oxford.
It furthers the University's objective of excellence in research,
scholarship, and education by publishing worldwide. Oxford is a registered
trademark of Oxford University Press in the UK and in certain other countries.

Published in Australia by
Oxford University Press
253 Normanby Road, South Melbourne, Victoria 3205, Australia

National Library of Australia Cataloguing-in-Publication entry

Author: Habibis, Daphne, author.
Title: Social inequality in Australia : discourses, realities and futures / Daphne Habibis,
    Maggie Walter.
Edition: 2nd edition.
ISBN: 9780195525410 (paperback)
Notes: Includes bibliographical references and index.
Subjects: Equality—Australia.
Other Authors/Contributors: Walter, Maggie, author.
Dewey Number: 305.50994

Edited by Kirsten Rawlings
Text design by Sardine Design
Typeset by diacriTech, Chennai, India
Proofread by Mei Yen Chua
Indexed by Frances Paterson
Cover image by Getty Images / James Lauritz
Printed and bound in Australia by Ligare Book Printers Pty Ltd

Brief Contents

Extended Contents

List of Figures

List of Tables

Acknowledgments

We would like to thank Susan Banks, Dr Di Heckenberg and Fiona Proudfoot at the School of Social Sciences at the University of Tasmania for their invaluable research assistance. Thanks also to the staff at Oxford University Press for their always helpful contributions: development editor Victoria Kerr and editors Jennifer Butler and Kirsten Rawlings.

Introduction

In preparing the second edition of this book, what is striking is the extent to which the trends we identified in the opening decade of the twenty-first century have become stronger despite changes in the political landscape. Australia is following global trends in the growth of inequality, and the barriers facing disadvantaged groups are growing as state support becomes less available, more tightly regulated and claimants are subject to more stringent expectations. At the end of 2007, when we completed writing the first edition of the book, John Howard's Coalition Government gave way to Kevin Rudd's Labor one. As we go to press on this edition, in 2014, the wheel has turned full circle and another Coalition Government is in power. In the period between the two editions the global financial crisis took place, and, although Australia bore the shock better than most nations, unemployment increased and, with it, an increase in poverty. Although there are important differences between Labor and Liberal policies, in many areas they are markedly similar. This may help to explain why our updated analyses show that, overall, neither Labor nor Liberal have succeeded in creating a more egalitarian nation.

At the heart of this book is the question of what kind of nation we want Australia to be. It shows that our response to global trends is creating an increasing disparity between the haves and have-nots. The book provides an examination of the contours of social inequality in Australia in the opening decades of the twenty-first century, using empirical analysis to raise questions about contemporary welfare discourses which support increasingly punitive approaches to disadvantaged social groups. We argue that while some aspects of the arrangements for social inequality have been remarkably static, they are undergoing significant transformation and that this has been accompanied by changes in societal and political values, explanations and beliefs about why inequality exists and what we should do about it. These two processes, the realities and the discourses, are not disconnected but, rather, are mutually constituting. How a nation and its citizens understand the arrangements for social hierarchy, its extent, causes and effects are closely tied to the political arrangements that shape its actual formation. What appears to be an objective process, tied to global trends, is socially constructed, with the policies formulated and implemented by the state, which plays a central role.

The term 'social inequality' has many meanings but at its most fundamental it is concerned with the distribution of social, economic and political resources and the impact these have on individuals and collectives. It can only be understood in relation to its opposite, social equality. The question of how much inequality should exist within a nation is fundamentally a moral one. There is no objective source to provide guidance, or some external benchmark against which reality can be judged, only arguments about the relative merits of greater or lesser egalitarianism. Contrary to assumptions that there is something inevitable about inequality and only so much that can be done about it, the evidence shows that the nature and extent of inequality arises from human actions, with public opinion, influential stakeholders and the state critical to the forms it takes. Social inequality is constructed by the past and present actions of individuals and by institutional arrangements, making our values and choices critical to its formation and sustainment.

Australia today is a nation undergoing immense change. Globalisation continues to have a profound impact on contemporary social arrangements, with both direct and indirect effects on social divisions within Australian society. The pendulum swing between greater and lesser inequality seems to have become fixed towards the inequality end of the continuum. The picture is complex, but *Social Inequality in Australia* provides some of the evidence that supports this claim. This growth in inequality is not occurring without public debate and resistance but the political context is one of a strong neoliberal discourse that argues against government interference in social and economic affairs and in favour of market principles as the main distributive mechanism within society. The strength of neoliberal discourse is evident in the cultural sphere, where the emphasis on individual achievement and the end of the age of entitlement is justified on the grounds of the importance of being competitive and an assumption that social position is the result of the unequal distribution of ability and effort. Although this discourse has continuities with arguments from an earlier era about the benefits of inequality and its causes in individual failure, today its roots lie in wider processes of individualisation that are linked to globalisation and which give it worrying power.

Part of the explanation for the strengthening of anti-egalitarian discourses is that inequality itself is increasingly individualised. Detraditionalisation has undermined collective sources of identity, such as class. In obscuring underlying collective arrangements that fix some social groups at the lower ends of social hierarchies, societal understandings of the causes of inequality are also individualised. This masks the visibility of the obstacles to improvement that some groups face, such as differences in access to quality health care, so that the causes of disadvantage are seen to be personal.

These trends towards greater inequality, and greater acceptance of it as a necessary feature of twenty-first century nations at the forefront of development, create a need for greater attention and public discussion. The shift away from more egalitarian discourses has worrying implications for the future of inequality in Australia. Located firmly on the egalitarian side of the argument, *Social Inequality in Australia* is an attempt to contribute to that debate.

Australia: Prosperous and unequal

To be a citizen of Australia today is to occupy a place of immense privilege. In 2013 the Human Development Index ranked Australia as the second-most-developed nation in the world; only Norway was more advantaged (United Nations Development Program 2013). According to the UN, Australians enjoy longer and healthier lives, have a better standard of living and better access to knowledge and education than almost every one of the 187 nations that comprised the 2012 index.

This enviable position has occurred in the context of the long period of prosperity Australia has enjoyed for over two decades. Despite the global financial crisis, which has caused so much suffering in other nations, Australia has experienced economic growth every single year since 1991. Unemployment is relatively low and most people are able to access work. The majority of Australians live comfortable lives. We also rank high on life satisfaction (OECD 2014). Yet alongside this rosy picture there are signs of a nation that is becoming increasingly divided into the privileged and the disadvantaged. Australia is in danger of becoming a nation of winners and losers (Leigh 2013; Rowse & Groot 2007; Schultz 2007). In the midst of great wealth there are some people who are doing it hard and who risk forming a new poor alongside the old poor, who have never gone away. The most visible of these groups are Australia's Indigenous people, whose position on almost every measure of development and well-being remains stubbornly low. Although there have been some improvements in some areas of health and education, levels of criminalisation continue to increase and Indigenous people remain the most likely, of all Australians, to be living in poverty, with limited access to adequate housing, employment and education. Despite decades of state policies aimed at improving Indigenous living standards, many Indigenous people still live in third-world conditions.

Although not comparable to the situation of the Indigenous population, there are also many other Australians for whom life is far from comfortable. While the wealth of those at the top has expanded greatly in recent years, the benefits have not trickled down very far. The living standards of ordinary Australians have improved but they have done so modestly, outstripped by the growth in salaries and share portfolios of the wealthy. The top 20 per cent of people have seventy-one times as much wealth as the bottom 20 per cent. They have five times more income. Australia's seven wealthiest individuals hold more wealth than the 1.73 million individuals who form the bottom 20 per cent (Richardson & Denniss 2014:2). As the cost of housing soars and the availability of affordable rental property shrinks, low income is exacerbated by the crisis in affordable housing. Many young people are locked out of the home ownership market, which is threatening Australia's status as a nation of home owners. Housing stress is growing as a result of excessive mortgage or rental payments. This, coupled with the availability of easy credit, has created an explosion in household debt.

These trends are reflected in contradictory accounts of how we are faring as a nation. Authors such as Tim Rowse and Murray Groot (2007) and politicians such as Andrew Leigh (2013) present an image of a deeply divided nation, with one part living a life of privilege and luxury in the city centres and wealthy suburbs while the other part lives on the margins in suburbs of vulnerability and disadvantage, forgotten until they erupt in disorder. This image contrasts with portrayals by authors such as Adam Creighton (2014), who suggests that poverty is a lifestyle choice and that claims of large numbers of people living in poverty are a 'charade' promoted by the 'welfare lobby'. The differences in these accounts are based on more than contradictory indicators about where the nation is headed and relate to disagreements about the kind of society we should become and the causes of advantage and disadvantage in postindustrial economies.

To understand these divergent interpretations it is necessary to place them in the context of the transformations that have taken place in Australia since the 1970s. At that time, Australia's political system was variously described as corporatist (Dean & Hindess 1998) or liberal-democratic (Esping-Andersen 1990). State intervention was widespread and included the regulation of the economy through centralised systems of tariff protection and arbitration, which ensured that the interests of capital and labour were well represented. High tariffs protected capital against overseas competition while industrial relations arbitration ensured that workers received a living wage. State-run services maintained the affordability of essential facilities, such as telecommunications, transport, gas and electricity. Welfare included a safety net for the unemployed, provision of low-cost housing for low-income groups, a universal system of free education that extended to tertiary level and a universal system of health care. Some of these arrangements had been laid down at the time of federation, but many were relatively new imports from European systems of welfare.

The nation was also undergoing a process of global transformation whose impact on social structure became more visible in the 1970s. Karl Marx's prescient observation in *The Communist Manifesto* that as capitalism developed 'all that is solid melts into the air' (1998 [1848]) proved prophetic. Until the second half of the twentieth century, class, gender and ethnicity were strong predictors of a person's future life, but this gave way to a more fluid system in which legal and social barriers to social mobility dissolved so that individuals had to choose how they wanted to live their lives. The state also retreated from the protective, balancing role it had developed in the latter half of the twentieth century. The nineteenth-century philosophy of laissez-faire re-emerged in the 1990s in the guise of neoliberalism, which became the dominant political and economic philosophy around which mainstream political parties organised themselves. In this model the state divests its responsibility for direct provision of care of its citizens, leaving this to market forces and expecting individuals to pay their own way with minimal state support.

In this new hands-off regime, trade barriers were reduced or dismantled and the centralised bargaining system was gradually wound down through the introduction of increasingly individualised forms of bargaining between workers and employers. The changed economic discourse also saw the state retreat from welfare provision. The wage-earners' welfare state, which had provided a fairly comprehensive safety net to those outside of the workforce and supplemented the income of those within it, diminished as the state's role in welfare became increasingly residual. From treating the welfare of all citizens as core government business, things changed so that welfare provision became increasingly treated not as a right but as a matter of unfortunate necessity. It moved to a tightly targeted system in which only the most vulnerable groups received support. This market orientation was associated with a restriction in public expenditure and increased measures of control, surveillance and review of social security recipients (Wacquant 1999).

The driving force behind these changes is globalisation. The demands of an increasingly connected social world are creating new challenges, risks and opportunities to which governments and citizens must respond. How we address these challenges is shaping the kind of society we will become. In *Globalising Inequalities*, sociologist Jan Pakulski (2004) analyses the impact of globalisation on inequality. He argues that globalisation is associated with complex, sometimes opposing, effects that, in advanced nations, create egalitarian and inegalitarian tendencies. The complexity and diversity of these forces explains the confusing picture of inequality in Australia today and places the nation at a crossroads.

On the international stage, globalisation has been a force for increased democratisation to the extent that economist Francis Fukuyama has argued that liberal democracy is now 'the final form of human government' (1992). The internet, along with social media, has empowered citizens through access to unprecedented levels of information as well as being the means of instant communication to a global audience. This has increased popular participation and provided new opportunities for the scrutiny of business and government. By providing an alternative, instantly accessible source of information and communication, electronic media have increased citizen knowledge and organisational capacity.

But other aspects of globalisation have tipped the balance of power towards elite groups, especially business. The size of business enterprises, their transnational structure and the enormous economic resources they control make them formidable players on the world stage, facilitating their ability to influence politicians and public opinion through direct and indirect pressure. Their economic weight undermines the democratic process, and enables them to manipulate governments towards policies of deregulation. Their global presence also places them beyond the reach of national governments, thereby reducing their exposure to corporate regulation. This increases their profits and minimises the likelihood that governments will implement redistributive taxation regimes through welfare provision. It is this that Pakulski is referring to when he observes that globalisation 'contains not only anti-egalitarian tendencies but also anti-redistributive immunities' (2004:166).

The waxing power of business contrasts with the waning power of labour, where the effects of globalisation have worked in the opposite direction. Globalisation reduces the solidarities of traditional associations, including those based on class. It has opened the labour market to diverse social groups, contributing to the progressive weakening of the trade union movement. The union movement has been an important source of working-class power, enabling it to influence industrial relations and to have some control over the workplace. Through the threat of industrial action the working class was able to resist the demands of capital and to stake its own claims. While its rewards were largely limited to white men, the union movement was the foundation of working-class resistance and of its claim to distributional entitlements. With the decline of trade unions the protections afforded to working people through processes of collective bargaining were weakened, leaving those in the secondary labour market especially exposed. Without these arrangements, groups such as young people, new immigrants and many women risk becoming the new poor.

Globalisation has similarly divergent social and cultural effects. The global expansion of capitalism carries with it individualising tendencies that on the one hand elevate human rights, but on the other create a push towards a new elitism. Respect for the individual has enhanced human rights and provided new opportunities for formerly excluded social groups. Anti-discrimination legislation has removed legal impediments to the equal treatment and participation of women, Indigenous and other ethno-racial groups, those with disabilities, and gay, lesbian, bisexual and transgender groups. Formal barriers to workplace participation have been removed and any form of discrimination is open to legal challenge.

Yet these pushes in the direction of egalitarianism are countered by opposing forces. State and labour market policies construct individuals as active agents, free from structural or situational impediments in making choices about how they will live their lives. As expectations of state provision have declined so have cultural expectations of collective responsibility. State support for disadvantaged groups has become tainted with notions of dependence and claims that welfare saps self-reliance and impacts on the nation's capabilities.

This aspect of individualism is evident in the appearance of arguments about the benefits of elitism and the need to encourage the pursuit of excellence if Australia is to maintain itself in the global economy (Joe Hockey, cited in Morgan 2014). The knowledge economy and the ideal of the clever country lends itself to individualised notions of citizenship. Sociologist Richard Sennett (2006) links this emphasis to the 'new capitalism' that now dominates the global stage. Old capitalism was predicated on the image of large, stable bureaucracies that provided predictable benefits and encouraged a life within institutions. New capitalism requires a highly mobile, innovative and mutable workforce, able and willing to embrace change, new knowledge and new horizons. While this new culture is not bereft of social ties it is associated with a fluidity and openness that runs counter to the collective ideals that pervaded the second half of the twentieth century.

Contemporary Australian elitist discourse is distinct from that of earlier forms. It is posited on a foundation of minimal egalitarianism through residual welfare provision. This legitimates the claim of meritocracy that underpins liberal democracies. Since state support ensures that no one need experience absolute poverty or lack educational opportunity, those who fail are judged to have no one but themselves to blame. If some people work hard and are more capable than others, so goes the argument, why should they not reap the rewards? What justification is there for them to support those less capable and hard-working than themselves (Saunders 2007a)?

This acceptance of the merits of inegalitarianism means that in Australia today inequality is not necessarily viewed as a social blight. In a social system embedded in neoliberal market-based ideologies, inequality is positioned as encouraging individual effort and aspirational ambition. Indeed, journalist Janet Albrechtsen (2007) has argued in *The Australian* that 'Inequality is not a dirty word ... (and) [T]hose trying to convince us that inequality is bad secretly dislike progress. Progress is born of competition and inevitably leads to inequality'. Under this rationale, inequality is not only inevitable, but also a societal positive. With the argument often concentrating on the rich rather than the poor, as Albrechtsen does, the affluent are relabelled as achievers and role models, and personal and corporate profit as wealth generation.

Within the economy, globalisation has provided new opportunities for enrichment but it has also reinforced old divisions and created new ones. The global marketplace offers unprecedented opportunities for wealth creation, unfettered by the regulatory barriers of governments. The well-paid jobs in the knowledge and finance sections of the economy provide those who have the education and cultural knowledge with a cosmopolitan lifestyle and considerable riches. Aspirationalism has become a key descriptor for an Australia in which full employment and high standards of living have generated a focus on materialism and competitive individualism. The extreme liquidity of financial markets has fed this, creating an insatiable demand for consumption, evidenced, for example, in the renovations boom (AMP.NATSEM 2012b).

But the reshaping of the labour market has left many groups out in the cold. The highly advantaged, highly skilled, educated and rewarded primary market is mirrored by an expanded insecure, casualised, low-skilled and low-paid secondary market. The latter is where the more vulnerable social groups are clustered, such as Indigenous people and early school leavers, who formerly would have entered the manufacturing sector as apprentices but are now more likely to work in the service sector in low-skill jobs. The access of many in these groups to the knowledge economy is limited. With limited economic and cultural resources available to them, these groups are the most severely affected by labour-market deregulation. Their employment in the casual sector leaves them especially exposed to economic downturns, to reductions in welfare provision and the lowering of the minimum wage.

Australia's economic prosperity is also heavily dependent on the commodities boom, which is now slowing, making the nation vulnerable to a global slowdown. The effects of global warming on food production, and on the agricultural sector more generally, raise the risk of inflation. This risk is exacerbated by high levels of household debt, declining levels of liquidity and the threat of rising interest rates. Although many of those in the bottom decile of income distribution do not identify as poor or disadvantaged, in the wrong economic circumstances their ability to just get by would be heavily compromised.

The changes that are taking place are tied to social developments so far-reaching that they have blurred the traditional distinctions between Left and Right. If governments fail to respond to the new economic order they run the risk that the nation will become a laggard in the race for development. This explains the attempts of mainstream political parties to capture the middle ground in Australia—both the Liberal–National coalition and Labor have embarked on programs of neoliberal reform. The transformation of the Australian economy and the winding back of the welfare state was begun by the Hawke–Keating Labor Governments, which held office between 1983 and 1996. These trends were accelerated by the Howard Government, which held power until 2007. Although the Rudd–Gillard Labor Government was elected on a more socially responsive agenda, it was accused of campaigning on a 'me too' approach that some argued made its policies indistinguishable from those of the Coalition and explain its electoral defeat in 2013. Both parties emphasise their fiscal conservatism and, although the Labor Party remains committed to preserving the bargaining rights of workers, it is also moving away from a reliance on trade unions as the mainstay of its support.

Despite being constrained by the *realpolitik* of global and national agendas, governments are critical players in how a nation responds to, and manages, pressures for greater or lesser inequality. As trustees of the nation's well-being, their regulatory role and control of the nation's resources has a direct impact on inequality through their redistribution of taxation revenue and the limits and supports they offer to business. Their formulation of social policy also affects how different social groups are constructed by political discourse and this flows through to public perceptions. Pejorative terms such as 'dole bludger' and 'no hoper' carry with them stigmatising effects that create and sustain individualised understandings of social exclusion. The role of the state is, therefore, critical to an understanding of inequality and its future directions.

Existing trends in political discourse and public policy suggest that, as a nation, we are choosing an increasingly inegalitarian direction. It is this perception that is the driving force behind this book. The views of writers such as Peter Saunders and others attached to right-wing think tanks such as the Centre for Independent Studies suggest that people choose to opt out of the new economy, preferring instead a life of marginalisation. Those who are winners, on the other hand, are to be lauded for their choice. This view of the world individualises success, arguing that those who make it into the elite do so through their own efforts and abilities. It suggests that social success and social exclusion are lifestyle options. The other view, which is where this book is positioned, sees social exclusion as an enforced outcome of situations and structures that have subjective and objective dimensions. One important aspect of this, often ignored by supporters of the neoliberal agenda, is that social exclusion carries with it a loss of power, leaving those on the margins with little space to voice their experiences or concerns.

In writing *Social Inequality in Australia* our objective is not to provide definitive answers but to assist informed debate by exploring the contours of inequality in Australia, based on the best available evidence and drawing on contemporary frameworks for understanding how and why it occurs. This is matched by a commitment to principles of social justice that seek to raise moral questions about the direction Australia is taking and to identify some of the risks faced by specific social groups, and by Australian citizens as a whole. We are especially concerned to provide a sustained review of the evidence on the unequal position of Indigenous people, to assist and inform debates about Indigenous life circumstances and the place of Indigenous people within the nation. The impetus for this focus is based in part on the observation that, as a social group, Indigenous people have been largely neglected within mainstream academic studies of inequality in Australia and in part because of the sizeable proportion of the Indigenous population that faces extreme disadvantage.

The conceptual framework of the study

The field of inequality today provides a rich array of approaches and concepts. Terms such as 'intersectionalities', 'complex inequalities', 'social divisions', 'difference', 'positionalities', 'identity' and 'Othering' vie with one another as analytical concepts for understanding the field. This conceptual diversity reflects the divergent and complex forms that inequality takes today and means that we have a large tool kit for interrogating whether and how, in a liquid world (Bauman 2000), ascribed social categories, such as 'woman' or 'Indigenous', can create collective effects that limit individual choice. This means exploring how the full range of cultural, social, economic and political factors intersect to shape existing arrangements. Reviewing the evidence on how structural and cultural barriers operate in areas such as social mobility or on how family change is linked to new forms of poverty, will help us to question assumptions about the causes of inequality and disadvantage.

Our work is directed by five groups of questions:

1 What are the main dimensions of social inequality in contemporary Australian society? How is marginality distributed and what are the causes of this?

2 How are these dimensions changing in the context of globalisation and a postindustrial society?

3 How is the distribution of Australia's social, political, economic and cultural resources reproduced across different social groups? What role does the state play in this?

4 How are subjectivities implicated in the creation of social inequality? What contribution do political and moral discourses make to its sustainment?

5 How does this analysis inform current debates about the kind of society Australia is, and what kind it can or should become?

To garner the empirical data to answer these foundational questions we use a combination of techniques. First, and primarily, we make use of Australian research and topical material such as media articles and commentary. Second, in arenas and sites where the existing data are limited, we undertake our own analysis of contemporary and robust social surveys such as the Household Income and Labour Market Dynamics in Australia (HILDA) survey, the Australian Survey of Social Attitudes (AuSSA) and the Australian Survey of Retirement Attitudes and Motivations (ASRAM). Third, we derive our own interpretation and understanding of some areas via a reanalysis and/or comparative combining of existing statistical sources, such as those from the Australian Bureau of Statistics (ABS) and the Australian Institute of Health and Welfare (AIHW). This three-pronged approach allows us to present a contemporary, unique and evidenced analysis of the current, emerging and changing dimensions and discourses of inequality in Australia.

The main theorist we will use is Pierre Bourdieu because his conceptual framework provides an accessible and effective way of capturing all the spheres of inequality and social division (Bottero 2005). Because we are dealing with secondary data it will not be possible to use his ideas in any rigid sense, but we will draw on his concepts of habitus, and of social, economic and cultural capital. Our use of Bourdieu also signals that we accept that the analysis of inequality needs to take into account both horizontal and hierarchical divisions. While we believe in the enduring significance of class we also acknowledge that it has become individuated and fragmented. We recognise also that consumption forms an important aspect of the expression and maintenance of inequality.

Cultural forces will also be explored through the idea of discourse. Discourses can be defined as ideas, values, beliefs and practices that are, in their expression, implicated in the constitution of social life while concealing their social origin. Discourses assign meaning and causes and, in so doing, act to shape our ways of thinking and reacting to aspects of the social world, including how we think and define social issues or problems. While the term is closely associated with the work of philosopher and social theorist Michel Foucault, our use of it does not imply attachment to Foucauldian theory or any other theory. Instead, it is used loosely to examine the intersection between collective understandings and social outcomes.

Another concept that will be evident in our vocabulary is the idea of clustering inequalities, as part of a framework for capturing how inequality is at once collective and individualised. This term signifies an understanding of social inequalities that have moved beyond the sharp-edged categories of structure, agency or culture, while also indicating solidities such as the extent to which disadvantage is spatially distributed. It conveys the multidimensional aspects of inequality and their overlapping, intersectoral nature. It recognises that there are very real effects of socially and culturally embedded factors that shape social lives while simultaneously acknowledging that their influence is neither equal nor independent; rather, the cultural operates within the social, providing an aura and, to a certain extent, a reality of wider individual choice but within structural boundaries of varying permeability and transparency.

Our theoretical framework therefore assumes that:

- the variables influencing the distribution of social resources are multidimensional and it is never enough to consider the role of a single factor
- these variables impact on one another in complex ways, that is, they are intersectoral, with no one variable likely to have ultimate determining power in shaping the overall distribution of resources
- while we might argue strongly for a particular interpretation of the data, the complex nature of social reality means that our conclusions are necessarily tentative
- individual subjectivities and collective variables such as class count. Although we live in a relatively open and rapidly changing social world, it is both possible and important to demonstrate that there remain observable faultlines in the social fabric of Australia. This means that the choices available to some social groups are different from those available to others and this is integral to the explanation of the social reproduction of inequality.

Organisation of the book

The book is organised into four parts. Part 1 covers the theoretical and historical context for the exploration of the questions that guide this study. Chapter 1 provides the historical context for the development of sociological ideas and debates about the study of social inequality. It explains why the study of social inequality has been reinvigorated and the need for the incorporation of structural as well as cultural accounts. Chapter 2 reviews classical theories of inequality and their modern formulations. It includes the work of contemporary theorists who use Marxist and Weberian models to create maps of the main social divisions within Australia today, and examines debates about how the boundaries between the classes have changed. Chapter 3 provides a detailed analysis of contemporary debates about the study of inequality and the main theoretical frameworks for understanding the three main domains of inequality: class, gender and race. The key theorist for this is Bourdieu.

Part 2 examines the three main spheres of inequality through a combination of theoretical and empirical analyses of the material, political and cultural dimensions of inequality in Australia. Chapter 4 answers the question of what the distribution of economic resources in Australia is and how this impacts on different social groups in the context of global economic restructuring. It examines how sociological frameworks for understanding poverty and social exclusion have developed from relatively straightforward models of economic inequality to more complex multidimensional ones that also take account of agency. Chapter 5 reviews the political dimensions of inequality. It outlines foundational sociological frameworks for the study of power and the relationship between this and other forms of inequality. It explains how the state's response to globalisation is implicated in the sustainment and creation of inequality and the differential impact this has on population groups. It outlines the transition from the welfare state to its postwelfare form, drawing a connection between increasingly punitive approaches to disadvantage and the creation of inequality itself. Chapter 6 examines the cultural sphere. It develops arguments about the role of consumption in social differentiation and reproduction, and highlights how subjectivities are involved in the construction of inequality. Ideas of the 'Other' and stigmatised identities are central to this chapter.

Part 3 considers sites of inequality. It focuses on knowledge, the labour market, the family, place and the body to explore how inequality and division are experienced in daily life. Chapter 7 reviews the nexus between education and technology in a globalised world and the impact on social and economic inequality. It examines how the knowledge economy operates as a reducer or reproducer of inequality, dependent on the equality of access to the education and skills needed to participate in this era of global technologies. Chapter 8 considers the central role of the labour market as a determinant of social resources. It points to its dual role as a vehicle for material prosperity and social mobility and as a reproducer and maintainer of disadvantage and social exclusion. It argues that the labour market's role has specifically Australian dimensions as well as being connected to wider global, social, economic and political changes. Chapter 9 examines the family as a major site of social inequality in contemporary Australia. It points to contradictory frameworks of the family as both a 'zombie category' (Beck 2002) and the bedrock of social organisation. It considers how the risks created by globalisation place pressure on contemporary families and how these impact on different family forms. Chapter 10 considers locational inequality. It explains how the places and spaces Australians occupy shape identity and life choices and how these are implicated in distributional inequalities. It reviews the centrality of home ownership to social well-being in Australia and the importance of state intervention in this area. As well as considering the housing affordability crisis the chapter raises debates about whether the urban environment is becoming more socially segregated, as symbolised by the retreat of the privileged into the secure enclaves of the gated community. It points out that while groups such as Indigenous people, young people and the mentally ill are especially vulnerable to homelessness, housing stress and environmental harm, those on middle and low incomes also face risks to locational security. Chapter 11, the final chapter in this part, focuses on the body as a site of inequality. It begins with a review of theories of the body that address notions of regulation and control. This is examined in relation to mental illness, gender and the state's interaction with Indigenous people.

Part 4 concludes the study. The last chapter, Chapter 12, summarises the findings and places them in the context of the questions that have guided the analysis. It argues that Australia is in an era of transition but that while the dimensions of inequality are changing these developments are neither even nor random. For this reason, cultural explanations of social inequality are unsatisfactory as they underestimate and fail to address the endurance of constants of inequality across multiple dimensions. There is an increasing clustering of the risks of inequality that is spatial and social. While opportunities for some groups—young and highly skilled women, for example—have opened, for others the divisions have deepened. In reviewing the implications for the future of inequality, Chapter 12 argues that while Australia continues to be economically prosperous these divisions may remain relatively residual, but the potential for further fracturing remains. In this uncertain environment, where the role of government is so critical, there is an urgent need for a revived discourse of an egalitarianism that challenges the dominance of individualising discourses by pointing to the uneven distribution of choice and opportunity.

PART 1

THEORISING SOCIAL INEQUALITY

1

○

SOCIAL INEQUALITY: A SHORT HISTORY OF AN IDEA

○

1.1　Introduction

This chapter sets the scene for our exploration of **social inequality**, defining the concept of inequality and its significance, and explaining how theories of inequality have changed in response to changing social conditions. It pays special attention to the challenge presented to traditional theories of inequality by the transition of Western liberal democracies to their current postindustrial form. And it addresses one of this study's guiding questions: how are the dimensions of social inequality changing in the context of globalisation and a postindustrial society? The next two chapters review in detail the main theories of inequality from classical times to the present day.

social inequality Refers to differences between groups of people that are hierarchical in nature. At its most basic it refers to the hierarchical distribution of social, political, economic and cultural resources.

The transition from an industrial to a postindustrial society represented a crisis for theories of inequality because throughout the modern period, the core concept for the field was closely associated with the modernist paradigm. David Lyon (1999) explains that class was one of the 'metanarratives' of **modernism** that sought to explain everything according to a single idea, and that this metanarrative became unsustainable in the conditions of postmodernity. Class is a collective concept that stresses the centrality of the economy and the objective nature of inequality. It is at odds with the fluidity of contemporary social arrangements and trends towards individualisation.

modernism Generally refers to the period since the Middle Ages and the Renaissance and is associated with the replacement of traditional society with modern social forms.

In the 1980s, as the influence of cultural studies within social theory grew, the study of social inequality came increasingly to be seen as an outdated approach to understanding social life. There were sociologists who argued strongly for the enduring importance of class and inequality but the direction of social theory was heading away from this kind of structuralist approach (Wright 1997). But by the 1990s new ways of understanding the field appeared, which accommodated new realities through a looser, more multidimensional framework.

1.2   Defining social inequality

The idea of social inequality refers to differences between groups of people that are hierarchical in nature. At its most basic, it refers to the hierarchical distribution of social, political, economic and cultural resources. A closely related concept is that of **stratification**, a more specific and technical term that refers to a model of social inequality that specifies the relationship between particular variables, such as wealth and social standing. Stratification refers to a systematic and enduring pattern of inequality that is transmitted across generations, built into institutions and practised in everyday activities. The most influential theory of stratification is that of Marx, who argued that all stratification systems are ultimately determined by the distribution of economic resources.

> **stratification** The existence in society of structured inequalities between groups in terms of their access to material and symbolic rewards.

Going deeper into the idea of social inequality, it is clear that establishing conceptual clarity is not straightforward. What kinds of inequality should the term include? Should it refer primarily to economic differences or are social and cultural differences also important? Should physical or health differences be included? What is the relationship between inequality and poverty and at what point should levels of inequality become a public concern? The measurement of inequality is also challenging. What should the level of analysis be—the individual, the family or some other unit, such as the household? How do you estimate the wealth of the rich when so much of their wealth is held in complex cross-national arrangements? These are just some of the questions that are implicated in the study of social inequality, and at different times and places the answers have varied, reflecting the way sociological ideas adjust to changing social arrangements. This variation is also because there is never any one way of looking at a social issue; rather, different concerns and interests lead to different questions and answers.

An important distinction in the study of inequality is the difference between distributional inequality and equality of opportunity or meritocracy. Distributional equality is concerned with the extent to which everyone receives a similar amount of economic resources. A concern with minimising economic, and sometimes also social, differences between individuals and groups is sometimes described as **egalitarianism**. Equality of opportunity focuses on the extent to which people have a similar chance to obtain rewards, with less attention paid to the effects this has on the distribution of wealth, income and influence. Egalitarianism is associated with socialism and communism while equality of opportunity has historically been associated with capitalist liberal democracies. Liberal democracies often claim to be meritocratic because the institutions of society are designed to ensure

> **egalitarianism** In the field of social inequality this term is usually applied to a concern with ensuring that economic and social differences between different social groups are minimised.

that everyone has a fair go so that social position is not based on privilege but on individual ability and effort. The term 'social inequality' is most widely used as shorthand for distributional inequality and it is in this sense that the term is used throughout this study.

1.3   Why inequality matters

Why should it matter if some people receive more advantages than others? Historically, it is inequality rather than equality that has been regarded as normal and natural. The argument that a just society is also an equal one was associated with the Enlightenment and the beginnings of modernity in the eighteenth century. Egalitarian ideals were closely tied to political ideals of democracy and the belief that a just society is one in which everyone should have their needs met and receive a good start in life.

The arguments for greater equality are ideological and practical. Proponents of egalitarianism point out that inequality violates principles of natural justice, damages human potential and creates problems that affect everyone.

Inequality offends the principle of egalitarianism that is fundamental to social justice. That some people should be privileged as a result of an accident of birth, and that for others the odds of achieving a good life are stacked against them, is unfair and a denial of human rights. Inequality is also inefficient because it reduces the potential for human development. The unequal distribution of opportunities for the development of individual and community capacity represents a loss to nations and to humanity in general. Inequality means that those at the bottom of the ladder experience disadvantage and poverty and carry health deficits that shorten and disrupt lives. People who are poor often miss out on quality education and fail to achieve their potential. This limits their future and curtails the contribution they can make to the development of their community.

There is also a strong association between poverty, crime and race. Merton argued that high levels of inequality create a sense of envy and resentment within communities, which leads to criminal behaviour as this is a way that excluded groups can achieve material success (Merton 1968). High levels of inequality are also associated with lateral violence—violence *within* disadvantaged groups. Middleton-Moz suggests that black-on-black violence arises from the sense of shame and anger Aboriginal people carry with them as a result of their oppression, which is expressed through dysfunctional behaviour (Middleton-Moz 1999). High levels of incarceration prevent people from living normal lives and have effects that ripple out to partners, children and neighbourhoods (Wacquant 2004).

High levels of inequality are an impediment to economic growth (Ostry et al. 2014). Nations with high levels of income inequality are inefficient because they limit potential markets, reduce human capital and constrain opportunities for investment and economic growth. Political and social inequality also hold back development through their association with political corruption (Bernstein 2013). In their influential book *The Spirit Level* (2009), Wilkinson and Pickett show that high levels of inequality affect everyone through their association with social 'bads' including high rates of crime and imprisonment, drug use, mental health problems and poor child well-being. They suggest that large income differences affect how people relate to one another and create 'broken societies' (2009:5).

Using secondary analysis of epidemiological data, Wilkinson and Pickett show that in wealthy countries, measures of the quality of life amongst individuals do not increase as national income per head increases. Instead quality of life is related to the level of equality within the nation, with higher levels of inequality associated with higher social dysfunction. Their analysis shows that, at any given level of personal income or education, an individual's quality of life will be higher in a more equal society, than that of an equivalent person in a more unequal society. Levels of inequality are also associated with higher levels of violence that affect everyone in the nation. The authors also show that race plays a critical role in shaping the impact of inequality. As the exclusion of ethnic minorities from education and job opportunities increases, so negative health outcomes increase for both black and white populations. It is not only the poor that benefit from higher levels of equality, but everyone in the society (2009:178).

Inequality is also inseparable from ideas of social division and the creation of a sense of distance and separation between social groups. It creates relations of domination and subordination that carry with them judgments about the value of different groups. In identifying some groups as inferior to others, inequality opens the door to processes of dehumanisation and the violation of human rights.

The view that inequality matters is not without its critics. Social libertarian Friedrich August von Hayek argues that social justice is a human invention and does not really exist (1976). This view is associated with neoliberalism, which suggests that the operation of the market should be the only real determinant of the distribution of wealth. This position is closely associated with the view that political, not economic, equality is what matters. So long as everyone is equal before the law and has equal political representation, then the distribution of wealth and privilege is unimportant. This argument ignores the political privilege that accompanies wealth and the fact that the views of those with few economic resources are usually poorly represented in public debate: compared with the wealthy or socially influential, they have little capacity to influence governments or shape policy agendas. There are many examples of this. In Australia the mining lobby was successful in substantially diluting the Gillard Labor government's mining tax. The policy was anticipated to reap $300 billion in revenue but actually gathered only $300 million (Ker 2013). In contrast, the severe opposition of many Aboriginal people to the Northern Territory Emergency Intervention in 2007 was not enough to prevent its introduction. This illustrates why the argument that it is poverty that matters rather than inequality is flawed. The view that it is permissible for some sections of the population to have enormous wealth if everyone has a minimum acceptable standard of living ignores the social and political injustices that tend to accompany excessive disparities of wealth.

1.4   Modernist approaches to the study of social inequality

When sociology first made its entrance as an academic discipline in the middle of the nineteenth century, the most influential theory of social inequality was that of Karl Marx (1818–83). By the turn of the twentieth century his ideas were joined by those of the other founding figures of sociology, Max Weber (1864–1920) and Émile Durkheim

(1858–1917). Marx regarded possession of capital (wealth that is used to produce more wealth) as the ultimate determinant of all forms of inequality, while both Weber and Durkheim believed political and social factors had an independent influence. As the twentieth century progressed, attempts to understand and explain social inequality mainly revolved around debates between Marx's economically deterministic model of class and Weber's softer, but still structural, model which saw economic resources as one of a number of sources of power that determined who received scarce resources. In these analyses the term 'social inequality' was used virtually interchangeably with stratification theory and, with the exception of functionalist theories, class theory was the major paradigm. To some extent, the terms 'class theory', 'stratification theory' and 'social inequality' were interchangeable terms.

Throughout the modern period, from the time of the Enlightenment until the Second World War, ideas about social inequality were central to sociology. Class operated as the most important concept within sociology, understood as offering the greatest explanatory power for understanding social formations. Until the mid-1970s, the idea of class was widely used to explain social arrangements and to understand how society changed. Although theories about the centrality of class and the extent of its explanatory power were contested, the idea that how people earn their living is central to their experiences and their destiny was the point of departure for many debates. Within the field of inequality Weber's more flexible and less deterministic model of inequality became the most widely used theoretical framework and existed alongside, rather than in opposition to, a Marxist framework. But as globalisation progressed, and the economy moved away from industrial production to service delivery, the weakness of these structuralist understandings of social inequality became more apparent.

These weaknesses derived from theoretical problems that had always bothered class theory but they became more exposed as the transformations associated with the move to a highly competitive, interconnected and fluid society, and the shift to a post-industrial economy, created a world in which the explanatory power of solid concepts such as class became increasingly compromised.

1.5   Postindustrialisation and debates on the death of class

agency and structure
Two key ideas used by sociologists to explain how social phenomena are derived from a combination of choices made by free-acting individuals (agency) and externally imposed social arrangements (structure).

The determinism inherent in Marx's argument that all social phenomena were reducible to access to economic resources was always highly contested, even among Marxist theorists, who pointed to contradictions within Marxist theory itself. One much discussed difficulty was described by sociologist Ray Pahl (1989, in Devine & Savage 2005:5) as the SCA problem, where S equals **structure**, C equals class consciousness and A equals **agency**. In a pure Marxist model, objective (that is, structural) class position gives rise to a particular kind of consciousness that determines how people will act (agency). Evidence for this was found in the development of the main political parties, each of which emerged out of class-based social movements. The working class formed the Labor Party and the middle and upper classes formed conservative parties, such as the Liberals in Australia. But closer investigation reveals that the empirical reality of class affiliation was not so neat, and many people supported political parties that did not represent their interests; many manual workers, for example, voted for the Liberal Party. The working class also failed to develop the radical consciousness Marx had predicted would eventually overthrow capitalism. With rare exceptions, trade unions followed a reformist path, focusing on redistributive issues, that is, how much workers receive for their labour, rather than challenging the principles behind redistribution and a rejection of capitalism as an economic system.

Marxists explained these failures through the concept of dominant ideology. This suggests that through their domination of the economy, the ruling classes are able to control culture so that the ideas that dominate society are those that benefit them. As a result, the working classes are unable to recognise the reality of their exploitation. The difficulty with this model is that it assumes that the influence of all other phenomena, most notably **culture**, is secondary to the underlying influence of the economy.

culture In contemporary sociology this term has taken the specific meaning of cultural production, in contrast to the material, technological and structural.

Although most stratification theorists continued to use class—operationalised in terms of the occupation system—as the main concept for examining inequality, it became increasingly apparent that the social transformations associated with postindustrialism were making the concept increasingly irrelevant. Throughout the industrial period, the existence of an upper, middle and working class, each defined in relation to their role in the production process, has been empirically defensible. The existence of the working class could be demonstrated across many variables: the nature and experience of their work was different from that of other classes; it involved manual labour that was dirty, dangerous and poorly rewarded, in marked contrast with the intellectual labour, clean, safe working environments and higher earnings of the middle class. To be a plumber or builder's labourer also carried less social prestige than being a professional such as a teacher, clerk or lawyer. There were also visibly distinct class cultures that were located in different geographical spaces.

Working class people tended to live in the industrial heartlands of cities. Their relationships with neighbours and family were different from those of the middle class, involving strong social networks based on frequent contact (Wilmott & Young 1962). Studies show the existence of distinct communities with a shared sense of social identity, rooted in common workplace experiences, close kin and neighbourhood ties, and recognition that collective action represented the best strategy for improving their situation (Metcalfe 1988). This was the sentiment that was the foundation of the trade union and Labor Party movements. There was a strong oppositional culture expressed in industrial action and resistance to right-wing political demands. While ethnicity and gender divided the working class, this was subdued under the **cultural hegemony** of white, male working-class culture. Contemporary studies such as social researcher Claire Williams' analysis of an Australian mining town offered rich accounts of these social spaces in which the significance of class analysis was not in doubt (Williams 1981).

cultural hegemony A term used by Gramsci to suggest that one of the ways in which the state wields power is by encouraging ideas that reinforce the status quo.

With the transition to a service economy the stability of these arrangements began to dissolve. The expansion of the service sector, together with the associated rise in educational participation, created high levels of social mobility and a growing number of people who identified themselves as somewhere in the middle. By 1980, research by sociologist Chris Chamberlain found that only 21 per cent of the Australian population identified as working class (1983). The collapse of the manufacturing sector meant that traditional areas of working-class employment fell into decline and those who could, moved to new areas and new jobs (Bryson & Thompson 1972; Bryson & Winter 1999). The suburbs expanded and began to be filled by a new, more individualised aspirant class whose loyalty was to their immediate family rather than to their fellow workers. A belief that poverty and class were things of the past began to emerge.

The sense that class no longer mattered was assisted by the increased visibility and significance of the horizontal divisions that cut across classes. While classes had always been divided by factors such as ethnicity, age and gender, a number of developments made these internal distinctions more apparent. These included the transformation of the labour force with the entry of increasing numbers of women and immigrants from non-English-speaking backgrounds (NESB) as well as the impact of the civil rights movements of the 1960s. The expansion of the service sector brought increasing numbers of women into the labour market, which challenged male dominance of the workplace and changed workplace politics and culture. The interplay between gender and class became more apparent, thereby exposing the limitations of class theory.

multiculturalism The acknowledgment and promotion of cultural pluralism in contrast to the cultural unification associated with, for example, assimilation policies.

The rise of **multiculturalism** in the period following the Second World War further fragmented the illusion of a homogenous class structure. Although there had always been ethnic minorities within the labour force the dominance of Anglo-Celts had made them relatively invisible. But the social turmoil that followed the end of the Second World War, together with the collapse of colonialism and a rise in egalitarianism, saw large-scale movements of population across national borders. In Australia, the demise of the 'White Australia' policy in 1973 led to rising numbers of NESB immigrants entering the country and taking their place alongside their Anglo-Celtic counterparts in the labour force. Multiculturalism, and the entrance of women into the labour force, began to fragment the cultural hegemony of the working class.

The 1960s civil rights movement of Indigenous Australians focused attention on their contribution to Australian identity and history. Citizenship gave Indigenous people a new visibility in Australian society and political culture, and raised questions about their place within the nation and what their relationship to the state should be.

These changes represented a challenge to class theory because dispelling notions of a unified working class also delegitimised claims of a unified working-class consciousness based on shared interests. Far from having a shared experience, the working class was revealed to be internally divided and fragmented. Resistance to the inclusion and representation of Indigenous Australians, women and immigrants within the white, male-dominated trade union movement, and the differential treatment of their labour through, for example, lower rates of pay or different employment conditions, showed that cultural and social differences were a source of divisions that were as significant as vertical divisions of wealth.

These developments provided fertile ground for social theorists sensitive to the failings of the traditional models of inequality. Feminists pointed out that class was not a gender-neutral concept but fundamentally masculinist in its focus on male experiences and domains. Most stratification theorists were male, which had led to myopia when it came to exploring sites of inequality. Fixated on the notion that the workplace and public politics were the only sites in which social life was shaped, they ignored the significance of the domestic arena. Feminist research on the role of gender in a wide range of settings suggested that it was gender, not class, that was the most enduring and significant source of inequality. A new wave of feminist research revealed the extent to which the workplace was permeated by gender issues, from characteristics such as the division of labour and pay differentials, to less acknowledged features such as everyday interactions and skills categorisation (Scott, in Crompton & Mann 1986:156). Although sociologists such as Juliet Mitchell (1971) and Sheila Rowbotham (1977) attempted to combine Marxist and **feminism**, class remained a fundamentally intransigent concept—too solid to incorporate the notion of gender.

> **feminism** A wide range of theories that place women at the centre of analysis.

Feminists also pointed out that the gender blindness about inequality extended to its measurement. In empirical measures of class by male social researchers, men were assumed to be the unit of analysis, with the contribution of women to the stratification system discounted. This was justified because occupation more or less equated with class, and men were the primary breadwinners. But the rise in the number of women in the labour market made it difficult for stratification theorists to defend this approach from the criticisms of their feminist colleagues. Although some, most notably British Weberian and stratification theorist John Goldthorpe (Goldthorpe et al. 1987), initially resisted revision and attempted to justify the exclusive focus on men, others responded by developing more inclusive measures.

The feminist critique did not end there. Working within a predominantly poststructuralist framework, a new wave of writers on gender and sexuality drew on the concept of **identity** to explore men's and women's subjectivities. They argued that there was no straightforward relationship between social position and consciousness and that identity was formed from multiple sources rather than one essential variable such as gender or class.

> **identity** The ongoing sense of self and the process of self-development and definition.

These arguments gained impetus from black feminists who accused white middle-class feminists of treating the category of gender in the same essentialist way as class had hitherto been treated. Feminist writer bell hooks accused white feminists of ignoring the situation of black women and challenged the view that social phenomena could be captured through any essentialising category, whether it be gender, class or race (1981). In Australia, Indigenous scholar Moreton-Robinson's study of Indigenous women and feminism revealed the extent of difference between the experiences and interests of Indigenous and Anglo-Celtic women (2000). These writers pointed to the fragmented nature of identity and the individualised and fluid way in which the experiences and consciousness of subjects was established.

globalisation The growing interdependence between different peoples, regions and countries, and the disappearance of national boundaries due to technological developments and communication becoming more instantaneous.

Sociologists have used different terms to describe the changed social conditions that accompanied the process of individuation associated with **globalisation**. These changes led to the argument that it is identity rather than class that should be the primary concept for understanding social life. For sociologist Anthony Giddens rapid social change has released people from their traditional social contexts. The values, beliefs and forms of social organisation that were once passed down through generations have lost their relevance and, in this social vacuum, people are forced to make choices without the support of ancestry or tradition. He argues that we now live in a world of 'reflexive modernity' in which individuals must engage in 'the project of the self' (1991). Our intimate relationships are no longer prescribed but based on personal choice and so are always subject to the principle of 'until further notice'.

liquid modernity Bauman uses this term to describe the fluid and swiftly changing nature of contemporary social arrangements.

Social theorist Zygmunt Bauman uses the term **liquid modernity** to capture this fluidity of social life. He argues that in any society there is always tension between having the freedom to choose who you want to be and how to live your life, and the security that comes with having your place ascribed by social arrangements. In the past, strong social norms and rigid social boundaries meant people were certain about where they belonged but lacked freedom to develop their own identity. Today the reverse is true. There are few social barriers preventing us from living any way we choose, but this comes at the cost of frail social bonds and the insecurity of living in a world where nothing can be taken for certain. Freedom is also distributed unequally, with those who are disadvantaged being trapped in situations where they have few choices and experience social exclusion.

Sociologist Ulrich Beck (1992) points out that this freedom to choose our identity is not one that is freely entered into but is imposed by contemporary institutional arrangements. While in the past, major institutions such as education and welfare allocated responsibility to collective institutions such as the family or the workplace, today they demand that people act as self-determining and self-responsible agents. We live in an individuated world but it is still our social environment that compels citizens to act for themselves.

1.5.1   From production to consumption

Closely associated with the shift from class to identity is a concern with consumption rather than production. In traditional stratification theory, understanding how people contributed to production—generally understood as how they made their living—was regarded as the most revealing social attribute, a position that implies the primacy of the economy. Today it is consumption rather than production that is the most striking feature of contemporary social life. Social identity is now established more by what we consume than by what we produce so for many theorists it is lifestyles rather than **life chances** that should be the primary focus of sociological interest, and this is closely tied to culture. Today we position ourselves in social space through the development of our aesthetic style.

life chances The material advantages or disadvantages and social and cultural opportunities that different social groups can expect within a particular society.

Unhindered by ascribed categories such as class, this positioning is relatively fluid and open to change. No longer fixed by the accident of geography, birth or biology, we can elect the groups with whom we wish to identify. From this perspective we can choose to be straight or gay, to support the Labor Party or the Greens, to be an Indy fan, follow Yogananda or become a committed feminist. Whatever our choice, it is associated with consumption patterns, such as how we dress or how we spend our leisure time, that serve as markers of being and belonging. The idea of a hierarchy of resources, of a world of haves and have nots, in which the economy serves as the key distributor of life chances, is replaced by a concern with different cultural forms.

The emergence of culture as the central feature of social life in a **postindustrial society** was closely tied to the growth in the power of the media and the knowledge economy. The post-Second World War period was characterised by an explosion in information technology, which played a major role in the process of globalisation. Time–space compression (Harvey 1990) is the process by which time and space shrink so that distant events, such as the war in Iraq, are experienced

postindustrial society
A social order based on a knowledge economy, in which services rather than manufactured goods are the primary products.

in real time across the globe. Communication is sped up through new technologies such as mobile phones, the internet and air travel, and a new global culture is created in which the media play a pivotal role. The high visibility and impact of the media, their integration with everyday life and their contribution to culture, make them essential objects of sociological analysis. Social theorists such as Stuart Hall (Hall et al. 1978; Hall 1997), who began his analyses within a neo-Marxist framework, embraced new paradigms to develop models of analysis that recognised the waning power of social structures.

The changing political landscape of the postwar period also contributed to the demise of class theory. As the century drew on, class-based politics declined in importance and voting preferences became increasingly detached from occupational position. Instead, identity politics emerged in the form of social movements, such as environmentalism, feminism and gay liberation. These movements were rooted in conscience politics rather than class location, further adding to the perception that class-based politics was a thing of the past.

The collapse of communism in the closing decades of the last century also had implications for class theory because it undermined the position of Marxist theorists. It led to claims that liberal democratic regimes had got it right and that market-led economies, balanced by the rule of law to ensure individual political and social rights, offered the best hope for humanity (Fukuyama 1992). The hopes that many left-leaning social theorists and activists had for a more egalitarian social order were replaced by a resignation to the seeming inevitability of inequality. In the West, socialist ideals, such as the provision of universal social care, appeared to be of declining relevance because of the persistence of poverty and disadvantage despite the existence of the welfare state. This made it very difficult to counter the arguments of the Right that the welfare state should be wound down because it encouraged dependence and was a waste of taxpayers' money.

These developments were important in moving academic attention away from a concern with division to that of difference. This was assisted by a sense that the expansion in middle-class jobs and the growth of consumerism had created a level of affluence that suggested the old inequalities of modernity had disappeared or were now so residual that they were of little academic interest. The changes in the experiences of women also had implications for the feminist movement. As women entered the labour force, their dependence on men declined, creating a new sense of independence and agency. Feminist paradigms of women as victims, subject to male oppression, came into question (Yeatman 1990). This corresponded with the rise of a new agenda of sexual difference derived from the experiences of gay men and lesbians. Both the feminist movement and the gay liberation movement moved away from an interest in gender inequality towards a concern with the construction of subjectivities and difference. This shift was also influenced by the development of postmodern and poststructural theory which rejected the possibilities for absolute truth and portrayed social reality as so relative and fragmented that it removed the subject as a coherent object of study. If there were no subjects then how was it possible to examine the social divisions between them (Derrida 1991)?

1.5.2   The death of class

For some stratification theorists the arguments of postmodernists and poststructuralists were too powerful to ignore. The view that class was a redundant concept was expressed in the 1980s and 1990s as the **death of class** debate. Sociologists Jan Pakulski and Malcolm Waters reviewed many of the arguments against the continued relevance of class and concluded that class 'can no longer give us purchase on the big social, political and cultural issues of the age' (1996:vii). They divided their analysis of the concept into three historical periods. The first period, 'economic-class society', is the classic period described by Marx: class relations are dualistic, oppositional and exploitative. There is a 'radically unequal distribution of property' (1996:88), with capitalists, whose wealth is predominantly inherited and rooted in property ownership, opposing industrial workers, who are organised for collective action and possess a revolutionary identity. In the second period, 'organised-class society', the sharp boundaries between classes begin to blur. The state emerges as a dominant interest group and the masses are organised into national-political groups; some diffusion of wealth occurs as occupational achievement overtakes inheritance as the primary source of wealth. This process continues into the third period, 'status-conventional society'. Globalisation, the collapse of state socialism and the growth of unemployment give birth to new status-based social divisions (1996:4). Privatisation and the new currency of intellectual knowledge further reduce the concentration and inheritance of wealth. Individual biography is what counts, with markets acting like casinos, where 'each individual is now their own market player ... what you get depends on how you perform' (1996:89). Even occupation has been displaced as the source of social position, which is instead determined by individual achievement. Consumption is the central expression of social position, which is now status- rather than class-based.

death of class Refers to the argument that class is of little relevance today because social collectives such as the working class have today become fragmented. There are no longer clearly defined social groups who share a common experience and who stand in political opposition to other social groups.

Pakulski and Waters concluded that although material inequality is still important, class has lost its currency as the master concept for explaining contemporary social life. It cannot explain the post-Fordist industrial environment, nor the postcolonial, postcommunist political landscape. It offers no purchase on **postwelfare states** or the emergence of identity politics and global political movements such as Islamic fundamentalism: 'Let class ... rest in peace, respected and honoured, but mainly relevant to history' (1996:153). Yet even though the death knell seemed to have been sounded on the field, new understandings and possibilities for examining social inequality were emerging, with a renewed emphasis on the need to understand its stubborn persistence.

> **postwelfare state** Challenges the ideas of welfare associated with the modern interventionist state, and promotes instead the benefits of the free rein of market forces.

1.6   Conclusion: Reinventing social inequality

The effects of three decades of a market model of social responsibility, and growing evidence of its damaging effects on the social fabric, have renewed concerns about social inequality. The idea that inequality does not matter, but that difference and **lifestyles** do, has become hard to sustain in the face of an increase in inequality in OECD countries (Vieira 2012). The failure of the excessive wealth associated with globalisation to trickle down to the lower reaches of society, the emergence of new groups of poor, and the stubborn persistence and sometimes worsening circumstances of other disadvantaged groups, such as Indigenous Australians, have led to a return to sociology's traditional concern with disadvantage.

> **lifestyles** Refers to patterns of consumption (goods, services and culture) that are not rooted in collective identities but emerge out of the impact of globalisation on self-identity.

Cultural theory has also been criticised because its arguments about the centrality of the individual and denial of the role of structural forces in shaping social outcomes has similarities with neoliberal views. Social researcher John O'Neill, for example, suggests 'a convergence of a postmodern leftism with neoliberal defences of the market' (1999:85). Implicit in the concern with difference rather than division is the assumption that in a postmodern world people make genuine choices about how they will live their lives. This position runs counter to a wealth of research that shows that for some groups the word 'choice' is a misnomer and that to suggest they are the exclusive architects of their fate is to deny the circumscribed circumstances of their lives. Questions of who gets what, and how and why they get it, remain critical sociological concerns.

Although the sociological gaze is returning to social inequality, it does so through a lens that is markedly different from that of a generation ago. It is characterised today by a diversity of perspectives and an emphasis on multiple positions. The ideas of Bourdieu are influential as a way of encompassing the role of culture and other non-economic forces in shaping inequality experiences and positions. Inequality is now understood as multi-dimensional, involving the interaction of diverse variables that include gender, ethnicity and class (Anthias 2001). Instead of a dominant paradigm such as neo-Marxism there is a more eclectic approach and an attempt to use whatever concepts and models work best for particular tasks.

Discussion questions

1   Define social inequality. How does distributional inequality differ from meritocracy?
2   What were some of the changes associated with postindustrialisation that challenged the notion of class as the primary determinant of social inequality?
3   What is meant by the claim that identity has replaced class as the key concept for understanding social location?

2

○

CLASSICAL THEORIES OF INEQUALITY AND THEIR MODERN DEVELOPMENTS

○

2.1   Introduction

Marx, Weber and Durkheim remain important to the study of inequality because, although contemporary theories have gone well beyond their ideas, they still represent an essential starting point for understanding the field. A review of the different but overlapping perspectives of Marx and Weber provides an introduction to arguments about the intersection between economic and non-economic spheres so central to current debates. The ideas of Durkheim have direct relevance to contemporary assumptions about how social position is achieved in liberal democracies.

In reviewing the ideas of the classical theorists and their modern developments, this chapter provides some answers to the first question that guides this study: what are the main dimensions of social inequality in contemporary Australian society? It explains the fundamental principles for outlining the main dimensions of inequality; principles whose context is European society in the nineteenth and early twentieth centuries, but that still have application for understanding contemporary Australia. This is apparent in the review of how contemporary stratification theorists have modified these ideas to provide a conceptual framework for an empirically based map of the Australian class structure based on an analysis of the occupation system. The final section of the chapter examines the question of class consciousness through a review of empirical studies on the willingness of respondents to identify with a particular class.

The social inequality theories presented in this and the following chapter are not geographically located in Australia. Although we (and others) apply them to Australian society, almost all these theorists are not Australian and they are very unlikely to have been considering the Australian context when developing their core theoretical positions.

social class Refers generally to the broad idea of a class grouping, or specifically to refer to people whose similar economic position is matched by a shared sense of social identity.

Even Pakulski and Waters, physically located in Australia, are global in their contemplation of the continuing relevance of **social class**. To what extent does this present a problem for attempts to theorise inequality in Australia? The central question is whether these theories can be generalised to underpin and inform the more empirical discussions on inequality in Australian society. The answer is yes and no.

In the yes aspect the general social theories used are connected to grand ideas in the Western tradition and therefore have relevance to the Western base of the majority of contemporary Australian life: politics, culture and society. The development of class theory by Marx, Weber and Durkheim in the nineteenth and early twentieth centuries has resonance with the class structure in Australia, in the past and at present, although these three theorists were physically and historically based in Western Europe more than a century ago. More contemporary critiques, such as those of feminist scholars on the absence of the female from inequality theories and the subsequent theoretical development of the gendered nature of much inequality, are valuable and applicable to the broader Australian context. Arguments about the effects of globalisation on contemporary arrangements for inequality are also broadly salient. Processes such as detraditionalisation and the increasing significance of consumption are being experienced throughout the Western world, and Australia is no exception. For these reasons, we make use of the generalised social theory tools available to us.

On the no side is sociologist Raewyn Connell's (2007) argument of the tacit positioning of social theory as universal although it is developed in specific places and societies. This place is almost always what Connell refers to as 'the metropole', that is, Western Europe and North America. Connell argues convincingly that modern social theory 'embeds the viewpoints, perspectives and problems of metropolitan society while presenting itself as universal knowledge' (vii–viii). In these generalised positions, the metropole is the centre and elsewhere is the periphery. The colonised world, including Australia, is absent except as a source of data and exotic examples, dichotomously juxtaposed with the social practices of Western (metropole) society. While such generalised theories can be used in the Australian context, it is our social circumstances that must be made to fit them, rather than the other way around. This squashing of Australian social realities into theories and frameworks developed in other places and based around other societies necessarily leaves gaps.

For Australian social inequality these gaps are significant. The most obvious is in relation to Indigenous Australia, the periphery of the periphery. Connell's thoughts provide at least a partial explanation for the otherwise inexplicable theoretical, even empirical, invisibility of Indigenous people from Australian studies of social inequality. But the gaps go wider. Australia is a society built on colonisation, dispossession, immigration and gradual national independence, and the development of a unique national identity. Considering social inequality in Australia without regard for this history and present actuality is to disregard the impact of the past on the present. The reality of this past resonates through our society and its social practices and formations, including those relating to social inequality. Therefore, in this book, we are cognisant that generalised social theory is inadequate for a complete socially and geographically located account of social inequality in Australia. Yet we are also mindful that theory required to do this has not yet emerged in an accessible form. We therefore take a, perhaps uncourageous, middle line, actively using Australian theorists to develop the specifically Australian nature of inequalities, while at the same time utilising the insights that the generalised social theories have to offer.

2.2   Classical theories of inequality

In sociology the attention paid to Marx, Weber and Durkheim, who had reigned as the founding triumvirate of the discipline, began to decline in the 1980s and today their ideas are often only briefly covered. But in the field of social inequality the work of these theorists, especially Marx and Weber, remains central. All the material considered in this chapter, and in much of the next, is rooted in their work.

Each of these social theorists wrote in the shadow of the Enlightenment and its aftermath and share the assumptions and concerns this implies. All were men, born into the material comfort of middle-class nineteenth-century European society and the discomfort of an era of profound, sometimes bloody, societal transformation. Their interest in social inequality stemmed from their attempts to understand this transformation, as well as its causes, future trajectory and implications for social relations. These concerns about social order and change were regarded as central to the vocation of sociology itself.

2.2.1   Karl Marx and the primacy of the material sphere

Marx's vision of a communist society in which everyone fulfils their potential, and need rather than greed is the principal for the distribution of wealth, power and honour, captured the imagination of generations of political activists and academics. The brilliance of his writing and the clarity, certainty and appeal of his vision led to social movements that influenced the destiny of millions of people.

Under the influence of the evolutionary model provided by the natural sciences, Marx believed that it was possible to uncover laws of social development. He developed an evolutionary theory of social change that he called **historical materialism**, whose premise was that, subject to some qualifications, it's the material conditions of society that lay the foundation for everything else. The type of political system, social relations and cultural forms and beliefs are ultimately dependent on how a society meets its material needs. The prevailing ideas of an era, its legislation and culture, are therefore closely tied to the technology and the social relations involved in the production of the materials used to support human existence. The term 'class' had been used by philosopher and sociologist Auguste Comte (1798–1857) to describe how social actors cluster around particular social variables. Marx used this term to describe those social groups whose common economic position could be linked to a shared sense of social

historical materialism
Marx's theory of social change, which posits that the material conditions of society lay the foundation for everything else.

identity. For Marx, it was this link between objective economic position and shared social consciousness that was the driving force behind social change. He argued that it was the interaction between class groups with opposing economic interests that drove social change.

Marx identified six stages of social development in Western social formations: primitive communism, slavery, feudalism and capitalism, which he predicted would be followed by socialism and communism. As a political activist he was most interested in understanding his own era—where it had come from and the direction in which it was headed. This meant understanding how capitalism had emerged out of feudalism and predicting its future transformation. Marx's belief in the possibilities of an egalitarian society was based on his understanding that, for the first time in human history, capitalist processes of production had the potential to eliminate **poverty** and hardship: the efficiency of industrial production meant that no one need do without. The reason why this potential was not being realised was because the existing relations of production divided citizens into haves and have nots. Capitalism is, therefore, the solution to social inequality (because it unleashes productive potential) and the problem (because it blocks equal distribution).

poverty The subject of much debate because whether an individual or group can be said to be poor is always a matter of subjective interpretation.

Marx pointed out that the production of wealth is not just a matter of technical knowledge but, crucially, involves different types of social relations organised around that production. What is distinctive about class societies is that these social relations of production involve unequal access to rights and powers over the productive process. With the exception of primitive communism, where there is no surplus wealth to distribute, all historical societies have institutionalised unequal access to wealth through the legitimation of private ownership of productive wealth. Those who own the productive wealth, such as agricultural land or factories, are able to impose a system of unequal economic exchange on the labouring classes, which further adds to their material advantage. Consequently, social antagonism, social exploitation and social division are endemic to the social relations of class societies.

Marx categorised social formations according to their type of social relations and technological knowledge. He argued that in Western civilisations the main types were the slave–owner societies of Ancient Greece and Rome; the feudal societies of the Middle Ages, which involved agricultural production and the serf–landlord relationship; and modern capitalist arrangements of industrial production and proletariat–capitalist relations. Marx pointed out that one of the distinctive features of capitalism is that the exploitative relationship between capitalist and proletariat is at once extreme and highly visible. It is extreme because, whereas in previous class systems the non-owners of productive wealth (those who must labour for their livelihood) retained some control over productive processes through, for example, their ownership of small landholdings, in capitalism the working class own nothing, not even the tools of their labour. This, therefore, makes them entirely dependent for their livelihood on employment in the factories and marketplaces owned by the **ruling class**.

ruling class A Marxist term that suggests that those who own and control the means of material production also control the state and the production of ideas.

Marx's argument about the increased visibility of the exploitative relationship between owner and non-owner of the means of production is complex. He pointed out that in previous systems the relationship between owners and non-owners of the means of production involved social as well as economic ties. Although highly unequal, the feudal system was one of mutual obligations and rights: although serfs were bound to the feudal lord for life, the lord was required to protect the serfs and they could not be displaced from the land. But in capitalism these social ties have dissolved and the only bond between capitalist and proletariat is economic; all relations are reduced to the cash nexus. Marx believed this brought a rawness and visibility to the relationship that would enable workers to understand its inherent unfairness.

This unfairness arose because in capitalism the labourer is not paid the real value of his labour power but instead is given only what he needs to meet his and his family's basic needs (Marx was not a feminist and the breadwinner was conceived of as male). The difference between the amount the worker takes home in wages and the value in the market of the goods he produces is taken by the capitalist as profit. Marx called this the 'surplus value' of the labour of the worker. This exploitation is further compounded because even the labour power of the worker is commodified. In previous historical formations, labour was regarded as an inalienable aspect of being human, which means it cannot be bought and sold, but in capitalism, labour is treated like a commodity, comparable to food or other consumables, and valued according to what the market will pay. It is just another entry in the calculus of profit.

Although there were features of the capitalist system that enhanced the likelihood of workers understanding their exploitation, Marx suggested that other elements worked to disguise this. He used the term 'ideology' to describe notions such as 'the market', which economists such as Adam Smith treated as an objective force. Marx pointed out that behind the 'invisible hand' of the market lay the actions of capitalists. Notions of democracy were subject to similar analysis. For Marx, the ideals of equality and freedom, which underpinned the emerging democracies of Europe, were ideological devices that masked inegalitarianism and exploitation. Marx believed that the contradiction between rhetoric and reality was a major cause of the **alienation** that pervaded capitalist nations.

alienation At the heart of this concept is the idea of something separated that should not be separated. In sociology its use implies a fundamental injustice and source of social ills.

Marx argued that contradictions such as these were inherent in the capitalist mode of production and that they would give rise to crises that would eventually expose the exploitation on which the system is based. One of these contradictions was capitalism's dependence on profit, which created a tendency for overproduction and a subsequent cycle of boom and slump. Marx predicted that as new technological developments increased the capacity for production so machines would replace the power of men. As the labour force declines, unemployment will grow and many people, including members of the middle class, will be unable to meet their basic needs. At the same time, the gap between rich and poor will grow ever wider, making the disparities of wealth more visible. This process of immiseration

proletarianisation The process by which some sections of the middle class, such as clerical workers, experience changes to their work that make them increasingly comparable to manual workers.

(increasing poverty) and **proletarianisation** (the middle class become working class) will lead to the birth of a revolutionary proletariat that, with the help of the middle-class intelligentsia, will bring about the collapse of capitalism.

Marx's predictions owed much to his analysis of the French Revolution, in which the attachment of the landed aristocracy to agricultural production had blocked the rising power of the industrial bourgeoisie, so giving rise to revolution. But Marx believed the capitalist revolution would be different from the French Revolution. In the French Revolution the bourgeoisie had replaced the church and landowners as the ruling class, so for working people, one form of exploitation had simply been replaced by another. Marx argued that the communist revolution would be different because it would get rid of the class system altogether and usher in a new era of economic, political and social egalitarianism. He believed that even the state, which historically had always supported the interests of the economically powerful, would 'wither away' and citizens would, for the first time, be responsible for their own decisions.

When reviewing Marx's writings on class it is essential to understand that his ideas varied depending on whether he was writing about his theoretical model or analysing an empirical reality (Giddens 1971). His theoretical model is the two-class structure of owners and non-owners of the means of production, locked in an antagonistic relationship, but his empirical analyses acknowledge a more complex reality. When analysing capitalism Marx identified a number of different classes, including the bourgeoisie, **petit bourgeoisie**, working class and lumpenproletariat. He also talked about class fractions, such as rentiers and entrepreneurs, who comprised the capitalist ruling class. He acknowledged the existence of emerging classes, such as the professional middle class, as well as remnants of classes from previous historical eras, such as the *Junkers*, Germany's landed aristocracy, who remained influential long after capitalism was established.

petit bourgeoisie The class of capitalist small-business owners. Marx used this concept to differentiate small- and large-business owners.

Marx used the terms 'class in itself' and 'class for itself' to distinguish between classes that exist objectively but whose members lack a shared social identity, and those classes that are both an objective and a subjective reality. A class exists in itself insofar as its members share an objective economic position, such as their dependence on the sale of their labour for survival, but they may have no consciousness of their common interests. In contrast, members of a class for itself recognise their common situation and so develop a shared identity, which is what makes them capable of acting together in pursuit of their collective interests. Marx pointed out that it is only when this shared social identity exists that classes become historically significant groupings—this insight is crucial to his analysis because of his emphasis on classes as real social forces with transformative capacity.

Marx's ideas have widely acknowledged theoretical and empirical weaknesses. His theories have been criticised for being teleological, historicist, scientist and monocausal. They are predicated on an evolutionary view of social development based on social laws and an assumption of an ultimate goal that does not exist. They overemphasise the importance of the economy as the ultimate determinant of social change.

Many of his empirical predictions have also proved inaccurate. The middle class has grown in size rather than collapsed, capitalism has proved extraordinarily stable, it is in non-capitalist rather than capitalist countries that revolutionary movements based on Marx's ideas have occurred, and most socialist regimes have proved ultimately unsustainable. The overall distribution of wealth has not become more equal, but improvements in living standards mean citizens in capitalist economies have their most basic material needs met. But these criticisms need to be balanced against the extraordinary insights Marx's ideas offer into the workings of capitalism and the conditions it engenders. Reading his work continues to have contemporary relevance and resonance with many aspects of social experiences and arrangements.

2.2.2   Weber: A multidimensional view of inequality

2.2.2.1   Weber versus Marx

Of all the modern social theorists, it is perhaps most true of Weber that his work represents a 'debate with the ghost of Marx'. Marx and Weber shared a similar concern with big picture issues about how social formations change, and both had much to say about social inequality. They lived in different periods and approached sociology with different objectives. Unlike Marx, Weber was a professional sociologist. Although both writers were politically active, Weber was a nationalist who worked within the political establishment, while Marx was a radical who tried to effect social change through the labour movement.

Weber wrote some forty years after Marx, when the contours of modernity were more developed. He witnessed the reformist direction taken by the workers' movement that Marx had sought to inspire to revolution. Weber extends and challenges Marx's ideas, which is especially evident in his argument that although class is best understood in terms of economic factors and is deeply implicated in creating and maintaining inequality, non-economic factors are also important.

Whereas Marx is best understood as a nineteenth-century thinker characterised by optimism about the possibilities that science offers for humanity, Weber has more in common with twentieth-century thought. Weber was not scientistic in the way Marx was, recognising that while science can tell us what is, it cannot tell us what we ought to do (1949). Science can tell us whether something, such as human cloning, is possible, but it cannot tell us whether we should actually perform it. Weber understood that science was incapable of providing answers to questions of value and morality (1946). And did he not share Marx's historicist and teleological view of history. He rejected the idea that societies were evolving in a particular direction, that there was an internal mechanism driving social change and that laws about its operation could be discovered. His famous study, *The Protestant Ethic and the Spirit of Capitalism* (1976 [1904]), was written with the intention of demonstrating the significance of contingent factors on the direction of social change and the independent power of culture. This study sought to show that capitalism was not the inevitable outcome of internal, economically driven, social processes, but the result of an elective affinity of social and economic characteristics. Just as there is no inevitability about the emergence of capitalism as an economic system, so there is no inevitability that it will be overtaken by a more egalitarian and just social system.

economic determinism
While especially associated with Marxism, this term refers to any approach that sees economic forces as the decisive determinant of social arrangements.

Weber's criticism of Marx's **economic determinism** extended to his theory of social action. Rather than seeing collective social action as the almost inevitable outcome of unequal class relationships, Weber argued there was no certainty that common economic interests would lead to class action. As with his broader theory of social change, Weber argued that whether a social class becomes a social movement is a matter for historical analysis and will always depend on the particularities of the moment.

Weber's two most important contributions to the study of social inequality:

1   His multidimensional model of inequality, which identifies differences in access to sources of power as the key explanatory factors, thereby granting equal weight to cultural (social), economic and political variables.

2   His emphasis on how economic resources are distributed, rather than how they are generated, as the principal explanation for economic inequality.

2.2.2.2   Weber's model

In an argument accepted by most contemporary social theorists, Weber argues that it is power rather than class that ultimately determines the distribution of resources in a given social formation. The sources of power are multidimensional, and although class is the most important source in capitalist stratification systems, in other systems other factors are more influential. The three sources of power Weber identifies are class, status and **party**, with party generally understood as referring to political organisation. For Weber, who gets what is determined by social, economic and political factors, and each of these must be understood as having an independent influence.

party The organised expression of class and status groups to support their interests. It is similar to, but broader than, the notion of political party because it includes organisational groupings such as trade unions.

There are also important differences between Marx and Weber's understanding of class. Weber agrees with Marx that class should refer to economic variables, but he regards the relationship to the market as the critical feature, rather than legal rights over productive property. In Weber's schema property ownership is significant because it represents a resource, comparable to education or skills, and this determines the relationship to the market. For Weber, it is the way resources are distributed that determines position in the social hierarchy.

status The social honour and prestige accorded to a person or groups by other members of society. Status may be positive or negative.

Weber used the term **status** to refer to the idea of social honour. In his terminology it is linked to the notion of *Stande*, the hierarchy of estates that formed the feudal system of stratification. These positions were fixed at birth and there was little the individual could do to move out of them. They were to some degree associated with a hierarchy of occupational groups that were inherited within the family, but Weber also noted that by definition status groups have a shared sense of social identity and this generates a common culture and lifestyle. The craft guilds of artisans in medieval Europe typify this type of social category: as well as controlling the labour market for specific skills, they offered their members a wide range of rights and privileges. Membership was associated with a particular lifestyle and patterns of behaviour that distinguished them from their peers. These occupationally based status groups are therefore also classes, a fact that Weber recognised in his concept of the social class, which is very similar to Marx's 'class for itself'.

For Weber, social classes are collections of people whose common economic position results in shared life chances, lifestyles and similar mobility patterns (1978 [1922]:302). These commonalities tend to lead to a shared identity and lifestyle so that they are simultaneously a class and a status group. But this does not mean that all status groups are classes. Whereas classes, by definition, form a horizontal band across the hierarchy of wealth, status groups cut across this band vertically because they include people with varying economic resources. They bring people together on quite a different basis from the class system and, in this sense, disrupt it. African Americans are a status group whose shared history as an oppressed racial group has been the basis of an important social movement in the USA. But although it is true that most of them are economically disadvantaged, a significant proportion are middle class. This vertical source of social solidarity has meant that the labour movement in the USA has been internally divided by racial difference, weakening its capacity to form a coherent social movement.

The idea of the social class also solves the problem of how to identify distinct classes. If classes are understood only in terms of their relationship to the market, then there are logically as many classes as there are occupational groupings. But by combining class and status Weber acknowledged that it is only when an economic collective also has a sense of shared identity that a socially significant group is formed. He argued that, according to this criterion, capitalism is comprised of a working class, a professional middle class of technicians, lower-level managers and specialists whose position is determined by their intellectual skills, small-business owners equivalent to Marx's petit bourgeoisie and an upper class of property owners. Thus, although Weber's identification of the sources of class power is different from Marx's, his image of the class structure is remarkably similar.

An important concept developed by Weber is that of **social closure**. Weber observed that when groups develop a sense of shared identity, they use this to control access to scarce resources through strategies of social inclusion and exclusion—this usually involves some claim to a monopoly over a particular area of social life so that only those who belong to a specific group can take advantage of it. These areas are not only economic, such as jobs or property rights, but also political, cultural and social, such as the right to bear arms and to vote. They also involve establishing social distance by, for example, placing restrictions on marriage partners or establishing rules around consumption, such as permissible or forbidden foods.

> **social closure** When groups develop a sense of shared identity and use this to control access to scarce resources through strategies of social inclusion and exclusion.

In a number of respects, Weber's theories provided a better theoretical foundation for the analysis of inequality in the twentieth century than those of Marx. By emphasising the market, Weber was able to account for the significance of non-material resources such as intellectual skills that were to form the knowledge economy. These ideas accounted for the growth in power and significance of the professional middle classes. His rejection of any form of economic determinism and his emphasis on status as a horizontal form of power cutting across the vertical hierarchy of class provided for the rise of identity politics, such as the women's movement. His belief in the contingent nature of social change and rejection of any form of historicism was also congruent with contemporary understandings of the possibilities for social science. In arguing that class position did not necessarily determine either social identity or social action he could also account for the political failures of the working class.

Contemporary Australia

SOCIAL CLOSURE IN THE HIGH COURT: JOBS FOR THE BOYS

The current process for selecting judges to the High Court has a 'clubby' feel, which gives the impression it is about who you know more than anything else, the shadow federal Attorney-General claimed last week.

Nicola Roxon has urged the government to consider gender, geography and philosophy when filling the looming vacancy in the High Court, which will need to be filled when Justice Michael McHugh retires in November this year.

In a speech to the ACT Women Lawyers' Association, Roxon called for a debate on reforming Australia's 'informal' and 'secretive' processes for judicial selection.

'Our High Court judges are selected on the say so of the Governor-General, acting on a recommendation of Cabinet. The *High Court Act* requires the Attorney-General to consult with the state counterparts in relation to appointment, but other than that there are no rules governing the process. The current Attorney-General has said he will consult with the Chief Justice, professional associations and possibly other judges. But these consultations are all informal and secretive,' Roxon said.

'I have a number of concerns with this opaque process—first and foremost, it has a clubby feeling to it. It generates a sense that selection to our most important bench is based more on who you know than any objective criteria.

'With no disrespect to the current Court, this sense of clubbiness cannot help but be confirmed when you note that all seven judges are men, five of them are from New South Wales, four graduated from Sydney University and three of them have been presidents of bar associations. It creates an impression that the pool for judicial appointments is small and closed,' Roxon said.

There should be a national discussion about improving the selection process, Roxon argued. 'Pointing to America in horror is not a sufficient reason to cling to the status quo. There are plenty of models that would provide more transparency and merit protection without the intense and often unfair scrutiny that occurs in the USA,' she said.

The diversity of High Court judges needs to be broadened, Roxon claimed. She reminded her audience of Justice McHugh's warning late last year that 'when a court is socially and culturally homogenous, it is less likely to command public confidence in the impartiality of the institution'. She said it would be fitting for the government to take this concern on board when picking Justice McHugh's replacement.

Source: <www.lexisnexis.com/community/lwau/blogs/top_stories/archive/2005/09/16/roxon-slams-old-boys-club-appointments.aspx>

Weber's multidimensional model of stratification was suited to a fluid, global world composed of diverse groups who were best understood as defined by their status characteristics. In the period after the Second World War, class remained an important variable in labour market dynamics, but of equal importance was the entrance of women and NESB groups. Immigration and changes in women's relationship to the market meant that the labour force could no longer be understood within the one-dimensional framework of class.

Weber's ideas provided powerful tools for the analysis of inequality. In the high tide of stratification studies in the 1960s and 1970s they were widely used, sometimes on their own, sometimes in combination with Marxist ideas. Together the two theorists formed the major paradigm for the investigation of inequality in the twentieth century.

2.2.3   Durkheim and structural functionalism

Although Durkheim favoured socialism as a political ideology, throughout most of the twentieth century his ideas were associated with conservative social theories. This is because he was concerned with the conservative question of how order was possible rather than with the relationship between social conflict and social change. Durkheim's interest was in how society was possible at all. His central question was: what is the source of social solidarity? His answer assumed a Hobbesian ontology that treated sociability not as a given but as requiring explanation. In this Durkheim differs from Marx, whose concept of alienation assumes sociability is a fundamental human trait.

Durkheim argued that society is made possible through the establishment of a moral order that socialisation ensures is accepted as natural and taken for granted. This forms the social glue that holds social actors together. He believed that sudden social change is problematic because it disrupts the moral order, which produces social conflict and disorder.

Durkheim's writings on inequality arise as a secondary aspect of his concern with the role of the division of labour in establishing social solidarity. Durkheim had an evolutionary view of social development, arguing that what differentiated traditional societies from modern ones was the degree of social differentiation and specialisation. Taking Australian Aboriginal societies as his example, Durkheim argued that in traditional societies social order was established because the relatively simple division of labour meant that their inhabitants shared similar experiences and this established a common morality and world view. He called this form of solidarity 'mechanical' because it emerged directly out of the shared experiences of the population.

Durkheim contrasted this with the 'organic solidarity' of modern societies characterised by high levels of functional differentiation and specialisation. As the division of labour increases, so the possibilities for shared understandings and a common world view diminish. The uniform religious beliefs of traditional societies give way to a wide range of other norms and values, none of which can claim the status of absolute truth. Rather than being based on likeness and shared experience, solidarity in modern societies is based on functional interdependence. Extreme specialisation means no one can survive on their own. Differentiation and division create high levels of interdependence and it is on this foundation that social solidarity is established.

For Durkheim, it is not the existence of inequality that is problematic but its legitimation in a way that preserves social order. Hierarchy within the division of labour is necessary and it must be accepted as normal and appropriate. He argued that what makes the attachment of different rewards to different social systems acceptable is an open system that recognises talent and hard work. His vision of an ordered society is that of a meritocracy. He wrote:

> What is needed if social order is to reign is that the mass of men be contented with their lot. But what is needed for them to be content is not that they have more or less, but that they be convinced that they have no right to more (1962:242).

Problems arise only if the system is not perceived to be legitimate. Whereas in the past the social hierarchy was justified on religious grounds as the natural order ordained by God, in modern societies it is justified on the basis of **meritocracy**. Durkheim agreed with Weber that credentialism was the central and appropriate mechanism for the distribution of resources but, unlike Weber, he regarded social conflict as a sign of dysfunction. In a normal society people accept the existence of hierarchy as part of an overall system for the distribution of rewards, understand how it operates and their place within it, and limit their demands to those that are appropriate for survival. Far from being a routine part of social relations, if social conflict occurs it is because of a crisis of legitimation that results from practices perceived to be unfair or from some other disruption to the system, which challenges the status quo.

meritocracy A society where social position is achieved through ability and effort rather than ascribed on the basis of age or social background.

Durkheim's ideas provided the foundation for the functionalist theory of inequality, which stressed the inevitability of inequality and justified its existence on the principle of equal opportunity. Although he believed that high levels of inequality were potentially disruptive, partly through their association with corruption, the potential radicalism of his ideas was lost in the period after the Second World War when they became associated with the extreme conservatism of sociologist Talcott Parsons.

Since that time Durkheim's explanation of inequality has not been widely used compared with the dominance of Marx and Weber. Nonetheless, his ideas offer a useful starting point for understanding why industrial relations in contemporary democracies are relatively stable, despite knowledge of extreme disparities of wealth. Durkheim's arguments about the damaging effects of corruption and cronyism provide a foundation for understanding the kind of conflict that sometimes spills over into movements such as anti-globalisation.

2.3   Theories of inequality in the modern period

In the period between the two world wars, sociology was influenced by two distinct trends: one was interpretivist, influenced by the work of the social psychologist George Herbert Mead, the other structuralist, coming under the increasing dominance of the work of Talcott Parsons. Although figures within the Marxist-orientated Frankfurt school were active at this time, it was not until the 1960s that their work became widely known. At this time, and in the period immediately following the Second World War, theories of inequality were largely framed within the conservative functionalist tradition, but in the period following the end of the Cold War, after the flourishing of the countercultural revolution of the 1960s and early 1970s, conflict theories came into prominence. The study of inequality then moved to the centre of sociological endeavour, with the works of Marx and Weber forming the theoretical foundation. The study of inequality during this period can be characterised as following two increasingly divergent paths, one questioning the appropriateness of structural approaches, the other remaining convinced of their relevance. The latter approach attempted to map the class structure through the application of theoretical models of the occupational structure. This became known as the employment aggregate approach. This approach is examined in this section because its **structuralism** fits within a modernist theoretical framework.

structuralism A term originating from linguistics, especially from Saussure and Chomsky—generally refers to any form of analysis or theory in which structure takes priority over agency.

2.3.1   Functionalism: Parsons, Davis and Moore and meritocracy

Traditional **functionalism**, as developed by Durkheim and Parsons, is based on an organic-model analogy: society is comparable to a living organism with needs that must be met for its survival. Just as the circulation system serves the purpose of transporting vital nutrients to the organs and other parts of the human anatomy, so a highly differentiated human society requires, for example, a well-developed transport system to carry goods from one area to another. The organic and social systems function to look after the needs of the system as a whole. Functionalist theory looks at all social phenomena from this perspective, arguing that if something has endured it must be because it serves a useful purpose—a function—for the system as a whole. There is a radical component to this view insofar as it insists that moral assumptions about whether social phenomena are good or bad should be cast aside. Traditional functionalists challenge conventional judgments about the undesirability of

functionalism Treats society as a system made up of self-regulating and interacting parts. It asks 'How is society possible?' and answers by examining the contribution each part of society makes to the maintenance of the whole.

some phenomena that have always been with us, such as prostitution and suicide, arguing that a certain amount of 'deviance' may be healthy. But, somehow, Parsonian functionalists always managed to turn their insights to a conservative end. American sociologist Kingsley Davis, for example, presented an unashamedly patriarchal interpretation of prostitution, arguing that it protected the institution of marriage (1937). The sexual desires of married men can be satisfied within marriage but unmarried men need an alternative source or they will tempt married women into infidelity. The function of prostitution, therefore, is to protect the stability of the nuclear family—but the double standard implied in this analysis is ignored. A similar denial of issues of power is evident in the functionalist argument that since social inequality has always existed, it must serve some useful purpose.

In the post-Second World War period, Parsons was the most significant figure in the functionalist tradition, and his ideas became the foundation for the dominant paradigm for understanding social inequality in the 1950s. This was the period of the Cold War, when fear of communist regimes, especially that of the Soviet Union, dominated politics. The activities of Senator Joseph McCarthy and the House of Representatives Committee for UnAmerican Activities meant that anyone suspected of having communist sympathies in the USA could be investigated and faced possible social and economic exclusion. The dominance of functionalism in this conservative period is not surprising since its image of a society based on a value consensus and open political processes justified and endorsed mainstream American—that is, male, white, Protestant—values.

Because the word 'class' was associated with the radical views of Marx and socialism it was not a favoured term in the functionalist lexicon. Instead, Parsons and his colleagues combined a conservative reading of Weber with Durkheim's argument about the existence of a consensus-based normative value system that accepted the existence of an economic, social and political hierarchy. Drawing on Weber's concept of status, functionalists conceptualised the stratification system as a hierarchy of social esteem. Parsons defined stratification as 'the differential ranking of the human individuals who compose a given social system and their treatment as superior and inferior relative to one another in certain socially important respects' (1954 [1940]:69). Today this use of Weber's concept of status as the foundation of the whole system of stratification is regarded as a distortion of his theories, which instead locate status as one of three sources of the unequal distribution of power. Parsonian functionalism presents a bowdlerised version of Weber's analysis of inequality.

According to Parsons the sources of status in all societies can be related to six key variables:

1   personal qualities, such as age, intelligence and beauty
2   family position
3   achievements, such as qualifications and skills
4   possessions
5   authority
6   influence.

Unlike traditional societies, in which ascribed characteristics such as the family are the primary source of social honour and position, in modern societies it is achieved factors such as educational and occupational achievements, personal qualities and possessions (understood as individually earned) that count. The labour market is the main mechanism for the achievement of position because this is where the value of these variables is assessed. The underlying assumption of this argument is that the allocation process is open and meritocratic.

Parson's image of the stratification system is of a hierarchy of graduated layers of occupationally based status groups with high levels of mobility between the levels, a model that assumes there is a consensus and acceptance of the rewards attached to each level. Rather than class conflict, exclusion and exploitation, the stratification system is conceived as rooted in a common value system into which all citizens are socialised from an early age. Functionalists regarded this in a positive light because they believed it created a well-ordered, functional society.

The empirical counterpart of these theories, social surveys that mapped the distribution of social esteem within the occupational hierarchy, found a close match between this distribution and the hierarchy of economic reward. This was taken as confirmation of the functionalist argument that economic differentials were based on collective valuations about the social worth of the various positions. Tension and conflict were interpreted as part of a process of continuing equilibrium maintenance, which required constant adjustments. In the stratification system these tensions stemmed from the inevitable influence of self-interest and, more broadly, competition over the values attached to different positions; however, because the hierarchy of values existed above and beyond the influence of any one individual or group, success depended on playing the game and conforming to the rules. In this way the stability of the system as a whole was maintained.

The most influential and succinct iteration of functionalist arguments on stratification is the essay 'Some Principles of Stratification', by sociologists Kingsley Davis and Wilbert Moore (1945). The authors argue that the high level of specialisation and differentiation that characterises modern democracies creates a demand for a wide range of abilities and skills. But since talent is not evenly distributed it needs to be matched to position. The problem, then, is how to do this in a way that is accepted as morally correct by the population. Davis and Moore argue that in Western democracies inequality is accepted because the process of allocation to position is open to competition. Equal access to basic services, including education and health, ensures a level playing field. Principles of equal opportunity, operating through the requirement for credentials, contain the effects of wealth and influence. In democratic nations an open system of selection ensures that the most talented individuals will have access to the most important and demanding jobs, while those with less talent will work in areas suitable for them. The system therefore works like a giant sorting mechanism, filling round holes with round pegs and square holes with square pegs. In this way, inequality works for the good of the system as a whole. It is only when rapid social change or unsettling external influences challenge the consensus that social conflict is likely to emerge.

The weaknesses of the functionalist tradition are obvious. The assumption of a value consensus and of a meritocracy were two areas that came under the most serious attack. Multiculturalism and the entrance of women into the workforce brought into prominence

social mobility The movement of individuals and groups between different socioeconomic positions.

questions about whose values were assumed, while studies of **social mobility** challenged the assumption of meritocracy. Nonetheless, the idea that we live in a classless society, that inequality is accepted because of value consensus and that anyone can make it if they try remain important justifications of inequality in liberal democracies today.

2.3.2   The conflict tradition

The rise of conflict theory in sociology in the mid-1960s was closely associated with the study of class. Within this tradition, debates focused on whether Marxist or Weberian approaches were best and on how changes in the occupational order were affecting the composition of the classes. Marxist theorists, in particular, faced the problem of how to account for the growth of the professional middle class which Marx had predicted would shrivel. The two most influential approaches were those of sociologists Erik Olin Wright (1997) and John Goldthorpe (Goldthorpe et al. 1987), who were critical of functionalist status approaches that merely map the rewards associated with different occupations. For these theorists the objective was to understand how labour market position (Weber) or the relationship to the means of production (Marx) explain the distribution of economic reward.

2.3.2.1   Neo-Marxist class analysis

Wright's interest in applying Marx's ideas to contemporary arrangements stems from an ideological commitment to Marxism and a political philosophy of 'radical egalitarianism' (2005:7). His work on class represents one of the most influential modern attempts to map the class structure, not least because it combines a theoretically rigorous application of Marx's ideas with empirical analysis through an international survey of the class structure called the Comparative Project of Class Structure and Class Consciousness. The aim of this project is to demonstrate empirically that 'class counts' and 'has systematic and significant consequences both for the lives of individuals and for the dynamics of institutions' (1997). Wright has also been able to contribute to important debates about the distribution and relations of class in contemporary liberal democracies.

In Wright's analysis class is defined as the unequal distribution of rights and powers over productive resources. He regards exploitation as the concept that is pivotal to Marxist class analysis. Exploitation refers to a type of interdependence between two groups that:

- is antagonistic because the benefits that accrue to one group 'imposes harm' on the other (2005:23)
- excludes the exploited from access to certain productive resources
- appropriates the labour power of the exploited to the advantage of the exploiters.

Since exploitation also involves control over the products and labour power of the exploited, domination is also a central feature of class relations.

Wright observes that in any social formation class arrangements are always complex. This is especially true in modernity because the state plays a central role in conferring rights and duties on different groups. The state's regulation of the labour market, its involvement in the provision and regulation of services, and its control over business and foreign investment mean that there can be no simple model of polarised class relations (2005:13). Nonetheless, exploitative class relationships still exist because of the legitimation of the private ownership of production. For this reason, class position is defined by that relationship, with exploitation as the central variable. Like all class theorists of the twentieth century, Wright sees the occupational order as the area in which these relations operate. As a consequence individuals are situated within a structured pattern of relations, with each class defined by its access to a different range of rights and powers over productive resources (2005:14). In this sense 'a class "location" is not "*a* class"; it is a location-within-relations' (2005:19).

Initially, Wright developed a six-class model of class, in which three groups were defined as occupying contradictory class locations, with one foot in the bourgeoisie and the other in the proletariat. This model identified three forms of control and exploitation: money, physical infrastructure and authority over people, with the upper class controlling all three, the working class controlling none and the middle class occupying the three contradictory class locations. In response to criticisms that this focused on relations of domination rather than exploitation Wright revised the model by identifying the exploitation of four types of assets: labour power, capital, organisational, and skills or credentials. This model produced a schema of twelve classes spread grid-like across the four axes of asset type. Of these, three are ownership classes (the bourgeoisie, small employers and the petit bourgeoisie), three are managers, three are supervisors and three are workers, who are defined according to whether they are expert, skilled or unskilled. An important feature of this scheme is that it includes non-manual workers within the working class.

2.3.2.2   Neo-Weberian class analysis: The Nuffield scheme

Although Goldthorpe's work on the class structure was not explicitly developed as neo-Weberian it is usually portrayed as deriving from a Weberian framework. Whereas neo-Marxists focus on exploitative relationships arising out of relations of production, neo-Weberians focus on life chances arising out of market relations.

Like Wright, Goldthorpe's scheme is an 'employment aggregate' approach that focuses on employment relations (Crompton 1998:55) in the form of market and work relationships. Market situation refers to those aspects of an occupation that relate to the market, including source and level of income, employment conditions and career prospects. Work situation refers to the relations of authority and control associated with the position (Goldthorpe 1980:40). This leads to a three-class model comprising employers, the self-employed and employees, each of whom has a number of subcategories. The service class is comprised of employers and high-level managers, professionals and administrators. The intermediate class is comprised of the petty bourgeoisie (small-business owners and self-employed artisans, with or without employees), farmers and self-employed workers in primary production, and skilled workers. The working class is comprised of non-skilled workers and agricultural labourers. This can be disaggregated into a seven- or eleven-class scheme (Erikson & Goldthorpe 1992).

Each class is defined by whether a labour or service contract applies. Labour contracts apply in positions that involve a high degree of supervision and low asset specificity, which refers to the extent to which the skills required for the job are transferable. This means that workers are easily replaced and surveillance can ensure that organisational goals are met. Service contracts apply in positions with a high level of asset specificity so that skills development, work performance and commitment to the organisation are rewarded with a range of salary, fringe and career advancement benefits.

2.4   Mapping class and inequality in Australia

The conceptual frameworks of Wright and Goldthorpe have been used to analyse the class structure of Australia. In the 1990s sociologist Mike Emmison used Goldthorpe's eight category model to produce a class map of Australian society, which also takes account of gender (1991; see Table 2.1). The dominance of women in Classes IIIa and IIIb, where they comprised over three-quarters of the gender composition of these groups, is notable. In contrast, men dominated the upper service class and the last three classes, especially the skilled manual class, of which they make up nearly 90 per cent of the gender composition. The location of Class IIIb is important because in some models routine non-manual workers are located in the working class. If they had been located there the size of the working class would have swollen from just over one-quarter of the sample to nearly one-third (Emmison 1991:41).

Table 2.1   Distribution of class and sex in the workforce: Goldthorpe model

Class		Men %	Women %	Total
I	Upper service, higher professional administrative and managerial, large proprietors	14.8	5.0	10.5
II	Lower service, lower professional administrators, managers, etc.; higher grade technicians, supervisors of non-manual employees	21.1	26.6	23.5
IIIa	Routine non-manual higher grade	4.1	18.2	10.3
IIIb	Routine non-manual lower grade: personal service workers	3.5	22.3	11.8
IVabc	Small proprietors, own account workers, non-agricultural, farmers, smallholders	12.0	8.7	10.6
V	Lower grade technical, manual supervisory	8.9	6.4	7.8
VI	Skilled manual workers	18.4	2.8	11.5
VII	Semi-skilled and unskilled manual	17.1	10.0	14.0

Source: Emmison 1991:43

Note: Figures have been rounded to the nearest decimal point.

Table 2.2 shows the distribution of these classes in the Australian population. Unsurprisingly, this schema produced a much larger working class than that of Goldthorpe, with the three groups who own no assets of any kind forming the largest class. If skilled workers are added into this group the size of the working class is increased to 44 per cent of the sample. Within the middle class there were two main groups. Experts comprised 11 per cent of the Australian population, with the smallest fraction of these being expert supervisors (2 per cent), most of whom were professionals without managerial responsibilities. The second group were non-expert managers and supervisors: skilled and unskilled managers and supervisors, who make up 31 per cent of the population. Owners make up a relatively small percentage of the class structure, with only 1 per cent of the sample forming the bourgeoisie.

Using the same data, Mark Western and Janeen Baxter applied Wright's Marxist model of class (Table 2.3).

Table 2.2   Distribution of respondents into Wright's multiple assets exploitation model*

Assets in the means of production					
Owners	Non-owners (wage labourers)				
1 Bourgeoisie—1%	4 Expert managers—6%	7 Skilled managers—10%	10 Unskilled managers—7%	+	Organisation assets
2 Small employers—4%	5 Expert supervisors—2%	8 Skilled supervisors—6%	11 Unskilled supervisors—8%	> 0	
3 Petit bourgeoisie—9%	6 Expert workers—3%	9 Skilled workers—12%	12 Proletarians—32%	–	
	+	> 0	–		

Skills/credential assets
Source: Emmison 1991:53

*Distributions are of people in the paid workforce; those excluded are unemployed, housewives, retired people, etc. (all data are weighted to ensure representativeness with census estimates; N = 1196).

Table 2.3   Class and weekly income in Australia, 2003

Class category	Percentage in workforce	Average weekly income ($)
Employers	6	1038
Petty bourgeoisie	9	774
Expert managers	22	1175
Managers	13	736
Experts	12	890
White-collar workers	21	517
Blue-collar workers	17	659

Source: Western & Baxter 2007:226

Wright's schema has been applied to data from the Australian Survey of Social Attitudes (see Table 2.3). This shows that those who earned the most were expert managers, followed closely by employers. It reveals a large income gap between employers and experts, followed closely by the petty bourgeoisie. At the bottom of the income ladder sit white-collar workers, most of whom are women in part-time employment, who earn less than half the income of employers and expert managers. Above them are blue-collar workers whose earnings place them closer to managers than to white-collar workers. Sociologists Mark Western and Janeen Baxter point out that the income differences in Table 2.3 would be even greater if the figures differentiated by gender and full-time and part-time work, and if, among employers, owners of larger enterprises were separated from small-business owners (2007:225).

2.5   Subjective understandings of inequality and social division

To what extent are Australians willing to identify with a particular social class? In the 1980s Chamberlain found that only one-fifth were willing to locate themselves in the working class (21 per cent), and around 28 per cent were unwilling to identify a class location for themselves. The remaining 51 per cent described themselves as middle class (1983). Similar findings were made by social researchers Jonathan Kelley and Maria Evans in a six-nation study that included Australia (1995). Kelley and Evans explained this tendency to identify as middle class as the result of reference group processes in which people see the world as an enlarged version of their reference group. Because the people with whom they interact are similar to themselves they regard themselves as 'average and unexceptional' (1995:158). The researchers argue that material forces are mediated by reference groups that create an image of hierarchy that denies the existence of sharp class distinctions and therefore works to reduce class conflict.

These findings are contradicted by those of the Australian Social Attitudes Survey conducted in 2003 (see Table 2.4). In this study only 9 per cent of respondents were unwilling to locate themselves within one of three classes and 41 per cent of respondents identified as working class, with just under 50 per cent identifying as middle class.

Table 2.4   Subjective class membership, 2003

Which social class would you say you belong to?	Frequency	%
Upper class	58	1.4
Middle class	2029	48.9
Working class	1703	41.0
None	363	8.7

Source: Australian Social Attitudes Survey 2003

The difference between this finding and that of earlier studies is partly due to methodological differences. Kelley and Evans employed a ten-class model, and the questionnaire itself did not use the terms 'middle', 'working' or 'upper' class. Instead, the categorisation of the groups into classes was done at the analysis stage with the researchers grouping all those falling in the middle eight ranges into the middle class. Since nearly 75 per cent of respondents fell into these categories it justified their claim that most people saw themselves as middle class. Using a different method, which included the option of a 'None' response, the Australian Social Attitudes Survey found that for over 90 per cent of Australians the term 'class' is a meaningful one and that they have some sense of their place within a three-class scheme. This finding supports claims that class remains relevant to contemporary social consciousness.

2.6   Conclusion

The models of inequality generated by the classical theorists were developed at the beginning of the modern era as part of the birth of sociology itself. It is not surprising, therefore, that by the 1980s they came to epitomise all that was problematic about modernist social theory and were eventually overwhelmed by later developments. Yet part of the argument of this book is that there remains a place for such approaches within contemporary social theory because empirical analysis provides evidence that meaningful divisions can be made between occupational groups and that these pattern life chances. Although most of these studies are not Australian, they demonstrate that, when it comes to these basic aspects of life experience, class does indeed count. Their weakness is that they take no account of subjectivities and, in their focus on occupation, ignore other areas of social life, including the domestic sphere. Broader understandings of processes of social exclusion that occur outside this arena therefore escape analysis.

These ideas are also important because, despite all the changes that have taken place in Australian society, we continue to live in a social system that has continuities with the period in which the classical theories of inequality emerged. The private ownership of wealth, albeit heavily corporatised, is still the foundation of the social order. Its distribution, though regulated by the state, remains fundamentally subject to market principles and there remains a large group of people whose control of their labour and its reward is quite limited. Although the word 'capitalism' has to be qualified with prefixes such as 'post' or 'new' it remains a helpful descriptor of the kind of arrangements in which we live today. So even though these ideas are in many ways outmoded they nonetheless contain significant explanatory power. Marx's ideas about exploitation, **ideology** and class domination maintain resonance with at least some aspects of today's social order. Similarly, Weber's insights into the distribution of social honour link directly with Bourdieu's notions of cultural capital. While functionalism has been far less enduringly influential than the ideas of Marx and Weber, the justification for inequality presented by Davis and Moore captures important assumptions about meritocracy that continue to underpin relations of inequality.

ideology A concept based on Marx's argument that in any age shared ideas or beliefs are used to justify the interests of the dominant social class.

Discussion questions

1   What does Marx mean by his distinction between a 'class in itself' and a 'class for itself'? Why does this distinction matter and is it relevant today?
2   Why is Weber's model of inequality described as 'multidimensional'? Identify two ways in which his understanding of class differs from that of Marx.
3   How do functionalist theorists account for the unequal distribution of power? Do you agree with this analysis?

3

○

TRANSFORMATIONS OF CLASS THEORY: FROM CLASS TO IDENTITY

○

3.1   Introduction

This chapter examines in some detail the debates and theories in the field of inequality that developed outside of stratification theory in the period following the Second World War. It concentrates on the challenge represented by the **cultural turn** and the emergence of new frameworks for understanding social inequality. It is therefore most closely concerned with the second of the questions that guide this study: how are the dimensions of inequality changing in the context of globalisation and a postindustrial society? A review of theoretical developments within the field of feminist and race and ethnicity studies are included in the chapter. Their critique of the limitations of traditional stratification theory played a critical role

cultural turn The transition within social theory from a concern with the economy as the main sphere of sociological interest towards a concern with culture, understood as an autonomous sphere.

in moving forward understandings of contemporary forms of social division, including recognition of the need for identity to be a key concept for understanding the individualised world of postindustrialisation.

The work of Bourdieu and his concepts of social and cultural capital are identified as crucial in enabling inequality theorists to adapt to the postindustrial environment. This chapter reviews central features of Bourdieu's ideas on inequality and links them to the work of a new wave of theorists. These new approaches employ a relational conception of class and conceive of inequality as a three-dimensional social space in which a range of variables contribute to social division. Class is understood as having ongoing relevance but it coexists with social and cultural dimensions. This multidimensional understanding of inequality also brings into prominence the role of subjectivities in shaping social relations since it is through the perceptions and images that social actors have of themselves and others that separation and distance are maintained.

3.2   The first wave: Early critiques of class theory

The theoretical challenge to traditional theories of inequality was rooted in debates that first emerged in the late 1950s. The expansion of the welfare state in Europe after the Second World War formed the context for arguments from the Right suggesting that Western nations were now classless. In *Class and Class Conflict* (1959) sociologist Ralf Dahrendorf argued that while Marxist theories of class were relevant in the first period of modernisation they had little salience in the postcapitalist economies now emerging in the West. The rise of the **service economy** and developments in technology were collapsing old unities and creating new groupings that lacked a sense of collective identity. Technology was fragmenting the working class, while the middle class was 'born decomposed' (1959:53), having always been individualistic in outlook. The power and unity of the upper class was eroding as a new breed of managers replaced owners as leaders of corporations. A further source of the decomposition of capital was the creation of the joint stock company, which diffused ownership among institutional and individual owners. Credentialism was replacing property as the main source of social honour and economic position. Meritocratic principles ensured an open society, and the extension of citizenship rights through the establishment of the welfare state had removed the traditional grievances of the working class. Class-based industrial conflict, in the form of strikes and protests, was now institutionalised through procedures of state-sponsored industrial arbitration and conciliation. Dahrendorf argued that these changes required a radical revision of theories of inequality and that Weberian theories of power and authority were more suited for the task than were Marxist theories of class.

service economy The decline of manual labour and the expansion of the service sector.

Dahrendorf's work was relevant to another argument about the impact of consumerism on working-class consciousness. The theory of **embourgeoisement** associated with social theorist and economist John Galbraith (1958) and sociologists Seymour Lipset and Reinhard Bendix (1959) suggested that affluence was eroding working-class consciousness, and that working-class people were becoming middle class in outlook and behaviour. Class conflict was being replaced by aspirationalism as the working class developed the privatised and instrumental attitudes typical of the middle class. Although this thesis was refuted by Goldthorpe and sociologist David Lockwood (1969) in their study of well-paid car factory workers in the new industrial towns of the United Kingdom, the idea that it was time for social theory to move beyond its nineteenth-century origins was now on the sociological agenda.

embourgeoisement One of the first theories to argue that class distinctions were declining. It appeared in the 1950s when mass consumption led to the claim that affluence was eroding working-class consciousness.

In 1973 sociologist Daniel Bell published his analysis of the emergence of a new postindustrial order based on cultural production. *The Coming of Post-Industrial Society* was in sympathy with many of Dahrendorf's observations but went further in its observations about the shift in the foundations of social organisation. Bell argued that the central organisational principle of the new social order was technical rationality and that knowledge, not property, was the new currency. Evidence for this lay in the dominance of the service sector in the economy and the entrance of women into the labour market. Bell agreed with Dahrendorf that Western democracies now operated on open, meritocratic principles and that credentialism, not property ownership, was the principle pathway to position and power. The unbridled power of market forces that had characterised industrial society was now constrained by an interventionist state that operated not as an instrument of class oppression but as an independent arbitrator, mediating between competing interest groups.

These ideas were vigorously contested by a new wave of Marxist theorists, many of whom were associated with the radical social and political movements of the time. Drawing on the humanistic writings of early Marx as well as the work of **critical theorists** such as Theodor Adorno (1973), Marxist philosopher Louis Althusser (1971) and political theorist Antonio Gramsci (1971), the absence of a radical working-class movement was explained as the result of the dominant ideology of the ruling class. Gramsci's theory of hegemony suggested that state power is used to encourage common-sense beliefs that create a false consciousness that reinforces inequality. This means that people have a false sense of what will advance them economically and socially. For example, the influence of popular culture has created a working class more interested in football and Hollywood than in attempting to change the system that, according to Gramsci, exploits them. These ideas were developed by cultural theorists Stuart Hall and Dick Hebdige at the Centre for Contemporary Cultural Studies in the United Kingdom, in their research on the media and working-class subcultures.

critical theory A number of theories, including Marxist conflict theory and the theories of the Frankfurt School, that have in common an attempt to challenge conventional understandings of social phenomena.

Despite the interest generated by these ideas it was evident that the dominant-ideology thesis was flawed. To writers investigating popular culture it was problematic to regard movements such as punk rock as false consciousness rather than an authentic expression of working-class culture. Marxism, however much revised, was unable to escape its theoretical limitations. In *The Dominant Ideology Thesis* (1980), sociologists Nicholas Abercrombie, Stephen Hill and Bryan Turner argued that if it had ever been the case that cultural forms could be reduced to an expression of ruling class domination, by the 1980s this was no longer tenable. The abandonment of Marxist class theory as the dominant paradigm in Australian and European sociology had begun.

3.3   The second wave: Postmodernity and poststructuralism

These developments gained further impetus from the arguments that emerged from postmodern theorists in the 1980s. Unlike the work of writers such as Dahrendorf and Bell, these arguments did not propose a classless society. Instead they suggested that globalisation was giving rise to new contradictions and conflicts that required entirely new frameworks for understanding social formations. The theoretical background of these ideas was the work of social theorists such as Anthony Giddens, Ulrich Beck and Zygmunt Bauman, whose concern was not so much to analyse social inequality but to decipher the new conditions that characterised advanced Western nations.

late modern theory Used by Beck and Giddens to signal their emphasis on the continuity with modernity rather than a radical break with it as advocated by postmodernists.

The main arguments of postmodern or **late modern theory** can be divided into social, economic, cultural and political spheres. In the social sphere, traditional inequalities of class are seen to have become fragmented, divided by other variables such as gender, ethnicity and sexual preference. In the economic sphere, the Fordist arrangements, characterised by factory production with workers lacking power or control over their labour, and strong trade unions, has given way to post-Fordist arrangements in which the workforce is flexible and multiskilled and industrial relations are individualised with workers representing themselves. Cultural production dominates industry and the production of identity, which is constructed through individual choice rather than being prescribed. Politically, the interventionist state of modernity has become the postwelfare state and market forces are allowed free rein. The morality of welfare dependence is challenged and citizens are constructed by the state as self-governing individuals, responsible for meeting their own needs. Underpinning these changes is a relentless drive towards constant transformation, which dissolves all solid ties and promotes individualisation.

3.3.1   Class and postmodernity

individualism The belief in the autonomy of the individual human being in social action so that whatever befalls a person or group is viewed as their individual responsibility.

Giddens and Beck were key theorists in documenting the rise of **individualism**. They use the term 'late modern' rather than 'postmodern' to emphasise their view that contemporary formations represent continuity with modernity rather than the radical break suggested by writers such as social theorist David Harvey (1990) and sociologist Alain Touraine (1974). Their theory of reflexive modernity describes a world in which the dynamics and contradictions of modernity force people and systems into an ongoing process of self-confrontation. For the individual, social existence takes the form of a self-directed project that is constructed reflexively through a process of self-monitoring. At the level of institutions and systems the constant creation of new knowledge also requires a continuous reappraisal of existing patterns of action.

Giddens describes how globalisation and the emergence of a postindustrial economy has led to the detraditionalisation of social life. In a runaway world of constant transformation, the past can no longer provide signposts for living. Instead of relying on the predetermined coordinates of our ancestors, we must continually reframe and reinterpret our understandings of who we are and where we are going. Since the goalposts are always shifting, individuals must look inward for signposts for action. Giddens describes this self-referential process as the 'project of the self' and regards reflexive 'self-identity' rather than class as the foundation of contemporary social existence.

Giddens' portrayal of a world rushing towards an uncertain destiny has much in common with Beck's account of **risk** society (1992, 2002). According to Beck it is risk that is the predominant characteristic of our times. Whereas traditional societies had their share of risks, these were localised, limited in impact and mostly determined by nature. In modern society they were usually products of class location, such as the health risks associated with poverty or the hazards of manual labour.

risk What characterises risk in late modernity is that it is generated by human activity, especially the application of scientific knowledge, it is uncalculable and it is global in its reach.

What distinguishes risk in late modern social formations is that it is generated by human activity, especially the application of scientific knowledge. Its impact extends spatially beyond national boundaries, and temporally into the future. While the management of risk is a characteristic feature of late modernity, it is inherently incalculable.

Beck's initial concern was with environmental risk but his later writings extended his arguments to include the sense of fear and uncertainty that occurs at the institutional level in relation to the management of potential global catastrophe, and also in our daily lives, through everyday anxieties such as fear of our neighbour or of the food we eat. The calculation of risk is, therefore, systemic and pervasive.

Beck and Giddens agree that, although classes still exist, the class-based movements that characterised modernity, such as the labour movement, have given way to 'lifestyle politics—the politics of life decisions' (1991:215), such as feminism and environmentalism. These movements are not rooted in collective identities but emerge out of the pressures that globalisation places on self-identity. They express lifestyle rather than life chances. They are less concerned with improving material conditions than with responding to 'those moral and existential questions repressed by the core institutions of modernity' (1991:223). Giddens also argues that elites have forged new transnational identities, while the strongholds of working-class solidarity have disappeared as industries have gone offshore and as women and immigrants have entered the labour force. The service class, on the other hand, has always been individualistic, achieving advancement through individual rather than collective effort. For Giddens, even the most impoverished sections of society do not form a cohesive segment, instead dipping into poverty for only limited periods (2001).

Although his conception of the postmodern subject differs, Bauman's account of the postmodern condition, in its depiction of a fluid, highly individualised world, has many similarities with those of Giddens and Beck. Bauman (2000) uses the term 'liquid modernity' to describe the uncertain and inchoate nature of the contemporary human condition. The solid self-constituting subject of modernity has become fragmented and mutable under the impact of consumption (Shilling & Mellor 2001:191–2). The idea of the working class, whose interests were simultaneously opposed to yet intertwined with those of the capitalist owners, belongs to the historical era of industrialisation. The belief in progress has also given way to a sense of uncertainty about what the future holds. The 'foundation of trust in progress is nowadays prominent mostly for its cracks, fissures and chronic fissiparousness' (Bauman 2000:133). Bauman likens the difference between the disciplined industrial worker of the modern era and the aesthetic attachment of the contemporary worker to that between pilgrim and tourist. Industrial workers are like pilgrims, solidly fixed to their project and on task for their lifetime. The contemporary citizen is motivated by short-term gratification and barely attached to the label 'worker'. Like a tourist, the worker today is driven by an aesthetic sensibility and a restless search for new experiences. Bauman argues that work has lost its centrality to contemporary existence and no longer provides a 'secure axis around which to wrap and fix self-definitions, identities and life projects' (2000:139). Just as the worker is light, so too is capital, being no longer encumbered by the burden of material production. It is ideas that now count. In the new equation of profit, consumers rather than workers generate wealth and, as a result, the holding power of labour over capital has shrunk.

Tourists trip lightly over the economy, fuelled by liquid capital and detached from solid ties to time and space through the mastery of technology. Lacking fixed attachments, consumption becomes their new centre of gravity. Yet even the attachments that are formed are fundamentally unstable because of a relentless drive for the next experience that must be met by a constant supply of enticing new products: 'the lid has been taken off human desires' (2005:79); these know no satisfaction and create a permanent state in which 'desire desires desire' (1998).

At the other end of the scale lies the flawed consumer, variously described by Bauman as the vagabond (1998), the underclass and the new poor (2005). Like the tourist, they are on the move but not through choice. They are the refugees, the criminals, the socially excluded, the flotsam and jetsam whom globalisation has left behind. They move, not through choice, but because they have nowhere to go. They are subject to constant surveillance and are locked out of contemporary sources of identity. They are constructed by the state as the enemy within and portrayed in popular discourse as incompetent architects of their own misfortune.

Between these two extremes lie four categories with an attachment to the labour market. Drawing on Reich, Bauman identifies routine labourers, those engaged in personal services, educators and functionaries of the **welfare state**, and the symbol manipulators who 'invent ideas and the ways to make them desirable and marketable' (2000:152). While the routine labourers are the most vulnerable of these groups and the least identified with their labour, 'from whatever side you look at it, the spectre of fragility and precariousness haunts all kinds of jobs' (2005). Although Bauman uses the term 'underclass', its connection with Marxism is more rhetorical than real. His key message is that we live in a world in which structures have dissolved, where self-motivated, self-centred, self-reflective individualism prevails.

welfare state The mechanism through which social policy is developed and delivered. In capitalist economies its main function is to allocate resources in a climate of conflicting claims.

The impact of liquid modernity on inequality has been captured by authors such as Standing, who argues that the casualisation of the labour market has created a new class he calls the **precariat**. The precariat comprise the rapidly growing number of people who are unable to find permanent jobs and face a lifelong existence of insecurity (2011). For Standing a key feature of the precariat is that they have none of the hard-won benefits of the labour movement of the 20th century and no

precariat Individuals who are unable to find permanent jobs and who face lifelong insecurity. They live on the economic edge, in a permanent state of debt.

occupational narrative to direct their lives. Their lack of rights makes them denizens rather than citizens. They have no superannuation, no medical leave, no rights-based benefits and they are subject to coercion by workfare. The demands for consumption mean they live on the economic edge, in a permanent state of debt. Their relationship to the state is one of supplicants—beggars—because, unlike the traditional working class, their exclusion from the labour market means they have no bargaining capacity with any agency of the state. Instead they depend on the discretionary power of bureaucrats for favourable treatment.

At the top of Standing's new class structure is the plutocratic elite, who are 'absurdly rich' (2011:7) and control and own most of the world's wealth. Beneath them are the salariat, who enjoy the fruits of stable employment and work in large corporations, government agencies and public administration, and the proficians whose technical and professional skills enable them to earn high incomes as consultants and independent agents. Beneath them are what remains of the working class, who work in secure manual occupations but have lost their sense of social solidarity.

Standing identifies three factions within the precariat. The first are those falling out of the traditional working class, who are not well educated and look backwards to the solid structures and certainties of the past. The second faction are the migrants and, in Europe, the Roma (gypsies). Their marginal legal status means they have few options for protest and instead maintain a strategy of keeping their heads down and maintaining a low profile because they fear expulsion. The third are the progressives: young, educated people who are denied a future because of the lack of permanent employment and a career, even when they have a degree. Each of the three factions has a distinct class consciousness but, according to Standing, all three contain a sense of anger at the denial of the means to a fulfilling life. In *A Precariat Charter* (2014), Standing argues that the conditions are in place for the precariat, especially the young, educated faction, to form a social movement and demand a change to the existing arrangements. Achieving this will involve three overlapping struggles. The first is the struggle for recognition of the idea that the unenviable position of the precariat is not the result of their individual failure but of a system that is stacked against them. The second is a demand for better representation and acknowledgement of their agency. Rather than being seen as victims, or in need of improvement, the precariat seek to be accepted on their own terms as capable of living a worthwhile life. The last struggle is for the redistribution of key resources—not necessarily economic, but which will allow the precariat to reproduce itself and create a more enlightened world. These resources include security, control of time, space, financial knowledge and education. Standing argues these demands should be the basis of a new Magna Carta that the world is badly in need of if it is to become more humane.

3.3.2   Poststructuralism: Foucault and discourse theory

The work of the postmodern theorists can best be described as diversionary in its effect on theories of social inequality. Their ideas drew attention away from the classical areas of the economy and the related solid inequalities of class to a new world of sociological concerns, such as environmental risk and self-identity. A related development was the

postructuralism Rather than seeing social forms as having solid foundations based on such things as economic arrangements, poststructuralist theories argue that they are constantly negotiated and subject to change.

discourse Discourses are particular scientific and specialist languages that comprise certain knowledges and ways of behaving. According to Foucault discourses are the main phenomenon of power.

impact of **poststructuralism**, whose emphasis on culture as the principal object of analysis, and rejection of the assumptions that underpinned the Enlightenment project, created yet another challenge for traditional class theory. Here, the work of Foucault was especially influential. His ideas offered an entirely new paradigm for understanding issues of power and inequality.

Foucault turned the sociological gaze towards culture, understood not as a kind of extrusion on the structural foundations laid down by the economy but as an autonomous force, shaped by language and signs. In this new analysis it is **discourse**, not class, that is the primary concept for understanding relationships of inequality. The assumption of a coherent subject is replaced by a fragmented notion of a subject who is constrained by relationships of power that arise not from economic imperatives but from culturally located symbolic systems. Knowledge replaces property as the locus of power. The researcher is conceived not as an observer uncovering some kind of objective truth but as deeply implicated in structures of knowledge and power. Since it is impossible to uncover the truth, attention must be diverted from an analysis of objective form to an analysis of how knowledge is constructed and the impact of this.

Foucault developed the idea of discourse to express the idea of systems of thought that constitute knowledge and establish ways of behaving. The idea of discourse joined that of identity in displacing the idea of class and class power from the vocabulary of critical theorists. It offered an alternative theoretical tool for understanding inequality that permitted a far more eclectic and flexible approach than that offered by Marxist theory. It provided critical theorists interested in cultural manifestations of inequality with a powerful new conceptual tool: feminists, race and ethnicity theorists and sociologists of the body embraced it. Freed from the materialist shackles of Marxism and the requirement to lay claim to the truth, poststructural theorists were able to explore the interpenetration and intersection of different forms of inequality and power operating across a wide range of spheres.

3.4   Fragmented identities: Gender, race and ethnicity

The historical dominance of class as the master concept for understanding social formations meant that throughout the modern period the dimensions of race and gender were largely invisible to sociology. With the advent of multiculturalism and the entrance of women into the labour market came new theories that sought to locate black men and women in the postcolonial landscape. Writers such as Stuart Hall, working in the area of race and ethnicity, and philosopher Judith Butler, in the area of gender, turned to poststructuralist theories for inspiration. Their studies spoke to a generation of new scholars whose understanding of inequality was shaped by the women's movement and the struggles for recognition and citizenship experienced by immigrant and other non-Anglo-Celtic groups, such as Indigenous Australians and African Americans. Although some theorists continued to work with the idea of class, the concept of identity came to be seen as a more appropriate tool for explaining individualised patterns of social division.

3.4.1   Transformations of gender

The historical neglect of gender within social theory is astonishing given that it is arguably the most pervasive of all forms of inequality. The complexity of gender relations has also made the field one of the most challenging. While men and women everywhere are socially differentiated they are also involved in complex relationships of dependence and interdependence. The male child is dependent on the mother, yet as an adult dominates women in the workplace. Women are more likely than their husbands to commence divorce proceedings, yet as single mothers they face a high risk of poverty. Women experience the glass ceiling in the workplace but working-class men, gay men and non-whites are subordinated by dominant constructions of masculinity. The history of gender theory is one that has involved a gradual accommodation in this fragmented and multidimensional field.

Theoretical concerns about gender inequality were rooted in observations about the decline of the nuclear family and associated concerns about single parents and child poverty, as well as the entrance of women to the workplace. These raised a series of important questions.

1   What is the explanation for women's secondary position in the labour market?
2   Why are women nearly always the primary caregivers?
3   Why, when they enter the labour force, do women enter the secondary labour market, in low-paid, casual and insecure positions? (Bottero 2005:110).

Second-wave feminist theory, which appeared in the late 1960s and early 1970s and is contained in the writings of theorists such as Juliet Mitchell (1971), used Marxist class theory to answer these questions. These theorists presented what, in some interpretations, amounted to a rather functionalist argument about the need of capitalism for a division of labour that relegated women to the domestic sphere as unpaid servants for the reproduction of human labour within the family. Women also socialised the next generation of workers for labour within the capitalist system. Since the class system was understood to be at the root of women's oppression, the solution lay in socialist revolution, which would simultaneously abolish both class and gender inequality.

Socialist feminism was fairly quickly critiqued by radical feminists who drew on the central idea of **patriarchy** rather than class and capitalism to explain women's oppression (Millett 1968; Delphy 1984). Radical feminists pointed out that since women everywhere, from remote tribal communities to Western democracies, are subordinate to and exploited by men, the class system cannot be the root cause. The problem, then, was not capitalism but men, whose greater physical strength enabled them to subjugate women. For feminist author

patriarchy At its most straightforward the idea of a society in which men as a social group dominate women as a social group, especially through the role of the father within the family.

Shulamith Firestone (1970), the solution was not revolution but advances in reproductive technology that would allow women to shed their role as bearers of children and enter the labour market on equal terms with men.

But the idea of patriarchy also proved inadequate. It could not account for the enormous variation in gender relations or for women's complicity in these arrangements. It left unresolved the paradox of male–female interdependence and their shared life chances within the family. It was also unable to shed light on the role of ethnicity in binding the genders. Black men and black women are subordinated to white Anglo-Saxon culture. While patriarchy was useful in pointing to a basic truth about gender relations, its explanatory power failed when it came to understanding specific gender arrangements.

Dual systems theory (Hartmann 1981) attempted to overcome these difficulties by bringing together feminist and class theory. Marxism sheds light on how capitalism disadvantages women, but its preoccupation with class ignores the need to address women's issues. Radical feminism is specifically concerned with gender politics but it offers a reductionist explanation of gender inequality as an outcome of biology. Its tendency to portray women as good and men as bad also offers no solution to the establishment of an egalitarian society in which men join women as equal partners. Economist Heidi Hartmann attempted to resolve these problems by suggesting that both patriarchy and class operate to create gender inequality. She added a materialist account to radical feminism's psychological one, arguing that, through organisations such as trade unions, men exclude women from the best jobs in the labour market. This relegates them to the domestic sphere and to financial and social dependence on men. Hartmann used cultural anthropologist Gayle Rubin's (1975) concept of the 'sex/gender' system to explain how patriarchy works independently of capitalism. The sex/gender system refers to the institutionalised system that allots resources, property and privileges to people according to culturally defined gender roles (Lerner 1986). Sex determines that women should be child bearers, but the sex/gender system makes them child rearers.

While Hartmann's ideas accounted for male sexism and the exploitation of both genders by capitalism, they could not explain the impact of gender on labour organisation. Hartmann's model separated the effects of patriarchy and class but other research was demonstrating the indivisibility of the social and the economic. Using case studies of the workplace, social researcher Alison Scott showed how gender affects the construction of occupational categories and forms of consciousness and action (Crompton & Mann 1986:156). Her work and that of other gender theorists demonstrated that gender

> influences the skill categorisation of job tasks, affects the status, income and forms of contract of certain jobs and affects men's and women's experience of work despite similar structural situations. It plays a role in dividing the workforce both structurally and politically.
>
> Source: Scott, in Crompton & Mann 1986:157

These studies demonstrated that the market does not act according to principles of instrumental rationality (that is, on objective criteria based on the maximisation of profit and productivity) but is strongly influenced by political and ideological forces. Gender and economic inequality are indivisible. This insight has far-reaching consequences for class and gender theory. Gender can no longer be understood as a separate realm but instead is integral to class formation, class processes and class identity (Bottero 2005:112). It collapses modernist notions of the dichotomies of gender–class, home–work and public–private, and supports poststructuralist arguments about the diversity of gendered experience.

This move away from the rigidity of class-based theories of gender received further impetus from the work of black feminists who protested against the sexism of the black civil rights movement and the racism of the women's liberation movement. In *Ain't I A Woman? Black Women and Feminism*, African American feminist bell hooks (1981) accuses the women's liberation movement of being a white, middle-class phenomenon, concerned with the gender issues affecting white, middle-class women. For hooks, the movement ignored the more profound issues of inequality affecting black women and poor women more generally; hooks points out that during the years of slavery in the USA black women were at the very bottom of the social hierarchy. As well as being subjected to the power of the male slave-owner they also suffered at the hands of their white mistresses and of black men. She was equally critical of the sexism of the civil rights movement for its use of masculinist notions that attempted to control women's sexuality and treated them as inferior to men. She argues that today, class, racism and sexism combine to keep black women in low status jobs and vulnerable to violence within their family and the workplace.

As the feminist struggle for women's emancipation declined and attention began to shift towards the diversity of women's experiences, poststructuralist theory came to dominate gender studies and the concepts of identity and discourse replaced those of patriarchy and class. The individualism implicit in the idea of identity created a more open space than that of either patriarchy or class in which to consider the divergent forces that shaped women's lives in the late twentieth century. The overlapping, intertwining and competing systems of gender, class and race could be acknowledged without the compulsion to give primacy to any one of these social forces. The idea of fractured or fragmented identities expressed this complex interplay and enabled social theorists to acknowledge the range of women's lived experiences.

Foucault's notion of discourse became widely employed by feminists seeking to account for women's **subjectivities**. The relativist stance of poststructuralism offered a theoretical framework which allowed feminist theorists to include women whose voices had formerly been excluded from academic analysis. The rejection of modernist notions of progress and metanarratives such as Marxism and liberation, enabled the everyday experiences of American Muslims (Gole 1996), working-class Liverpudlians (Skeggs 1997) and Indigenous people in Australia (Moreton-Robinson 2004) to be heard.

subjectivities How we see ourselves and our relations with others, based on our immediate and relatively limited understandings and experience of social life.

The development of the field of masculinities and queer theory gave further impetus to the deconstruction of gender and the further marginalisation of the concept of class for the understanding of inequality. In *Masculinities* (1995), Connell explores how gender is enacted by men. She develops the idea of hegemonic masculinity to explain how a particular cultural image of masculinity as the strong, self-determining man forms the dominant ideal against which all men measure themselves and are measured by others. While few men live up to this idealised model of male behaviour, its dominance subordinates alternative ways of enacting masculinity. Connell argues that while the idea of the social construction of gender has some merit it also suggests a misleading rigidity. Instead, she argues that gender is always enacted through bodily practices that require reflexive monitoring and performance. While Connell acknowledges the influence of social structure, her ideas about performance and the dynamic nature of gender moves her some distance from modernist gender theory.

The idea of the performativity of gender is further developed by Butler (1999). Originally locating her work within queer theory, Butler argues that gender is only meaningful insofar as it involves performance. With this argument she removes the last vestiges of solidity from the notion of gender and separates it entirely from its association with sex.

> When the constructed status of gender is theorized as radically independent of sex, gender itself becomes a free floating artifice, with the consequence that *man* and *masculine* might just as easily signify a female body as a male one, and *woman* and *feminine* a male body as easily as a female one.
>
> Source: Butler 1999:10

For Butler, then, there is no such thing as female, even at the biological level. The body is a site of social transformation, hence there is no essential maleness or femaleness. Not only is the link between class and gender dissolved, but gender as a coherent concept also disappears. In this formless world the concerns of the researcher are necessarily transferred from inequality in the material sphere to difference in the sphere of culture.

3.4.2   Race and ethnicity: Towards postcolonial theories

3.4.2.1   Developing theories of racial inequality

Although modernist theories of inequality were almost as blind to race and ethnicity as they were to gender, sociologists have always challenged the notion of race, arguing that there is only one, human, race. They refer to the work of biologists, including geneticists, that shows that there are more differences within so-called racial groupings than there are between them. The denial of the existence of races is also supported by the repeated failure of attempts to provide a consistent taxonomy of racial groups. Instead, sociologists argue racial divisions result from a process of '**Othering**', in which dominant groups create a sense of social distance through claims of racial distinction.

Othering This term was first popularised by Said who used it to explain the way in which the West turned the land, culture and peoples of the East into objects for study and colonisation.

In the USA in the 1970s the changing social context of the civil rights movement and the seeming intransigence of black disadvantage brought the issue of racial inequality to the fore. This formed the basis of theories of race that drew on Marxist concepts of capitalist economic exploitation, ideology and class. These ideas were valuable because they offered an explanation for the economic aspects of white colonial power that authors such as sociologist Andre Gunder Frank (1966) argued formed the foundation for Western development. Ideas similar to dual systems theory were developed to account for the combined effect of gender and race. Sociologists Stephen Castles and Godula Kosack (1973) argued that black workers provided the capitalist economy with a source of cheap labour during its expansion in the colonies and later, as a result of migration, within the colonising nation. From the 1950s immigrant workers formed a reserve army of labour, employed on very low wages to do the work that the local workforce, cushioned by welfare and well-developed mechanisms of industrial arbitration, were reluctant to do. Lacking the protection of trade unions or citizenship rights, these immigrant workers could be expelled to their homeland when they were no longer needed. The capitalist economy reaped a double benefit from this practice because the employment of immigrant labour kept wage rates low, but the state was absolved from long-term provision when their usefulness to the labour market wore out. From this perspective, black people form a racialised faction of the working class that is even more disadvantaged than the white working class (Miles 1982).

These arguments were also used to explain the failure of the working class to challenge capitalist exploitation because colour (and gender) divided it into factions, thereby undermining working-class solidarity. The trade union movement played an important role in this factionalisation by excluding non-white people from the benefits of employment (Cox 1970).

The strength of these theories lay in their exposure of the disadvantages, both economic and other, experienced by non-white workers within Western economies and the origins of this in colonialism. They also drew attention to the failure of the working-class movement to take up the cause of non-white workers. But these ideas were reappraised when inequality stubbornly persisted despite the extension of citizenship rights, and they came under postmodern critique. In Australia Indigenous people retain their status as an excluded minority despite decades of effort to change this. In the USA the growth of an African American middle class does not alter the fact that skin colour remains fundamental to social experience and location. In the United Kingdom, Afro-Caribbeans remain ghettoised spatially and within the labour market. These analyses suffered from the same problems as Marxist theory more generally. The thesis of a reserve army of labour was functionalist in its claim that racist exploitation was caused by the need of the capitalist economy for a cheap labour force; it was also deterministic. Nor could it account for the varied role of race and ethnicity in relations of domination and subordination across different historical periods and settings. It also shed no light on cultural dimensions of race relations and the critical role played by subjectivities.

Hall identified this weakness when he pointed out that modernity had generated multiple sources of identity, of which ethnicity is only one. He argued (1992) that modern people are 'mongrels' in the eclecticism of their sense of self because it is derived from overlapping and 'imagined communities' derived from a range of sources including national identity, political affiliation, class and gender. Hall's work and that of similar sociologists reinvigorated sociological understandings of race by locating them within the framework of postcolonialism. In the process they jettisoned the baggage of Marxist class analysis.

3.4.2.2 Race, whiteness and privilege

An important point made by postcolonial theorists is that studies of racial inequality in liberal democracies have hitherto left unexamined the position of the dominant racial grouping, whites. Yet a full understanding of racial inequality requires bringing both blackness and whiteness into view (Cowlishaw 2004). By turning the academic gaze onto whiteness, the unspoken assumption that race studies are about colour is turned upside down.

The absence of whiteness from debates or discourses of inequality has been primarily related to its social invisibility. Moreton-Robinson (2004:75) argues that whiteness forms the base of 'an invisible regime of power that secures hegemony through discourse and has material effects', both positive and negative, on the everyday life of individuals and groups. Despite its omnipresent effects, whiteness remains invisible and unnamed as a racial category. Although racial identity is a predominant signifier of inequality of life chances and outcomes, discussions of race have been blind to whiteness: the term 'race' is reserved for non-whites. Being white is aligned with being normal, and normality means belonging to no racial group.

Just as non-whiteness is linked to **social exclusion**, deprivation and poverty, so whiteness can be linked to a domain of social privilege, white privilege. Social researcher Derald Wing Sue (2003) defines white privilege as the unearned advantages and benefits that accrue by virtue of a system that holds white experiences, values and perceptions as the norm. Its attributes include the automatic conferring of dominance on those who are white, with non-whites subordinated in a descending relational hierarchy. In Australia, white Anglo-Celts sit at the top of the hierarchy, followed by other white, English-speaking groups, and then those from Europe, with western Europeans outranking those from eastern and southern Europe. In the bottom half of the hierarchy are people from Asia, then, at some distance, those from the Middle East, especially Muslim groups. Indigenous Australians occupy the lowest rung (Walter 2007). A group's position in this racial hierarchy is directly linked to its capacity to access, and to be deemed a deserving recipient of, Australian society's social, economic, political and cultural resources.

social exclusion The exclusion of groups or individuals from participation in mainstream social and economic life.

Crucially, and precisely because it is so deeply socially embedded, the invisible realm of white privilege enables its beneficiaries to remain oblivious to their privilege. In analysing how this operated in her own life, researcher Peggy McIntosh (1990) equated white privilege to an invisible, weightless knapsack of special social provisions—maps, passports, codebooks, visas, clothes, tools and blank cheques—that she could count on cashing in but of which she was unconscious of possessing. Despite her liberal views on race, she found unpacking this knapsack a confronting experience as she discovered fifty daily conditions of privilege she had previously taken for granted. These varied from the broad social conditions of feeling welcomed and normal in the usual walks of life and not having to educate her children to be aware of systemic racism for their own protection, to personal aspects such as being able to talk with her mouth full without observers attributing this to her race.

The imperviousness of the veil that cloaks white privilege lies in the tie between whiteness and individualism. The individualisation of those who are white renders their whiteness invisible. Non-whites are seen first as part of a racial group and only second, if at all, as individuals. On the cover of Alexis Wright's 2006 Miles Franklin Award-winning novel *Carpentaria*, it is noted that Wright is one of Australia's finest Aboriginal writers. Yet Peter Carey, also an award-winning Australian writer, is never described as a white Australian or even an Australian of European descent. As Chambers (1997, cited in Nicoll 2004) posits, the invisibility of the racial category of whiteness can only be maintained by atomising whiteness. By distributing it among individuals, the common whiteness of those individuals remains unperceived and unexamined. Whiteness is normalised. In place of visible white privilege is a discourse of meritocracy that allows the privilege of the dominant group to be viewed as the result of individual merit and deservingness.

By interrogating the concept of whiteness, critical race theories point out the contrast in the lived experiences of blacks and whites. Being white means not having to deal with—or even think about—race. Being non-white means being unable to ignore it. To be Indigenous in contemporary Australia is to be racialised in all aspects of life and to experience daily the negative effects of Indigeneity. White Australians, while perhaps empathising with the situation of Indigenous people, generally fail to see such positioning as the mirror reflection of their own everyday experience of white privilege. White people have the luxury of not exploring themselves as racial or cultural beings (Wing Sue 2003). The silent dichotomous contrast between whites and blacks in Australia has provided the justification for the dispossession, vilification and differential treatment of Indigenous people in the past and in the present (Moreton-Robinson 2004).

The individualised, invisible nature of whiteness means that white-dominated policies, discourses and debates are viewed as essentially unaligned to any special interest group. As social researcher Fiona Nicoll states (2004), the individualist discourse ironically ensures that individual investments in the collective primacy of white people remain invisible. Such discourses, policies and debates are deemed racially neutral and objective in their formulation and enactment. When Pauline Hanson wrapped herself in the Australian flag while vilifying Asians and Aborigines, it was an act that was essentially reasserting white privilege: a politics of whiteness. Yet although her racism against Aborigines, Asians and Muslims was publicly discussed and condemned in many cases, her racism in favour of whites remained unremarked. This enabled her white critics to avoid any scrutiny of their own and others' racial and cultural selves and consequent white privilege. Even when specifically racially based, it is the race of those who are not white that is examined.

3.5   Reviving class: Bourdieu

The cultural turn in social theory generated within sociology a sense that, in Western countries at least, a concern with inequality was anachronistic. It was not just classes that had dissolved under the impact of globalisation but also the subject itself, and with it the moral concern that had accompanied the study of inequality. Still, there remained sociologists and social theorists whose concerns about inequality were given renewed impetus with the growth of inequality that occurred in the closing decades of the twentieth century. Yet it was apparent that new models were required that acknowledged the changed social environment within which relations of domination and subordination are now played out.

The key theorist who provided the conceptual tools for moving the field forward was sociologist and anthropologist Pierre Bourdieu. Bourdieu wrote across a number of disciplinary and empirical fields, including anthropology, philosophy, sociology and education, and inequality and cultural studies, and this contributed to his influence. His work acts as a bridge across a number of domains: theoretical and empirical, structural and poststructural. While agreeing with poststructuralists on the impossibility of separating subject and object, he rejects the relativism of poststructuralism, instead maintaining a critical stance. Bourdieu argues for a reflexive sociology in which the sociologist, while never an objective observer, can nonetheless utilise particular theories and methods to throw new light on the subject.

Bourdieu's lifelong work was to bring within one theoretical framework both subjective experience and the constraining force of society that shapes and limits possibilities for action. One of the strategies he used was an examination of social practice rather than focusing on either the individual subject or the organisational features of social life. This, together with his acknowledgment that we are all situated within culture (Robbins 2000:xi), enabled his work to straddle the structuralist–poststructuralist divide.

3.5.1   Bourdieu's model of inequality

While Bourdieu might resist the construction of his writings on inequality as amounting to a model, since it suggests a rigidity of ideas and their application that he explicitly rejects, it is still helpful to use the term to refer to key aspects of his writings on inequality and social reproduction. The appeal of his work lies in his original approach to understanding difference and division while remaining grounded in many of the important insights of his intellectual predecessors. Key features of his model of inequality:

1   An understanding of social hierarchy as a three-dimensional social space constructed by different forms of capital: social, economic and cultural.
2   An understanding of the social in relational rather than structural terms while being nonetheless fundamentally conflictual in character as actors draw on a range of sources of capital to compete with one another for position.
3   Recognition of the centrality of cultural consumption as a major determinant of class.
4   Acknowledgment of the agenda-setting power of institutions.

In certain respects, Bourdieu's understanding of social class is similar to that of Weber. Like Weber he regards non-economic factors such as knowledge and beliefs as independent sources of social power while also regarding economic power as having the greatest weight. He also agrees with Weber that one form of power can be translated into another, with economic power again being the most common form of conversion. But he differs from Weber in that his model of inequality is, first, a holistic one that combines multiple dimensions of class so that 'it becomes a metaphor for the total set of social determinants' (Brubaker, in Shilling 1991:657), and second, a relational one that emphasises the way class position is always mediated through cultural knowledge. While Weber emphasises the importance of the subjective, for Bourdieu it is not so much what people believe about their class position as how their forms of consumption serve as signifiers of social position.

> One only has to bear in mind that goods are converted into distinctive signs, which may be signs of distinction but also of vulgarity, as soon as they are perceived relationally, to see that the representation which individuals and groups inevitably project through their practices and properties is an inevitable part of social reality. A class is defined as much by its *being perceived* as by its *being*, by its consumption—which need not be conspicuous in order to be symbolic.
>
> Source: Bourdieu 1984:483

Bourdieu developed a number of conceptual tools to explain how these features play out in everyday life. Here we will examine four of the most important: habitus, cultural capital, social capital and the field.

3.5.1.1   The habitus

The **habitus** represents Bourdieu's attempt to overcome the agency–structure divide. It provides a framework for understanding how social structures operate at the level of individual practice. The most commonly used term to describe the meaning of habitus is 'social disposition', which refers to the set of beliefs, attitudes, skills and practices possessed and employed by individuals in their daily lives. The habitus is closely associated with class position. Bourdieu writes: 'Social class is not defined solely by a position in the relations of production but by the class habitus which is "normally" (i.e. with a high statistical probability) associated with that position' (1984:372).

habitus A patterned way of thinking about the world, a set of values and orientations that derive from groupings in society. It describes how individuals develop attitudes and dispositions.

Bourdieu combines this structuralist analysis with a social psychological one, arguing that the habitus is not a set of attributes and attitudes that is consciously worked out. It operates unconsciously through internal beliefs that direct action but which are nonetheless derived from external social forces. An idea that is often compared to that of the habitus is sociologist Alfred Schutz's notion of the lifeworld; sometimes the two terms are used interchangeably. Like the habitus, the lifeworld refers to the predispositions and resources possessed by individuals that enable them to function in their everyday social milieu but, unlike the lifeworld, Bourdieu emphasises the ties between the habitus and social class, with each class having a characteristic habitus. It is this link that prevents the idea from being psychologically reductionist.

Bourdieu defines the habitus as 'systems of durable, transposable dispositions, structured structures predisposed to function as structuring structures, that is as principles of the generation and structuring of practices' (1977:72, from Smith 2001:136). Social reproduction is understood as a process that takes place in dynamic interaction with others. The structuralism of the concept is therefore diluted by the relationalism this implies. Social position only has meaning insofar as it implies relationships with others. It is within the habitus that structure becomes agency. Positions do not exist as objective locations but are self-consciously created by actors, individuals, groups and classes who gauge their position in relation to others and seek to modify it. It is through this activity of position-taking that the construction of difference comes into play (Robbins 2000:37) and it is within the habitus that this process is enacted. While the habitus is shaped by collective forces, it exists at the level of the individual; it is for this reason that events are contingent and never predetermined. The process of taking a position is also always a cultural process, enacted through cultural practice. This idea offers social inequality theorists an important theoretical tool for exploring how cultural practices are implicated in relations of hierarchy and domination.

3.5.1.2   Cultural capital

Bourdieu's solution to the economic determinism of Marxist class theory was to extend the notion of capital to include cultural, symbolic and social power, thus moving away entirely from Marx's unidimensional model of inequality. For Bourdieu, these resources serve not as determinants of social position but as the currency actors employ in their socially directed interactions.

cultural capital Suggests that culture operates as a resource that can be possessed, similar to economic goods and wealth, to create hierarchies in society.

In locating **cultural capital** as a resource equal in importance to that of economic capital, Bourdieu was acknowledging that culture serves as the medium through which actors identify and make distinctions between themselves and others. The possession of cultural knowledge serves as a signifier of group membership; it is through this that practices of social exclusion operate and social hierarchy is reproduced. Bourdieu's understanding of cultural knowledge is broad, including cultural practices such as manners and patterns of speech as well as the possession of formal and informal knowledge. Formal knowledge operates as a form of social closure through credentialism, which serves as a gatekeeper to occupational position by limiting access to those who hold the necessary qualification.

While formal practices operate through institutions, informal practices operate through everyday cultural practice but with similar effects. How you behave with others, your likes and dislikes connect you with some groups and distance you from others. It is through cultural practices that social identity is expressed. Bourdieu argues that the adoption of taste preferences and cultural affiliation is not a reflection of class position, as suggested by traditional Marxists, but 'position-taking in action' (Robbins 2000:xiv). This process operates through the creation of social distinctions, based on differential cultural knowledge and involving judgments of others according to cultural markers. Bourdieu's most famous study, *Distinction* (1984), is subtitled *A Social Critique of the Judgement of Taste*, which expresses precisely Bourdieu's argument that group membership is developed and sustained through cultural practices that artificially define some people as insiders and others as outsiders.

Bourdieu's study was based on survey material collected in France in the 1960s. His objective was to investigate the link between different forms of cultural practice and educational capital and social origin. Bourdieu divides cultural practice into two forms, illegitimate and legitimate. He argues that this distinction is not objective but is a product of a dominant cultural order in which judgments of taste create and sustain social hierarchy. Just as economic capital can be accumulated, so too can cultural capital, in the form of credentials and through the acquisition of the cultural knowledge of the dominant class. Although there is no intrinsic value to different forms of cultural capital, the dominant class maintains its position by successfully positioning its cultural knowledge as the only legitimate form. It is both an expression and a determinant of social position.

3.5.1.3   Social capital

Social capital refers to the social networks and sources of support available to actors as a resource. Bourdieu defines it as 'the aggregate of the actual or potential resources which are linked to possession of a durable network of more or less institutionalised relationships of mutual acquaintance and recognition' (1986:248). Social capital expresses the idea that who you know counts and, like cultural capital, is a reflection and source of social position. Bourdieu argues that one of the characteristics of the dominant class is its deliberate cultivation of social networks, especially through the education system. Attending the same elite private school creates social bonds between students that are carried through to adulthood, helping to sustain a sense of a shared social world and encouraging mutual support and promotion. The effect is to create a sort of club for the rich in which only those who went to the right schools and have the right cultural knowledge and connections can join. These social networks are used to provide opportunities to access highly rewarded social positions. The operation of social capital serves as a system of mutual exchange through which the wealthy transmit their social position to their offspring.

social capital Refers to the social networks and sources of support that are available to people to draw on as a resource; the nature of one's social capital signals one's social position.

3.5.1.4   Field

Bourdieu's idea of **field** is a spatial metaphor to explain the arena in which actors compete for advancement. It refers to domains of social life, such as politics, medicine and industry, in which struggles for social position are enacted. While the field has similarities with the idea of the market it denotes relations of domination and subordination as well as exchange relations between buyers and sellers (Swartz 1997:120). Bourdieu defines a field as:

field Bourdieu's explanation of social life as an arena in which actors compete to locate themselves. It refers to domains of social life in which struggles for social position are enacted.

> a network or configuration, of objective relations between positions. These positions are objectively defined, in their existence and in the determinations they impose upon their occupants, agents or institutions, by their present and potential situation (*situs*) in the structure of the distribution of species of power (or capital) whose possession commands access to the specific profits that are at stake in the field, as well as by their objective relation to other positions (domination, subordination, homology, etc.).
>
> Source: Bourdieu & Wacquant 1992:97

Field vs market?

Fields are the social space in which goods, knowledge, status and services are produced, circulated and accumulated (Swartz 1997:117). Although they exist at the level of institutions, Bourdieu (1984) conceives of them as actively constructed by actors who draw on their habitus to access the resources that circulate within them. Fields include formal institutions and areas of social life such as the scientific community where certain forms of knowledge and practice prevail and are accepted as valid. It is within fields that actions have meaning and receive recognition (Robbins 2000:xiv). This takes place in two ways: 'People secure recognition for themselves within the assumptions of one field, but they also "trade" that recognition for recognition within a different field altogether' (Robbins 2000:xiv). A well-known celebrity or media commentator, for example, can gain political power by becoming a politician, as in the case of Peter Garrett whose rock-star status facilitated his transition to Labor Party frontbencher. Struggles occur within and between fields and subfields on collective and individual levels using the currency of different forms of capital and according to the laws or mechanisms that operate within specific fields.

3.5.2   Bourdieu's influence

Bourdieu's ideas have had a profound influence on the study of contemporary forms of social inequality. His concept of cultural capital has provided the basis for attempts to revitalise understandings of how class inequality operates in a postindustrial world. His ideas of field and habitus represent an important development in attempts to move beyond the agency–structure dichotomy.

Bourdieu's ideas are not without criticism. His analysis of culture leaves him open to the charge of cultural elitism, and his work suggests an acceptance of bourgeois cultural ideals as valid and working-class ideals as inferior or non-existent. In *Distinction* he suggests the limited resources available to the working class inhibit development of a cultural aesthetic. This denies the value and integrity of popular culture and suggests that cultural validity adheres only to the activities of the higher classes.

Bourdieu is also accused of being a structuralist, despite his efforts to move beyond dualist explanations. His writing emphasises the hidden forces that shape actors' lives, despite their best efforts to exert agency. In much of Bourdieu's work it appears that the working classes are forever trapped in the class locations into which they were born.

On the other hand, Bourdieu's multidimensional model of class captures the way that all forms of action, whether economic or social, are always embedded in social relationships. Although many theorists work outside his model of inequality it remains an essential reference point for understanding the contemporary workings of inequality and division.

3.6   Locating inequality today

The influence of Bourdieu across the field of social inequality can be traced across a range of different approaches but there also remain theorists attached to classical models or who draw on entirely different foundations. While not exhaustive, it is possible to identify four main approaches in the field.

1   Theorists who remain attached to classical approaches that draw on Marxist or Weberian models of inequality to draw maps of the stratification system and to analyse patterns of social mobility, such as in the work of Goldthorpe and Wright (see Chapter 2).

2   Theorists working within class theory, such as sociologists Fiona Devine, Harriet Bradley and Simon Charlesworth who, in varying degrees, draw on aspects of Bourdieu's work to incorporate cultural aspects of inequality.

3   Cultural theorists, such as Bev Skeggs and Diane Reay, who use Bourdieu's concepts of class, cultural capital and the habitus to examine the social space in which various aspects of inequality are enacted.

4   New paradigms for the study of inequality, which, while drawing on the classics, incorporate the insights of survey research to generate new models of inequality and social division. The work of sociologists David Grusky, Jesper B. Sorenson and Charles Tilly are examples of this approach.

Charlesworth, for example, provides a phenomenological account of how globalisation has transformed the lives of working-class people living in the industrial areas of northern England, where they have been left out of the opportunities for prosperity offered by the postindustrial economy. Charlesworth uses Bourdieu and philosopher Merleau-Ponty to provide a 'living archaeology' (2000:9) of the lives of his respondents based on data drawn from extended interviews and conversations. The idea of class is the central concept but it is explored through concepts such as habitus, practice and **reflexivity**.

reflexivity Describes how the knowledge we gain about society can affect the way we act in it.

Devine's (1997) approach to the study of class has been largely structural, but she also draws on Bourdieu's ideas of social and cultural capital in her analysis of how middle-class parents in the USA and United Kingdom draw on their cultural and social capital to ensure that their offspring do not slip down the ladder. In *Class Practices: How Parents Help Their Children Get Good Jobs* (2004) she uses in-depth qualitative interviews to discover the everyday micropractices used by doctors and teachers to help their children into middle-class careers. Her account illustrates how class can be combined with a fully social analysis that takes account of everyday practice.

Approaching class from the opposite end to that of stratification theorists such as Devine, scholars such as Skeggs and Savage extend the work of British cultural theorists to incorporate a class perspective into their analysis. These authors write about class processes without relying on collective notions of class identity. In her study of working-class women who trained and worked within the helping professions in England in the 1980s, Skeggs argues that the discourse of 'respectability' serves as a cultural representation of class that positions classes in relationships of inferiority and superiority. Popular discourses of respectability are organised around the values and practices of the middle class so that being working class means not being respectable. Working-class women, therefore, shrink from identification with a working-class identity since it is a polluted cultural ideal.

A major theme of Skeggs' study is a critique of feminist theory's rejection of class, which she asserts is 'completely central to the lives of the women' (1997:161) and their relations with one another. Like Charlesworth, Skeggs argues that working-class people experience feelings of being devalued and worthless. While the women in her sample attempted to establish respectability through various practices, such as enrolling in a course of study or dressing in a certain style, their access to the kinds of capital that assisted this were limited because they had limited trading potential. Skeggs argues that 'respectability is one of the most ubiquitous signifiers of class' (1997:1), and that it is usually the concern of those who are seen not to have it. She argues that the construction of working-class women as non-respectable is a form of **symbolic violence**, generated through the media and other forms of symbolic representation. It devalues and delegitimises the already devalued capital of working-class people and works to keep them in subordinate positions (1997:10). She suggests it is ironic that the pollution of the idea of working class with notions of disreputableness makes the women reluctant to claim a working-class identity and leads them to construct themselves in individualistic ways.

symbolic violence Any violence that is exerted upon people in a symbolic rather than physical way; an example is a woman being treated as inferior in the workplace.

Savage offers a similarly culturalist analysis of class. In *Class Analysis and Social Transformation* (2000), Savage shows that class continues to have salience in a post-traditional society, operating through individualised class cultures. Although class does not appear to operate as a collective source of social identification, class structures continue to impact on people's life chances (2000:xii). People are still aware of the existence of classes but they hesitate to talk about them or to locate themselves within the working class. For Savage the work of social inequality theorists should be about understanding the intersection between class location and cultural identity.

3.7   Conclusion

The ideas of **postmodernism** and poststructuralism transformed the field of inequality by offering new ways for understanding social relations in contemporary social conditions. Yet for many theorists of inequality these insights were only accepted with difficulty. For most of the 1980s and 1990s the majority of stratification theorists were on the defensive, certain that class theory remained important but struggling to defend it against claims of its obsolescence. Their concern that it retain its place within social theory was based as much on their commitment to social justice as on their belief that it was a vital tool for understanding contemporary social life. To reject the idea of class and the significance of structural inequality seemed a betrayal of concerns that had been important for generations of scholars.

postmodernism The belief that society is no longer governed by history or progress and that it is highly individualistic and pluralistic.

The cultural turn had given rise to a new generation of social theorists whose interests seemed to have little to do with ideas of disadvantage and exclusion. Even feminist theory, which had historically been deeply concerned with issues of oppression and subordination, had moved towards a new agenda of subjectivities and social difference. Yet by the end of the twentieth century inequality was once again recognised as an area of importance and theories of inequality approached the area with a wider range of concepts in which class and identity, **production and consumption**, lifestyle and life chances were all recognised as being important terms in the vocabulary of inequality theory and research.

production and consumption Today it is consumption rather than production that is the most striking feature of social life. The liberation of the individual from structural constraints means that social identity is reflexively constructed through consumption.

Yet while even conservative organisations such as the IMF recognise the damage caused by excessive inequality to the national and global economy (Ostry et al. 2014), the jury is out on whether this will lead to changes that will reverse the current direction of a growing gap between the rich and the poor.

Discussion questions

1   Explain the meanings of 'reflexive modernity' and 'liquid modernity'. How do these ideas challenge traditional theories of social inequality?

2   Explain the meaning of the term 'discourse'. Do you agree that in developing this concept Foucault provided a powerful new framework for understanding inequality? Why is the idea of discourse so relevant for understanding inequality today?

3   Why do critical race theories analyse the normativity and invisibility of whiteness as a way of understanding social inequality?

4   In your own words, explain the meaning of the following terms: 'habitus', 'cultural capital', 'social capital' and 'field'. Why is Bourdieu sometimes described as a bridge between modern and postmodern theories of inequality?

PART **2**

SPHERES OF
INEQUALITY

○

○

4

○

THE MATERIAL SPHERE

○

4.1   Introduction

Despite the transition to a postindustrial society, how we earn our living and how much economic capital we have remains central to social existence. Possession of economic capital is a primary determinant of life chances, everyday experience and feelings of well-being. Children who grow up in poverty are more likely than their wealthier peers to have poor educational and career outcomes, higher rates of imprisonment, poorer health outcomes, and poorer subjective well-being (Vinson 2007; Walter & Woerner 2007; Headey & Wooden 2007). Economic position is also closely correlated with lifestyle factors such as sport preferences and selection of intimate partners (Bourdieu 1984; Bennett et al. 1999). Economic capital is the easiest of all forms of capital to convert into other forms, such as cultural or social capital: money can buy social standing, especially for the second generation, while lack of it undermines the ability to maintain the lifestyle that accompanies privilege. And while in contemporary society the traditional bonds to family and social networks have been loosened, inherited wealth remains a common feature among Australia's richest people, such as Gina Rinehart, Jamie Packer and Rupert Murdoch and their families. Other data, however, indicates that while established wealth remains significant, old money is increasingly diluted by new money as new groups located outside Australia or drawn from new businesses in the knowledge economy, join the ranks of the wealthy (Gilding 2004).

Australia emerged largely unscathed from the recent global financial crisis, which significantly impacted material well-being and inequality in the USA, United Kingdom and European countries. In the context of two decades of relative uninterrupted economic growth, how material capital (interpreted here to refer to income and wealth) is distributed is pivotal to understanding contemporary inequality. This chapter addresses the first and third guiding questions of this book by asking: what are the main economic dimensions of inequality in Australia?; and how is the distribution of Australia's social, political, economic and cultural resources reproduced across different social groups?

The chapter begins with an overview of how material well-being is distributed in Australia. Discussions of material well-being inevitably lead to an examination of its opposite, poverty. Poverty is a highly contested topic and as a necessary prelude to considering why some have gained while others are experiencing hardship, we must explore the ideological discourses that contribute to understandings of poverty, and how these are practically translated. The chapter then reviews the current winners and losers in the material stakes alongside consideration of the vexed question of whether inequality is decreasing, increasing or remaining stable in Australia, and whether it is possible to have increasing inequality without an increase in poverty. Such judgments inevitably involve ideological interpretations, even if they remain unspoken, and so this chapter also addresses the fifth organising question of this book: how does this analysis inform current debates about the kind of society Australia is, and what kind it can or should become?

4.2   The dimensions of economic inequality

Analyses of privately held economic capital normally distinguish between wealth and income. Wealth is usually defined as total assets minus total liabilities, what an individual or other unit of analysis such as household, family group or company holds at a given moment in time, and includes assets such as real estate, shares, savings, cars and works of art. Wealth is a vehicle for further economic capital accumulation through investment or as a supplement or substitute for income. It also safeguards against future hardship should income diminish. Income, in comparison, refers to any flow of money over a given period of time that derives from employment or investments. It includes wages, the superannuation contribution of employers, dividends from shareholdings and rents from investment properties. It can be measured as wage income, taxable income, gross or total income, net income and equivalent family income. Income can be converted to wealth if it exceeds expenditure and is saved or invested. The ratio between holdings of wealth and income varies with social location. High economic capital means greater wealth relative to income while low economic capital means little, no or negative wealth (debts) relative to income.

Accurately measuring privately held economic capital is a complex task. Methodological difficulties include accounting for the range of economic resources, accurately estimating value and selecting the most meaningful unit of analysis. The invisibility of some forms of economic resources, and the variability in how economic resources are defined, especially those held by the super-rich, is also a problem. As a result of under-reporting, especially if assets are held overseas, wealth estimates based on government sources, including income tax data, probably underestimate the economic capital of the wealthy, as do those based on self-reported survey data.

4.3   Economic inequality in comparative perspective

Data on economic inequality need to be located within the broader social and economic context. Living standards (including housing costs), economic conditions such as the availability of credit, and labour market conditions all play a critical role in shaping how economic resources translate into experiences of wealth or of hardship, low social status and social exclusion.

4.3.1   Income inequality in Australia

How does the distribution of economic capital in Australia compare with that in other countries? The earliest attempt to compare levels of national inequality was conducted by the OECD in the early 1970s, although results were limited by the available data. Australia was found to be relatively egalitarian, sharing the top spot for an equitable distribution with Japan and Sweden, while the most unequal countries were France and the USA (Sawyer 1976).

When analysing changes in economic inequality over time it is helpful for comparisons to express the resource being measured as a single number. Three widely used measures are the **Gini coefficient**, the Relative Income Poverty percentage, and the top 10 per cent versus the bottom 10 per cent approach. The Gini coefficient is a single unit measure in which 0 equates to a situation of perfect equality where all the economic resources are distributed equally. A situation of perfect inequality in which one economic unit owns all of the resources while the rest own nothing is represented by 1. The Relative Income Poverty percentage is the share of the population of a given country with an income of less than 50 per cent of the respective median income. The top 10 per cent versus the bottom 10 per cent calculates the average income of a nation's top 10 per cent of income earners as a multiple of the average income of that nation's bottom 10 per cent. Data across these three measures from 1995 and 2010, compiled from OECD data, are displayed in Table 4.1.

Gini coefficient An inequality measure in which 0 equates to perfect equality and 1 equates to perfect inequality (where one unit owns all the resources and the rest own nothing).

Table 4.1 Income distribution and poverty in high-income economies

	Gini coefficient		Relative Income Poverty percentage		Top 10% versus bottom 10%	
	1995	2010	1995	2010	1995	2010
Australia	0.309	0.334	11.4	14.4	7.7	8.9
Canada	0.289	0.320	10.7	11.9	7.2	8.9
Japan*	0.323	0.336	13.7	16.0	10.2	10.7
New Zealand*	0.335	0.317	8.4	10.3	8.9	8.0

	Gini coefficient		Relative Income Poverty percentage		Top 10% versus bottom 10%	
	1995	**2010**	**1995**	**2010**	**1995**	**2010**
Norway	0.243	0.249	7.1	7.5	5.4	6.0
UK**	0.340	0.341	10.5	10.0	8.9	10.0
USA	0.363	0.380	16.7	17.4	12.5	15.9

*Data from 2009
**Data begins in 1999
Income after taxes and transfers, adjusted for difference in household size

Table 4.1 shows that the differences between nations in income distribution are not small. Measured by the Gini coefficient the most unequal nation (USA) has a relative income poverty rate of 17.4 per cent in 2010; that is, 17.4 per cent of the population live on incomes below 50 per cent of the median income, compared to just 7.5 per cent of the population of Norway. On the 2010 figures, however, Australia has the second-highest relative income poverty rate, with 14.4 per cent of the population with income below 50 per cent of the median income and a Gini coefficient of .334. The USA also has the largest gap between the top and bottom of income earners, with those in the top 10 per cent earning nearly sixteen times the earnings of the lowest 10 per cent.

The key point from this table is that in a majority of the countries listed, including Australia, inequality is rising. The comparison of 1995 to 2010 data also shows that the Australian level of inequality in terms of income distribution and poverty appears to be increasing at a faster rate than other countries on several dimensions. In 1995 the Gini coefficient for Australia ranked fifth highest out of the seven countries listed, higher only than the coefficients of Canada and Norway. In 2010 the Australian Gini coefficient ranks at number four of seven. Australia's position on the Relative Income Poverty measure is the same in 1995 as it is in 2010, the third highest after the USA and Japan, but the proportion of the Australian population with income under 50 per cent of the median has increased the most, by 3 percentage points, during the fifteen years. Australia's current Relative Income Poverty rate of 14.4 per cent is also higher than the OECD average of 11 per cent (OECD 2013a). On the final measure, the ratio of top to bottom income has risen in Australia from 7.7 times to 8.9 times since 1995. Canada and the USA are the only countries with a larger increase in this ratio.

The increasing disparity in income distribution is part of a long-term trend, with the richest 10 per cent of Australians gaining almost 50 per cent of the growth in income over the last three decades. OECD figures also indicate that between 1980 and 2008, 22 per cent of all growth in household income in Australia went to the richest 1 per cent. (Though income inequality is not nearly as stark as that found in the USA, where the richest 10 per cent are estimated to have gained 80 per cent of all growth in individual income between 1980 and 2008 (Colebatch 2013).) On international measures of income, Australia is trending consistently to greater, not lesser, material inequality.

ABS data (2013a) show that the gross household income per week in Australia varies significantly across the income range. As shown in Figure 4.1, while there is a very large disparity between the bottom and the top 20 per cent of households, the gap between those in the fourth and the highest quintile is also large, with the highest quintile of households having an income nearly double that of those in the fourth quintile. Those in the top income bracket quintile are, therefore, significantly richer than those in other income quintiles.

Figure 4.1   Australian gross household income per week 2011–12

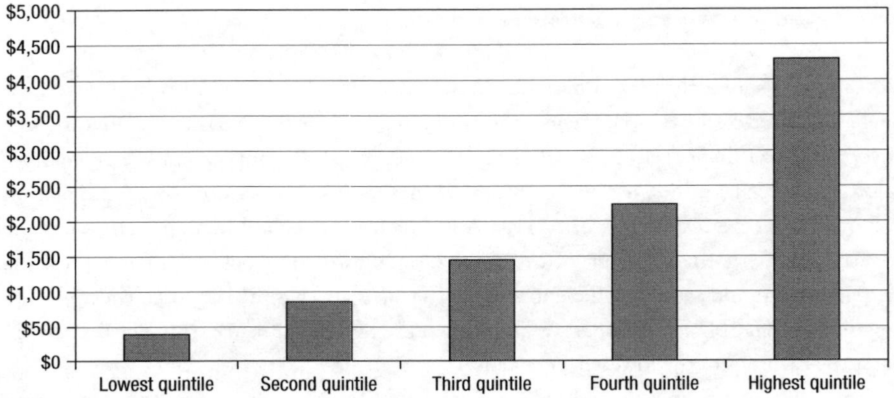

Source: ABS 2013a

4.3.2   The distribution of wealth in Australia

Other analyses indicate that overall wealth and income in Australia has been growing strongly. In real terms and in comparison to trends in other OECD countries, Australian individual and household incomes have risen substantially over the last fourteen years, with particularly strong growth in 2009–10. The Productivity Commission (Greenville et al. 2013) attribute this rise to growth in labour force earnings, labour force growth and increased hourly wages. Growth in real income, however, has not been equally distributed across the Australian population. Data from the Australian Treasury (Fletcher & Guttmann 2013) indicate a higher growth level for those in the fortieth, eightieth and ninetieth percentiles. For example, while the real income of those in the bottom 10 per cent of income earners in Australia grew by around 48 per cent from 1995 to 2011, those at the fortieth percentile saw their incomes rise by more than 60 per cent as did those at the ninetieth percentile. Age group is a factor in this growth, with the same authors finding that couples without children aged between 55 and 65 (the baby boom generation) have had the sharpest level of growth, suggesting that this group has been particularly well placed to benefit from increased labour force participation and a period of strong growth in investment income.

Wealth is a net concept that measures the extent to which the value of a household's assets exceeds its liabilities (ABS 2013a). Data released by the Australian Bureau of Statistics (ABS) estimates the mean Australian household net worth in 2011–12 at $728,000. The assets of the vast majority of Australians are largely comprised of owning their own homes (average value $370,000) and their superannuation (average value $132,000 per household). But, like income, wealth is not evenly distributed. As Figure 4.2 indicates, the median household worth of those in the lowest quintile is just $31,205, compared to $2,215,032 for the highest quintile, a ratio more than 70 times lower. These figures reduce when different household sizes and composition are taken into account, but they remain substantial. The wealthiest 20 per cent of households account for 61 per cent of the total household net worth while the poorest 20 per cent account for just 1 per cent (Stanford 2013).

Figure 4.2   Australian household net worth 2011–12

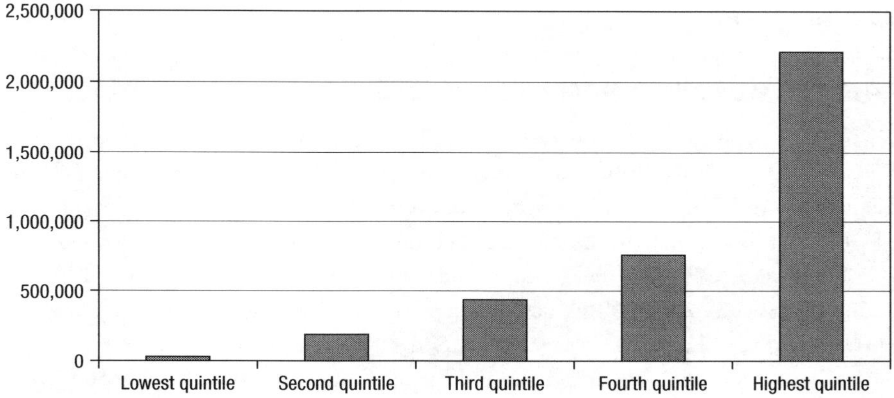

Source: ABS 2013a

These figures do not of course tell the whole story. Households can be asset rich and income poor, and this is especially the case for older Australians, many of whom own their own home, often in areas that have seen dramatic increases in property values, but may be reliant on the age pension or superannuation for the bulk of their income. This pattern is borne out in analysis by the ABS (2013a) of net worth data from 2011–2012, which reports that the average age of the household reference person in the high net worth group is 57 years compared to 54 years for those in the third (middle) quintile and just 41 years for those in the lowest net worth group—this indicates the influence of age in the accumulation of wealth. Alternatively, households can be low wealth and low income, raising the likelihood that people living within those households experience poverty.

4.4   Discourses and debates: Defining poverty

Poverty as a concept and as a lived reality is causally linked to material inequality. Poverty is also a central concept for sociological understandings of society. Its generation and reproduction has been at the core of social enquiry since Marx, Weber and Durkheim pondered these issues in the eighteenth and nineteenth centuries. At a basic level poverty refers to a lack of material resources that encompasses the idea of living below an acceptable minimum standard. Despite the centrality of poverty to empirical and theoretical explorations of inequality, the term is not simple to define. Determining exactly what poverty means, where it begins and ends and how best to measure it, are complex and contested tasks. At the centre of such disputes is the fact that poverty and inequality have ideological, political, economic and moral dimensions.

The first hurdle in examining poverty is deciding how to understand the concept. Poverty has myriad interpretations, and the following section outlines some of the key divisions in how poverty is perceived and defined. These contested definitions provide a basis for understanding how different interpretations shape public discourses on this aspect of social inequality.

4.4.1   Absolute and relative definitions of poverty

The sharpest definitions of poverty are those relating to absolute and relative poverty. In essence, the terms capture the difference between extreme poverty, in which the sustainability of life itself is threatened, and poverty that is more relative to the standard of living of a broader society. The concept of absolute poverty was first used by sociologist Seebohm Rowntree (1901) in his London study of poverty. The United Nations (1995:57, cited in Harris et al. 2001:260) updated this concept to define absolute poverty as severe deprivation of basic human needs, including food, safe drinking water, sanitation facilities, health, shelter, education and information. Its identification depends not only on income but also on access to services. In developed nations such as Australia, the relatively high standard of living means that there is seldom theoretical discussion about absolute poverty. Yet a glance around our society reveals a number of groups for whom the United Nations' definition of absolute poverty might be applied. The most prominent are Indigenous people, especially but not exclusively those living in remote communities. The poor infrastructure, substandard and overcrowded housing, inadequate sanitation and water supplies and lack of basic services are indicators of absolute poverty (Walter & Saggers 2007). People who are homeless or at risk of **homelessness** and many people with mental illness or mental disability would also fall into the category of those who experience absolute poverty.

homelessness Primary homelessness refers to those who have no secure home, location or place. Secondary homelessness refers to people who stay temporarily with friends and relatives. Tertiary homelessness includes people living in boarding houses.

In contrast, relative poverty can be applied more broadly within Australian society. Social researcher Peter Townsend (1993) points out that poverty is more than a question of 'mere physical efficiency'; it also concerns the relative dimensions of insufficient income to afford roles, activities and relationships considered normal in the individual's society. The Australian Council of Social Service (ACOSS) provides a three-tiered definition. The first tier refers to a lack of basic necessities and the second refers to socially defined necessities. These first two tiers highlight the contextual nature of a relative definition of poverty. Socially defined necessities are resources, both goods and services, that people in a society cannot reasonably live without. In modern day Australia these include a healthy diet, warm, dry, secure accommodation with good sanitation, and adequate clothing for warmth and of sufficient quality for the wearer to not stand out as different from peers. Necessary household items might include an automatic washing machine, a car, refrigerator and possibly electronic and technological goods such as a television, a computer and a mobile or a landline telephone. Lack of access to regular medical and dental treatment would also be encompassed by this definition. The third aspect of the ACOSS definition identifies the role of choice: the lack of necessities must be caused by limited material resources (an inability to afford), not personal preference. While a car, say, would be a social necessity for a family living in a regional town or an outer suburb where there is limited public transport, it may not necessarily be regarded as essential for inner-city dwellers.

Contemporary Australia

FEMALE, OLDER AND HOMELESS

The Age newspaper (May 2014) reports the case of a hard-working retired nurse aide, who found herself homeless when the owner of her run-down flat raised the rent beyond her capacity to pay. She is, according to a report commissioned by the Mercy Foundation, just one of the increasing number of older women who are experiencing homelessness. Rising housing unaffordability, higher rental prices, the lower levels of superannuation accumulated by women because of child-bearing and -raising responsibilities, and lower female wages all contribute to a high vulnerability to homelessness for older women. With Australian women over the age of fifty-five years having, on average, less than half of the superannuation of men and with less than 1 per cent of rental properties affordable by people on low incomes, homelessness among older women is expected to rise as more retire and become reliant on pensions and other government benefits. The article also taps into the impact of the crisis in affordable housing in Australia. More than 750,000 households are in housing stress which, as in the case of the retired nursing aide, has spilled over into growing numbers of homeless people (see Chapter 10). Each year an estimated 80,000–100,000 households are evicted from their rental accommodation; among them are many children (Beer & Randolph 2006).

4.4.2   Subjective and objective poverty

The existence of low economic resources does not always mean that people identify as being in poverty. How people experience economic hardship therefore forms an important debate about whether poverty should be defined externally (**objective poverty**) or whether the individual or group's experience of being poor or not poor (subjective poverty) is most relevant.

objective poverty Poverty as determined by external criteria against which the situation of individuals and groups is measured.

Objective poverty is determined by defined criteria against which the situation of individuals and groups is measured. Defining a household or individual as objectively poor centres on whether the household's or individual's standard of living, level of income or ability to access social and material resources falls against pre-determined poverty measures such as income-based poverty lines. Those below this level are defined as poor, and those above are deemed not to be in poverty. Subjective poverty concerns the way people actually experience situations of low wealth and income, how they feel about their daily lives and how it affects their families. Some people may be objectively poor by nearly all measures but deny they live in poverty. Others, while not meeting poverty criteria, feel poor and experience distress due to lack of income or ability to access what they perceive as necessities of an adequate standard of living (Dean 1992).

4.4.3   Poverty as capabilities and functionings

Another perspective on poverty relates to capabilities and functionings. The economist Amartya Sen argues that it is not so much the level of material resources an individual or a household can access that determines poverty but the sort of life that they are able to lead. Within this concept, 'functionings' refers to what a person can attain in relation to a satisfactory standard of living, participation in society and achievement of self-respect. Capabilities denote the choices that are open to a person to decide on the type of life they wish to lead (Lister 2004:1–16). Under this perspective, the lives that people can and do lead are related to the choices available to them and to their ability to access and make use of such choices. The importance of Sen's conceptualisation is that it reminds us that lack of material resources in themselves do not cause poverty; rather, it is the role of such resources in enabling individuals to lead certain types of lives and attain different levels of functionings that relate to poverty. Therefore, Sen argues, poverty should be defined not just in terms of income, material resources or standard of living but also in terms of capability failure; that is, the failure of basic capabilities to reach certain minimally acceptable levels (Sen 1992:109, cited in Lister 2004:16).

4.5   Measuring poverty

When researchers try to measure poverty, they must take into account the different definitions of poverty. The changeability in determinations on what should be counted, the unit of analysis chosen and the treatment of intangible resources such as social capital, mean that measuring poverty inevitably involves subjective judgments. This variability results in the design and utilisation of many different measures of poverty. Some of the more common are outlined below.

4.5.1   Money measures of poverty

Poverty is most often measured by level of cash income. Income is a relatively accessible indicator that enables comparisons to be made within populations and across time. Poverty is usually determined by whether income falls below or above a selected **poverty line**.

The first Australian survey of poverty was conducted by Professor Ronald Henderson, with a poverty line set at the basic (minimum) wage plus child endowment, or 56.6 per cent of average earnings. Henderson's 1971–72 study found that before housing costs, nearly 18 per cent of Australians were poor; and just over 10 per cent, with incomes more than 20 per cent below the poverty line, were very poor. These figures dropped after housing costs were taken into account, to around 10 per cent of Australians being poor and around 7 per cent falling into the very poor category (Australian Government 1975:15). The before and after housing costs distinction is significant because housing costs, whether rental or mortgage payments, impact significantly on how much income is available for other expenditure (see Chapter 10). While the age pension provides only a minimal income, high rates of home ownership among aged pensioners mean that older Australians tend to drop out of poverty figures once housing costs are taken into account. In contrast, recent immigrants and single parent families rarely own their own homes and their vulnerability to poverty is more visible in after-housing-costs figures.

poverty line A measure used to define a certain income level, below which people are said to be living in poverty.

Poverty lines are still used in Australia. The quarterly poverty lines published by the Melbourne Institute of Applied Economic and Social Research use an updated version of the Henderson poverty benchmark. In the September 2013 quarter, the poverty line for a couple with at least one partner working was $674.71 per week inclusive of housing (Melbourne Institute of Applied Economic and Social Research 2013). Using this poverty line, all individuals or households reliant on a government benefit for income, other than age or disability pensioners, had income below the poverty line. A single adult on unemployment benefit as their only source of income ($310 per week in September 2013) is $194.38 below the relevant poverty line of $504.38.

Other institutions and researchers use different poverty lines; the poverty line of half the median income is one standard. The National Centre for Social and Economic Modelling and the OECD use a poverty line of half the median income, although in the European Union people and households with income falling below 60 per cent of median income are regarded as at risk of poverty (EAPN 2014). The major critique of poverty lines is that while they enable precise and relatively easily useable measures of poverty, there is no way of objectively deciding at what point a given level of income equates with poverty. This makes the setting of the poverty line a politically sensitive matter. Just a small move in the placement of the line can make a huge difference in how many people are deemed to be living in poverty.

4.5.2   Broader measures of poverty

Measures of poverty that look at money income are criticised because they do not capture other aspects of deprivation and provide little insight into the underlying dynamics behind the generation and maintenance of poverty (Fincher & Saunders 2001). Income received is also not a direct reflection of expenditure. But determining poverty via the measurement of expenditure is constrained by the difficulty of collecting reliable and representative data (Travers & Richardson 1993).

In recognition of these limitations, a wide variety of non-money measures has been developed. Some researchers examine the level of immediate material hardship, such as in the ABS question that asks respondents if they would be able to raise $2000 for something important within a week. Others recognise the analytical advantages of indicators measured in income terms but argue for a fuller definition of what constitutes income. Broader definitions of economic resources can include way of life items such as capital assets, the value of employment benefits in kind, the value of public social services in kind and private income in kind, as well as cash income. Economist Robert Goodin and his colleagues (1999) use an income model that incorporates labour income, asset income, private transfers such as gifts and child support, public transfers such as social security payments and owner-occupier imputed net rent.

The concept of deprivation, built around an index of items regarded as necessary, takes a broader approach to poverty and is taken as an indicator of unmet need. Updated regularly from its original format in the 1970s, the list of items varies from society to society. In Australia an index has been developed by researchers at the Social Policy Research Centre (Saunders & Wong 2009) based on a list of items that were regarded as essential by more than 50 per cent of respondents. These include basic needs and capacities such as warm clothes, bedding, a substantial meal once a day, adequate accommodation and domestic facilities such as a decent and secure home, heating in at least one room, a washing machine and television, risk protection items such as insurance and basic emergency savings, capacity to participate in social events, access to health care and basic children's needs such as a separate bed for each child, hobby and leisure activities and new school books and school clothes. Using this measure, the researchers found that sole parent families faced the highest level of deprivation in 2008, followed by single people of working age.

4.5.3   Does the way we measure matter?

It is of crucial importance to understand that the way poverty is defined and measured influences the estimates obtained. The more comprehensive the definition of material well-being and the larger the income group (individual or household), the more income inequality between groups tends to be reduced. Trigger (2003:37), for example, comparing the level of poverty over time and between different household groups, found that poverty trends are extremely sensitive to the choice of the indicator. Where direct income was used, the level of poverty in Australia increased between 1975 and 1984, but fell between 1984 and 1994. With a broader measure the same trend is seen, but poverty levels looked higher in 1993–94. Similarly, sociologists Peter Travers and Sue Richardson (1993:39) found that different measures significantly changed the household income rankings. When only equivalised income is used, widows were as poorly off as the divorced, but when a broader concept was used, especially one that included housing, divorcee households were more than twice as likely to be poor.

4.6   How many are poor? Ideological dimensions

The multitude of ways poverty can be defined and measured creates varying estimates of how many Australians experience poverty. The critique around this divergence is heightened by the fact that estimates of poverty also necessarily involve judgments about the appropriate (and inappropriate) social and political response to poverty. Table 4.2, drawn from poverty data provided in the 2004 *Senate Report on Poverty*, demonstrates how different measures and definitions affect poverty estimates. Although all are based around accepted definitions and measures, the results range from more than four million to one million Australians living in poverty. These results dramatically affect how the problem of poverty is perceived.

Table 4.2   How different measures of poverty affect estimates of poverty

Estimation source	Poverty (%)	Numbers estimated to be in poverty in Australia (in millions)
Henderson Poverty Line	20–23	3.7–4.1
St Vincent de Paul Society	14	3
Australian Council of Social Service	15	2.5–3.5
Smith Family	13–19	2.4
Brotherhood of St Laurence	7	1.5
Australia Institute	5–10	1.2
Centre for Independent Studies	5	1 (in 'chronic poverty')

Source: Adapted from *Senate Report on Poverty* 2004

The explanation for the disparity is that each result is based on a range of assumptions about poverty. The Centre for Independent Study (CIS) estimate, for example, is based on the idea that relative poverty is not a legitimate concept and poverty should be examined only in terms of absolute poverty. In line with this standpoint the CIS also downplays the societal and individual impacts of poverty, arguing that most of those listed as being in poverty are only transitionally poor (that is, only poor at that particular time), or are only 'notionally poor' because of the under-reporting of true income (Hughes 2002; Saunders 2004b; Saunders 2007b). In contrast, the high estimates of poverty that find up to one in five—or four million Australians—living in poverty is based on an updated Henderson Poverty Line. The findings of the Brotherhood of St Laurence come from a measure that categorises people as poor if their income falls below half the national median income. This produces a more conservative estimate of poverty, around 1.5 million Australians or about 7 per cent of the population.

Estimates of poverty also have political and ideological dimensions. Those in favour of a full market economy are keen to demonstrate that poverty is not rising, or at least not substantially. Those concerned about the impact of neoliberalist social and economic policy are keen to show that these policies are causing rising poverty and a clustering of inequality. The debate is deeply divided. The CIS argues that poverty in Australia is largely an invention of those academics and agencies who study it and who, they argue, have a vested interest in exaggerating the problem in order to attract more research or program implementation funds. In turn the CIS is perceived as being ideologically driven by a commitment to hard-line market capitalism, which leads it to disregard any evidence that the market causes poverty or hardship.

More recently, arguments about how poverty 'should' be defined have been reignited, with a correspondent from *The Australian* newspaper, Adam Creighton, accusing the welfare lobby of maintaining a 'poverty charade' (Taylor 2014). The dividing line, again, is whether it is relative poverty or absolute poverty that is perceived as the most valid indicator. The fact that different studies produce different estimates is not an indication that the studies themselves are flawed; rather, it indicates that poverty studies based on different data will produce different estimates. Understanding how those estimates are derived enables us to critically evaluate their validity.

4.6.1   The discourses of the causes of poverty

Competing understandings of what poverty is and how it should be measured link directly into arguments about its causes and how its presence can be reduced. Although slightly blurred around the edges, the demarcation lines around competing explanations of poverty and arguments about forms of intervention, including the role of the welfare state, can be divided into three main theoretical streams: poverty as an individual attribute, culture of poverty explanations, and structural explanations.

4.6.1.1   Poverty as an individual attribute

Theories that locate the causes of poverty within individual characteristics such as behavioural choices implicitly perceive the individual as responsible for their own poverty. From this perspective, poor people have something wrong with them that is more than a lack of money. Within this proposition there are a number of interwoven concepts. The first stipulates that poverty is the result of deficiencies within the individual—laziness, profligacy, poor self-discipline and lack of personal competency, for example, and particularly a lack of work effort. The essential problem is a lack of self-reliance (Yeatman 2000; Henman 2001b).

Concern about the work ethic and the morality of the poor is not new—examples of this can be traced back to at least the fourteenth century (Bryson 1992; Dean & Taylor-Gooby 1992). Mingled with these older theories are more postmodern explanations of poverty as related to identity and consumption: poverty as the consequence of the choices people make. In the most extreme form of this view, poverty is the natural and deliberately chosen consequence of irresponsible behaviour. The Centre for Independent Studies, for example, argues that what we have in Australia is mostly behavioural poverty, a situation in which joblessness and low income are essentially lifestyle choices. According to psychologist Lucy Sullivan (2000), the aim should, therefore, be to ensure that the poor and jobless choose paid work by reducing the lifestyle attractions of welfare dependency. The key criticism of such an explanation of poverty is evidence provided by high welfare spending nations that have low levels of poverty. If poverty were basically about lifestyle choice, then Scandinavian countries should have relatively more people in poverty than exist in liberal welfare states such as the USA and Australia.

4.6.1.2   Culture of poverty explanations

While linked with theories about poverty as an individual attribute, the **culture of poverty** thesis contains unique components. The thesis was initially developed in the USA during the 1960s by anthropologist Oscar Lewis (1967), who defined a culture of poverty as 'a sub-culture with its own structure and rationale, as a way of life which is passed down from generation to generation along family lines' (Lister 2004:106). Although Lewis emphasised that this culture functioned as an adaptation by and a reaction of the poor to their marginal position in unequal societies, the

> **culture of poverty** A concept to describe how extreme poverty results in values, attitudes and behaviours among the poor that ultimately condemns them to an intergenerational cycle of poverty.

idea that poverty is developed and maintained generationally by the poor themselves, who are different in their values, attitudes and beliefs from the non-poor, has found widespread public and political appeal. Variations on the culture of poverty thesis regularly reappear in political discourses (Lister 2004). The perceived dangers of a transgenerational joblessness— that those raised in households where the adult members are dependent on welfare will be socialised into the norm of welfare dependency—fits this explanation.

4.6.1.3   Structural explanations of poverty

In contrast to individual or culture of poverty explanations, structural explanations position the economic, political and social system as the cause of poverty. From this perspective, forces embodied in our society's social, economic and political institutions pattern the way resources and opportunities are distributed in a way that privileges some while limiting the opportunities and resources available to others. The result is that advantage and disadvantage and, consequently, inequality, become entrenched within different social groups. Structural explanations, therefore, move the focus away from the individuals who are poor to examine the system that produces winners and losers.

Structural explanations are also unique in that they point to the social processes inherent in poverty and inequality and the social relations between the poor and non-poor. Specific structural factors include major factors such as globalisation, the policy outcomes of neoliberal philosophies and class, gender and ethnicity-based social divisions. Minor arenas of disadvantage such as local labour markets, community settings and infrastructure and housing are also identified as impacting structurally on poverty levels (Lister 2004). The basic point of a structural explanation is its argument that it is impossible to address poverty without exposing and addressing the social, economic and political factors that cause it.

4.6.2   Evaluating competing explanations of poverty

Structural versus individualistic or cultural explanations of poverty roughly equate to a debate about the role of individual agency, that is, to what extent can poverty as a social outcome be defined as either a product of the autonomous, purposive action of human agency or of social, economic and political processes and structures? The answer is complicated by the embeddedness of individual behaviour in the social environment (Walter 2007). As choices are inextricably entwined in their social settings it is very hard to differentiate when an action or choice is a result of personal agency, when it is a reflector of intransient social arrangements or when it is a mix of both. The choice of a young person to leave school early, for example, has very real consequences for future opportunities and outcomes; the chances are that they will experience low income and wealth over their lifetime. While they may be aware of this, and while governments may put in place measures to promote continued educational participation, their habitus is most often one in which the education system is not where they feel comfortable or does not seem relevant to their lives. The vast majority of early school leavers are from families who also left school early and are disadvantaged, so their access to cultural capital relevant to prolonged educational participation is quite limited. So while they are making choices, they are doing so within a particular set of circumstances that make remaining in school or continuing to tertiary education an unfavourable option.

According to Giddens (1991) the key to ascertaining the respective roles of agency or structure is the extent to which a group has the power to exercise control over their own lives despite their subordinate position in the wider hierarchical political, economic and social power relationships. If those in poverty have choices and opportunities available and realistically accessible to them, then their poverty might be deemed, at least to some extent, to be about choice or individual failure to capitalise on opportunities. If, however, a group or individual is without the power, opportunity or capacity to significantly change their own life circumstances, then allocating the causation of poverty to personal agency or cultural choices risks pathologisation, thereby adding stigma and shame to situations of structural disadvantage (Lister 2004). Consider the two social groups most regularly positioned as poor: Indigenous people and lone parents—does their subordinate and disadvantaged position, along with the way they are positioned in dominant discourses, realistically mean that they have ready access to options that would enable them to lift themselves out poverty? As will be shown throughout this book, these groups' current position in the socioeconomic hierarchy—economic, ideological, moral and social—heavily constrains their life chances and their capacity for broad social agency.

4.7   Material inequality and poverty

The linking of poverty measures to normative relative definitions such as median income makes a close link between inequality and poverty. Such linking makes sense in that it is inevitable that any social system that permits the existence of high levels of entrenched inequality also creates a situation in which some people will be at the bottom of the ladder and will experience poverty, deprivation and injustice (Gans 1976). The problem is that the two concepts, although highly connected, are still distinct. Poverty not only entails having less than others but is also associated with exclusion because of inadequate resources. Growth in inequality, therefore, does not necessarily mean a growth in poverty. Inequality increases if the rich are getting richer at a faster rate than those at the bottom, but this does not mean that those at the bottom are necessarily experiencing greater levels of poverty. Equally, poverty may increase even as inequality is reduced.

The separation of a growth in inequality from the growth of poverty is central to current political debates on poverty and inequality. Peter Saunders of the CIS (2004b), for example, argues that data indicating rising inequality do not mean that poverty is growing. The growth in the income of the rich effectively raises the position of the mid-point, so it is not that those in the middle are slipping back, rather, they are just not increasing their level of affluence at the same rate as the rich. Affluence is being shared, it is just not being shared equally. Yet, as shown by the rising proportion of Australians living on incomes below 50 per cent of the median income (14.4% in 2010), the rates of those in poverty on this standard measure is rising.

So is inequality increasing or decreasing? While our earlier analysis of OECD data over the last fifteen years would indicate that it is increasing, the difficulty in making a valid diagnosis is linked to the variation in whether we are referring to absolute or relative disparities. While the position of low-income groups has improved in real terms over the last two decades, in relative terms it has declined because of the extent of growth at the top. Data discontinuities related to changes to data collection techniques by the ABS further complicate the picture, making it difficult to fully interpret the data for the last decade (Harding et al. 2007). But while it remains unclear whether inequality is growing or not, the evidence does indicate that a significant percentage of Australians are not participating in the general prosperity of the nation and that, simultaneously, the wealth of those at the top has been growing disproportionately to those of middle- and lower-income and -wealth groups.

4.8   Chronic and transitory poverty

Another complicating factor is the temporal dimension of poverty. While we know that chronic poverty—that is, poverty experienced over an extended period—has a negative effect on life chances and outcomes, not all poverty is chronic. Many people experience transitory poverty, which is a low or very low income over a relatively short period only. Students are the classic example: many have very low incomes during their student years but as they complete their studies and enter the job market their incomes rise and few experience poverty again over their life course. The impact of transitory poverty is negative but does not have the same life-course effects as chronic poverty. So the effect of poverty is more than the level of an individual or household's wealth and income but how long such low income is experienced. Chronic and transitory poverty are also not dichotomous. A household with irregular employment and income, such as families of casual or seasonal workers, might move in and out of poverty on a regular basis. The question is, then, what proportion of those on low income at any given time are likely to remain on low income over an extended period? There is little research available but a study by Rodgers and Rodgers (2010) using data from the longitudinal Household Income and Labour Dynamics (HILDA) survey estimate the average poverty rate in Australia from 2001 to 2007 to be 10.5 per cent of the population. Of this, 6.2 per cent were deemed to be in chronic poverty and 4.3 per cent in transitory poverty. The life-course group most at risk of chronic poverty were older Australians, and those most likely to experience transitory poverty were young adults. The researchers used their own definition of a poverty line, so these results are not directly comparable to other reported estimates, but they do indicate that poverty is more than just low income and that the pejorative effects of poverty accumulate over time.

4.9   Material winners and losers

In some respects, the debate about whether inequality is growing is misleading because it misses the real point of the lived reality of material inequality. Alongside evidence of growth in private sector wealth, there are indications that many Australians are doing it hard.

4.9.1   The winners

The global financial crisis, which included a dramatic reduction in the value of share markets around the world, including in Australia, affected the rich as well as the poor. The share of total income of the top 1 per cent of Australian earners dropped from 10.1 per cent in 2007–08 to 8.6 per cent in 2008–09. But this decline started to reverse the next financial year, with the top 1 per cent of Australian earners increasing their percentage of total income to 8.9 per cent in 2009–10 and up to 9.2 in 2010–11 (Leigh 2013). And despite the global financial crisis, the growth in private wealth over the last two decades has been fuelled by the increased value of equities. In November 2007, just before the global financial crisis, the Australian share market S&P/ASX reached a new high of 6800 points. After the crash its low point was 3120 points. By early 2014 the S&P/ASX had reached 5400 points, still below pre-GFC highs but showing a dramatic recovery since late 2007. Once again, solid returns were available to those with large investments in the stock market. The rising value of stocks and equities is given as the main reason for the increase in the number of millionaires in Australia: their number was up to 1.123 million people in 2013, an increase of 38,000 since 2012.

But the biggest winners remain Australia's CEOs. In 2013 the wealth of the top executives of S&P/ASX companies rose by an average of 16.7 per cent, more than quadruple the rise for most other Australian earners. One executive recorded a rise in remuneration of 233 per cent. The average CEO remuneration is now $3.2 million per annum, up from $2.7 million in 2012. Extremely high salaries, however, do not alone explain the high wealth of the executives of Australia's largest companies. The BRW Executive Rich List 2014 shows that the wealthiest hundred executives all hold shares in their company worth far more than their salaries. For example, Tony Alford, chief executive of the Retail Food Group, had an annual remuneration of $716,000 in 2013 but held shares valued at $101.8 million (Xavier 2014). Such large jumps are part of a long-term trend, not a one-off case. Australian economists Anthony Atkinson and Andrew Leigh's analysis of the income tax returns of top income groups since 1921 found the income shares of the top 5 per cent fell from the 1920s until the mid-1940s, rose briefly in the postwar decade and then declined until the early 1980s. Since then they have risen rapidly. By 2002 the income of the richest 1 per cent was the highest it had been at any point since 1951, while that of the richest 5 per cent was at its highest point since 1949 (Atkinson & Leigh 2006). Atkinson and Leigh attribute much of this growth to the massive salaries given to Australian CEOs since the 1990s at a time when marginal tax rates have also declined (2006). The trend towards paying corporate heads huge salaries has occurred across the OECD. An American study showed that in 2005, CEO pay was 411 times that of an average worker, up from 107 times in 1990 (Lever 2007). This growth is partly because of the deregulation of financial markets and partly because of the internationalisation of the market for CEOs in the context of massive company profits and the tying of CEO salaries to performance targets.

Contemporary Australia

WHO ARE THE RICHEST PEOPLE?

The BRW Rich 200 list names the following people as the ten richest in Australia in 2013, and lists their estimated wealth and the primary source of that wealth.

1 Gina Rinehart (resources): $22,020,000,000
2 Frank Lowy (property, investment): $6,870,000,000
3 James Packer (entertainment/gaming, investment): $6,000,000,000
4 Anthony Pratt and family (manufacturing, investment): $5,950,000,000
5 Ivan Glasenberg (investment—global commodities trading): $5,610,000,000
6 Harry Triguboff (property): $4,950,000,000
7 Wing Mau Hui (property): $4,820,000,000
8 John Gandel (property, investment): $3,700,000,000
9 Andrew Forrest (resources): $3,660,000,000
10 Christopher Wallin (resources): $2,800,000,000

Source: BRW 2013

Generationally, baby boomers (those born 1946–64) are winners overall. This generation is wealthier than any previous generation, thanks to rising housing prices and government reforms to superannuation, which minimise taxation. Baby boomers are estimated to hold half of the nation's total household wealth even though they comprise only one-quarter of the population (AMP.NATSEM 2007). The ABS (2013a) estimates the mean household net worth of Australian couple-only households where the reference person is aged fifty-five to sixty-four years as $1,266,000 in 2011–12. This net worth is the highest of all household groups, more than five times the mean household net worth of one-parent-family households with dependent children ($251,000), nearly triple the mean net worth of couple-with-dependent-children households ($459,000) and eight times the mean net worth of lone-person-aged-under-thirty-five households ($160,000). Much of the net worth of those aged fifty-five to sixty-four is in housing, with 55 per cent of this group owning a home without a mortgage and another 34 per cent owning a home with a mortgage. Added together, nearly 90 per cent of this group are home owners, compared with just 37 per cent of lone parents with children.

4.9.2   The losers

Despite disputes around definitions and causes of poverty, we find that the poor, no matter how they are counted or measured, are still virtually the same groups identified by Henderson back in the early 1970s (Australian Government 1975:18). The usual suspects of poverty in Australia remain: Indigenous people, the unemployed, income support recipients, sole parents, large families, aged renters, recent immigrants and refugees and people with disabilities. The only real major change from the 1970s is the emergence of 'new poor': low-paid, part-time and casual workers who also experience periods of unemployment.

As shown in Table 4.3, women are slightly more likely to have low income than men, children are the age group at greatest risk of living on low income, migrants from non-English speaking countries have higher rates of poverty under this measure than other Australians, more than a quarter of those people disabled with a core activity restriction have income below 50 per cent of the median, and more than a third receiving a social security payment, pension or benefit as their main source of income are poor.

Table 4.3   Proportion of groups with income below 50 per cent of median income 2009–10

Sociodemographic group		<50 per cent of median income %
Gender	Female	13.5
	Male	12.1
Age	Under 15	17.3
	15–25 years	12.0
	25–64 years	11.3
	65 plus years	13.2
Family type	Lone parent	25.0
	Couple, no children	8.4
	Couple, children	9.0
Ethnicity	Australian born	10.0
	Migrant from non-English speaking country	15.8

Sociodemographic group		<50 per cent of median income %
	Migrant from English speaking country	11.7
Disability	With a core activity restriction	27.4
Main income source	Wages	5.2
	Social security payment	36.5

Source: ACOSS 2013

The higher rate of low income for those aged under fifteen years is likely related to the high proportion of sole parents with income below the 50 per cent median level. In 2010, it was estimated that 575,000 children (17.3 per cent of all Australian children) were living below the poverty line (ACOSS 2013). In the same year, 43 per cent of Parenting Payment (Single) recipients (the main income support payment for sole parents) did not have secure housing, 57 per cent could not pay a utility bill in the last twelve months and 56 per cent lacked even $500 in emergency savings. Such levels of deprivation have implications for educational and economic participation, and for the achievement potential of children being raised in sole parent households (ACOSS 2013). Data from the 2011 census of population and housing found that sole parent families make up more than 22 per cent of all families. With more than one in five children in a sole parent household at any given time, and more experiencing life in such a household at some period during their childhood, there are serious implications for the future well-being of many Australian citizens.

Contemporary Australia

RISE OF POVERTY IN SOLE-PARENT HOUSEHOLDS

A research report using data from the longitudinal Household Income and Labour Dynamics in Australia (HILDA) survey found that the number of single parent households in poverty is rising (reported by the ABC, Norman 2013). Analysis found that 24 per cent of children living in single-parent households are living in poverty, compared to 7.6 per cent of those living with two parents. This result signifies a rise of 15 per cent in poverty among single-parent households since the HILDA study began collecting data in 2001. The researchers attribute this rise in poverty to changes in welfare policy for sole parents begun in 2006 and continued by successive governments, which moves single parents from higher sole-parent-specific benefits to the lower Newstart payment once their youngest child turns eight. Newstart payments also have a tougher income test, which particularly affects those working part-time.

Another clearly identifiable group more likely than other Australians to experience poverty is Aboriginal and Torres Strait Islanders. That Indigenous people have been left behind in the rising tide of economic prosperity is not in dispute. The connection of Indigenous material inequality to cultural dislocation and social and political exclusion means that for many, if not most, Indigenous people, poverty is intergenerational and sustained across the lifecycle. The extreme nature of Indigenous disadvantage is an additional factor. For most Australians with few economic resources the experience of poverty takes the form of exclusion from the lifestyles considered normal for the nation. Nationally, data from the 2011 census (ABS 2012a) establishes that the national Indigenous population is far younger than the non-Indigenous population, with a median age of twenty-one years compared to thirty-eight years. Median Indigenous personal income is 62 per cent of that non-Indigenous median personal income. Median Indigenous household income is less than 80 per cent of non-Indigenous household income although average Indigenous household size (3.3 persons) is substantially larger than non-Indigenous household size (2.2 persons). Aboriginal and Torres Strait Islander households are nearly four times as overcrowded as non-Indigenous households and are far less likely to be owned by the occupants. Data from the 2011 census also shows that only 36 per cent of Indigenous people nationwide own their own home (with or without a mortgage) less than half the rate of non-Indigenous households (78 per cent).

National statistics such as these obscure the complexity and diversity of the many Aboriginal and Torres Strait Islander peoples living across Australia. Importantly, poverty is not limited to the quarter of the Indigenous population living in remote communities. The three-quarters of the Aboriginal and Torres Strait Islander population living in metro or regional areas remain substantially less materially equal that their non-Indigenous co-residents. Despite policy measures such as Close the Gap and the many other policies aimed at reducing Indigenous disadvantage, Aboriginal and Torres Strait Islander people, regardless of where they live, remain the poorest group in Australia (Walter 2008). An example is the Aboriginal and non-Aboriginal people of Perth: Table 4.4 compares socioeconomic data on the Aboriginal and non-Aboriginal populations of Perth drawn from the 2006 and 2011 censuses of population and housing.

As can be seen in the table, across housing, education, unemployment, personal and household income and home internet connections, Aboriginal households in Perth are significantly disadvantaged. Perth's Indigenous families and households are far less likely to own their own homes and are heavily concentrated in public and private rental. Over one-quarter of Perth's Aboriginal residents live in public housing compared to under 4 per cent of non-Indigenous Perth residents. Overcrowding is also a problem, with around one in eight Aboriginal people in Perth living in a household with six or more residents, compared to one in thirty-six non-Aboriginal residents. Aboriginal people are around half as likely to be educated to Year 12 level or its equivalent and only 6 per cent of Aboriginal youth were attending university in 2011 compared to 23 per cent of non-Indigenous youth. The Aboriginal unemployment rate is more than three times as high as that of non-Indigenous residents, and personal and household income is substantially lower. The other feature of this table is that between 2006 and 2011 there is very little evidence of a decline in relative disadvantage between the two groups. There is little improvement across the indicators between the two census years, except in the rate of home internet connection. Even in a major capital city, closing the gap between Indigenous and non-Indigenous people appears to be a very long way off.

Table 4.4   Aboriginal and non-Indigenous socioeconomic comparison: Perth 2006–11

Socioeconomic variable	Aboriginal 2006	Aboriginal 2011	Non-Aboriginal 2011
Home ownership/mortgage	41.5%	41.5%	71.4%
Public rental	28.0%	27.2%	3.5%
Private rental	30.4%	31.3%	24.7%
Households 6-plus residents	12.0%	12.1%	2.8%
Home internet	42.0%	70.0%	84.5%
Educated to Year 12 or equivalent	21.3%	30.5%	57.0%
Attending university aged 18–24 years	4.6%	6.0%	23.4%
Unemployment rate	16.1%	17.5%	4.8%
Median personal income	$327	$407	$683
Median household income/average household size	$258	$355	$571

Source: Data derived from 2006 and 2011 census community profiles (Perth Indigenous area)

Although Indigenous Australians are unequivocally poor by any of the standard measures, identifying the economic correlates of their position does not do justice to the complexity of Indigenous poverty. Economist Boyd Hunter (1999) established that material deprivation and living in overcrowded conditions are found even among relatively high-income Indigenous households. Regardless of income level, Indigenous people experience poorer health and housing outcomes and higher levels of criminalisation than their non-Indigenous counterparts. Indigenous individuals, families, households and communities do not just happen to be poor: Indigenous poverty and inequality are directly related to the history of black–white relations in Australia and the consequent capacity of Indigenous people to access the economic, social, cultural and human capital resources of our society.

This does not mean that factors such as low income, low educational attainment and limited employment options are not important, just that they must be understood within the context of the experience of Indigeneity. Indigeneity itself is central to the explanation of the low economic position of Indigenous people, with other factors interwoven and interpreted through this (Walter 2007). Cultural loss is central to this. It is difficult to do justice to the dimensions of this loss in a few short lines, but it includes loss of land, which had particularly egregious effects since land was not only the source of Indigenous livelihoods but was also central to Indigenous cultural and spiritual identity. The declaration of *terra nullius* had a symbolic dimension in its denial of the very existence of Indigenous people and their ancient traditions and customs. This loss of culture has been compounded by the systematic denigration of black people and black ways by past generations of white Australians, which continues in various forms today. The removal of Indigenous children in the name of welfare and civilisation was part of this, leaving a legacy of trauma that remains a live memory for many Indigenous individuals and communities.

4.9.3   Australian views on material inequality

What are the views of Australians about the current levels of material inequality? To what extent do they perceive them to be fair? Analysis of data from the Australian Survey of Social Attitudes (AuSSA) collected in 2009 shows that a significant majority of Australians agree that material inequalities are too high in Australia and have increased substantially over the last two decades. Figure 4.3 displays these data, divided by gender.

When asked whether they thought the differences in income in Australia are too large, just over 70 per cent of men and 76 per cent of women agreed; 56 per cent of men and 62 per cent women also agreed that ordinary people did not get a fair share of the nation's wealth; and 48 per cent of men and 54 per cent of women agreed it was the government's responsibility to reduce differences in income. These data suggest that a substantial majority of Australians regard the current income distribution in Australia as too unequal and a smaller, but still solid, majority feel that ordinary people do not get their fair share of wealth, but that only around half of Australians see income redistribution as a government responsibility.

Figure 4.3   Attitudes to economic inequality in Australia

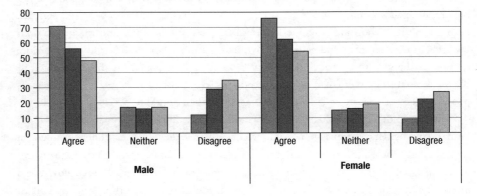

Source: Figures derived from AuSSA 2009 data

The other pattern in these data is the gendered differences. Although the overall pattern of responses was the same, women were significantly more likely to agree with each statement than men. This result is common in surveys of attitudes, with women holding more egalitarian attitudes than men overall.

Contemporary Australia

○   ○   ○

WORKING WA FAMILIES, SOME ON DOUBLE INCOMES, ARE STRUGGLING TO BUY FOOD

In January 2014, the *West Australian* newspaper (Emery 2014) reported that Foodbank, a not-for-profit organisation, was noticing a rise in demand from low-income workers. The group's chairperson reported that some of those seeking help were double-income families who were struggling under the burden of mortgages, utility and schooling bills, leaving them unable to always afford groceries. He said 'It's the hardest phone call they ever make, having to call for help. You know, "We've paid our mortgage, we've got credit cards, all that sort of stuff, but we're struggling for food on a weekly basis". You can hear the quiver in their voices when they talk to you.'

Foodbank's End of Hunger report last year showed a big shortfall between demand and supply, with more than 16,000 West Australians turned away from charities each month because of a shortage of food supplies.

4.10   Social exclusion

4.10.1   What is social exclusion?

Low income and poverty involve much more than economic disadvantage. The multidimensional nature of material inequality includes negative social participatory aspects, such as a lack of voice, powerlessness, shame and stigma, the denial of rights and diminished citizenship. These aspects are inherent in and compounded by exclusion from social resources, broader dimensions that are recognised in the recent shift in poverty research away from income indicators to measures of social exclusion, and in the social policy trend towards social inclusion.

As the term infers, 'social exclusion' relates to exclusion of people or groups from participation in mainstream social and economic life. The idea of social exclusion not only suggests a departure from normal living standards but it also seeks to understand the processes behind their creation and reproduction. Social exclusion recognises the social aspects of poverty and the existence of power relations. The exclusion of some groups from socia resources can operate as a means of securing the privileged position of others

(Burchardt et al. 2002). These negative social relations are reinforced by how those in poverty interact with the wider society and vice versa. The concept of social exclusion, therefore, includes the social processes involved in the underlying causes of poverty and inequality as well as the outcomes of low resources (Fincher & Saunders 2001:9).

Like poverty, social exclusion is not easy to define. Rather, it draws together different theoretical concepts of poverty and inequality—researchers have argued that it is more useful to develop a general conception of social exclusion than to pursue a precise definition (Burchardt et al. 2002; Saunders 2003; Bradshaw 2003). Poverty researcher Ruth Lister (2004), for example, argues that social exclusion can be most usefully understood and used as a multifocal lens that illuminates aspects of poverty, as a way of looking at poverty, rather than an alternative to it. Conceptions of what constitutes social exclusion thus tend to vary in the elements they include, but all highlight the multidimensional nature of exclusion, and the concept has been adopted into social policy across many Western nations. Saunders and Wong (2009) report that social exclusion emerged in social policy thinking in France during the 1970s in relation to the plight of those who were long-term unemployed or otherwise excluded from the labour market. In the 1990s and 2000s the concept has become influential in Britain, Ireland and across the European Union. In Australia the concept was picked up by state governments and at the federal level in 2008 when then-Deputy Prime Minister Gillard announced the development of a new policy framework based around social inclusion.

One British study (Gordon et al. 2000) identifies four dimensions of social exclusion: impoverishment, which denotes income below poverty income thresholds; labour market exclusion, which refers to joblessness within households; service exclusion, which refers to basic services such as power and water as well as external items such as transport, shopping and financial services; and exclusion from social relations, which incorporates a range of measures such as non-participation in common social activities due to costs, isolation from family and friends, perceived lack of social, physical and emotional support, disengagement from community activities and reduced ability to participate in social activities beyond the household.

In Australia, studies of social exclusion are relatively recent. The most prominent was carried out by the Social Policy Research Centre at the University of New South Wales and non-government community organisations: it examined deprivation and social exclusion using data from three surveys, two conducted in 2006 (one community sample and one sample of community sector clients) and one in 2008 (community sector clients). The researchers rate twenty-seven indicators of social exclusion, classified into three broad areas (Saunders and Wong 2009:13):

- disengagement—lack of participation in social and community activities
- service exclusion—lack of access to key services when needed
- economic exclusion—restricted access to economic resources and low economic capacity.

The project's key finding to date is that more than 20 per cent of Australians are affected by social exclusion in one form or another. Among the project's key findings are that economic exclusion was most commonly experienced, followed by disengagement and service exclusion, and that three-quarters of the 2008 client sample experienced five or more forms of exclusion and 40 per cent experienced twenty or more. The study also highlights the corollary between vulnerability to exclusion and being a member of a social group known to have a consistently high risk of experiencing poverty and disadvantage: Indigenous people, the unemployed, those renting public housing and sole-parent families fare comparatively poorly across ten indicators of exclusion (Table 4.5).

Table 4.5   Comparative selected indicators of exclusion by social group

Area of exclusion	Indicator of exclusion	Sole parent families %	Unemployed people %	People with a disability %	Indigenous Australians %	Single older people %
Social exclusion	No regular social contact with other people	29.5	29.2	35.1	22.6	0.0
	Did not participate in community activities	28.8	44.3	32.0	31.0	14.3
	Could not go out with friends and pay their way	61.0	64.0	61.5	51.3	26.0
Service exclusion	No access to a local doctor or hospital	12.9	14.2	15.4	12.5	0.0
	No access to a bank or building society	12.8	10.9	12.8	10.5	0.0
Economic exclusion	Couldn't make electricity, water, gas or telephone payments	56.3	44.1	43.8	46.1	13.6
	No child care for working parents	74.0	74.7	78.2	70.0	N/A
	Doesn't have $500 in emergency savings	88.7	89.5	81.2	94.0	15.8

(continued)

Table 4.5   Comparative selected indicators of exclusion by social group (continued)

Area of exclusion	Indicator of exclusion	Sole parent families %	Unemployed people %	People with a disability %	Indigenous Australians %	Single older people %
	Has not spent $100 on a special treat	29.4	21.1	26.3	28.4	16.7
	Lives in a jobless household	82.8	92.0	87.3	77.1	N/A
Average exclusion rate		47.6	48.4	46.2	44.5	12.9

Source: Adapted from Saunders & Wong 2009:60

Of particular note is the way different groups are affected by different aspects of exclusion. People with a disability are most affected by social exclusion while sole parents and Indigenous people are most affected by economic exclusion. The relatively low rate of exclusion across all the indicators of single older people is perhaps reflective of the sample. All respondents were clients of community sector organisations, and the services that older people receive from such groups, such as meals on wheels, or home maintenance services, are not directly tied to economic resources or low income.

4.10.2   Social exclusion as a contested topic

The broader concept of social exclusion is not immune to political and ideological arguments. The Centre for Independent Studies labels social exclusion a chaotic concept. It argues that the inclusion of cultural, political and other dimensions as well as economic well-being make the measure so broad that anybody would qualify as socially excluded on at least one measure. On one level this criticism has validity: the broader the constitution of social exclusion, the wider the definition becomes. Yet it misses the key point that what the concept of social exclusion aims to do is capture the multidimensional aspects and outcomes of disadvantage as well as recognising the cumulative implicit and explicit social processes involved in the creation of poverty.

Other poverty researchers, while supportive of a broader social exclusion approach, point to dangers in an uncritical adoption of the term. Lister (2004) notes a tendency in British social policy to team social exclusion with what is proposed as its conceptual opposite, 'social inclusion', a term often equated directly with labour market participation. This pairing reduces the solution to social exclusion to putting the socially excluded into market work. This criticism is particularly pertinent to Australia because the federal and state governments establish social inclusion units that are often modelled on the British experience. Such reduction risks losing the vital complexity and focus on interactions inherent in the concept of social exclusion.

Another risk is a tendency to focus on the individual at the expense of the structural aspects of social exclusion. This leads to a divergence in the term's meaning. Rather than thinking about social exclusion as a concept that encompasses what happens when people or areas suffer from a combination of linked problems, individuals are labelled as 'socially excluded' and the explanation for such exclusion is sought in the behavioural and personal deficits of the individuals themselves. The ABS (2004), for example, uses the term in its analysis of multiple disadvantage, which includes items such as health, education level, labour market involvement, financial hardship, experience of crime and individual family and community support. The examination of such disadvantage is undertaken in individual terms without specific regard for the services or community and social infrastructure aspects of social exclusion. As Saunders (2003:5) argues, viewed as an individual attribute, social exclusion can become 'a vehicle for vilifying those who do not conform and an excuse for seeing their problems as caused by their own "aberrant behaviour"'.

4.11   Conclusion

Material inequality and social exclusion are deeply political subjects, with their contestability centring on what the concepts actually mean. Decisions about definitions are founded not just on neutral measures but also on the moral, social and political dimensions of the terms and the discourses that surround them. These interpretations mean that the attributed causes of inequality and social exclusion and preferred policy action depend on the ideological perspectives from which they are viewed. The supremacy of neoliberalist discourses and policy directions in Australia mean that inequality and social exclusion are largely explained by individualistic and cultural discourses, which hold the individual responsible for their poverty and at the same time promote market-based solutions as the most appropriate and effective response, especially those that involve greater participation in the labour market. These same discourses question the link between poverty and entrenched inequality and argue against the idea that inequality, in itself, is a negative social outcome. It is here that the largely unspoken aspects of these discourses come to the fore.

The inverse is also seen to apply. If those who are the losers in the arena of material capital are responsible for their own position and remediation, then the winners are also responsible and deserving of their success and, as importantly, not responsible or liable for reducing material inequality or its outcomes. Indeed, under these frameworks, material inequality is seen as promoting individual enterprise, with the uneven distribution of material benefits the just reward for individual effort and ability. To intervene in this process would be to undermine core market values of individual responsibility and the work ethic.

Older social democratic understandings perceive inequality as a negative consequence of a competitive market economy. Solutions from this perspective revolve around support programs and income and wealth redistributive measures. Material inequality is seen as a societal responsibility, with all members of a society, and especially the privileged, as morally and economically bound to contribute to reducing the negative consequences of material inequality. Reducing inequality is regarded as a social good, with all benefiting, not just the poor.

Regardless of arguments over who or what is poor and who or what is responsible and whether inequality is socially detrimental or a meritocratic outcome, in Australia, according to all mainstream measures, the same social groups remain vulnerable to poverty. The entrenched nature of the patterns and trends strongly suggest, as will become more obvious in later chapters, that it is group status or social positioning rather than individual effort that is the largest determinant of material disadvantage. Aboriginal and Torres Strait Islander people, the unemployed, income support recipients, sole parents, large families, aged renters, immigrants and refugees, and people with disabilities are consistently and heavily over-represented among those deemed to be poor. This suggests that changing debates and discourses around poverty and material inequality have done little to alleviate the position of these groups. What has changed is that they themselves are now held responsible for their position, and the social, economic and political contexts in which poverty is embedded have been obscured.

Discussion questions

1   Identify two theories that explain poverty and disadvantage as individual or cultural problems. How do these ideas differ from a structural explanation of poverty?

2   Go online to find research undertaken in the last two years that provides information on levels of poverty and disadvantage in Australia. Which groups does the research suggest are most vulnerable to poverty? What are some of the social determinants that explain their position?

3   The Centre for Independent Studies claims that relative poverty is not a legitimate concept and that poverty only exists when it is absolute. What would you say to either defend or disagree with this claim?

5

○

THE POLITICAL SPHERE

○

5.1   Introduction

As well as materially, inequality is also situated politically. Our political systems operate within social systems, and political institutions, as embodied in the state, are central to both. As such, the political dimensions of inequality are most evident in the recognition of and response to inequality by the Australian state. The relationship between inequality and the state is direct but constrained. The role of the state in redistribution makes it the key actor shaping the distribution of resources within the nation: the state's policies relating to education, the labour market and welfare impact directly on the experiences of individuals and families, influencing their opportunities, economic wealth and social standing. Yet it must be acknowledged that the state is not completely free to fashion policy as it sees fit, if it ever was. In Australia, as in other Western nations, policy is increasingly shaped and influenced by global conditions and imperatives that place pressure on the state to act in directions that, in their current configurations, tend to increase social division and inequality.

This chapter's discussion of the political dimension of inequality addresses questions two and three of this study's five guiding questions. Question two asks: how are the dimensions of inequality changing in the context of globalisation and a postindustrial society? This is an issue central to any exploration of the political dimensions of inequality. Contemporary political discourses and their redistributive effects are heavily influenced by global conditions and imperatives, and by the restructuring of society to meet the demands of a postindustrial society. Question three asks: how is the distribution of Australia's social, political, economic and symbolic resources reproduced across different social groups? How is risk distributed? This is answered through an examination of how state intervention impacts on different social groups, thereby underscoring the significance of state power. State policies inevitably affect different groups in different and often inequitable ways. Central to the argument is the understanding that not all social groups have equal power to influence the policies developed and implemented by the state. The least powerful social groups generally have the least political influence, which increases their vulnerability to the negative impacts of global forces. Alternatively, and as importantly, those groups with the highest rates of social, cultural and economic capital can have political influence well beyond that of those further down the social and economic scale.

In this chapter, the term 'the political sphere' means much more than the activities of political parties. It refers to all aspects of government, government structures and public affairs in Australia, including public and social policy, political debate and discourses. In relation to the production and reproduction of inequality, its focus is the relationship and interaction between the nation state and key social groups.

5.2   Definitions of power

Understanding the political dimensions of inequality requires a focus on the distribution and exercise of power in society. Weber defined power as 'the chance of a man or a number of men to realise their own will in a communal action even against the resistance of others who are participants in the action' (Gerth & Mills 1948:180). While this definition is certainly helpful, highlighting the coercion that underpins the exercise of power and its oppositional nature, it is limited in its recognition of the varied ways in which power is manifested. A more radical view of power is provided by the sociologist Steven Lukes, whose analysis of the '**three faces of power**' acknowledges power's hidden aspects (1974).

three faces of power
This model was developed by Lukes to explain how power operates directly and indirectly.

Lukes argues that power operates within different planes and levels, and identifies three core dimensions that develop in complexity, with the third dimension of power being the hardest to detect but the most effective. According to Lukes, power can—and is—utilised by social actors and institutions across a range of dimensions and in a range of different ways.

5.2.1   One-dimensional view of power

Lukes' (1974) first dimension of power concerns its overt and deliberate use to enforce the preferences or decisions of one group over those of another or others where there is an observable conflict of interests. Similar to Weber's definition of power, the one-dimensional view describes how power is exercised by one individual or group to make another individual or group comply with its wishes. It refers equally to the power of the police to legitimately direct the behaviour of the nation state's citizens and use force if necessary to extract compliance, such as in riot situations, to the power of the state to require employers to pay workers a minimum wage through the capacity to apply negative sanctions such as fines for non-compliance.

5.2.2   Two-dimensional view of power

Lukes' (1974) second dimension of power is more subtle than use of direct force and refers to the ability to not only make decisions but to also control the political agenda. Control of the agenda negates the necessity of direct force by its capacity to ensure that potential issues of conflict, either as express policy preferences or as grievances, are kept out of the political process. The two-dimensional view of power is more subtle than direct coercion but no less effective in exerting control. The history of the state's blindness to women's issues and resistance to addressing issues such as adequate child-care provision are an example of this form of negative power, which is exerted through the failure to act. While women's groups have repeatedly raised the child-care issue for nearly forty years, until recently it failed to get onto the agenda of either major political party. The invisibility of this issue meant there was no overt conflict between the interests of female workers and other interest groups, including employers. The second dimension of power is thwarted when a public issue gains voice in the public sphere. The placing of maternity leave firmly on the political agenda through the implementation of the Paid Parental Leave Scheme in 2011 by the Labor Government has seen the proposal of an even more generous maternity leave scheme by the incoming Coalition Government.

5.2.3   Three-dimensional view of power

Lukes' (1974) third dimension is the power to shape, influence and determine the wants of others. This most effective and insidious use of power prevents conflict arising by convincing the less powerful that the interests of the powerful are also their interests. As Lukes (1974:24) argues, 'to assume that the absence of grievance equals genuine consensus is simply to rule out the possibility of false or manipulated consensus by definitional fiat'. Lukes also rejects the idea that power can be exercised by one group in the real interests of another group. Rather, he argues, only the first group is able to identify its own real interests, and this can only be done through 'exercising choice under conditions of relative autonomy and, in particular, independently' (1974:33). An example of the third dimensional use of power by the state is the development and promulgation of discourses that create the impression that the course of action taken is the only one possible. Phrases such 'the end of the age of entitlement' are used to create the impression that cuts to public programs cannot be avoided and that such cuts will be borne by all. Other options, such as raising taxes, are thereby rendered invisible, even though public attitude surveys regularly find a majority of Australians want government to spend more on public services. For example, in an annual survey of public attitudes towards taxation and government spending, Hetherington (2013) found that more than 60 per cent of respondents support more public spending on services and only about 12 per cent support a reduction in government spending on public services.

5.2.4   Critique

The advantages of using Lukes' radical view of power as a theoretical framework for analysing the political dimensions of inequality are threefold. First, the perspective recognises as a core value that the social, political and affiliated economic interests of different groups are more likely to be conflicting than complementary; that is, social and state interventions often result in one group being privileged over another. Second, Lukes clearly identifies that the winners and losers of such conflicts of interest are not evenly dispersed. In the context of the key role of the state as a distributor of economic, social and political resources, Lukes acknowledges that the more economically, socially and politically powerful a group is, the more likely it is that its interests will be recognised and supported by the state. The dominant discourses of the state and the society tend to legitimise this uneven distribution of social and political power. Third, Lukes' perspective recognises that the state is not a neutral arbiter but an entity of power in its own right. This perspective provides the theoretical foundation for an examination of the role of the state in the maintenance and perpetuation of existing patterns of social, economic and political privilege and exclusion, though not all of these are immediately apparent to those involved, especially those whose interests are being harmed or overridden.

Lukes' perspective also has limitations. The first is connected with its primary alignment with a conflict perspective. Dividing the social and political worlds into basically two groups, the exploiters and the exploited, oversimplifies the complexities of the positioning of social groups within our society. Also, his focus on the material and economic context misses other important aspects, such as cultural factors and the meanings and understanding people bring to their interpretation and actions in the social and political worlds. Power is a very complicated concept. Even groups with little or no access to political or social power often muster significant levels of resistance to the wishes of the more powerful group. The eventual addition of maternity leave to the national social policy agenda demonstrates that power in the political sphere can sometimes be successfully overcome.

5.3   The state and power

While it's not the only key player in the exercise of power, the state occupies a central role. For Weber, it is not just its status as the final arbiter of the exercise of power that is the defining feature of the state, but also that its claim to this position is successful. In other words, what defines state power is that it is authoritative power, accepted as legitimate by those who are subject to it. The state not only establishes the rules that all citizens and institutions must play by, it also has the power to ensure compliance. Implicit in the concept of authoritative power is a set of institutionalised arrangements, such as the parliament, courts, police and military, that legitimise and support the use of power by the state (Orum 2001). The decisions of the state are thus enforced by a legal, administrative and bureaucratic framework that ensures that anyone who resists these arrangements faces a range of sanctions. The state can enforce compulsory education by taking the parents of children who do not attend school regularly to court; it can fine those who break the road rules or suspend their licences or even have their car confiscated to force compliance.

The use of power and authority by the state is also distinct because its exercise is more complex than one group imposing its political will on others. Political and social power, like all power, is variable in its application and visibility. The way the state responds to the differing needs of social groups and the way these needs are socially perceived highlight the different relationships of power that exist between different social groups and the state.

By definition, social relationships of unequal power are political; not all segments of the population have the same power to elicit and shape the state's response to their needs. More critically, the state is not a neutral player or arbiter in the allocation of social resources; rather, its exercise of power tends to mirror and reinforce existing power relations. Access to and control of social resources is competitive, and social relationships between groups reflect this. The results of these social contestations establish as well as reinforce social divisions. For example, the state's public policy response to the ongoing public and political debate on the provision and level of government funding to private schools (see Chapter 7 for more details) can either entrench, exacerbate or reduce inequality in the level of access to high quality education among Australian school students.

5.3.1   Theorising the state's use of authoritative power

The state includes not only the government but also the opposition, public service, state corporations, central financial institutions and regulatory commissions such as the Reserve Bank, the courts, military and police services, state and federal parliaments, politicians and political parties. Theoretical perspectives on the nature of state power and its relationship to social and political inequality vary substantially. The core differences reflect the origins of theories in the tumultuous social and political upheavals of the eighteenth and nineteenth centuries. In the period of the French and Industrial Revolutions and of the rise of a new political order in the New World of the Americas, political sociology's founding theorists Karl Marx, Max Weber, Émile Durkheim and Alexis de Tocqueville all sought to make sense of their rapidly changing social and political world.

5.3.1.1   Karl Marx (1818–83)

Marx was the first of the major social theorists to explain political life in terms of social variables (Goertzel 1976). Although his writings concentrate on the capitalist economic system, Marx's work also incorporates a critique of the state's exercise of authoritative power, arguing that it is a central player in the creation and sustainment of social inequality. To Marx, the economic means of production and the place of the individual or the group within it—one's social class—explained and determined the individual's or the group's life chances and their access to political and economic power. From this perspective, all societies are divided into two groups, the exploiters and the exploited, and the more political power is controlled by the exploiter group the more exploitative the society's economic relationships become. Marx rejected the liberal ideal of the state as an objective or neutral arbiter of conflicting social and political demands. Instead he argued the state was a reflection and expression of class power. In *The Communist Manifesto* he famously described the state in a capitalist society as merely the executive arm of the bourgeoisie (Marx & Engels 1998 [1948]). By this he meant that the state arose as a means of establishing, legitimating and maintaining the power of the economically dominant class. Far from being neutral, it was centrally concerned with making decisions that benefited the ruling class, though this *raison d'être* is masked by the ideology of liberal democracy, which portrays the state as the expression of popular will.

5.3.1.2   Max Weber (1864–1920)

Weber's writings and theories are centrally concerned with the role and workings of the nation state. In Weber's view the economic and the political are intricately intertwined to the extent that the means of administration of a society are as important in shaping that society as are the means of production. Weber's key theoretical insights focused on the nature of the state itself and its connections to other social institutions. The modern state, Weber argued, is made up of two central features, the bureaucracy and groups of influential officials. These are intimately linked. The bureaucracy provides the organisational and administrative apparatus to implement the laws and policies on behalf of the state. The expert officials, through expert knowledge and skills in political ascendancy, come to dominate key positions (Orum 2001). In contrast to Marx, who saw the state as the instrument of the economically dominant group, Weber saw the state as an independent source of power—but this did not make it a neutral player. Instead, it was concerned with its own interests, which might or might not coincide with those of other social groups. From this perspective the state is a separate source of power within the nation, and one that is of considerable significance. In Weber's view it was the pre-eminent and most powerful institution within modern society, whose unique position enabled it to wield power in a way not open to other social institutions or groups. Weber further theorised that political questions and activity are always fundamentally about the distribution, maintenance or transfer of power.

5.3.1.3   Émile Durkheim (1858–1917)

Durkheim's most influential writings in the field reflected his central concern with social order and social solidarity rather than with the state or political power per se. He focused on the workings of civil society and argued that its survival depended on the existence of shared beliefs and values. He argued that modern societies were characterised by a high level of social differentiation within the division of labour, creating high levels of individualism. This broke down the mechanical solidarity that existed in traditional societies where shared experiences gave rise to shared views. Instead, social cohesion was achieved through the interdependence generated by different social roles. He used the term 'organic solidarity' to describe this.

Durkheim regarded the state as a central player in the creation of social order through its role of moral regulation. Through its exercise of authoritative power, the state established the normative standards and values necessary to control the tendencies within modernity toward moral individualism. He saw these standards as generated from both above and below through the independent actions of the state as an agent of social change, and from the expression of the common moral sentiments of citizens (Giddens 1994:194). But he also believed occupational associations have a critical role as a mediating layer between the state and civil society, ensuring that democracy prevails without requiring the state to give up its role as the ultimate source of power.

While Durkheim was more concerned with the state's moral regulatory role than with its redistributive role, he nonetheless emphasised the need for genuine meritocracy, and the need for inequality to be set at a level that was accepted as fair by the population. Where this was not the case then disorder and dysfunction were likely to prevail.

5.3.1.4   Alexis de Tocqueville (1805–59)

Alexis de Tocqueville's key contribution to the study of power is his insight into the workings of democracy. De Tocqueville was intrigued with the development of democracy, especially that emerging in the USA, and wanted to understand how and why American society had managed to create a new set of political and social institutions. The key to democratic development in the USA, according to de Tocqueville, was a strong social infrastructure of voluntary associations such as local political and other social groups, coupled with the concept of free speech embodied in a free press. While recognising the potential for democracy to create a meritocratic, liberal, modern and orderly society, de Tocqueville also believed that social equality under democracy had its limitations and dangers. He observed that the democratic values of freedom and equality did not apply equally across the racial groups, as Native Americans and African Americans were subject to widespread inequities. He also recognised the danger of what he termed 'the tyranny of the majority'. As all citizens are equal, only the greatest number can effectively wield authoritative political power. This imbalance, de Tocqueville argues, threatens both freedom and equality in democracies by leaving the interests, opinions and ideas of the minority, or minorities, vulnerable to exclusion (Orum 2001).

5.3.2   Contemporary theories

Apart from Foucault, whose ideas are considered elsewhere in this book (see Chapters 3 and 11), the major sociological theories on the state's use of power tend to be more or less aligned with one of the classical theorists. Each theory presents a competing paradigm and each contains implicit assumptions about the way the social and political world actually is and how it operates. In turn, these assumptions shape the type of questions the perspective raises and the way they are answered. Each theory also presents a different argument on how power is distributed and used within modern societies. Although each theoretical perspective has developed its own variations, only the major components are presented here.

5.3.2.1   Conflict perspectives

Theories influenced by the writings of Marx reflect the central idea that the social and political arena is one of conflict between competing social groups and classes. In the classic Marxist political economy model, for example, political life is interpreted as a reflection of economic forces. For Marx, the state is more concerned with retaining the status quo in power distributions and access to social and economic resources than in redressing social and political inequalities. Indeed, from a Marxist perspective, the state has a vested class-based interest in maintaining and perpetuating current patterns of social, economic and political privilege and deprivations. Marxist perspectives see contradictions and conflict as inherent in political and social systems. More importantly, the stability of the social and political system is reflective not of consensus but of the direct domination of the business sector over everyone else, including the state itself. From this perspective, 'common values' are not consensually agreed, but express the values of the ruling class and they are 'enforced by the state using "symbolic"' if not actual violence (Bottomore 1993:6).

The strengths of Marxist perspectives are twofold. First, they recognise that the social, political and economic interests of one group are more likely to conflict with than complement the interests of other groups. Second, the winners and losers of such conflicts of interest are not evenly dispersed. The more economically powerful a group is, the more likely that its interests will be recognised and supported by the state. The major criticism of Marxist perspectives is that they place too much emphasis on the economic realm at the expense of recognition of the complex interconnectedness of the broader social and political world (Goertzel 1976).

Despite these criticisms, the idea that a ruling class exists has been the subject of significant investigation. In their study of the development of classes in Australia between colonial settlement and the 1970s, Connell and Irving argue that it was led by the state but was for the benefit of the capitalist economy and of the social elite consisting of pastoralists, other landholders and business leaders. Together these groups amounted to an Australian ruling class. By the middle of the twentieth century, overseas competition, the decline of the rural sector and democratisation had reduced the internal cohesion of Australia's upper classes and increased the independent power of the state. By the 1970s the industrial ruling class remained, but internal divisions and changing social conditions had made it highly susceptible to crisis (Connell & Irving 1980).

More recently, research by sociologist Malcolm Alexander (1998) has found that foreign ownership and control of the Australian economy has diluted the concentration of economic power among Australia's wealthiest groups. Sociologist Michael Gilding comes to a similar conclusion. His interviews with forty-three of Australia's 200 individuals and families who appeared in the 1999 issue of *Business Review Weekly*'s annual Rich List revealed that most had made their fortunes after the Second World War rather than inherited it. But he also found that there existed an established elite group with a high degree of internal unity. Almost all of the individuals within this latter group came from white, Anglo-Saxon Protestant (WASP) backgrounds, sent their offspring to the same schools, married within the same group, joined the same exclusive social clubs, had similar political views and were directors on the same company boards. Gilding's respondents suggested there was a degree of class-based cohesion among this group that was used to exclude the new elite, who tended to be from Irish Catholic, Jewish and Mediterranean backgrounds. One of these 'outsiders' described how this operated:

> There is still a class thing. There still is the old English mentality. There still is the Melbourne Club. There still is the upper crust in Sydney. They're the ones who run politics; they're the ones who run the social activities; and they're the ones who run the money in Melbourne and Sydney.
>
> Source: Gilding 2004:138

But unlike earlier accounts that suggest that the establishment wields considerable exclusionary power, Gilding reports that the members of the new elite are quite dismissive of the power of the established elite, regarding them as an irrelevant anachronism who had no effect on their capacity to accumulate wealth or to use their global personal and organisational connections to pursue their political interests. This research suggests that if Australia ever did have a unified upper class, its political influence has been weakened as a result of globalisation and new sources of wealth.

5.3.2.2   Elite theory

Elite theories are characterised by a belief that while there is a concentration of power within a nation, the sources of that power are diverse and plural. While some theories explicitly reject Marxist ideas about the power of business, others sympathise with Marx's views but disagree with his argument that state and business leaders act in unison.

Classical elite theories argue that aspects of human nature make rule by elites inevitable and that such rule is necessary for the effective functioning of society (Goertzel 1976). The justification for the monopolisation of power and authority by a small minority rests on the assumption that elites possess superior personal qualities. Elites form a united, cohesive power minority who make the major decisions on behalf of the masses, whom they consider to be uninterested in, and incapable of, self-government. Classical **elite theory** was first developed in the eighteenth and nineteenth centuries by Italian theorists Vilfredo Pareto and Gaetano Mosca, both of whom argued, from slightly different standpoints, that as not all people are created equal, in the interests of society those with the most abilities, especially the capacity to garner economic wealth and political power, should rule. For Pareto the psychological qualities of the elites to harness and make use of power was their distinguishing feature; for Mosca, the socially derived intellectual and moral superiority of the elites set them apart from the masses.

> **elite theory** A political theory that argues that power is held by one or a number of relatively small groups who owe their position to specific social, political or economic factors.

Another classic example of elite theory is Charles Wright Mills' study of power in the USA in the 1950s. In *The Power Elite* (1956) Mills argued that power in America was concentrated in the hands of a triumvirate comprised of the military, business and federal government. Instead of seeing the risks inherent in this situation and recognising their exclusion from political decision-making, ordinary citizens preferred to immerse themselves in their private lives, unable to make the connection between their experiences and the decisions of their politicians. This argument was enormously influential and had much in common with Marxist arguments about the concentration of power in the hands of a few. Australian elite theory took a different view about the distribution of power, tending towards a more benign interpretation. Social researchers John Higley, Desley Deacon and Don Smart's (1979) empirical study of the distribution of power in Australia identified three circles of influence drawn from a range of arenas but dominated by political and business leaders. Despite this finding, the study took a consensual view, arguing that recruitment to this elite is relatively open and its existence is inevitable and in the interests of society as a whole. There is no concentration of power across different sectors, and political influence is limited to the specific areas of elite interest. More recently, sociology professor Michael Pusey (1991) analysed the power of the public service in Canberra. He identified an elite of influential public servants who share a social background of privilege—Pusey concluded that this influential group is neither open nor is their power held or wielded by public consensus.

5.3.2.3   Pluralist models

Pluralist models of power and the state are linked to the theoretical work of Weber and his understanding of power in modern Western states. Pluralist models take as a central assumption the view that Western democracies are open structures in which social groups compete for access to social and economic resources. These groups are led by elites whose role is representative rather than controlling and who risk being replaced unless they satisfy their constituents that they are performing in the group's interest. The state acts as a neutral, independent arbiter, reviewing the merits of each claim on its resources in terms of the interests of the population as a whole. While pluralist models recognise that power is not evenly diffused, they argue that it is sufficiently balanced between a broad range of representative groups (business, labour, welfare) to preclude the dominance of any one group in the state's decision-making processes. The citizenry can also influence the state through political demonstrations, submissions, petitions, strikes and other social actions: under pluralism, power is exercised legitimately rather than coercively. This system of competitive checks and balances is further enhanced by the wide range of roles, interests and group affiliations of most citizens. The role of the state in pluralist models is to be representative and to perform governing functions on behalf of the society.

Pluralism's major strength is its demonstration of the diffused nature of power. By drawing attention to the way different groups compete at different social levels for power we are able to recognise the occurrence of decision-making across the political and social spectrum. Conversely, the model's major weakness is its lack of recognition that different concentrations of power are held by competing groups. By focusing on the exercise of formal power, other ways of exercising power are ignored. Also, by assuming the state is a neutral arbiter, pluralism overlooks power differentials between groups in their ability to influence and shape the state's decisions.

5.4   Globalisation and the state

Contemporary explorations of state power must necessarily locate the state's actions in the context of globalisation. Sociologist Gary Teeple (2000:179) defines globalisation as the arrival of 'self-generating capital at the global level'; that is, capital, represented by the transnational corporation, is increasingly free of national loyalties or controls. This highlights the independent power of transnational business corporations and the economic constraints imposed by the global economy. To compete in this context, nation states must alter their aims, political agendas and policies to facilitate an enabling framework for global capital. It is this imperative that underpins the adoption of neoliberal policies by successive Australian governments because such policies privilege private property and market economic forces. Neoliberal ideologies centre on a commitment to minimise the role of the state and maximise that of the market. The term 'economic rationalism' is used in Australia to describe the dominance of neoliberal ideas that posit the market as the most efficient mechanism for allocating social and political resources. **Neoliberalism** has now infiltrated policy directions across all sectors, not just the economic. The result is a change in focus from direct involvement of the state in the redistribution of social and economic resources to one in which market economic principles pervade most areas of social policy and determine distributions and services. Take the power industry as an example: the Australian states have progressively sold off their publicly owned power generating and distribution networks. The result is that there are now multiple private or semi-private power companies operating within and across states. The rationale is that the market will determine an appropriate price for power.

> **neoliberalism** A commitment to minimise the role of the state and maximise that of the market. Neoliberalism believes the market to be the most efficient mechanism for allocating social and political resources.

This change from interventionist to market-influenced policy has significantly altered the state's historical commitment to egalitarianism and income redistribution (Pusey 1991). Under neoliberalist policies, long-established social and political institutions are being reformed and replaced with market-friendly alternatives. In Australia these include industrial relations institutions and practices, widespread deregulation of the labour market and financial systems, and increasing privatisation of public services such as education and health. The changes wrought are pervasive and unlikely to be reversed by changes of government; indeed, much of the change occurred under the Hawke and Keating Labor Governments. The changes represent a fundamental transformation in the mode of production, with the neoliberal agenda forming the 'social and political counterpart to the globalisation of production, distribution and exchange' (Teeple 2000:5).

The removal of economic protection has been accompanied by a parallel removal of social protection. Under market economy principles, social policy aimed at reducing poverty and inequality moves from an emphasis on the redistribution of income by the state to one reliant on the market. The remediation of inequality is transferred from the public to the private sphere, that is, from the state to the market. In this framework, poverty reduction is not a direct goal of the state. Rather, it is assumed to flow automatically from heightened economic activity which, it is believed, will reduce welfare dependence and increase economic self-reliance.

5.5   Neoliberalism and the transformation of the welfare state

5.5.1   Introducing the welfare state

The primary significance of the state in reference to social inequality is that it is *the* key mechanism for the redistribution of economic resources. The main mechanism by which this is achieved is the taxation system, through which government redistributes taxation income to individuals, groups and institutions by means of direct cash transfers or service provision. Cash transfers are often targeted at specific groups, such as older people, first-time home buyers or couples with children, with the aim of cushioning them against economic hardship or facilitating access to a necessary resource, such as education. Services are usually universal provisions, such as health and education, which build the infrastructure necessary for the development of human and material resources. Such development includes ensuring that the nation has a suitable workforce that can take its place in the global economy. The 'social wage' is the term used to refer to this transfer of wealth. The policies developed by governments in relation to the social wage are critical determinants of the extent of inequality within the nation. Harding (2005) has demonstrated that it is government transfers that have ensured that levels of inequality, as measured by the Gini coefficient, have remained relatively stable in this period of radical change.

The welfare state is the main, but not the only, mechanism through which the redistributive role of the state operates. It is the site of the development of policy on how taxation income should be allocated and from where it is delivered. The type of welfare state a nation has significantly influences that allocation. One of the effects of the influence of neoliberalism in the last three decades has been a radical restructuring of the Australian welfare state.

The welfare state has been built around sociologist Thomas Humphrey Marshall's (1950) concept of social citizenship, defined as 'the right to the prevailing standard of life and the social heritage of society'. The modern welfare state emerged during the twentieth century as part of democratic welfare capitalism. The social fallout from the 1930s Great Depression and concerns about social upheaval following the Second World War were the catalysts for its introduction. Capitalism, at the time viewed as the most efficient and effective economic system, was also deemed unable to adequately regulate itself to ensure social stability. The *Beveridge Report* was a key document in forming the blueprint for the modern welfare state. Written for the UK government in 1942 it aimed to abolish the five 'Evil Giants' of want, ignorance, squalor, disease and idleness. Beveridge also suggested five propositions to justify state intervention, among them the abolition of extreme inequality in wealth and possessions, equality of opportunity for all children and the centrality of the family as the main source of social well-being and social stability.

The economic policies of economist John Maynard Keynes were influential in determining how the welfare state would operate. Keynesian economics argues that the state should intervene in underperforming economies by expanding social welfare spending—in this way, the nation can spend its way back to economic health. The poor are supported in hard economic times and unused resources are mobilised to restart the economic cycle (Jones 1983). Keynesian economic policies were effectively adopted by governments across the Western world and were the underlying philosophical basis of the modern welfare state until the 1980s.

5.5.2   Welfare state regimes

While the welfare state is common to Western industrialised nations, its form varies. Sociologist Gospa Esping-Andersen (1990) classifies three major welfare regime types: liberal, corporatist and social democratic. His typology is based on the extent to which markets are privileged over the state as the primary site for welfare provision. In highly commodified welfare states, labour is treated as a resource that can be bought and sold and individuals must sell their labour on the market to meet their essential needs. In decommodified regimes the state provides essential services as a universal right to all its citizens and the role of the market is diminished: the high level of social protection provided by the state frees individuals from reliance on paid work for survival.

In this analysis, Australia, Canada, New Zealand, the United Kingdom and the USA form a distinctive cluster of liberal welfare regimes. In liberal welfare regimes, social policy is used to uphold market and traditional work ethic norms, with modest and means-tested benefits aimed at a residual group of welfare recipients. In Esping-Andersen's words, 'Entitlement rules are therefore strict and often associated with stigma; benefits are typically modest' (1990:26).

The corporatist welfare regimes of countries such as Germany, France and the Netherlands also have highly regulated social welfare systems in which entitlements are based on status differences, generally related to position in the labour market. More decommodified than liberal welfare regimes, the level of social rights available in corporatist systems are determined by status and class. Corporatist regimes are also guided by the principal of subsidiarity, in which the state is seen as a support, not a replacement, for family or companies in welfare provision.

The third type, social democratic welfare regimes, are the most decommodified; Scandinavian countries such as Sweden, Norway and Denmark most closely fit this model. Social assistance is extended to all, the labour movement is seen has having significant power and the market is de-emphasised. There is also a high emphasis on all adults participating in the labour market to allow for the high rate of taxation needed to finance universal welfare (Esping-Andersen 1990).

Although categorised as a liberal welfare state regime, Australia's welfare system is distinctive. Australia has a residualist system of entitlement, based around means-tested, low-level payments expended from income tax revenue. Eligibility is based on an individual's employment, family status and income and all recipients are paid at the same rate. In contrast, welfare programs in other Western nations tend to provide universal but variable protection based on contributory social insurance (Castles 2000). The unique nature of the Australian welfare state is linked to its history. Castles (2000) points to the coincidence of a strong economic performance with a politically strong labour movement in the late nineteenth century. The result was a fair and reasonable wage, defined as one that 'met the needs of the average employee regarded as a human being living in a civilised community' (Higgins 1992, cited in Castles 2000). State and federal arbitration commissions set minimum standards of pay and conditions, and wages were supported by tariffs from foreign competition. While this model enhanced the security of Australian workers, it was, as Bryson (1992) notes, effectively only achieved for male workers. Male benefits were linked to the labour market, with payments made to those who were unemployed, disabled or past retirement age. In contrast, women's eligibility was linked to the entitlement status of their male partner. The arrangements for welfare within Australia until the 1980s have often been described as 'the wage-earners' welfare state' because of the dependence on the market for social provisions, but the limited provision for women leads Bryson to argue that it is more aptly described as 'the male wage-earners' welfare state'. The word 'white' could also be inserted because Indigenous peoples were specifically excluded from eligibility in all social security legislation up to and including the immediate post-Second World War period.

5.6   The emergence of the postwelfare state: Ending the age of entitlement

It is ironic that the point at which Australia was moving closer to a social democratic welfare regime occurred only a few years before the first critiques against the welfare state began to appear. In the early 1970s the Whitlam Labor Government (1972–75) introduced a number of measures that moved welfare provision closer to universal provision. Measures including universal health care (Medicare), the sole mother's pension (now parenting payment single), and national worker rehabilitation and compensation schemes were introduced, as was increased social spending, particularly in health and education. But these developments took place at a time of growing concern at the spiralling costs of welfare as well as changes in the dominant economic discourse underpinning the welfare state. Rising inflation and unemployment, a greater frequency of marital breakdown and increased labour market participation of women contributed to the growing critique of the costs of welfare. As the Hawke–Keating Labor Governments (1983–96) embraced the idea of a free market economy as a response to globalisation (Jamrozik 2001), welfare reform came onto the political agenda. A 1985 review of the Australian welfare system preceded a policy shift to a tighter targeting of welfare payments and increased measures of control, surveillance and review of social security recipients (Shaver 1998). The core of the wage-earners' welfare state, centralised wage fixing, was also challenged by the introduction of the enterprise bargaining system via the *Industrial Reform Act 1994* (Cwlth) (O'Connor, Orloff & Shaver 1999).

From the mid-1990s the welfare reform process in Australia dramatically accelerated. The election of the Howard Government in 1996 resulted in significantly more market-oriented social and economic policies, with a consequent shift to a more residual and moralistic welfare state focused on need, deservingness and work incentives.

The rationale for the need to overhaul the Australian welfare system was, and is, the same as in other English-speaking countries. The growth in 'welfare dependency' and the 'culture of dependency' were identified as worrying trends; increasing proportions of workforce-age people, dependent on social security payments, were taken as evidence of the welfare system's failure. Figures cited for the first major overhaul in 2000 indicated that between the 1980s and 1998 numbers of welfare recipients rose from around 10 per cent to 18 per cent. It was also argued that the Australian welfare system was rooted in the past and that it embodied outdated assumptions about the structure of work, families and gender roles. The new approach was described in one policy document as the government's commitment to maintaining and enhancing the safety net for those who need it, while ensuring that support does not go unconditionally to people with the capacity to contribute to their own support and to the community (Newman 2000:6).

The final report of the Welfare Reform Reference Group, 'Participation Support for a More Equitable Society' (more commonly known as the 'McClure Report'), was completed in July 2000. Its stated aims were 'to develop policies and strategies to strike a better balance between providing a strong safety net and allowing all Australians to participate fully in the workforce where they are able' (Newman 2000:3). In 2001 the subsequent Welfare Reform Package, *Australians Working Together*, was released. This package included the introduction and broadening of mutual obligation principles right across the welfare system (Centrelink 2001). The incoming federal Labor governments from 2007 onwards did not dismantle any of these welfare changes, but added more restrictions, especially for single parents. From 1 January 2013, all sole parents who started receiving parenting payment before July 2006 were subject to the same rules as newer sole parents: their eligibility for parenting payments ends when their youngest child turns eight years of age (Department of Human Services 2013). Thus, while there are still important distinctions between the major political parties regarding the extent and scope of welfare reform they believe to be necessary, they both accept the fundamental principle of residualised welfare, and consider the market to be the main mechanism for social security.

Patrick McClure was asked to deliver another report to the Government on how to overhaul the welfare system in 2014. Again the key rationale was that reliance on the welfare system is growing too quickly and that too many people are welfare dependent. Minister Kevin Andrews is cited as saying that more than one in five Australians receive an income support payment, that the number of people on the Disability Support Pension had increased by more than 100,000 between 2007 and 2013, and that there was an increase in 132,000 people receiving Newstart Allowance over the same period (Probono Australia 2014). The 2014 McClure report is expected to recommend a simplification of the welfare payment structure, reducing the number of payments from more than twenty to four, with a single payment for all people of working age. Access to benefits on the basis of disability is also expected to be targeted: access to the Disability Support Pension is likely to be restricted to those with a permanent impairment and no capacity to work (Karvelas 2014).

A key feature of the welfare reforms from the early 2000s to the present has been the linking of discourses of individual responsibility with those of welfare dependency. Social researchers Hartley Dean and Peter Taylor-Gooby (1992) point out that welfare dependency encapsulates three discrete but interrelated ideas: first, that people react in a simple economistic calculus of cash benefit against work effort so that the evasion of work is in direct proportion to the size and accessibility of income support payments; second, that this behaviour is linked to cultural attitudes among particular types of people; and third, inappropriate dependency is seen as a moral affront to society's values in relation to the work ethic. Defining what constitutes welfare dependency is not straightforward. Social researcher Peter Whiteford (1997) attempted to define welfare dependency but came up with more questions than answers, such as: At what level of receipt of income support does one become welfare dependent? Does the label apply to those who earn some of their own income? If so, at what point does a recipient stop being welfare dependent? A significant proportion of people on Newstart Allowance or Parenting Payment Single are actually in the labour force, but do not have enough paid work to reduce their entitlement to zero. Are these people welfare dependent?

The associated policy outcomes also sit within an individualising explanatory framework. 'Mutual obligation' is the presumed obligation held by all those who receive financial support from the welfare system that they must do something in return (Saunders 2000). In welfare reform discourse, this obligation translates to work effort. Under this rationale, the primary purpose of mutual obligation is to link welfare payments with compulsory work requirements—thus, the goal of social policy should be to overcome dependency by promoting equal citizenship based on participation in paid work (Murray 2001). The policy rhetoric of mutual obligation, Yeatman (2000) contends, is a rediscovery of the social in the face of market failure, but a conception of the social that is radically individualised.

Contemporary Australia

O O O

LEANERS OR LIFTERS?

The 2014 Federal Budget is supported by a discourse that Australia has too many 'leaners', people relying on the government, and not enough 'lifters', those supporting themselves and contributing to society and the nation. Thus there was a need to end the age of entitlement. But determining just who is reliant and who is contributing are not always straightforward propositions.

Item 1

Are high-income earners paying their fair share of tax? In 2012/13, only 2 per cent of income earners in Australia returned a taxable income of more than $180,000 per annum despite the Australian Tax Office listing more than 2600 high wealth individuals; that is individuals controlling wealth of $30 million or more. Of this group, 5 per cent paid no tax in 2010 and the rest contributed only 2.5 per cent of the tax paid by individuals in Australia. This low proportion of total tax contribution is attributed to the ability of high-wealth individuals to structure their affairs so that they can support their lifestyle without producing resources that attract taxation. Taxation can also be deferred through the use of business entities located in foreign tax jurisdictions, and family trusts can also be used to minimise tax liability.

Source: Hodgson 2014

Item 2

The Abbott Government has declared an end to corporate welfare on the basis that companies, like individuals, must bear the responsibility of their market-related decisions, activities and circumstances. In 2013/14, taxpayer-funded subsidies have been withdrawn or denied to Australian car manufacturers and SPC Ardmona, among others. So, is it now true that corporate welfare has ended in Australia? It would seem not. In 2014 the fuel tax credit scheme still provides high levels of subsidy to two business types in particular: the pastoral industry and the mining industry. In 2011, business claimed $5.2 billion under this scheme. Of this, $2 billion dollars was claimed by the mining industry.

Source: Holmes 2014

5.7   Social policy and the state

Social policy is all policy aimed at, or that has an impact on, social conditions or social issues. In effect this means nearly all policy. Family policy that provides additional support for families with only one wage earner, or education policy that opens the way for full-fee paying university places, or housing policies that provide grants for first homebuyers are easily identifiable as social policy and their implications for inequality are readily discernible. The social dimensions of ostensibly economic or industrial relations policies are also important and in each case the social impact of the policies can be assessed for their inequality implications. Less amenable to being measured is the impact of a lack of policy. Yet the absence of social policy is an integral component in assessing the state's response to inequality. For example, until very recently the idea of a national scheme to provide services for Australians with a disability was not on the political agenda, despite the lobbying of national and state disability organisations and families of people with a disability.

The practical ways in which social policies affect inequality vary, and this variation centres on three key causes. First, social policies can affect different segments of the population quite differently, creating winners and losers. The reduction of funding for public housing in recent years has had a disproportionately negative affect on the poorer and disadvantaged sections of society. At the same time, those with housing investments have benefited as increased demand for private rental accommodation has driven up rental incomes and housing prices. Second, social policy can operate as a way of ordering the competing interests of different groups in a society. Policies on drinking in public places, for example, are theoretically aimed at all people but are most likely to affect those with limited access to private spaces. Primarily, such sanctions will be applied to young people and in some areas will specifically target Indigenous people. Third, policies that do not seem to have a social dimension can result in significant, often unanticipated, social impacts. Changes in industrial relations policy were the catalyst for changed working schedules in the mining industry, such as lengthening of shifts. While such arrangements suit mining companies' schedules, the consequent social impacts on miners, their families and communities can include increased fear of work accidents, increased strains on families, and higher levels of relationship breakdown and parenting difficulties.

The making of social policy is a political process. It is also, as sociologist Adam Jamrozik (2001) argues, the practical mechanism for the allocation of society's resources. This allocation is shaped by a nation's dominant values, objectives and goals, which traditionally include values and objectives such as equity, equality, social justice, fairness, social support, and reduction of poverty and disadvantage. Few would argue against the importance of such concepts and some of them are likely to be articulated in nearly all social policy formulation. The critical question is how these concepts and values are defined and translated into actual social policies? The answer varies with different political ideologies and eras. Social policy is developed, influenced and determined by changing philosophical beliefs and dominant discourses, economic conditions and global trends. The values and objectives expressed in social policy will, therefore, be powerfully influenced by the dominant discourses prevailing within the nation at a given time.

5.8   Discourse and social policy

According to political scientist Carol Bacchi (1999), social policy is, by definition, discourse because of its socially constructed nature and its capacity to define the way an issue is understood and responded to. But discourses don't just exist. There are many competing discourses and all discourses are not equal. Foucault (1984, cited in Bryson 1992) draws attention to the essentially political nature of discourses, whereby institutional and social structures enable some discourses to be more influential than others. The unequal status, power and resources of different social and political participants impact on their capacity to frame the discourse, the consequences of which can be seen in the influence of particular discourses in shaping social policy; the discourses of the powerful are most likely to be dominant. An example of the influence of dominant discourses is the way different groups are assigned definitional positions such as 'needy', 'disadvantaged' or 'deserving'. How the political discourse presents the needs of a group determines whether assistance is viewed as legitimate.

This differential labelling of the same behaviour depending on the group an individual belongs to is important for understanding the social construction of policy. The politics of representation is inherently related to such interpretations. To determine how social status and representations are implicit in policy solutions, Bacchi (1999) poses a number of questions about social issues. First, how the issue is represented is important. Is it defined in terms of group entitlement or group deficit? The presuppositions or assumptions underlying this representation then need to be identified, as do the effects they have on how the groups involved in the issue are constituted within it. The question of who benefits and who is disadvantaged should be asked as well as what issues are left unproblematic in this representation. Finally, consideration is needed of how policy responses might differ if the issue or the group involved were thought about or represented differently.

5.8.1   The beneficiaries of welfare

The dominant discourse of welfare constructs it as targeting those members of society who, by choice or circumstance, are unproductive. There is, however, an alternative model for understanding what constitutes welfare and who its beneficiaries are. From this second perspective, welfare is defined as any form of cash transfer or service provision to an individual or social group. According to this definition, welfare includes a much broader range of beneficiaries than just direct recipients of cash and should extend to those benefits derived from the market. This form of welfare provision takes forms that may be less visible, yet are often more generous than transfers such as pensions, and the beneficiaries are more likely to come from wealthier social groups. Occupational welfare is an example of this: here, tax concessions and other benefits such as superannuation are provided to individuals in the workplace.

This broader understanding of welfare is described by Jamrozik, who, like many social policy analysts, categorises it into three main types:

1   provisions related to income distribution and redistribution
2   provisions related to divisible collective goods and services—that is, good and services that can be allocated to individuals or groups in society
3   indivisible collective goods and services that are shared by all and cannot be allocated individually.

While some of these provisions, such as pensions and benefits, are provided by the state, others are provided by the private sector. Some, such as working conditions, are provided by the state and the market. The important point is that this model of welfare provision shows how, in a market economy, it is almost impossible to separate out the beneficiaries of social policies—all benefit, although the specific forms might differ. Jamrozik argues that understanding welfare as any form of the analysis of the allocation of resources by governments becomes relatively meaningless if allocations by the market are not included. If we only focus on the individual direct allocation of resources of the state, we may develop a misaligned picture of who benefits.

5.8.2   Representations and discourses in action

An example of the operation of these different discourses of what welfare is and who deserves to benefit from it is provided by anthropologist Gillian Cowlishaw (1999), who uses subsidies for education as an example of how the representation of the group is fundamental to how the issue and its solution are interpreted. Cowlishaw examines how the issue of the schooling needs of rural and remote children is differently socially represented in relation to two groups, graziers and Aboriginal families, who vary significantly in social status.

While their children are still at secondary school, the parents of many of the Aboriginal students are eligible for an Abstudy payment, an allowance that is meant to encourage school attendance and to help Aboriginal families cope with the expenses of education. The grant, which is heavily means tested, has not kept pace with inflation: the rates of at-home and school-term allowances have not risen or been adjusted for inflation for years. Aboriginal students in rural and remote regions can access additional Abstudy monies to subsidise boarding school fees. In the Bourke region, where Cowlishaw undertook her research, Abstudy allowances are the source of much resentment from poorer white families, who see these payments as grossly unfair. Cowlishaw reports that teachers at the local schools express their frustration that the grant does not produce obedient or grateful students.

Another very common payment, the Isolated Children's Allowance, is made to subsidise education in most rural towns. This allowance is mostly income-test and asset-test free and is largely paid to graziers (primarily, if not all, middle class and of Euro-Australian background) who send their children out of the area for school including to private boarding schools in the capital cities. Monies can be accessed to subsidise boarding fees as well as the costs of keeping a second home in the city, up to nearly $15,000 per year. In Cowlishaw's analysis, the amount of taxpayers' money expended on the Isolated Children's Allowance was significantly more than that spent on Abstudy, both of which are paid via the welfare system from Centrelink.

Table 5.1 outlines these allowances for 2014 and whether they were subject to parental income tests. As can be seen, the Abstudy payments for parents of secondary students, apart from those whose children are boarding, are very modest. They add up to less than $1000 per annum if all allowances were accessed, and all are subject to Centrelink's stringent income and asset tests. The allowances for isolated children undertaking distance education are much more generous and are not income or asset tested. The allowance for boarding school fees are the same for both sets of parents, but the payments for parents of isolated children are mostly free of income tests and these parents can additionally claim the second-home allowance.

Table 5.1   Abstudy and Isolated Children's Allowance 2014

Assistance for isolated children	Per child per annum
Boarding allowance (not income or asset tested)	$7667.00
Additional boarding (income tested but not asset tested)	$1466.00 ($9133 maximum total boarding allowance)
Distance education allowance (not income or asset tested)	$3833.00
Second home allowance (not income or asset tested)	$5806.00 (maximum 3 per family)
Abstudy (secondary schooling)	
School term allowance (income and asset tested)	$540.80
School fees allowance (at home): turning 16 before 1 July in school year (income and asset tested)	$78.00
School fees allowance (at home): under 16 at 30 June in school year (income and asset tested)	$156.00
School fees allowance (boarding): maximum rate (income tested)	$9133.00

Source: Department of Human Services 2014a, 2014b

What fascinated Cowlishaw in her research was that one of these payments attracted acute resentment from local people and was seen as pandering to the 'underserved' needs of a special interest group, and the other did not. In fact, the assistance for isolated children was rarely mentioned in the town at all and certainly never discussed as a subsidy. Cowlishaw's attempts to enquire about who was receiving the payment and the amount expended created great discomfort and, at times, an aggressive response. This clearly raises the question of why Abstudy payments were resented when financial assistance for isolated children was paid without regard to the income or asset base of the parents. Cowlishaw argues that the differential labelling of similar education cash subsidies—one as welfare, one not—reflects how the two forms of subsidy are legitimated and reinterpreted through meanings associated with their recipients. The payments occupy different spaces in the local discourse as well as in the realms of policy. The unproblematised status of those in the pastoral industry means that subsidies to this group are viewed as a social right not a social problem. Almost by definition, though, payments to Aboriginal parents for education costs are deemed problematic, unfair and at taxpayers' expense—as such, they are resented.

It is obvious that the very different representations of these two groups of parents is at the core of the dramatically different way that their entitlements to educational subsidies were viewed. Such representations are associated with the level of social power and influence each of these groups hold within Australian society and its political realm.

5.9   Conclusion

The political dimension of inequality is most apparent in how the distribution of power among social groups intersects with their respective ability to legitimately access social resources. As discussed in this chapter, people with significant levels of power and influence are highly advantaged in staking their claims. Conversely, those with little power, such as Indigenous people, have difficulty establishing their claims, despite their manifestly unequal position within Australian society. And while the Australian state is the key player in the allocation of social resources, via social and economic policy, and is the central arbiter of competing claims for those resources, it is not a neutral arbiter. In addition, it uses authoritative power in how it reacts and responds to inequality; the representations and status of the different claimants can be seen in the state's response to those claims. In determining how social resources are allocated, the state remains influenced by dominant social discourses around deservingness. As a result the needs of the less powerful tend to be framed by social policy discourses that emphasise the deficits of those in need. This allows the status quo of privilege and power to remain undisturbed and reduces the capacity of the less powerful to influence the social policy that affects them and their life chances.

Globalisation and the restructuring of Australia along globally determined lines into a postindustrial society also impact on how the state interprets and responds to issues of inequality. The outcomes of the postindustrial transformation are not equally distributed and, while opportunities have been increased for some, much of the change has further embedded the traditional faultlines of inequality. The rising influence of globally dominant discourses, especially neoliberal discourses, have over the last two decades shifted the response to inequality from the state from one of state-related intervention and redistribution to a more market-influenced residualist role. A focus on individual responsibility and market-oriented responses has underpinned the large-scale reform of the Australian welfare state. In turn, the discourses of welfare reform can be connected with the ideological perspectives that inform the dominant discourses of poverty and inequality discussed in the previous chapter. Neoliberalism and the associated imperatives and demands of Australia's place in the global economy therefore reinforce the inequality outcomes of power distribution. Market-aligned social policy means that notions of deservingness and non-deservingness now mediate the state's response to inequality, with the power of the different social groups determining their opportunity to shape policy outcomes and understandings of entitlement in their own interests.

Discussion questions

1   What are the three faces of power identified by Lukes? Find an example that illustrates the three faces of power from online or print newspapers.
2   Explain some of the key characteristics of neoliberalism. How has neoliberalism influenced changes to the welfare state?
3   Why does Bacchi argue that social policy is fundamentally a form of discourse? Illustrate her argument with an example of a current social policy.

6

○

THE CULTURAL SPHERE

○

6.1   Introduction

Cultural practices are deeply implicated in sustaining social inequality and social division because it is through culture that identity is formed. Language, lifestyles, values and beliefs also serve as signifiers to others and ourselves about where we belong in the social universe. Our everyday actions and patterns of consumption signal which tribe we belong to and which we regard as outsiders and possibly risky.

The conditions of postindustrialisation have seen an increase in the importance of cultural identities. As the constraints of ascribed identities have been loosened, so people look to cultural resources to construct their own, individuated one. Culture offers a source of stability, a hook around which the answer to the question 'Who am I?' can be organised. But with this offer comes the potential for social distance, division and exclusion since the answer also identifies who I am not, and it is here that the traditional divisions of gender, race and class play a part.

This chapter points out that the term 'culture' has multiple meanings and that its use within sociology has changed over time. Current usage emphasises the role of culture in creating social distinctions between different groups. In considering the way cultural difference forms one of the main axes for processes of inclusion and exclusion, the chapter looks at how culture differentiates groups across multiple axes of social formation. The different cultural practices of women and men and of the working and middle classes, for example, are embodied in language and lifestyle, and form visible lines of distinction.

The most important social theorist to recognise the significance of culture in the creation of social faultlines was Bourdieu and it is in this chapter that his influential study, *Distinction* (1984), is reviewed. In this work Bourdieu reveals the existence of a cultural hierarchy that, through its association with class, serves to maintain social divisions. This is expressed through the consumption patterns and stylistic choices that differentiate social groups, differences that may appear trivial or superficial but that create social barriers that can be difficult to cross.

Because lifestyles are implicated in the expression of identity the chapter pays close attention to the role of subjectivities in the creation of social hierarchies. It considers how moral discourses create notions of respectability and self-worth that are experienced as personal yet located in collective social forces. The chapter argues that moral discourses are often fuelled by media representations and used to justify the differential treatment of groups whose different cultural practices lead to their identification as outsiders. The power of these constructions is enhanced through their internalisation by subordinate social groups, adding further barriers to their chances of social inclusion.

A key goal of this chapter is to demonstrate how deeply cherished beliefs can be manipulated to create irrational and socially harmful processes of social exclusion. Cultural power works through our prejudices and preconceptions, and makes false equations between what is normal and what is right. The creation of moral identities is one of the ways in which this is achieved. This argument is linked to contemporary debates about multiculturalism and changing perceptions about the meaning of multiculturalism and the effects this has on current directions in immigration policy.

6.2   Understanding culture

Many meanings are associated with the term 'culture'. In everyday discourse it is often used to refer to high culture, in the sense of cultured; that is, the cultural practices of the middle and upper classes, such as listening to opera and going to the theatre. Its broadest meaning within the academic literature is the anthropological one in which culture is used in opposition to nature. In this sense, culture refers to all forms of human creation, material and immaterial. As well as created artefacts, it comprises all forms of knowledge, including beliefs, values, language and symbols. In sociology the term has come to be used in a more restricted sense that contrasts cultural production with the material, technological and structural (Smith 2001:3). Sometimes the term is used in a way that overlaps with that of the social, but it may also be used more specifically to refer to ideational knowledge, as in Bourdieu's distinction between cultural and social capital. The different uses of the term requires attention to the context in which the term used in order to gauge its meaning.

As an expression of collective identity, culture forms one of the main axes around which processes of social inclusion and exclusion revolve. Culture establishes social norms about behaviour, which, when transgressed, may result in social disapproval. When different cultures intermingle the question of which culture is regarded as legitimate comes under scrutiny and notions of cultural dominance and subordination come into play. Throughout history some social groups have been on the receiving end of negative social appraisal by other, more dominant groups. The process by which one culture is delegitimated and denigrated by another is captured by literary theorist and cultural critic Edward Said in his concept of the 'Other' (1978). Said coined this term to describe the process of mythmaking and negative stereotyping that accompanied the colonisation of the Arab world by Britain and other Western powers. He argues that Western imaginings have historically denigrated Arab peoples, treating them as objects of study in ways that have shaped public and academic discourse about them. While these imaginings have borne little resemblance to the real world of Arab peoples, they have established discourses about their unfitness for Western civilisation and were used to dissect, invade and dispossess them from their lands and cultural heritage.

But ethnic identity is not the only domain of cultural practice. Gender, age and class also form axes around which identity revolves and so form the basis of exclusionary social practices. Often this takes the form of notions of moral worth and intellectual capacity, which coalesce around the different lifestyles, values and beliefs of different groups, forming a patchwork of difference and division that is part of our daily experience.

The complexity that culture introduces to the patterning of inequality complicates the neat image of hierarchical class division that dominated classical sociology. While class forms a hierarchical axis of inequality, with different groups ranked according to possession of economic resources, culture forms a horizontal axis that cuts across it. This means that two groups that share the same economic position may have different cultural practices that cut across it and this is a source of social distance and distinction. Our sense of identity is expressed through our cultural practices, such as what we wear, the food we eat, how we talk, our values and beliefs and the activities in which we engage. Two schoolgirls may sit next to one another in class and have parents who work in similar occupations but if one covers herself and wears a veil while the other exposes her body, their different cultural homes are immediately visible. While each style of dress may derive from an active expression of identity, it locates each subject in distinct social spaces and conveys a message about their affiliations and the relations between the two. While one form of embodiment is perceived as culturally legitimate, the heightened tensions of a post-September 11 world make the other an object of suspicion. Depending on the nature of our imaginings, difference can become division.

6.2.1   Culture, identity, lifestyle and division

The relationship between culture and lifestyle is mediated through patterns of consumption that are experienced as derived from our individual personality yet are linked to social forces such as ethnic identity or possession of capital. As well as cultural knowledge and economic resources, the capacity to live a desired lifestyle also requires certain social connections. Consumption patterns express aspirations and are used to position subjects in relation to others. One of the first social theorists to explore these interconnections was the nineteenth-century economist Thorstein Veblen (1857–1929). In *Theory of the Leisure Class* (2006 [1899]) Veblen provides a satirical account of America's aristocracy. He argues that the main activity of America's elite is not production but leisure and the conspicuous display of wealth. Veblen suggests that it is through conspicuous leisure and **conspicuous consumption** that different groups position themselves in the social hierarchy. At the top of the social order are the parasitic aristocracy whose lives revolve around the conspicuous display of wealth. Beneath them are the middle and lower classes who are productive but whose ambition is to achieve the leisurely lifestyle and wasteful consumption practices of the wealthy.

conspicuous consumption
A conspicuous display of wealth. Today the term is used to refer to any form of excessive consumption used by different groups to position themselves in the social hierarchy.

In Veblen's opinion, the American lifestyles of his day were little different than those of the 'barbarians' of the past. He suggests a parallel between the way triumphant male leaders of the past displayed their women as 'trophies of war', and the practices of the American business class of his day whose wives were prevented from engaging in paid labour. Their busy performance of 'household duties or social amenities' served as a demonstration to others that they had no need to occupy themselves with 'anything that is gainful or that is of substantial use' (2006[1899]:281).

Bourdieu was the first modern sociologist to explore the link between consumption, lifestyle and inequality. The ideas contained in his influential work *Distinction* (1984) have parallels with Veblen's work insofar as both authors criticise the upper class and are concerned with the relationship between lifestyle and social position, but the concepts and methods the two authors use to analyse this relationship are different. Bourdieu also offers a more detailed and systematic account of the way taste establishes social distance.

In *Distinction* Bourdieu explored the way that cultural markers serve to differentiate groups from one another and create a hierarchy of aesthetic sensibility. Expressions of taste, manners and morals define social identities and form the basis of the evaluation of social worth. But although cultural practices are closely tied to class location, Bourdieu believed that they also form distinctions within economic groupings. The upper, middle and working classes are internally divided by different distributions of economic and cultural capital. Within the bourgeoisie, business owners and financiers possess a high degree of economic capital but relatively little cultural capital, while the reverse is true of intellectuals such as writers, artists and university professors.

For Bourdieu cultural capital is an independent source of social position and can be converted to and from economic capital. In an earlier work, Bourdieu argued that the main mechanism by which this is achieved is through the education system (Bourdieu & Passeron 1990). The upper and middle classes reproduce their social position by sending their offspring to expensive private schools where, in addition to the formal curriculum, they develop their knowledge of middle- and upper-class culture. According to Bourdieu this cultural knowledge is as important as formal qualifications when seeking middle-class jobs. Working-class children who go to state schools gain a particular form of cultural knowledge that equips them for working-class rather than middle-class jobs. Even if they gain the necessary qualifications to enter the professions, their different cultural power will mean they are relatively disadvantaged when they enter the labour market. Its role in the transmission of cultural knowledge makes the education system an important site for the conversion of economic capital to cultural capital. Upwardly mobile people from working-class backgrounds can purchase the cultural power they lack within the family by sending their offspring to expensive private schools. When families invest in education they are purchasing formal and informal knowledge, which makes an important contribution to the establishment and maintenance of family position.

In *Distinction*, Bourdieu argued that in France there is a sharp distinction between high and low culture that justifies and maintains the social exclusion of the working class from wealth and power. By establishing upper-class cultural knowledge as legitimate and working-class knowledge as illegitimate, members of the working class are disadvantaged.

But working-class people are unable to see that their academic failure is due to cultural subordination and instead define themselves as incapable. The education system is implicated in this because it legitimates middle-class knowledge and devalues the cultural practices of working-class people. Bourdieu described this as a form of symbolic violence because it disguises structural inequality as individual failure. Although Bourdieu focuses on lifestyles rather than life chances he stresses their interconnections because likes and dislikes are influenced by class-based habitus. Consequently, taste is not merely a matter of personal preference but locates us in a hierarchical social order.

Bourdieu's study, while very influential, is not without criticism. One concern is that while he aims to provide an account that transcends structuralism, he constantly emphasises the influence of class and structural forces on behaviour. Another concern is whether his findings are able to be generalised beyond 1960s France. In an age of mass consumption, for example, is it still possible to point to a hierarchy of taste (Lamont 1992)? Bennett et al. (1999:201) also argue that French culture was insulated from the forces of globalisation, which was having a large impact on other nations, such as Australia.

In *Accounting for Tastes: Australian Everyday Cultures* (1999), Bennett et al. attempted to reproduce Bourdieu's research in contemporary Australia. They based their analysis on a national survey conducted in 1994–95 in which they mapped a wide range of cultural practices with the objective of identifying the extent to which these are socially patterned by variables of class, gender, age, education and ethnicity. They described cultural practices as located within forms of cultural and social power that mark social positions and contribute to unequally distributed cultural life chances. The labour market plays an important role (including part-time or permanent employment) in this since engagement is mediated by these variables. This is linked to lifestyle through the association between work and leisure because the workplace is often an important source of personal friendships.

These findings differ from those of Bourdieu in a number of ways. Bennett et al. found no simple dichotomy between high and low culture that also corresponds with relations of power. Instead there is a variety of positions between culture and power, with competing cultural distinctions corresponding to different social divisions. Although patterns of cultural difference are repeated and consolidated across cultural domains, they are organised differently according to levels of cultural and economic capital and the influence of variables such as age, gender and class. Another point of disagreement relates to the role played by education in reproducing inequality. While Bourdieu argued that middle- and upper-class people sought cultural knowledge for their offspring by sending them to a private school, Bennett et al. found that this was of relatively little relevance to parents: what mattered to them was the social capital offered by the school.

6.2.2   The cultural omnivore

Bennett et al. drew on researcher Richard Petersen's distinction between the **cultural omnivore** and **cultural univore** (Bennett et al. 1999:187) to explain some differences in cultural practice between the elite and the mass. They note that while those with high levels of education have musical tastes that are wide ranging and inclusive (the cultural

cultural omnivore/univore
Cultural omnivores have the ability to move between different cultural realms. In contrast, the cultural practices of the cultural univore are more restricted and localised.

omnivore), those with less education have more restricted musical tastes (the cultural univore). Emmison elaborates on this in a discussion of the concept of cultural mobility, defined as:

> The differential capacity to engage with or consume cultural goods and services across the entire spectrum of cultural life, an ability which is itself premised upon an unequal, class related distribution in cultural competence. Cultural mobility, then, is the ability to move at will between cultural realms, a freedom to choose where one is positioned in the cultural landscape.
>
> Source: Emmison 2003:211

cultural mobility The extent to which different social groups are able to move more or less freely between different cultural realms.

Emmison argues that **cultural mobility** is an important aspect of social division and inequality in postindustrial economies because of the association between high levels of cultural competence and high levels of social reward. The *Accounting for Tastes* study found that although the cultural practices of some social groups were inclusive, in the sense that cultural competency (that is, knowledge about cultural practices) stretched broadly across both high and low culture, those of other groups were more restricted and covered a relatively narrow range. Cultural omnivorousness was strongest among people with higher levels of education, urbanites, women and young people. It was especially strong among members of the professional and managerial classes. In contrast, although univorousness occurred among higher and lower social classes it was most strongly associated with low education and the manual working class. Cultural omnivorousness, and therefore cultural mobility, is thus associated with higher class location. Emmison's point, in contrast to Bourdieu's argument about the dominance of high and low culture, is that it is levels of cultural mobility that distinguish between the classes.

6.2.3   Bourgeois lifestyles

The work of Bourdieu and Bennett et al. is unusual in its scrutiny of the middle and upper classes. While the lives of the poor have been subject to excessive academic scrutiny, there has been less investigation of the middle and upper classes. Yet such studies are of great importance because of the need to understand how their cultural power is used to maintain advantage over others and because of their influence on policy and public discourse. The cultural practices of the middle class are examined in David Brooks' *Bobos in Paradise: The New Upper Class and How They Got There* (2000) and Andrew West's *Inside the Lifestyles of the Rich and Tasteful* (2006). These studies lack systematic empirical analysis but point to the dominance of new cultural elites in the USA and Australia respectively.

By 'bobos' Brooks means bourgeois bohemians, whose intellectual influence positions them as one of the USA's dominant groups. They combine the wealth of the traditional bourgeoisie with the idealistic, liberal attitudes and lifestyle of 1960s counterculture hippie-bohemians. They are the 'vineyard-touring doctors, novel-writing lawyers, tenured gardening buffs, unusually literary realtors [and] dangly earringed psychologists' (2000:61).

Brooks argues that their position is not based on inherited wealth but on their education and intellectual capacity. Their extreme wealth locates them close to the established upper class but they distance themselves from this predominantly conservative group, instead sporting disestablishment views: they reject the conspicuous consumption of the seriously rich and seek a lifestyle in line with their liberal beliefs, which does not translate into the rejection of consumption but, rather, virtuous expenditure on goods that they can justify ethically and which demonstrate their good taste. They would never wear mink but an expensive triple-layer, third-generation Gore-Tex shell parka is an everyday garment.

Brooks presents a comic picture of the bobo lifestyle, contending that their expenditure is not as virtuous as they claim but is just as wasteful and excessive as that of the conservative upper class they reject. Their concern with authenticity is also compromised by their concern with status and their position as the cultural trendsetters of the nation. Yet although Brooks mocks the pretensions of the bobos and their attempts to live an ethical life amid gross consumption, he also approves of them and sympathises with their concern to live a good life and to establish some moral boundaries around consumption patterns. For Brooks bobos are praiseworthy because their mushy liberal attitudes create the right balance between conformity and progressive creativity.

While Brooks' study is more journalistic than academic, his work illustrates how cultural approaches to the study of social difference gloss over the realities of inequality. Apart from the absence of systematic empirical research it also fails to consider the structural inequalities of class, race and gender that underpin the wealth of the bobos. Behind his 'comic sociology' (2000:back page) is a valorisation of the bobos and an ideological claim to the moral validity of an individualistic and elitist model of inequality. Brooks' claim that it is 'genius and geniality that enable you to join the elect' (2000:14) ignores his acknowledgment elsewhere that this select group were mostly born into the upper middle class. Unlike Bourdieu, whose study of the lifestyles of the rich demonstrated the hidden cultural forces that support structural inequality, Brooks trivialises the impact of the concentration of wealth in the hands of the few. He presents a misleading account of how wealth and influence are achieved and supports stereotypes about the openness of US society.

West's account of a segment of the Australian upper middle class has some similarities with *Bobos* but, unlike Brooks, is concerned with the political implications of divergent tendencies within this group. West agrees with Brooks that the character of those close to the top of the class hierarchy has changed. The dominant class of WASPs has been infiltrated by Catholics, Jews and second-generation immigrants as a result of a more meritocratic social system. But West argues that Australia has yet to see real bobos who combine creativity and commerce in the way described by Brooks. Instead, the upper middle class is engaged in a lifestyle war between two new and opposing fragments: the culturalists and the materialists. While neither are a power elite in the sense that they control the economy, they hold considerable cultural power as well as everyday economic power through their positions as senior managers, technocrats, professionals and public servants. The culturalists are similar to the bobos in their combination of affluence and left-wing ideology. They share with the bobos a concern with authenticity and good taste but because they know 'the world is unequal and unjust' (2006:11) they also struggle with the contradictions their affluence brings. In contrast, the materialists have an uncritical understanding of their success as due entirely to their own efforts. They are competitive, and material success is their main goal in life. Their purchases are not a demonstration of aesthetic judgment but rather an expression of conspicuous consumption. Both groups desire and possess cultural power but the materialists also desire financial capital which gives them greater economic power. Both groups influence cultural trends, one towards a counterculture that exults the 'real thing' (2006:70), the other towards transient trends designed to ensure that they remain ahead of the middle class as a whole.

West claims that the culturalists were in the ascendant in the years of the Keating Labor Government (1991–96), but under the Howard Coalition Government the materialists dominated, as their beliefs were championed by the Liberal Party for which individualism is a dominant ideal. Because the political ascendancy of neoliberalism extends beyond party politics the materialists' values and aspirations also resonate with those of the broader community. In contrast, the ideals of the culturalists lack the support of a major political party and so their influence is diminished.

West draws attention to the growing traction of a political philosophy of elitism in the nation's consciousness. As explained in the introduction, elitism can be understood as an effect of the rise in individualism that accompanies globalisation and economic rationalism. It is implicated in the introduction of full-fee-paying university courses, in federal government support of private schools and in the industrial relations reforms that shift the balance of power towards business by reducing the possibilities for collective bargaining. It is evident in newspaper articles extolling the virtues of elitism, in the work of thinktanks such as the Centre for Independent Studies and in the blame-the-victim policies of welfare conditionality. West's argument reinforces the view that elitism is becoming normalised within sections of the Australian population and leading towards a society that blames the socially excluded for their unenviable situation.

6.3   Imagining the 'Other'

The images that social collectives hold of themselves and others is a central feature of social identity and plays a major role in patterns of social inclusion and exclusion. These imaginings are not morally neutral but carry with them social estimations of worth. Notions of social honour and stigma adhere to social location so that to be working or middle class, for example, carries with it certain representations that are always socially constructed and contested. Those images that become normalised and enter the cultural mainstream contribute to dominant discourses that help to create and sustain social division and difference. To self-describe as a 'bogan' may be a source of pride among sections of the working class, but it becomes a disabling term on the lips of the middle class. Images of the 'Other' convey strong cultural messages about what is normal and legitimate and what should be excluded and marginalised. These negative images form beliefs and discourses that justify differential treatment and associated forms of social exclusion.

6.3.1   Scientific racism and its consequences

An early account of how a society imagined hierarchy was provided by the social historian Eustace Tillyard in his depiction of sixteenth-century Elizabethan England (1952). This understanding formed the foundation of racist policies in the colonial age and even today resonates in some arguments about relations between ethnic groups.

In Elizabethan England all creation was conceived of as ranked along a divinely ordained 'great chain of being' that stretched from heaven downwards to earth and beyond. At the top of the hierarchy was God, followed by the angels, the stars, the elements, humans, animals and plants in strict succession. Tillyard explains that, for the Elizabethans, order was equated with hierarchy. Nature had been designed by God in an orderly way and to permit disorder and chaos to prevail was evil.

According to Tillyard, the Elizabethans believed that human arrangements had been divinely ordained in the same way as nature. As the sun ruled in the heavens so the monarch ruled on earth; to disturb political arrangements was to induce sickness, failure and social dysfunction. In this way, religious belief was employed to justify and support social hierarchy and inequality. In an alignment between priest and politician, those who challenged the social order were accused of sanctioning chaos and engaging in sinful action against God, nature and humanity.

The Age of Reason, or the Enlightenment, refers to the period in European history, commencing around the middle of the seventeenth century, when the close association between church and state began to dissolve and religious beliefs were replaced by a belief in science as the dominant epistemology in European society. The notion of hierarchy remained but rather than being supported by religious ideology it was supported by a pseudoscience of race that took the form of **biological essentialism**, which classified the human species into a hierarchy of development and so justified white domination over black. By the nineteenth century a distorted version of Darwin's theory of evolution located white people at the peak of civilisation while non-white people were distributed beneath them. Africans and 'Oceanic Negroes', as Indigenous people of Australia were often known, were located at the bottom (Reynolds 2005:68).

> **biological essentialism** The belief that biology determines social behaviour.

In the nineteenth and twentieth centuries scientific racism justified the colonisation of continents, including of Australia. The idea of it being the 'white man's burden' to bring civilisation to the world masked practices of enslavement, economic exploitation, political domination and social control. In Australia this justified the declaration of *terra nullius*, the displacement and control of the Indigenous population and the denial of citizenship rights to them and other non-white workers such as the Chinese and the Afghan camel riders who provided essential services in the Australian outback. Dehumanising ideologies are evident in nineteenth-century descriptions of Indigenous people as 'but one degree removed from Brutes ... less elevated above the inferior animals than in any other part of the known world' and 'the last link in the great chain of existence which unites man with the monkey' (White 1981:8).

In the early twentieth century, racist evolutionary theories appeared in the form of the eugenics movement. Founded on the false claim of the existence of pure racial groups this condemned the mixing of races on the grounds that it harmed natural evolutionary processes. Terms such as 'half caste', 'mulatto' and 'quadroon' were used to describe patterns of racial mixing. All those of 'mixed blood' were regarded with social opprobrium. The term 'miscegenation' was coined to suggest that intimate relations between black and white peoples, especially between black men and white women, was a form of social and biological pollution that damaged human evolution and produced physically and mentally degenerate 'mongrels' (Reynolds 2005). Colonial governments used these ideas to manage genetic inheritance by passing laws and regulations that controlled the sexual liaisons of black peoples.

Negative portrayals of ethnic groups have been used to justify appalling violence and oppression throughout history, but the most systematic and extreme expression of this was the Nazi Holocaust in the 1930s and 1940s. Nazi ideology about the superiority of the Aryan race was used to legitimate the attempted genocide of millions of Jewish people as well as others deemed to be unfit for survival, including homosexuals, gypsies and political dissenters. In *Modernity and the Holocaust*, Bauman (1989) argues that the unprecedented systematic, calculated brutality against those deemed by the Nazis to be unfit for civilisation was an expression of the rational bureaucratic techniques central to modernity itself.

In Australia belief in the inevitable extinction of 'the savage races' (Reynolds 2005:71) and fear of the 'degeneracy' caused by 'half castes' was used in the first half of the twentieth century to justify government policies of protectionism. Under these policies Indigenous people were placed on reserves, light-skinned children were removed from their families and in many jurisdictions interracial marriages were strictly controlled. Removal was sometimes based on an attempt to 'breed out colour' from the Indigenous population and so to ensure its demise. The racial inheritance of populations was carefully calculated by those responsible for the program, with some accounts calculating this down to the last two decimal points (Reynolds 2005).

6.3.2   Imagining the working class

Claims of the natural superiority of one group over another extend beyond race to class and gender. Images of women as weak, irrational and emotionally unstable were used for centuries to exclude them from public life. Similar images of the inferiority of the working class justified the division of paid labour. The belief in the natural superiority of the aristocracy and business leaders and the incapacity, instability and dangerousness of the working class was deeply entrenched in political and social culture in Western nations until relatively recently. Much of the debate about the extension of universal suffrage (the right of all adults to vote) centred on whether women and the working classes were worthy of carrying the responsibility of electing their own government. In this case intellectual and moral capacity was linked to property rights since the right to vote at that time was based on property ownership.

The denigration of working-class culture and people was reflected in the morals and manners of nineteenth-century society. At all times servants were required to maintain the appropriate social distance from their master despite the intimate nature of many of their tasks; domestic servants were often expected to avert their faces when unexpectedly encountering their employer (Davidoff et al., in Bottero 2005:28). Sociologist Wendy Bottero quotes the twentieth-century social commentator and novelist George Orwell's description of the attitudes of the upper classes to their social inferiors: 'This is what we were taught ... *the lower classes smell*' (Bottero 2005:29).

In the first period of settlement, images of the Australian working class as feckless and inferior were intertwined with notions of depravity and vice that stemmed from the nation's status as a convict colony. These negative images later competed with other, more favourable views that portrayed Australia as a great country whose positive environment would create a new generation of morally upright citizens (White 1981:27). White argues that in Victorian Britain there were two main attitudes within the middle class to working-class immigrants: that migrants were lazy and incompetent and their difficulties and failures were due to their personal inadequacies, and that it was the failures of the British social system that forced people who were ill-prepared and ill-suited to emigrate to a harsh and bitter land (White 1981:37–8).

The aftermath of the Second World War saw an ideology of egalitarianism influencing political culture, partly spurred on by the atrocities of the Holocaust. Within Australia, mass consumption and the expansion of the service sector brought to prominence notions of a classless society. Yet Australia's national identity remained conservative. Despite high levels of urbanisation and a nation built from the labour of men and women from diverse cultural backgrounds, the national imagining was of the bush, the beach, strong, white male bodies and Protestant values (Phillips & Smith 2000). This white, male, Anglo culture formed the foundation for exclusionary government policies, such as the White Australia immigration policy. Within the trade union movement the voices of groups who did not fit the cultural norm, namely, women, Indigenous people and non-Anglo immigrants, were also suppressed.

The way in which class distinctions draw on notions of respectability is evident in sociologist Ken Dempsey's study of a small town in rural Victoria in the 1980s. Dempsey analyses how the idea of the outsider fractures social relations along race, class and gender lines. Although his respondents portrayed their community as cohesive and inclusive compared with the non-egalitarian and impersonal relationships of the city, Dempsey found that some people were caricatured negatively as belonging beyond the boundaries of the community (1990). 'Respectable locals' were distinguished from 'blow-ins' and from long-term residents whose lifestyle and values were deemed to threaten the quality of the town (1990:29). Just as it was common among the nineteenth-century middle class to distinguish between the respectable and disreputable members of the working class, so Dempsey's respondents identified a category of poor people as 'no hopers', people who 'belonged' to the town in the sense that they had lived there for as long as anyone could remember but were socially marginalised. For the 'decent community members' of the town these no hopers were antisocial, 'lazy buggers' who don't work, are always in trouble with the police, drink too much and neglect their properties and children. Dempsey found that this group was isolated from the 'respectable' citizens and subject to ridicule and social exclusion. They, in turn, felt deeply stigmatised and found living in the town a painful experience. They believed their faults were exaggerated and misrepresented and that those condemning them had little understanding of their real situation.

Today terms such as 'losers' and 'dole bludgers' might be applied to such people to describe their 'immoral' lifestyle and to distance them from 'ordinary' working people. This demonisation of the unemployed has a long history. Even Marx regarded the workless poor as morally bankrupt; his notion of the *lumpenproletariat* was condemnatory. He described them as 'thieves and criminals of all kinds, living on the crumbs of society, people without a definite trade, vagabonds, people without a hearth or home' (cited in Giddens 1971:38).

In the nineteenth century poverty was closely associated with criminality. The criminologist Cesare Lombroso presented a phrenological account of criminality that suggested its roots lay in atavism, a form of primitive development caused by evolutionary throwback and reflected in the physiognomy of criminals. But his prejudices about the essential nature of men and women led him to provide a different account of the criminality of women. Since women had never developed to the same evolutionary stage as men, atavism could not be an explanation of their criminal behaviour. Instead it stemmed from their possession of an excess of male biological characteristics (Lombroso 1895). They were thus doubly condemned, for not only were they criminal but they also failed the test of femininity.

Research on the working class has focused less on their patterns of consumption and more on working-class culture and its relationship to poverty and social mobility. The idea of cultures of poverty, based on an anthropological account of the life of a poor Mexican family (Lewis 1961), was influential in American sociology in the 1950s and 1960s. Lewis describes how extreme poverty results in values, attitudes and behaviours among the poor that, while understandable, ultimately condemn them to an intergenerational cycle of poverty. The argument has been criticised because although it is sympathetic to the difficulties imposed by poverty, it ultimately offers an individualistic explanation of its origins in inappropriate attitudes within the dispossessed.

Similar ideas about the role of values and beliefs in maintaining disadvantage are found in researcher Charles Murray's claims about the existence of people 'living on the margins of society, unsocialised and often violent' (2001:2). The underclass contains not only a criminal element but also includes parents who mean well but give nothing back to the community and whose children engage in antisocial behaviour. Murray explains that rising crime rates are caused by a decline in moral values, the breakdown of the nuclear family and the consequent rise in teenage pregnancies among the 'lower class'. According to Murray, these children, born into welfare dependence and lacking a stable father figure, grow up undersocialised and undisciplined and become the criminals of the future. Murray's argument is a plea for the return of conservative social values, including the traditional family structure; he also blames social exclusion on the behavioural characteristics of the poor. In this view, the social problems associated with marginalisation are not understood as arising from the complex web of circumstances that circumscribe the lives of the poor but from psychological characteristics generated by inadequate childrearing. The lack of services, lack of economic resources, lack of opportunities, lack of self-esteem and lack of cultural knowledge are ignored.

6.3.3   The uses of language

Language is an important source of cultural power and it is through its use that images of hierarchy are established. Language carries meanings and emotions. It forms the basis of social definition and social action and is reflexive, acting back on the subject while fixing the object in social space. The nuances of language serve as markers of identity, with the turn of phrase, the accent and the emphasis positioning the subject in relation to others. Language therefore expresses social location. Speaking with the 'wrong' accent identifies and excludes; speaking with the 'right' accent opens the door to privilege. Hearing one's own language creates a sense of belonging but that sense of pride and belonging is not necessarily shared by the broader community. Language acts simultaneously as a weapon and a shield, excluding and harming as words build barriers or bridges, create worlds opaque or penetrable to outsiders, and serving to heal or hurt.

The media play an important role in creating the language of exclusion through their reduction of complex realities to simplified binaries such as black/white, young/old, Muslim/Christian, Australian/unAustralian, which are then joined to estimations of moral worth such as degenerate/civilised, strong/weak, dangerous/safe, normal/abnormal, respectable/rough, rational/irrational and dirty/clean. This contributes to the creation of images of the 'Other' as abnormal, distant, outside and not us. In some popular discourses, to be a Muslim is to be unAustralian, different, untrustworthy, dirty and dangerous (Poynting et al. 2004; see 'The uses of language: The Cronulla riots' in this chapter). Social odium is attached to different social groups in ways that are accepted, in varying degrees, as natural, obvious and unquestioned, which then feeds the invisible social boundaries that separate and divide and become the basis of discrimination and social exclusion.

It is through the use of language that the 'Other' is objectified and distinguished from 'us'. Through language, the kaleidoscope of individual realities that make up the 'Other' are meshed into a single, threatening entity. The objects of these constructions are reduced to an essentialised imaginary person who is 'not like us' and who can, therefore, be treated with disdain. Their difference and outsider status provides the moral justification for social discrimination and exclusion. In *The Exclusive Society* sociologist Jock Young describes this as a process of cultural essentialism that 'allows people to believe in their inherent superiority while being able to demonise the other, as essentially wicked, stupid or criminal' (1999:109).

Contemporary Australia

THE USES OF LANGUAGE: THE CRONULLA RIOTS

On 11 December 2005 the beaches at Cronulla in south Sydney were the scene of violent confrontations between people of Middle Eastern appearance and a 5000-strong crowd of white, mostly young Anglo-Celtic Australians who had

(continued)

gathered to protest what they saw as the take-over of 'their' space by non-locals of Middle Eastern origin. At least thirteen people were reported injured and twelve were arrested and the incident and its aftermath were widely covered in the media (Poynting 2007:160).

The events followed the pattern of 'deviancy amplification', first identified by sociologist Stan Cohen, with an initial, relatively minor event being fed by media reaction into a series of violent confrontations. The initial incident occurred when three off-duty lifesavers taunted a group of four young men of Lebanese background. In the ensuing fight two of the lifesavers were assaulted. This event was widely reported in the media, partly because it fuelled long-standing tension between the relatively wealthy Cronulla locals who regarded the beach as theirs and 'outsiders' from the western and south-western suburbs, many of whom were from Lebanese Muslim backgrounds.

As tension built up during the week some media sources mounted a campaign demanding a crackdown on Middle Eastern 'thugs' and 'grubs'. Poynting argues that it was not only journalists and shock jocks who used this language, but also politicians. The language they used mirrored that of the participants in the violence and resonated with earlier images of the Muslim 'folk devil', who is portrayed as threatening the moral order of Australian society. Poynting argues that when then Federal Health Minister Brendan Nelson stated that Muslims should accept Australian values or 'clear off', it echoed in the chants of the vigilantes at Cronulla who cried 'Fuck off Lebs! … Let's keep our country clean! … Fuck off kebabs!'

Poynting suggests that this use of language to portray Muslims as dirty, troublesome and dangerous outsiders gave the vigilantes 'permission to hate' and was an important contributor to the tensions and violence at Cronulla (2007:160).

6.3.4   The hidden injuries of race and class

The stigmatisation associated with moral discourses that divide populations into the respectable and the disreputable has effects that help us to understand some of the subjective aspects of marginalisation and their relationship with social reproduction. In the 1970s, sociologists Richard Sennett and Jonathan Cobb (1972) argued that a class society, in which manual labour is devalued, carries with it hidden costs in the feelings of self-blame and shame experienced by the working class about their position in the social order. The lack of dignity in their lives is associated with a class system that explains inequality as personal failure on the grounds of the existence of equality of opportunity. Sennett and Cobb point out that the Western humanist tradition, which constructs humanity as fundamentally equal, achieves the opposite effect when combined with a misplaced belief in meritocracy. The belief that no one is fundamentally any better than anyone else is combined with the rhetoric that anyone can make it if they try—thus, the burden of blame for failing to achieve equality is placed at the feet of the individual.

In their study of manual workers, Sennett and Cobb found that this group is aware that the likelihood of achieving a high social position is heavily weighted towards the already privileged, but societal claims of egalitarianism and the existence of limited social mobility create a sense of personal failure, the effect of which is to create within workers feelings of self-blame, anger, fear, hatred and subordination. These conflicting emotions are detrimental to the individuals who experience them and also work to reinforce their subordinate position. This is how Sennett and Cobb describe how manual workers make sense of their inferior status:

> The institutions may be structured so that he wins and I lose, but this is my life, this is thirty or forty years of being alive that I am talking about, and what I have experienced in school and at work is that people are supposed to understand what happens to them in life in terms of what they make of themselves. I see this man, who I know is no better than I, being treated better by others—even I treat him that way. Much as I know it isn't right, much as I rebel against his putting on airs and trying to act superior, there is a secret self-accusation implanted in me by my very belief in our basic equality. Even though we might have been born in different stations, the fact that he is getting more means that somehow he has the power in him, the character, to 'realize himself', to earn his superiority.

> Source: Sennett & Cobb 1993 [1972]:255–6

Sennett and Cobb's argument has similarities with Bourdieu's (2001) notion of symbolic violence in its description of how symbolic power, in this case the markers of respect that are accorded to one group and denied another, become internalised by subordinate groups. The result is injury to the self-worth of these groups and the legitimation of a fundamentally unjust social order. Sennett and Cobb highlight the existence of a symbolic order of respect and dignity, which parallels the economic order of wealth and plays an important part in the perpetuation of unequal social arrangements.

These ideas are employed by Cowlishaw in her analysis of black/white relations in Western Australia. She argues that Aboriginal people in Bourke experience racism on a daily basis and that this forms part of their everyday experience (2004). While this sullies white people through the violation of Australian norms of egalitarianism and tolerance, for black people the shame attached to racism is far more extreme and constantly disrupts their efforts to assert social honour, even within their own communities (2004:32). The stigma experienced by whitefellas is largely symbolic but for black people it is directly linked to feelings of self-worth and hopelessness. Respect and its denial have emotional effects that internalise social difference and generate feelings of empowerment and disempowerment, entitlement and self-blame, resentment and subordination. It individualises inequality and, in denying its embedded quality, contributes to its masking and ongoing reproduction.

The damage caused by the burden of disregard experienced by marginalised social groups also has serious and far-reaching effects on their physical and mental health and has been implicated in their early mortality (Barnes et al. 2008). Discrimination has been shown to cause stress and depression (Ferdinand et al. 2013) and to lead to hypertension and cardiovascular disease (Lewis et al. 2006; Williams & Neighbors 2001). The exact mechanisms by which these damaging effects occur are still being unravelled but one explanation is that being a racial minority leads to greater stress, partly because of coping mechanisms that may involve unhealthy behaviours but also because of the physiological effects of anticipating racism following repeated experiences and memories of racialised attacks (Anderson 2013).

Recognition of the harm caused by discrimination has led to legislation against any form of behaviour that treats people unequally or unfairly on the basis of their race, colour, descent or national or ethnic origin in different areas of public life. It also prevents racial vilification in which words, gestures or conduct are used in a way that is likely to offend, insult, humiliate or intimidate an individual or group on the basis of their race, colour, national or ethnic origin. In Australia, Section 18C of the *Racial Discrimination Act 1975* (Cth) deals with racial vilification and is designed to protect people from the harm that can be caused by discrimination, the denigration of other groups and the stirring of racial hatred involved in hate speech. The legislation does not involve the imposition of any financial penalties on offending parties but instead is designed to promote conciliation through the Australian Human Rights Commission. Racial vilification legislation is seen by those concerned about racism as an essential tool in the promotion of racial harmony and prevention of harm and division within the Australian community. However, because it seeks to prevent racist behaviour it is open to constructions that it denies freedom of speech and this has resulted in pressure to remove or dilute its provisions—see the feature below for an example of this.

Contemporary Australia

RACIAL VILIFICATION VERSUS FREEDOM OF SPEECH

In a series of articles and blog posts, *Herald Sun* columnist Andrew Bolt argued that many fair-skinned people who claimed Aboriginality were doing so because it was now fashionable to be Aboriginal or because it provided access to benefits of some kind. He named a number of prominent Aboriginal public figures he believed this applied to (Bolt 2009).

Nine of these public figures brought a class action against Bolt and the *Herald Sun*, arguing that the articles and blogs contravened Section 18C of the *Racial Discrimination Act*, which states that it is unlawful for a person to do an act, otherwise than in private, if: the act is reasonably likely, in all the circumstances, to offend, insult, humiliate or intimidate another person or a group of people; and the act is done because of the race, colour or national or ethnic origin of the other person or of some or all of the people in the group.

The Aboriginal litigants won their case, and the *Herald Sun* was required to publish a corrective notice explaining why Bolt and the company contravened the *Racial Discrimination Act*. The judge explained that the purpose of this was to 'redress the hurt felt by those injured, restore esteem and social standing, inform the public of the gravity of the wrongdoing and help prevent racism' (Crook 2011).

The judgement resulted in public debate about whether the *Racial Discrimination Act* interfered with freedom of speech, with Liberal politicians declaring their determination to change the *Act* so that it would not be possible for someone like Andrew Bolt to be sued in this way again. In 2014 the Liberal Government moved to repeal sections 18B, 18C, 18D and 18E and insert new sections which state that the judgment about whether an act is likely to have vilified or intimidated someone should be made 'by the standards of an ordinary reasonable member of the Australian community, not by the standards of any particular group within the Australian community'. They also introduced far-reaching exemptions to the application of the law so that it 'does not apply to words, sounds, images or writing spoken, broadcast, published or otherwise communicated in course of participating in the public discussion of any political, social, cultural, religious, artistic, academic or scientific matter'. The strength of community backlash against the change led to the decision of the Abbott Government to back down from its proposed legislation.

6.3.5   Multiculturalism, immigration and discourse

Multiculturalism and immigration are areas in which discourses have played an important role, contributing to how immigrants are constituted within the political and cultural sphere in ways that flow through to the nation's immigration policies and to everyday interactions. The cultural mix of people immigrating permanently to Australia has altered significantly over the past five decades, with the most distinct change occurring over the last decade. Immigration has always been important to the Australian nation state. In 2011, overseas-born residents constituted around one-quarter of the Australian population. More than half of them were born in Europe, nearly one-quarter in Asia, and smaller proportions in Oceania (mainly New Zealand), Africa, the Middle East and the Americas.

The pattern of immigrant source countries has changed over the last half century and is a reflection of global conditions as well as Australia's population needs. During the 1950s and 1960s, the high proportion of immigrants from Europe reflected the role Australia played in resettling people displaced by the Second World War. At the end of the 1960s, the growing proportion of immigrants born in the United Kingdom and Ireland was accompanied by substantial immigration from southern Europe (Yugoslavia, Greece and Italy in particular). From the late 1970s, immigrants became increasingly likely to have been born in countries of the Asia–Pacific region, such as New Zealand, Vietnam, China and India. In 2011–12

India and China were the leading birth countries of permanent migrants to Australia, with the United Kingdom in third place (see Table 6.1).

Table 6.1   Main source countries of Australia's Migration Program

Country of citizenship	Migration Program visa places 2011–12
India	29,018
People's Republic of China	25,509
United Kingdom	25,274
Philippines	12,933
South Africa	7,640
Other Countries	84,624
Total	184,998

Source: Department of Immigration and Citizenship 2012

To be accepted as an Australian immigrant people need to qualify under one of Australia's three main immigration programs: the skilled immigration program, open to those who hold work qualifications and skills that Australia needs; the humanitarian immigration program, through which people are selected for immigration on humanitarian grounds, with selection often made from refugee camps in other countries; and the family reunion program, through which immigrants already with residence in Australia can sponsor other members of their family. New Zealand citizens are also able to immigrate to Australia outside of these three programs.

In 2011–12 Australia received just fewer than 200,000 permanent migrants, which represents considerable growth since the 1990s. In the 1990s the predominant migration category was family reunion but today it is skilled migrants, with almost two-thirds of migrants being from this category and only 7 per cent (13,759) from the humanitarian program. Another important change has been the increase in temporary migrants, of which there are almost three times as many as there are permanent migrants: these temporary migrants are comprised of almost a quarter of a million foreign students, 223,000 working holiday makers and 125,000 people on temporary long-stay business visas. As with permanent migrants, people born in India and China make up the greatest numbers of temporary migrants (Department of Immigration and Citizenship 2012).

assimilation The process by which immigrants are expected to surrender their own culture and adopt the lifestyle and culture of the dominant group.

A policy of multiculturalism prevailed in Australia from the 1970s to the 1990s, replacing earlier policies of **assimilation** and integration. Social researcher Jock Collins (1991) notes that the term has come to mean much more than an empirical description of the multi-ethnic makeup of the Australian population; it is also a philosophy that encompasses an ideology of cultural dualism. In this sense, multiculturalism can be described as a discourse on the place of immigrants within Australia. Its status in this regard is reflected in Collins' observation that, despite agreement between the major political parties and acceptance by many ethnic organisations, multiculturalism remains a contentious concept.

The first major critique of multiculturalism was made in the early 1980s by Melbourne historian Geoffrey Blainey, who argued that by embracing multiculturalism Australia was effectively abandoning its British heritage and history and that cultural dualism expressed under multiculturalism meant that Australian–British culture was no longer the paramount national identity. In effect, he was saying that Australians were in danger of losing the primacy of their own culture, and were under threat of being taken over by other cultures, especially Asian. As he noted in the Melbourne *Age* in 1984, 'Sadly, multiculturalism often means Australians come second'. From Blainey's perspective multiculturalism was costly and divisive, and had given rise to an 'ethnic industry' that diverted taxpayers' money from 'Australians' to serve minority interests.

During the 1990s this critique was echoed by and gained political reality via the emergence of Pauline Hanson's One Nation Party. Again, the rhetoric focused on the threat to national identity—its 'Australianism'—posed by immigrants, particularly those from Asia. Along with Aborigines, these groups were seen as getting entitlements over and above those of ordinary Australians. Since 2001 the focus has switched sharply from a fear of Asianisation to a concern about the cultural problems and non-assimilationist practices of immigrants from the Middle East, especially Muslims. September 11, the war on terror, the large numbers of Middle Eastern asylum seekers arriving by boat in the early 2000s and, more latterly, the Cronulla riots have all added to a fear that Australian culture is being swamped, this time not by Asians, but by Muslim peoples.

The dominance of the discourse of multiculturalism is now under serious challenge. Prime Minister David Cameron of the United Kingdom, Angela Merkel, Germany's chancellor, and the former president of France, Nicholas Sarkozy, have argued that multiculturalism has failed and that instead there should be a requirement for integration into the mainstream community. These developments have occurred mainly in response to concerns about Islamic extremism but are also supported by the work of political scientist Robert Putnam. Putnam argues that increased immigration and ethnic diversity are associated with lower trust, lower social solidarity and lower happiness. He writes: 'The effect of diversity is worse than had been imagined. And it's not just that we don't trust people who are not like us. In diverse communities, we don't trust people who do look like us' (Putnam 2007). His solution is not to close the door to migrants but to improve strategies for integration, including ensuring all immigrants to the USA learn to speak English, and developing symbols of national unity (Lanzarotta 2008).

In Australia these developments can be seen in a new emphasis on integration as the new ideal for the behaviour of immigrants. This idea, that incoming peoples and their cultures be integrated into the dominant Australian culture, is evident in public policy measures such as the introduction of new test requirements for citizenship applicants, which require an understanding of Australian history, culture and values, as well as the raising of the standard of English needed to qualify for a skilled immigrant visa (ABC 2007a). Simultaneously, a core principle of multiculturalism, the recognition of the value of other cultures and their right to coexist alongside Australian culture, is being increasingly politically and publicly questioned. Certainly the use of the word 'multiculturalism' has slipped out of the public lexicon—a sure sign of a changing discourse—to be replaced by terms such as 'linguistically diverse' and 'diversity'.

6.3.6   Multiculturalism, elitism and the enemy within

One of the factors influencing the trend against multiculturalism is the creation of stereotypes of marginalised groups who threaten the normality of the 'Australian way of life'. Ideas of the 'unAustralian' have entered public discourse (Smith & Phillips 2001) and are associated with the construction of immigrants and refugees as dangerous and undesirable. Perhaps the most prominent expression of this kind of phantasmagoria is that of the bearded, Arab fanatic plotting to wreak terror in the street. Morgan and Poynting argue that there is a long tradition within mainstream Australian culture of the creation of Arab migrants as 'folk devils' who threaten the social fabric of Australian communities (2012). A series of rapes that occurred in Sydney in 2002 are an example of this. In the moral panic that followed the first reports, the stories were immediately racialised. The rapes were explicitly linked to the ethnic background of the perpetrators so that Arab culture itself was on trial. To be of Arab descent was to be inherently suspect, uncivilised and treacherous. Even looking like an Arab opened the door to suspicion:

> They invade our shores, take over our neighbourhood and rape our women. They are
> all little bin Ladens and they are everywhere: explicit bin Ladens, closet bin Ladens;
> conscious bin Ladens and unconscious bin Ladens; bin Ladens on the beach and bin
> Ladens in the suburbs. Within this register, the Arab, like the Jew of the Nazis, is
> intolerable as such. Even a single Arab is a threat.
>
> Source: Poynting et al. 2004:xx

Although there was no evidence that the rapes were linked to the values, beliefs and traditions of local Arab communities or with Arab culture in general, or that racial hatred was the primary motive, whole communities were subjected to ideological denigration and Arab immigrants were marginalised and excluded.

Collins et al. (2000) argue that even though young, second-generation Australians from non-English-speaking backgrounds may identify as Australians, they are subjected to an ideology of racism and social control that insists on treating them as 'Other'. In these conditions of social exclusion and economic disadvantage young men from ethnic minorities may turn to one another for support. The group becomes a site for the construction of a particular type of identity (working-class, masculine) that values physical prowess, assertiveness and group loyalty. Acts of collective violence become a form of defence and of resistance to Anglo-Australians and other ethnic groups. But, as with the resistance of Indigenous people, this does not resolve the problem; instead, it exacerbates it by further reinforcing the negative stereotyping and social reaction that produced it in the first place. Racism, economic marginalisation and a particular type of working-class masculinity combine with the young men's struggle for identity and social space to recreate their disadvantage. Collins et al. (2000) argue that it is these structural forces that shape ethnic violence rather than the cultural factors suggested by the media. Similar arguments are presented by Lentin and Titley (2011) in their analysis of the strength of the public discourse that multiculturalism has failed. They argue that the focus of public attention on the difficulties and dangers of multiculturalism serves to displace the crises that arise from the tensions within global neoliberalism. This provides a means of disciplining 'immoderate populations at home, to secure borders against risky migrants and transnational agitation and to oppose Islamic "totalitarianism" on its benighted terrain' (2011:47).

Stereotypes of the dangerous, immigrant 'Other' have serious consequences. They are implicated in public acceptance of policies and political acts that violate human rights and threaten Australia's image of itself as a tolerant country. In 2001, public acceptance of claims that refugees threw their children overboard and scuttled their boat in an attempt to gain asylum provided the environment that permitted policies of harsh treatment towards refugees seeking asylum on Australian shores, including excising thousands of islands from the Australian immigration zone, the prolonged detainment of refugees in prison-like conditions at refugee campus such as Nauru, and the creation of a class of temporary citizens through the use of temporary protection visas (Marston 2003). These stereotypes are also implicated in the reframing of multiculturalism from a positive benefit for the nation to its portrayal as divisive and a threat to social cohesion in its denial and denigration of Australian culture (Roth 2007). Within the criminal justice system, fear of the enemy within has permitted the passage of new laws that the Human Rights and Equal Opportunity Commission has argued erode civil liberties (von Doussa 2004). These include twelve-month control orders on terror suspects, restricting their movement and enabling tracking, preventative detention for suspects in the event of an attack, increased police powers to stop, question and search those suspected of taking part in a terrorist attack, fines of up to $3000 and possible jail terms of three to six months for people who refuse to hand over documents, and the creation of a new sedition offence for advocating violence against the community. These stereotypes have also damaged everyday interactions between immigrant and Anglo-Australian communities. A study by Poynting found that the level of racism experienced by Muslims increased significantly following the September 11 attacks. These interactions form the foundation for the kind of violence experienced at Cronulla in 2005 (see the earlier feature in this chapter titled The uses of language: The Cronulla riots).

6.3.7   Australian attitudes to multiculturalism

While it is not hard to find examples of incidents that suggest there is more than an element of racial intolerance within the Australian polity and citizenship, Australian social theorists Bob Hodge and John O'Carroll argue for a more complex picture, and this is supported by surveys of Australian attitudes to multiculturalism (2006). Rather than understanding multiculture (their preferred term) in terms of simple binaries they argue that it is just as easy to point to incidents that suggest positive attitudes to immigrants as it is to find negative ones.

This ambiguity is also present in surveys that show very mixed results in Australian attitudes towards multiculturalism. A national study of attitudes towards racism found that 89 per cent of Australians support cultural diversity, 84.4 per cent believed that there is still racial prejudice in Australia, and 85.6 per cent believed something should be done to minimise or fight racism in Australia. But the same survey found that 77.7 per cent of respondents believed humankind is made up of separate races, 41.4 per cent believe there are cultural groups that do not fit into Australian society and only 49 per cent often or very often mix with members of other cultural groups in social life (Dunn et al. 2011). This ambiguity can be seen in the public acceptance of harsh policies towards asylum seekers. Under the Howard Government new provisions were introduced that saw the excising of some islands, including Christmas Island, from Australia's migration zone, and the creation of offshore immigration detention centres at Manus Island and Nauru. Asylum seekers are detained there in often difficult conditions while their claims to refugee status are assessed. The successful re-election of the government following its refusal to allow the Norwegian vessel the *Tampa* into Australian waters because it would have meant accepting 438 refugees who had been rescued by the boat, also supports the view that at this time Australians were taking a hard line towards immigration (Poynting & Mason 2006).

Under the Abbott Coalition Government, policies have become even tougher: information about boats that have attempted to reach Australian shores is not provided to the media, and a new regime of turning back boats to where they have come from has been introduced. Since 2001 the proportion of survey respondents wanting lower levels of immigration has been declining and the majority believe that immigrants open Australia to new ideas and cultures and are good for the economy, jobs and employment. This transition to a more benign attitude towards immigration and multiculturalism has taken place in a time of continued economic prosperity that may have alleviated concerns about job shortages and about the effects of immigrants on the economy (Goot & Watson 2005). It is also possible that this attitude is connected to heightened public concerns about the curtailment of civil liberties and the involvement of Western nations in human rights abuses domestically and overseas. The case of David Hicks, who was held without charge for nearly five years in the USA's military detention centre at Guantanamo Bay, Cuba, on the grounds that he was a terrorist, illustrates this shifting attitude: initially hostile public attitudes in the wake of September 11 gradually muted in response to Hicks' prolonged illegal detention and allegations of maltreatment.

6.4   Conclusion

For most of its existence sociology has been concerned with understanding the power of material forces in determining social arrangements, while the power of culture has been largely overlooked. Bourdieu's importance as a social theorist within the field of inequality is largely because his analysis of culture revealed the existence of a cultural hierarchy which exists alongside the economic order and which empowers some groups over others through the establishment of a hierarchy of knowledge. Cultural power is symbolic power, formalised through the possession of credentials and in the informal signs conveyed by manners and behaviour. In drawing attention to the latter Bourdieu highlights how the status order is manifested in daily interactions through the manipulation of symbols such as language, dress and the often unspoken rules of behaviour, and shows that this is critical to the maintenance of horizontal and vertical social divisions.

An important extension of Bourdieu's insights into the role of cultural capital in the creation of inequality is his concept of 'symbolic violence'. This idea of the social harm enacted on subordinate social groups through their absorption of individualistic understandings of social hierarchy provides insight into the corrosive effects of negative discourses on subjectivities. Similar ideas are presented by Sennett and Cobb in their analysis of the hidden injuries of class.

As well as contributing to an explanation of class inequality, these understandings make an important contribution to the explanation of race and ethnic relations. Cowlishaw demonstrates how the long history of racism experienced by Indigenous people in Australia creates stigmatised identities that are absorbed within Indigenous communities and contribute to their feelings of hopelessness, frustration and resentment. This further damages black–white relations by adding internal barriers to the external ones that already exist. The negative effects of the creation of moral identities can also be traced in the way stereotypes of the ethnic 'Other', especially those from the Middle East, have been played out in the media, contributing to perceptions that the policy of multiculturalism is failing and should be replaced by policies with an insistence on integration. But such policies attempt to recreate an imaginary past of a homogenous white culture rather than reflecting the diverse reality of today. While the survey evidence on the increasing acceptance of the benefits of multiculturalism suggests that this shift does not reflect the majority view, incidents such as the riots at Cronulla in 2005 and the increase in racist acts against people of Muslim appearance following September 11 suggest that xenophobic forces remain powerful within the nation. In a world facing an unpredictable future, where the one certainty is that we live with unquantifiable and unpredictable risk, the shift from popular to populist is one that is easily made. Understanding how easily cultural forces can be drawn on to demonise the 'Other' assists in challenging such tendencies.

Discussion questions

1   What is scientific racism and how has it been used to justify the denial of human rights to Indigenous peoples and other ethnic minorities? Do these ideas have any currency today?

2   What role do morals, values and behaviours play in the maintenance of social distance and exclusion between different social groups? Illustrate your answer with examples from a TV show or a movie.

3   Explain the meaning of the term 'the hidden injuries of race and class'. Do you agree with the argument that they exist?

4   What does survey research suggest about the accuracy of claims that Australians don't support multiculturalism? What is your own view on immigration and why?

PART **3**

SITES OF INEQUALITY

○

○

7

○

KNOWLEDGE, EDUCATION AND TECHNOLOGY

○

7.1   Introduction

In an increasingly globalised world the social and economic value of education and knowledge is rising exponentially. Accompanied by myriad new technologies that make globalisation possible, almost every aspect of life, work and communication is being transformed. Within this new environment the education system remains the central disseminator of knowledge and skills. Education also holds a unique position as both a core societal institution and a fundamental social resource. But the relationship between education, knowledge and inequality in this new global terrain is not straightforward. Knowledge can operate as a reducer or reproducer of inequality, dependent on the equality of access to the education and skills needed to participate in this era of global technologies. There is no doubt that the current generation of young Australians is better educated than previous ones, and that education is the link to occupational and consequent upward social mobility within the globally transformed Australian labour market (see Chapter 8). If we look at trends in who acquires the education needed to prosper and participate in the information age, we can see clear and long-standing patterns of privilege and deprivation. In Australia, as elsewhere, those already privileged on indicators such as household income are demonstrably far more likely to acquire higher level educational outcomes than those from lower socioeconomic backgrounds.

The social resource and social institutional functions of education are intimately tied into the workings of the Australian state. The state's role in shaping educational institutions and setting the framework for how education is socially allocated means that debates around the role of knowledge, technology and education are essentially political. The discourses inherent in such debates play out through their interaction with the state in the dominant ideas that influence education policy. Recent policy debates about proposals to send high-achieving Indigenous children away from their communities to boarding schools, and about the changes to the levels and ways that public and private schools are funded by the state, demonstrate competing discourses. Also, although policy in this arena is only implemented at the state and territory or national level, such policies increasingly interact at the idea, development and outcome level with the global market forces and technologies that increasingly dominate our everyday world. The focus of this chapter, then, is the nexus between education, technology and our increasingly globalised world and the impact on social and economic inequality.

This discussion directly addresses the third question of the study's guiding questions: how is the distribution of Australia's social, political, economic and cultural resources reproduced across different social groups, and what role does the state play in this? It asks how the dimensions of inequality are changing in the context of globalisation and a postindustrial society. Responses to the first two questions (What are the main dimensions of social inequality in contemporary Australian society? How is marginality distributed and what are the causes of this? How are these dimensions changing in the context of globalisation and a postindustrial society?) are also developed as they apply to the arenas of education, knowledge and technology, all key sites for the manifestation of inequality in contemporary Australia. The examination shows that the distribution of education, knowledge and technology resources and the resultant social privilege or deprivation are not spread evenly across different social groups. Rather, while change has occurred in relation to the spread of educational inequality, the inequality that remains is highly clustered. Especially in relation to gender, embedded divisions of inequality based on class, location and race are still highly visible and may be becoming even more entrenched.

7.2   Theorising education and inequality

The relationship between education and inequality has long been of theoretical interest to social researchers. The explanations of this link have varied, with the contestation centring on the concept of social reproduction. The key question is whether the education system is meritocratic and thereby allows those with ability and fortitude to succeed regardless of social background, or whether it operates to socially reproduce inequality across the generations.

Pierre Bourdieu is the major social theorist in this area. According to Bourdieu, education is a field of struggle over access to social resources where hierarchies are maintained through access to different forms of capital: the different levels of educational attainment among different social groups can be directly related to the amount of cultural, social and **symbolic capital** they possess. The individual's or group's levels of social capital or access to resources or social networks, cultural capital (the acquisition of dominant cultural knowledge, tastes and preferences that differentiate the

symbolic capital A form of value that means nothing in itself but is dependent on whether other people believe someone possesses it.

social classes) and symbolic capital (the social status and prestige accorded to individual groups) all play a role in such distribution. Bourdieu also identified 'academic capital' as a key factor, arguing that this specific educational capital is 'the product of the combined effects of cultural transmission by the family and cultural transmission by the school (the efficiency of which depends on the amount of cultural capital directly inherited from the family)' (1984:23).

The major role of the education system is, according to Bourdieu, cultural reproduction, and the culture that the education system reproduces is the culture of a society's dominant classes. While such culture is positioned as superior, its dominance stems from the ability of the powerful to impose values and legitimacy on their own cultural preferences rather than from any innate superiority. Defining social, cultural and symbolic factors as capital also highlights their usability as a way of achieving social privilege. Under such reasoning, students from privileged backgrounds are automatically advantaged within the education system as they have been socialised into the dominant culture. The value of Bourdieu's theoretical frame is that it rebuts meritocratic assumptions by taking into account the core social reality: students access education from very different starting points. Or, as sociologist Wendy Bottero (2005:251) would have it, the less advantaged always have a greater distance to travel to achieve the same goals.

7.3   An overview of education in Australia

The Australian system is similar to those of other Western countries in that it is made up of primary, secondary and tertiary sectors. In 2013 there were 9393 schools in Australia, 70 per cent of which were primary, 15 per cent secondary and 15 per cent combined primary and secondary schools, down from 9562 schools in 2008 (ABS 2013c). Despite the small reduction in number of schools, the number of students enrolled in the education system is impressive. According to the ABS, in 2012 there were 3,624,605 full-time school students, 1,790,000 students undertaking vocational education and training (VET), around 390,000 apprentices and trainees and 1,192,700 higher education students. Even allowing for overlap, these figures indicate that a significant proportion of the Australian population is currently undertaking education or training.

Australian schools are divided into public and private sectors, with most being government (public) schools. Nationally in 2012 the majority of primary schools (76.8 per cent) were government, as were the majority of secondary schools (74 per cent). The Northern Territory had the highest proportion of government schools (80 per cent), the Australian Capital Territory had the highest proportion of Catholic schools (23 per cent), and Western Australia had the highest proportion of independent schools (13 per cent) (ABS 2013c).

In the past twenty years a clear pattern of students moving from the public to the private system has emerged, with a marked decrease in the proportion enrolled in government schools. In the last ten years this trend has accelerated with the number of students attending (non-government) Catholic and independent schools increasing by 11 per cent and

37 per cent respectively between 2001 and 2011, compared to just a 1.3 per cent increase in student numbers in government schools (ABS 2011). The gradual rise in the number of students attending private schools is depicted in Figure 7.1.

Figure 7.1   Number of students by school type, 2003–13

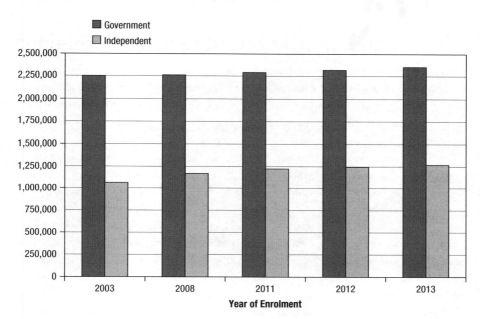

Source: derived from ABS 2013c:18

In the current system, most young Australians attend school until at least the age of sixteen, with the retention to Year 10 being almost 100 per cent (Collins et al. 2000:32). The retention of students through Years 11 and 12 has also risen but the upward trend seems to have plateaued. In 2013 the national retention rate for students from Year 7/8 to Year 12 was 81.6 per cent, up slightly on previous years, but similar to the retention rate in 1994. While the Year 12 retention rate for female students is still higher than that of male students, the gap between males and females has been slowly closing. In 2006 there was a difference of 11.7 percentage points between males and females but in 2013 the difference was 7.8 percentage points (ABS 2013a, ABS 2013c).

In its tertiary sector, Australia has thirty-nine universities (of which thirty-seven are public institutions and two are private) and numerous colleges, including more than sixty technical and further education (TAFE) colleges. A rising number of institutions, such as Charles Darwin University, are dual-sector, providing both higher education and vocational education courses. The proportion of Australian students continuing to higher education is gradually rising: in 2011 there were approximately 929,000 people enrolled in higher education, up from 719,000 in 2001 (ABS 2012b). This rise is part of a more general trend in educational participation among Australians of all ages. On an international comparison, Australia ranks slightly higher than the OECD average for secondary- (84 per cent compared to 82 per cent) and tertiary-level attainment (45 per cent compared to 39 per cent) (OECD 2013b).

7.4 Education, knowledge and life chances

A population's education and knowledge levels are broadly perceived as being directly linked to individual, economic and national benefits. As one indicator, the ABS measures the attainment of formal non-school qualifications and the levels of educational participation as indicators of whether life in Australia is getting better: the headline indicator is the proportion of the population who have a vocational or higher educational qualification. On such measures, Australia is indeed progressing. The proportion of people aged fifteen to sixty-four years with a non-school qualification increased from 47 per cent in 2001 to 57 per cent in 2013, with the proportion of people with a bachelor degree or above increasing from 17 per cent to 25 per cent in the same period (ABS 2013d). For the nation, a highly skilled labour force translates into a robust, adaptable economy able to take advantage of global economic opportunities; for individuals, educational and skill attainment translates directly into labour market access. As noted by Kelly, Bolton and Harding (2005:2), 'education has proven to be the silver bullet for Australian workers, directly translating into job opportunities'.

The importance of education to economic and national progress and individual success underscores the life-chance risk to those with low educational achievement. In a knowledge-based society, the highly educated gain privileged access to rewards linked to the possession of knowledge and skills. Conversely, those with low educational outcomes are vulnerable to economic and social marginalisation, risk that is most clearly observed in the translation of educational achievement into labour market access. Low educational attainment is linked to labour market marginalisation for both younger and older workers. Early school leavers (before Year 12) are likely to face prolonged periods of unemployment and those who do find work are likely to be limited to part-time, low-paid, casual employment (Senate 2004; Dusseldorp Skills Forum 2006). The decline in manual and manufacturing jobs in recent decades means that work opportunities for those with low levels of education are limited, and this particularly affects older workers. Those pushed out of manual positions by economic change often experience difficulty in finding other work (Weller & Webber 2001).

Other research indicates that in times of higher employment the prospects of younger workers, in particular, improve. Marks' (2005) study of school-to-work transitions found that within four years of leaving school over 70 per cent of those who did not go on to tertiary study were engaged in full-time employment. However, there is a clear correlation between employment and educational qualifications. As shown in Table 7.1, at the national level those with higher levels of education have both lower levels of unemployment and higher rates of labour-market participation.

Table 7.1   Australian employment outcomes by level of education, May 2013

	Unemployment rate %	Participation rate %
Degree	3.3	87.1
Diploma	3.8	84.2
Certificate	5.8	83.8
School leaver	7.8	65.8
Australian population	5.7	76.9

Note: degree includes bachelor and higher degrees; diploma includes advanced diploma; school leavers include those without non-school qualification.

Source: ABS 2013d

Structural adjustments in the economy due to changes in technology and the reorganisation of the workplace have led to fewer work opportunities for people with limited qualifications; a pattern that is likely to increase in a world where high-value workers are expected to possess a sophisticated set of skills and to be able to quickly acquire and interpret new knowledge. James (2002), for example, notes that the working lives of young people completing their education today will extend forty years into the future and beyond. The skill sets needed for workers towards the middle of this century will likely be very different than those required in its second decade, but those with developed skills will be more easily able to adapt to changing needs and technologies.

7.5   Accessing and using information technology

The limiting aspects of low educational attainment are also evident in data relating to the use of information and communication technology (ICT). ICT and the knowledge required to maximise its use are key to successfully operating in the globalising world. Questions around ICT and inequality relate to whether technology operates to reduce or reproduce inequality in our society. Does technology such as the internet lead to an egalitarian forum for access to knowledge and for voices to be heard? Is there a digital divide, with the rising importance of such technologies reinforcing existing social divisions and inequities? Should those people who are already poorly positioned in relation to access to knowledge and education just add information poverty to their catalogue of other poverties while the already privileged also become the information rich?

At first glance, current data indicate that those predicting an equalising effect of technology are more likely to be correct. While groups with the most social resources were the first to access and use these technologies, over time their use has become far more general. In 2013, more than 90 per cent of the 7.3 million Australian households with internet access had a broadband connection. However, access varies by location, with household proportions of internet access ranging from 89 per cent in the Australian Capital Territory to 78 per cent in Tasmania. The presence of children is also influential: 96 per cent of households with children under fifteen years of age have access to the internet, compared to 78 per cent of households without children under fifteen. Internet usage is also part of most Australians' daily lives. More than four out of five households (81 per cent) accessed the internet at home every day and a further 16 per cent accessed the internet at home at least weekly (ABS 2013e).

Closer examination of usage data, however, reveals persistent patterns of inequality across most of the usual dimensions. While there is little gender difference in access to ICT, high income earners, people with higher levels of educational attainment, people living in capital cities and people aged fifteen to twenty-four all register relatively higher levels of access, and these divisions do not appear to be lessening. ABS (2013e) data indicate that 97 per cent of those earning more than $120,000 per annum are internet users compared to 77 per cent of those earning less than $40,000. Similarly, the majority (96 per cent) of those with a bachelor degree or above were internet users, compared to 75 per cent of people educated to Year 12 or below. Agewise, those in the fifteen-to-seventeen age group had the highest proportion of internet users (at 97 per cent) compared to 46 per cent of those sixty-five years or older. Locationally, 85 per cent of households in capital cities have internet access, versus 79 per cent of those outside major metropolitan areas, although the location gap is reducing (ABS 2013e). In remote areas only 20 per cent of households were connected to the internet.

Indigenous people are also substantially less likely than other Australians to have internet access in their homes. For example, analysis of ABS 2011 census data shows that in the regional town of Dubbo, New South Wales, 60 per cent of the Indigenous population have household internet access compared to 70 per cent of the non-Indigenous population. In Perth, using the same data source, 70 per cent of Indigenous households had internet access compared to 83.5 per cent of non-Indigenous households.

The patterns of inequality in internet access, therefore, fall along the same faultlines as other dimensions of inequality. Those who are poorer, less educated, older, living in regional or remote areas and/or Indigenous are less likely to have household internet access and are therefore less likely to be able to reap the benefits of access to higher-level ICT skills that are aligned with greater labour-market success.

Contemporary Australia

SCHOOL LEAVING: MORE EDUCATION OR MORE JOBS?

The 2014 Federal Budget outlined major changes to the benefits available to those aged under thirty years who are unemployed. Under a policy shift described by its proponents as 'earn or learn', young job seekers applying for Newstart of Youth Allowance would have to undergo a six-month waiting period before they became eligible for any payments and would also have to participate for twenty-five hours a week in the Work for the Dole Program. Once they have been on the payment for six months they would have to wait another six months for further payment unless they undertake training or study (Jabour 2014).

This policy is being introduced into a labour-market environment where youth unemployment is more than double the national average. The policy proponents argue that the new rules will encourage young people to raise their skill and educational levels and therefore be more able to enter the labour market and stay employed.

Critics argue that, rather than penalising those who are unemployed, we need new approaches to education and training as a way of overcoming high rates of youth unemployment. Arguing that entry-level jobs have dried up since the global financial crisis, academic John Spoehr (ABC 2014a) states that as a society we have to be careful that we do not create the conditions where young people will find it very difficult to find entry-level jobs at the beginning of their careers.

7.6   Patterns and trends: An educational divide?

As a group, young Australians are better educated and better skilled than earlier generations. Participation in tertiary education has jumped substantially: more than 44 per cent of twenty-five to thirty-four-year-olds have a tertiary qualification, compared to about 30 per cent of fifty-five to sixty-four-year-olds (AMP.NATSEM 2012a:2). The increase in educational attainment, particularly completion of Year 12 or equivalent, is noticeable across generations: it is clear that Gen Y (those aged twenty to thirty-four years) has achieved higher educational outcomes than older Australians, with 66 per cent of Gen Ys completing Year 12 compared to around 40 per cent of the baby boomer group (AMP. NATSEM 2012a:10).

As such, individuals and the nation are better placed to compete and participate in the increasingly technology-driven and globalised world. A closer look at Australian education data, however, reveals a picture of patterned differences between groups within our society in relation to this overall trend. Ongoing research has established that in all sectors of the education system, from primary to higher education, educational success is influenced by the gender, socioeconomic background, geographic location, ethnicity and school sector of the student (Fullarton et al. 2003; Considine et al. 2005). Moreover, educational inequality is clustered, with the educationally privileged tending to be privileged in other social and economic realms as well. Similarly, the educationally disadvantaged are often weighed down by multiple factors implicated in social inequality. The following section provides an overview of the clear differences in educational outcomes between differently located social groups.

7.6.1   Socioeconomic status

socioeconomic status
A measure of standing in the community that generally relates to an individual's, family's or group's relative income, occupation, wealth and education.

Socioeconomic status is a measure of standing in the community and generally relates to an individual's, family's or group's relative income, occupation, wealth and education. As such, socioeconomic status has a pivotal role in educational inequality. Not only does it exercise a significant and independent effect on the educational outcomes of students, it also features as a central element in other aspects of educational inequality, compounding and amplifying their impact, both negative and positive.

A trend among recent equity studies is the stress on 'compound disadvantage', the overlap between low socioeconomic status and other forms of social inequality such as gender, ethnicity, disability and rurality (Ferrier 2006:2). One study, for example, finds that rurality and low socioeconomic status combine to produce the greatest educational disadvantage (NBEET 1999). Disentangling the role of the socioeconomic positioning of a student's family from other factors, such as gender or rurality, is not a simple process. While, for example, boys in general underachieve at school in comparison to girls, boys from poorer backgrounds do much worse than boys from higher-income families. For this reason, socioeconomic background is discussed first in this section, and its overarching role should be kept in mind in relation to the discussion around other identified factors.

Despite the general rise in educational levels, the level of increase among those from lower socioeconomic backgrounds is not keeping pace. Young people from poorer families are staying longer at school than they did in the past but their educational achievement remains well below that which would be expected if they were increasing their educational participation at the same rate as other young people (Ferrier 2006). Students from lower socioeconomic backgrounds are only half as likely to go on to higher education. In Victoria, for example, in 2012 only 45 per cent of final-year secondary school students from lower socioeconomic backgrounds enrolled in a bachelor degree compared to 60 per cent of those from high socioeconomic backgrounds (Gale & Parker 2013).

The pathways by which socioeconomic status influences educational outcomes are complex but include financial as well as attitudinal aspects. A large-scale study of senior Australian school students (James 2002) found that attitudes towards the relevance and attainability of a university education are socially stratified. While gender and geographic location had some effect, socioeconomic status was the major predictor of student perspectives. Although over 90 per cent of students expressed an interest in higher education, only 42 per cent from lower socioeconomic backgrounds thought themselves likely to enter it compared to 70 per cent of higher socioeconomic students. The reasons fell into three categories: relevance, academic suitability and cost.

- Lower socioeconomic students tended more to the belief that TAFE would be more useful, expressed weaker interest in university course options, had less confidence that their parents wanted them to go to university and had a stronger interest in earning income as soon as they left school
- Lower socioeconomic students had less confidence that their results would be high enough or that they were undertaking the subjects needed for their course preferences

- Lower socioeconomic students were more likely to believe that university fees were unaffordable and that their families could not afford to support them through a higher-education course

The authors conclude that for young people from low socioeconomic backgrounds, lower rates of educational attainment can be explained by the 'cumulative effect of the absence of encouraging factors and the presence of a stronger set of inhibiting factors' (James 2002:xi). These conclusion are borne out by ABS (2011) data that found that people aged twenty to twenty-four years were more likely to have attained a Year 12 qualification if both their parents/guardians had attained Year 12 (90 per cent), compared with one or neither parent/ guardian having attained Year 12 (78 per cent and 68 per cent respectively).

Socioeconomic status also influences the types of schools students attend. This is important because a student's school type has a consistently predictive effect on education outcomes. In 2012, 76 per cent of students in government schools, 82 per cent of students in Catholic schools, and 92 per cent of student in independent schools completed Year 12 (ABS 2012b). These differentials are obviously implicated in the climbing rates of enrolments in independent schools. Evidence suggests that it is predominantly higher socioeconomic students who are making the switch from public to private schooling. Researcher Dev Mukherjee (1999), in analysing the socioeconomic background of students enrolled in government, Catholic and independent schools, identified clear socioeconomic differences. Using data from census collection districts, he found that, as socioeconomic status increased, the proportion of students enrolled in government schools fell while the proportion in independent schools rose. Government schools enrolled slightly more students from low socioeconomic backgrounds than high socioeconomic backgrounds, while a large proportion of students at independent schools came from high socioeconomic status families.

Research + migrants students!

& will this be having the same effect in 'attitude' than enrolls? Uni enrolls?

Contemporary Australia

○ ○ ○

A DIVIDE IN ACCESS TO HIGHER EDUCATION?

The sector in which the greatest educational effect of low socioeconomic status is found is in tertiary education. Research has found that the share of university places occupied by people from low socioeconomic backgrounds had remained at approximately 15 per cent (compared to 25 per cent of the total population) for more than twenty years despite an expansion of access to higher education during that period (Centre for the Study of Higher Education 2008). The same study also concluded that people from low socioeconomic backgrounds are particularly underrepresented in the professional fields of study, comprising less than 10 per cent of postgraduate students. Further, underrepresentation was most marked in the prestigious Group of Eight universities, with a fall over time in the proportion of people from low socioeconomic backgrounds attending those universities. These

(continued)

results are particularly pertinent in light of proposed changes to the higher education system announced in the 2014 Budget, which will see the rate of student fee contribution increased and a higher interest rate applied to HELP loans for students. Such changes may reinforce or exacerbate the current barriers faced by those from lower socioeconomic circumstances when considering tertiary education.

7.6.2   Gender

Australian education data indicate that female students tend to outperform male students at all levels. At the primary and early secondary level, girls' attainments exceed those of boys in reading and writing. The OECD (2012) reports that while the average reading performance of Australian fifteen-year-olds is higher than the OECD average, Australian girls outperform Australian boys. Gender differences are less obvious in mathematical literacy, where testing of Australian fifteen-year-olds finds little or no difference between the mean scores of boys and girls (PISA 2012).

Gender differences in educational attainment continue through to the senior secondary and tertiary level. In 2010, the Year 12 completion rate for young women was 83 per cent compared to 73 per cent for young men (ABS 2011), a disparity that has been evident since 1994 (ABS 2006a). On average, male Year 12 students attain lower marks than females, although the proportion of high achievers is more evenly spread. Gendered subject choice preferences are also clear at Year 12, with boys more likely to be enrolled in the physical sciences and technical and computer studies, and female students more likely to be involved in the humanities, arts and languages. Pathways postschool also differ by gender. The ABS (2006a) found that 43 per cent of Australian women aged fifteen to nineteen are in full-time education compared to 35 per cent of young men, and women now constitute 53 per cent of those enrolled at university. In 2012, 60 per cent of graduates from Australian universities were female (ABS 2013c).

These data raise questions about the changing role of gender as an explanatory factor in educational inequality. While girls have traditionally been seen as educationally disadvantaged, Australian girls and young women are now achieving more than Australian boys and young men at outcome and qualification levels. But an examination of gender educational inequality needs to consider past patterns as well as current outcomes. The current trend is a reverse of the situation of previous generations, when young men were more likely to complete their education and with higher skill levels. This legacy is evident in education patterns among older Australians. In 2003, only 51 per cent of women aged twenty-five to sixty-four held vocational and higher educational qualifications compared to 60 per cent of men. Now, even at the whole-population level, the gender educational gap is closing: between 2002 and 2012 women increased their rate of vocational and higher educational qualifications by 50 per cent to 65 per cent, while for men the increase was from 59 per cent to 68 per cent; a 14 percentage-point range compared to 8 percentage points for men (ABS 2013c). There is now just a 3 percentage-point gender difference and it looks likely that the proportion of women with post-school qualifications will exceed that of men in the near future.

Does this mean that the mantle of educational inequality has passed from females to males? The answer is not clear cut. While Australian male students are being academically outperformed by Australian female students, an examination of students' postschool options indicates that young men have greater job choices and therefore less need to continue with education. ABS data (2006b) show that the rate of full-time employment for young men is nearly twice that for young women. Similarly, Marks (2005) finds that among young Australians who do not go on to university, the full-time employment rate is significantly higher for males, with more females unemployed or working part-time.

Subject selection is also influential in gender-based postschool options. Girls' overrepresentation in subjects such as the arts and humanities has been linked to the greater likelihood of young women being in part-time or casual employment, despite their higher academic outcomes (Redmond 2006). For example, female numbers in undergraduate architecture and building courses have not risen over the last ten years but remain at about 38–40 per cent; in engineering they have stayed at about 14 per cent. In information technology the proportion of female enrolment has actually fallen, from 23 per cent to 15 per cent, since 2003 (Maslen 2013). The under-representation of women in all areas of ICT is particularly relevant, because such choices have life-course impacts. Without high-level ICT skills, women remain outside the employment and education options in global, high-status technological fields. Family responsibilities also have an impact. So, overall, although young women now have a superior educational attainment level to young men, they remain disadvantaged in the labour market in terms of having higher levels of unemployment, low-paying jobs and short-term and part-time work.

Despite this, the comparative underachievement of boys and young men in the Australian education system remains a concern. The research evidence suggests that lack of achievement is related to the lack of relevance school has for many boys rather than a lack of ability. Social researchers Faith Trent and Malcolm Slade (2001) found that boys felt that schools did not listen to them, treated girls better, did not offer courses that boys were interested in and offered little of relevance or value to their later lives. As a consequence, the authors argue, many boys are caught in a downward spiral of disaffection, resentment and resistance to school. Boys' relative poor performance and alienation from schooling is not limited to Australia. OECD data indicate that in every participating country boys underachieve in reading literacy in relation to girls and are more likely to be disaffected with school (DEST 2003). Considerable policy efforts have been expended to re-engage boys in the schooling process and reduce their educational lag over the last decade. In 2002, a House of Representatives inquiry into the education of boys found that concerns for boys' education were largely justified and inadequately addressed by existing policies. Policy initiatives since implemented include:

- a program to identify and showcase successful practices in the education of boys (DEST 2003)
- a program to provide positive male role models in education
- a focus on literacy and ICT that aims to improve boys' learning outcomes and engagement with the schooling process (ABS 2006a).

7.6.3   Location

A student's geographic location is also a significant influence on schooling completion rates and transition to tertiary education. Rural and remote students do not complete Year 12 or go on to higher education at the same rate as their urban counterparts. According to the ABS (2011), in 2010, young adults (twenty to twenty-four years) were more likely to have attained Year 12 if they lived in major cities (81 per cent) compared with inner or outer regional areas (67 per cent) and remote or very remote areas (64 per cent).

Locational educational inequality starts well before senior secondary school. Results from the OECD's Programme for International Student Assessment (PISA) show that while Australian students perform very well, this overall performance masks clear evidence of underachievement among rural students. Children from metropolitan areas perform above the OECD average, but those from rural and remote areas fall below it (ABS 2006c). These types of results led researchers such as Pegg (2007) to argue that there is an educational divide between rural and metropolitan education. Rural higher-education participation rates, while influenced by geographic distance, also reflect differences in family and community attitudes about the relevance of education. According to James et al. (1999:ix) these differences are socioeconomic rather than locational. James (2002) found that students in rural or isolated locations are less likely to see the relevance of schooling than are urban students. Further, rural lower socioeconomic status students reported less interest in school overall than did middle or higher socioeconomic status rural students or urban low socioeconomic status students. In relation to university aspirations and attitudes, rural students at all socioeconomic levels are more likely than urban students from the same socioeconomic background to view university as really only for the wealthy and are less likely to regard completing a university degree a good investment for the future. These attitudes may also be affected by the lack of tertiary education institutions within their own localities.

Students from regional and rural or remote locations face additional barriers in accessing education. Most rural and remote areas and many regional areas have poor educational facilities and opportunities in comparison to metropolitan centres. For most students from these areas, university requires leaving home, community and family, taking up different lives in 'unfamiliar circumstances, in untried locations' (Alloway et al. 2004:249). Such leaving has social and financial consequences. It is often beyond a family's financial capacity, forcing the young person to be reliant on paid employment so they can cover their living expenses. It is also difficult personally; students may need to move away from the family home long before they may otherwise have chosen to live independently. A lack of occupational models can also lead to a more limited world view and understanding of what opportunities might exist among rural students (Alloway et al. 2004).

The location of the cities and regional areas was also important: 59 per cent of young adults in the Northern Territory have achieved a Grade 12 education compared to 86 per cent in the Australian Capital Territory. And tertiary education participation rates in the ACT are considerably higher than in Tasmania. But a study by sociologist Stephen Lamb and colleagues (2004) found that the gaps between the states and territories are considerably diminished if population differences are included. Mature-age students, for example, add more than 7 per cent to the apparent retention rate to Year 12 for Tasmania; the apparent retention rate of the Northern Territory is also increased if the high numbers of the Indigenous population are taken into account. Still, such modelling does not explain why Tasmania has so many mature-age students or why having a high Indigenous population in the Northern Territory automatically means that educational levels will be lower. Such factors have social, not naturally occurring, explanations.

7.6.4   Ethnicity

7.6.4.1   Non-English-speaking-background students

Although traditionally considered an equity group, recent data suggest that the educational lag of students from non-English-speaking countries is, in aggregate, relatively small or no longer obvious. People from non-English-speaking backgrounds are more likely to participate in Year 12 but are slightly underrepresented in tertiary education compared to Australian-born students (Gale & Parker 2013) and have slightly lower results in tertiary education (Ferrier 2006). Recent immigrants (those who arrived within the last ten years) from non-English-speaking countries have slightly higher access to higher education than Australian-born students do. In line with populations of relatively recent immigrants being concentrated in state capitals, universities in those cities have higher ratios of non-English-speaking background students than do regional universities. Immigrant students at regional universities also appear to face higher barriers to success than do metropolitan immigrant students. While retention rates of non-English-speaking-background students at major city universities are similar to those of native English speaking students, for those studying at regional campuses, the retention rate is slightly lower. However, students from non-English speaking backgrounds are more likely to attend a Group of Eight university than a regional or other university (Gale & Parker 2013).

The reason for the relative educational success of recently arrived immigrants is likely aligned with changes to Australian immigration policy and practice. The ABS (2004) reports that levels of educational attainment have increased across successive waves of immigrants to Australia over the last three decades. Of immigrants who arrived between 1987 and 1997, 61 per cent had vocational and higher educational qualifications compared with 51 per cent of those who arrived between 1981 and 1989. The increase in the skilled immigration component and the decline in the family reunion program explains at least part of this trend. This trend is likely to continue into the future, as further reductions in family reunion migrant programs came into effect in 2014.

7.6.4.2   Indigenous students

The educational gap for Indigenous Australians is extremely high, a disparity that is especially significant given the very young demographic profile of the Indigenous population—it has a median age of twenty-one years, compared to thirty-seven years for the non-Indigenous population; and over 40 per cent of Indigenous people are below the age of fifteen compared to 20 per cent of the non-Indigenous population (ABS 2012c). Educational inequality for young Indigenous people will, as a result, have ongoing negative social and economic consequences for decades to come.

In 2013 there were 182,636 Aboriginal and Torres Strait Islander students attending school full-time in Australia, an increase of nearly 5 per cent from 2012. This rise continues a trend over the past ten years with Aboriginal and Torres Strait Islander full-time students now accounting for over 5 per cent of all full-time students (ABS 2013b; the Indigenous population makes up only 2.5 per cent of the Australian population). But Indigenous students have far lower rates of Year 12 and equivalent attainment than do non-Indigenous Australians and the continuation of this disparity underpins the Council of Australian Governments' (COAG) aims to halve this gap by 2020. There are signs of some improvement, but not nearly enough.

Indigenous students are much more likely to leave school early: three times as many Indigenous as non-Indigenous students leave school before Year 11 (MCEETYA 2006). The apparent Year 12 retention rate of Indigenous students stood at 55 per cent in 2013 compared to 83 per cent for non-Indigenous students. Within these rates, Indigenous girls are staying on at school longer than Indigenous boys: the retention rate for girls was 58 per cent in 2011 compared to 52 per cent of boys (ABS 2013b). Indigenous versus non-Indigenous academic performance differences are apparent from the earliest schooling years, with Indigenous students often less prepared for the school environment when they begin school. As such, policy makers suggest that more effort in preschool and the early school years may lead to academic outcomes and participation rates closer to educational parity (ABS 2006c).

Indigenous/non-Indigenous inequalities persist across geographic locations. Figure 7.2 uses data from the 2006 and 2011 censuses of population and housing for Dubbo, a regional town in New South Wales. While education levels for the whole population in Dubbo are lower than average, Aboriginal education rates are still well behind those of the non-Aboriginal population. Yes, Year 12 achievement levels went up between 2006 and 2011 but not by a lot, and while the disparity in attendance at TAFE is not high, very, very few young Aboriginal people in Dubbo are accessing higher education, despite the presence of a campus of Charles Sturt University in the town.

Explanations of the educational inequality of Indigenous Australians are complex. Improving Indigenous educational outcomes is not just a matter of more effort on the part of Indigenous students and their parents; factors linked to the current and historical poverty and social exclusion of Indigenous people within Australian society must be included. The 2007 Western Australian Aboriginal Child Health Survey (WACHS) highlights the unique difficulties Indigenous children face in accessing and utilising the education system to best advantage.

WACHS found three key factors associated with lower Indigenous academic achievement. The first is absences from school. The median absent days of Western Australian Indigenous children is more than triple that of non-Indigenous children. But non-attendance is not just about truancy: factors such as being in a family experiencing multiple life stress events, emotional or behavioural difficulties, difficulties sleeping, and living in an isolated area were all associated with school absences. Another key factor was the level of the primary carer's education. Indigenous students whose primary carer had not attended school were the least likely to have average or above-average academic performance. Conversely, those with a primary carer who had thirteen years or more of education were far more likely to achieve academically. Indigenous parental education has historical discrimination links.

Figure 7.2   Aboriginal and non-Aboriginal educational level 2006 and 2011: Dubbo, New South Wales

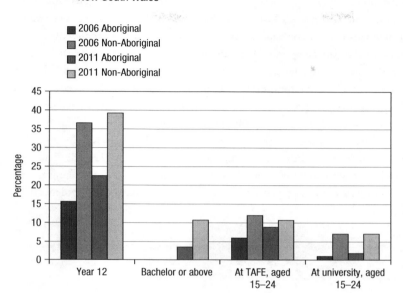

Until the 1950s, Indigenous children in Western Australia, among other locations, were widely excluded from the education system. The third factor was emotional and behavioural difficulties. Around 17 per cent of Indigenous children aged four to seventeen in Western Australia were rated at high risk of clinically significant emotional or behavioural difficulties. The majority of these students were also rated as having low academic achievement. In light of these complexities, recent policy interventions such as the Northern Territory government plan to develop antitruancy contracts with Indigenous communities seem simplistic.

The WACHS data do not canvas the difficulties faced by Indigenous students in an education system that is developed by, for and around the dominant non-Indigenous culture. Studies in this area find that Indigenous students at all levels, and their families, often feel alienated within and by the education system. Indigenous students who make it through to university enrolment are the survivors of a long process of attrition. Apart from the well-established factors of high levels of socioeconomic disadvantage, rurality and limited family and individual exposure to the personal and broader benefits of higher education (see Biddle et al. 2004; Encel 2000; DEST 2005), Indigenous students face other obstacles to educational achievement and participation. These include lack of physical access to educational institutions, individual and cultural isolation and alienation, dissatisfaction with courses of study and educational delivery modes, inflexibility of education systems, unfamiliarity with and lack of confidence in academic requirements and skills, lack of access to educational resources, lack of family support, high rates of household crowding and family and personal disruptions, participation-linked financial problems, the personal, family and financial burdens of spatial relocation and the pull of community and family commitments (Bourke et al. 1996; Bin-Sallik 2000; White 2000; Bunda & McConville 2002; Biddle et al. 2004).

Patterns of early school leaving significantly reduce the participation rate of Indigenous students in postcompulsory education. In 2011, 1.6 per cent of new university enrolments were Indigenous, a rate significantly lower than the proportion of the eighteen to twenty-four-year-old population who are Indigenous. However this rate does represents a trend of slow increase in the participation of Indigenous people in higher education (Gale & Parker 2013): the rate of Aboriginal and Torres Strait Islander people aged fifteen to twenty-four attending a higher-education institution more than tripled between 1986 and 2011. But a huge disparity still remains. In 2011, just one in twenty Aboriginal or Torres Strait Islander fifteen to twenty-four-year-olds were studying at this level, compared with one in five non-Indigenous people of the same age (ABS 2013k). However, the story does not end at enrolment: data indicate that Indigenous students are more likely than non-Indigenous students to drop out before the end of their course. In 2010 the retention rate for Indigenous students was just 65 per cent, compared to 79 per cent of all students (Gale & Parker 2013).

Contemporary Australia

EDUCATIONAL EQUALITY IN THE NORTHERN TERRITORY

Federal MP Warren Snowden stated in 2007 that as many as 5000 children in the Northern Territory, the vast majority of them Indigenous, had no access to any kind of mainstream secondary education. According to Minister Snowden, until 2001 there were no secondary schools outside NT urban centres. The problem extends to the primary education that is provided. Although for most of the students English is a second language, the schools are not staffed to accommodate this and even where secondary schooling is being provided, the curriculum reflects previous inequities. On a recent visit to a bush school Minister Snowden observed that teenagers in middle and upper secondary schools had a low reading ability and were being taught a dressed-up primary curriculum. Minister Snowden blames the state of secondary education for non-urban children in the Northern Territory on a legacy of under-resourcing by previous territory governments and a lack of interest in the educational outcomes of these children by the federal government (Cowan 2007).

The final report of the review of Indigenous Education in the Northern Territory, *A Share in the Future: Review of Indigenous Education in the Northern Territory*, was released by the Northern Territory Minister for Education in May 2014 (Wilson 2014). It contains fifty-one recommendations covering the span of educational levels from the early years through to primary school and the delivery of secondary education, along with recommendations relating to the support structure of schools, including attendance, community engagement, student well-being, behaviour management, workforce planning, funding, and the roles and responsibilities of teachers, principals and the Department of Education.

The previous major review of Indigenous education in the Northern Territory was *Learning Lessons*, released in 1999. The authors of that report, noting the exceptionally poor results for Indigenous students, argued that the loss of a further generation could not be tolerated. The young people who were then being born are now of secondary school age and many are illiterate and disengaged. Indigenous young people as a group are now as poorly served by their education system as those referred to in the 1999 review; thus, we are now having the same conversation that accompanied the earlier review (Wilson 2014:3).

The inequality question here is whether these reports represent a move towards reducing educational inequality for Indigenous children and youth in the Northern Territory or whether the actions being taken are restricted to merely identifying the same problems again and again.

7.6.5   A polarisation of education and knowledge

Education in Australia has undergone a massive expansion in recent years. Increases in participation are at the upper end of the education system, with fewer early school leavers and higher enrolment numbers in tertiary-level education and training. Yet despite the growth, educational inequalities remain, and are highly patterned in ways that seem entrenched in our society. As Bottero (2005) points out, while the overall level of educational attainment has increased substantially in all Western countries, there is little evidence that this change has led to greater social equality. Indeed, what seems to be occurring is a polarisation of educational and knowledge outcomes for Australians.

Increasing levels of education in Australia reflect the needs of a postindustrial society for a workforce whose skills go well beyond those of literacy and numeracy. The transition from a primary and manufacturing economy to a service economy requires a flexible, multiskilled workforce that can meet the requirements of a highly competitive, global economy. Numerous government and private sector reports have stressed the role of knowledge in establishing Australia's future as the 'clever country' (see, for example, Watson 2003). For this reason, postcompulsory education is now a normal part of a young person's experience.

Yet education is also increasingly expensive and higher education costs are primarily borne privately. The stringency of the parental means test for Youth Allowance, the primary income-support payments for students, alongside an age of independence of twenty-five years for students, mean that young people with parents on limited income are disadvantaged in their ability to access higher education. For many families, supporting a young person through postsecondary education is a significant, if not impossible, financial burden. As noted in the earlier sections on factors related to educational outcomes, the division between the education-enabled and the education-disabled are bound into the planes of class, race, location and gender.

Accessing higher levels of education is also associated with significant levels of poverty. The *Report on Poverty and Financial Hardship* (Senate Community Affairs References Committee 2004) found that students had a mean annual income of one-third of the average Australian. The only options for students whose families cannot afford to support their tertiary study are to leave home long enough to qualify as independent for Austudy or to combine their study with employment. Data indicate that the average full-time student works fifteen hours a week in mostly secondary-labour-market, casual, low-wage jobs (James et al. 2007). The juggling independent living, poverty, part-time work obligations and study that poor students must do translates into higher rates of course drop-out and more difficulty in achieving at their optimal level. For some groups in Australia this is particularly difficult: although tertiary students in general are poor, Australian research into the financial status of higher-education students found that Indigenous students are particularly disadvantaged (James et al. 2007).

7.7   Interaction with the state

As a social resource, Australia's education system is fundamentally shaped by its relationship with the state. Education at all levels—federal, state and territory—is predominantly supported by state funding, and its content, shape and accessibility are directly impacted by policy and funding decisions made by the state. In line with other major state policy arenas, free-market principles have, since the late 1980s, emerged as a guiding philosophy in education policy. Neoliberal policies have been embraced by governments of all political persuasions, a market-based influence that has been particularly strong over the last decade. Therefore, despite the general acceptance of education and training as a national and public good, education is also an arena for social and political debate. At the centre of such debates is the way the state interacts with and shapes policy for the education system and the result of this on patterns of educational inequalities. The following sections examine several of the most prominent discourses. The first is the rising costs of education, especially as they relate to the HECS system, and the advent of full-fee paying students and courses within Australia's higher education system. The second is the ongoing debate about the funding and respective roles of the public and private educational systems within Australian schools. Each of these topics has at its centre ideological clashes over how education should be funded and the role of market-based choice for education consumers. Each of these areas has also been impacted by policy changes following the election of the Abbott Coalition Government in September 2013, and are likely to see even more change over the government's term of office.

7.7.1   Higher Education Contribution Scheme

The Higher Education Contribution Scheme (HECS; later renamed the Higher Education Loans Program, HELP) was introduced in 1989 by the Hawke–Keating Labor Government. HECS sought a contribution from students to the costs of their education, and so replaced the free tertiary system brought in by the Whitlam Labor Government during the 1970s. The contribution amounts of HECS have increased over time and depend on the course undertaken. In 2012, HECS costs ranged from $5648 per annum for nursing (up from $3998 in 2007) to $9425 per annum for law (up from $8333 in 2007;

Norton 2012). Students may either pay their HECS/HELP debt upfront, for which they receive a 25 per cent discount, or defer payment until their earnings reach a certain point. In 2011–12 that point was $47,196 per annum, up from $30,000 per annum in 2006. Rates of repayments are then dependent on the level of income the student is receiving. The HECS/HELP debt was not subject to interest but was increased each year in line with CPI to maintain the real value of the debt.

Changes brought about under the 2014 Federal Budget mean that from July 2016 graduates will begin to repay their debt when they start earning $50,638. In contrast to earlier times, students will be charged interest on their HECS/HELP debts 'at a cost that reflects the costs of the Government borrowings ... with a maximum rate of 6 per cent' (Australian Government 2014). This means that those who delay, or are delayed, joining the labour market will accrue additional debt through interest being added to the original amount. Concerns have been raised by community organisations and unions that women and those from lower socioeconomic backgrounds may be disproportionately affected by this change. The postbudget statement by the National Tertiary Education Union, for example, stated: 'The imposition of real interests charges make the changes highly unfair to graduates who take career breaks, most particularly women who take breaks to have children' (2014).

How much higher-education students pay for their education via HECS contributions is a disputed issue. While the proportion of the actual cost of an education paid as HECS/HELP debts is regularly cited in government policy statements as around 25 per cent, this figure is disputed. For example, estimates are that in 2013 those undertaking a nursing degree paid about 31 per cent of the cost of their course; those studying law paid around 84 per cent; and medical students paid about 32 per cent (Norton 2012). Under the 2014 Federal Budget changes, the situation will become very fluid. Not only does the federal government plan to reduce its funding for Commonwealth Supported Places at universities by 20 per cent, it has also removed the limit on how much universities can charge students for courses. The National Tertiary Education Union argues that under these changes a medical degree could cost up to $200,000 and a law degree could cost up to $125,000 (2014). Another concern is that this move may create a two-tier university system in Australia, with the more prestigious Group of Eight universities being able to charge high fees and still draw students, while being able to offer scholarships to high-achieving students, and the other universities not having the financial capacity to do either. A related issue is that for the first time in Australia, private educational institutions will be able to attract public funds. Under proposals outlined in the 2014 Federal Budget, the Australian Government will provide direct financial grants to students studying at any registered Australian higher-education provider, including private universities and private colleges (Australian Government 2014).

These changes to HELP fees and repayment arrangements, the uncapping of fees universities can charge students, and the support of private universities and colleges introduce a strong and growing private component into what had been a predominantly publicly funded higher-education system. It will take a number of years to evaluate the inequality implications of these changes. But the discourse that underpins the move to a more market-based higher-education system is aligned with the broader influence of neoliberal policy. Such policy clashes, ideologically and practically, with previous dominant discourses of education as a national and public good. Social researcher John Tomlinson (2004) argues that divergent views of how education should be funded and constructed vary by conceptions of who is the prime beneficiary of education. From a neoliberal perspective the prime beneficiary is the student and, therefore, education options should be mediated by the market. This viewpoint is reflected in government papers relating to the changes of 2014, which state in part that the changes 'share costs fairly between students—who benefit from a university education—and the taxpayers who support them' (Australian Government, 2014:2). Such discourses have been in the ascendancy since the late 1980s.

The alternative perspective sees education as benefiting a range of entities. While the individual benefits directly, so too do employers of graduates and all citizens who make use of the services and products that are available from those graduates. As such, education is seen as benefiting the nation overall and should be regarded as a national investment, with allocation of places in the education system based on merit and open competition between students, rather than on ability to pay fees. From this viewpoint, the contribution of students via income foregone while studying, the expenses of HECS/HELP, books and other costs and mental labour expended in acquiring skills and knowledge are deemed an adequate contribution in relation to their personal gain (Tomlinson 2004).

The early evidence on previous market-related changes to higher education in Australia suggests that such policies do operate to entrench existing education inequalities. While commentators such as Norton (2000) argue that higher HECS rates do not contribute to educational inequality because early statistics show that the proportion of poorer students has not declined after HECS rises, the status quo should not necessarily be viewed as success. Low socioeconomic students are already significantly under-represented in higher education, a pattern that remained static throughout the 1990s. Rising HELP debts are likely to add a further barrier to those already sensitive to the costs of education. Additionally, the likely high fee rises for many of the higher-rating courses, such as medicine, veterinary science and dentistry, will also discourage those with less means from entering these courses. Such places will only be available to those with the means to pay for them. The result seems destined to be a redistribution of university places from the less to the more privileged.

7.7.2   Public and private schools

The relative public funding of private and public schools has become a major issue in recent years. Groups such as the Australian Education Union claim that the extra public money going to private schools is being used to reduce class sizes and provide a standard of education not affordable by the public sector. The result, it claims, is a polarisation of the education system between rich and poor families (Smith & Tomazin 2007:1). On the other side of the argument, increasing public funding to non-government schools is seen as redressing some of the imbalance that occurs when parents pay the costs of their children's private education. Such choices, it is argued, reduce costs to the public purse. The choice by these taxpayers to pay fees rather than rely on public funding thereby reduces public education costs, enabling more money to be expended on public schools.

Regardless of the veracity of the debates around public funding and private education, the shift of students from the public education system into the private has inequality implications. An exodus of students from higher-income families results in public schools having higher concentrations of students whose backgrounds and disabilities make them relatively costly to teach (Vickers 2005).

Social researchers David Hayward and Alexis Esposto (2004) undertook an analysis of federal government education funding. Their aims were, first, to ascertain whether the rise in federal funding to non-government schools could be explained by rising numbers of private-school students and, second, to determine how non-government schools had fared under the rises. They concluded that federal funding increases to non-government schools went well beyond that which could be explained by changing enrolment patterns, and that while all schools received more funding, overall the biggest beneficiaries were non-government schools. Within this group the wealthiest schools had done the best.

Proponents of public funding for private schools argue that the existence of such schools enables parents to exercise educational choice, but such choice comes with a sizeable price tag, one that many parents are financially unable to choose. As discussed earlier in this chapter, such costs are reflected in the socioeconomic status of the parents of children who attend the different school types. School choice is not independent of household income and means.

7.8   Education, social reproduction and social mobility

In contemporary Australia, education emerges as the boundary marker between workers with access to good quality jobs and those relegated to the lower end of the labour market (see Chapter 8). The question, then, is whether access to higher levels of education is leading to a more fluid society, where enterprise, merit and education are rewarded within the labour market. The answer lies in whether Australia has high levels of social mobility and, if it does, whether this is increasing. Can individuals and families, with application and the acquisition of the right skills, move easily through the social strata, regardless of their social origin?

While this question cannot be answered comprehensively in Australia due to the lack of longer-duration longitudinal studies, economist Fred Argy (2005) suggests that the answer is mixed. Using overseas data as predictors of Australian patterns he finds that a significant 30–40 per cent of the population can expect to rise, over their lifetime, to a higher income and occupational rank. These trends, he contends, reflect rising education opportunities, economic liberalisation and the results of policy such as antidiscrimination legislation. Intergenerational mobility patterns, that is, from one generation to the next, are less fluid. The positive correlations between parental occupational and educational status and that of their children remain very strong. Such a correlation reflects structural factors, such as the advantages of superior social location and access to positive social networks, as well as more individual factors, such as the passing on of values around education. So, a relatively mobile society exists in terms of the chance of individual occupational achievement while the socioeconomic location of an individual's family of origin remains a strong predictor of later occupational outcomes.

Relational aspects of social arrangements are also a vital ingredient of the social reproduction of education. Devine's (2004) study of GPs and teachers in the United Kingdom and the USA provides some insight into this because she looked at what middle-class parents did to ensure their offspring reproduced their own social position. She found that her respondents went to great efforts to assist their children through the education system, mobilising their social networks for information and advice about choices at every stage of their education, from good nurseries through to good universities. They drew on their social capital to enlist the aid of friends and colleagues to find out which establishments would be most advantageous for their children and what strategies they needed to employ to ensure that their children attended these establishments. Their assistance extended into the labour market, where they drew on close and loose ties to secure entry into jobs with good prospects. They also ensured that their children mixed with 'nice' children, that is, children who had professional parents who valued educational success. These activities were not necessarily consciously strategic but were part of everyday life. Their values were also passed on to their children, whose hopes and plans were influenced by the professional world of their parents.

Devine thus demonstrated that academic success was only part of the equation—when it came to making the transition from education to the labour market social networks played a critical role. But she also found that parents' efforts were not always successful and that many parents, especially those in lower-middle-class positions, struggled to assist their children to reproduce or improve their social location. Similarly, in Australia, middle-class parents increasingly place an emphasis on ensuring that their offspring achieve strong educational outcomes that will guarantee they are well placed when they enter the labour market (Pusey 2003).

The pattern of wealth transmission appears to be shifting away from the direct transfer of economic wealth through inheritance to the transfer of cultural capital. Lack of inherited cultural and academic capital is likely, despite economic prosperity and a growing labour market, to translate into a lifetime of precarious employment options: to intermittent, low-skill, casual or part-time work.

7.9   Conclusion

Educational opportunities have expanded in recent years, raising the options for upward social mobility for increasing numbers of Australians. The knowledge economy and the global market have created new opportunities where knowledge and education are increasingly valuable assets and commodities. In this new environment, education and knowledge are also increasingly important to an individual's labour-market and material-wealth prospects. Education can, therefore, be the vehicle to improving an individual's and their family's social and economic position. Yet access to and capacity to make use of such opportunities remains patterned at the aggregate level. While education can and does serve as a vehicle for social mobility its position as a key factor in social reproduction remains strong. Rather than operating as a social equaliser, the current trend towards and requirement for high levels of education and skills may have little effect on or, indeed, may actually increase overall levels of existing inequalities. Social reproduction remains a powerful force.

There is also evidence of a clustering of privilege and disadvantage. The already privileged still have the first and best access to educational options and the privilege that such options bring. The evidence suggests that the cultural capital that leads to educational success is transmitted generationally by the family and social milieu. Those with the most educational and other social advantages are in the best position to assist their children to the same privileged position through passing on attitudes and expectations around education and being able to purchase better access to social resources via options such as private schooling and paying university fees. It is in the middle class where this transfer of cultural capital is strongest. The middle class appears to be the primary beneficiaries of the rising value of and increasing options for education, with middle-class females in particular benefiting. This transfer of cultural capital is supported and assisted by policies that increase funding to private schools and the adoption of market-related practices within the education system. The private-school system also ensures the socialisation of wealthier students into the dominant culture.

Conversely, just as educational advantage can be inherited, so too can disadvantage. For many, especially poorer, working-class, Indigenous and regionally located families, the rising value of education and knowledge in the postindustrial society magnifies the impact of lower educational aspirations and achievements. The evidence discussed here shows that a lack of social, cultural and symbolic capital results in significant disadvantage within the education system. Market-related policies such as full-fee-paying courses and private-school support, which link educational choice with ability to pay, reinforce the barriers to academic capital among disadvantaged groups. The consequent disadvantage in the labour market in terms of social power lines resonates through the life course.

Discussion questions

1   What contribution can Bourdieu make to understanding why the proportion of people from low socioeconomic backgrounds participating in higher education has remained stable for over twenty years despite an expansion of access to higher education during that period?

2   Is the rise in information technology increasing or decreasing educational inequality?

3   What are the arguments for and against government financial support of private schools?

4   Overall educational attainment has increased substantially in all Western countries but there is little evidence that this change has led to greater social equality. What do you think is the explanation for this?

8

○

THE LABOUR MARKET

○

8.1   Introduction

Participation in the Australian labour market is increasingly diverse in terms of its structure and conditions. This significantly affects life and work patterns. For Australian workers, employment can be full-time or part-time, permanent or casual, and have regular or changeable shifts or hours. Conditions of employment are also impacted upon by the changing legislative and policy frameworks in which the labour market operates. Award conditions are no longer the standard for an increasing number of Australian workers; many now work under contracts or specific enterprise bargaining agreements. Rather than the traditional pattern of continual full-time participation from youth until retirement, Australians' working lives are now far more likely to be punctuated by exit and re-entry. Labour market careers are likely to include periods of **unemployment** or time taken out for parenting responsibilities, carer responsibilities, a return to study, or travel.

unemployment Rates of unemployment measure the proportion of people over the age of fifteen who are available for work and actively looking for it but cannot get a paid job.

The implications that this diversity has for inequality can be contradictory. The trajectory of a working life remains largely dictated by which sector of the labour market it is spent in, and the skills and qualifications and, to some extent, the gender of the individual worker. The labour market increasingly offers individuals substantial career and material benefits and opportunities. Working lives can be dominated by positive career prospects, attractive remuneration, job security and tangible and intangible rewards associated with occupation. For some, the labour market can also be a vehicle of social mobility. It is possible to rise from a relatively deprived socioeconomic background to achieve high labour-market status and the social benefits that accompany that position.

But the labour market also directly reflects and reinforces existing social inequalities. Although merit is rewarded, the labour market continues to display the traditional patterns of privilege and disadvantage, which are easily discerned within the labour market's hierarchy. For some groups, working life is increasingly insecure and poorly paid, with few opportunities for advancement or development. Despite the dramatic restructuring of the Australian labour market since the 1980s, knowing a person's gender, age, partnership status, parental status, socioeconomic background and ethnicity still allows for a reasonably accurate prediction of their likely labour-market status and work conditions.

The labour market, then, is an arena of social mobility as well as a reproducer and maintainer of societal inequality. It operates as a potentially equalising force as well as a reflector of pre-existing fault lines. In this chapter the analyses of these facets of the labour market address the first three guiding questions of this book: it provides answers to the question of what the main dimensions of social inequality are in Australian society, how these are changing in the context of globalisation and post industrialisation, and how resources and risks are reproduced across different social groups. The labour market is a societal site of inequality that has specifically Australian dimensions as well as being connected to wider global social, economic and political changes. The labour-market risk associated with these changes is not evenly distributed, but clustered around the lower skilled, women with family responsibilities and Indigenous Australians. Emerging changes, such as using offshore labour and national skills shortages, are likely to further alter the shape and structure of the Australian labour market.

8.2   The restructuring Australian labour market

The breadth and diversity of employment conditions demonstrates the increasing diversity and changeability of the Australian labour market, which in turn reflects the dramatic changes that have occurred in its structure, shape and participation patterns over the last twenty years. The statistical picture of the Australian labour market over this period is one of large-scale employment growth alongside increased levels of labour-market participation. In 1980 the Australian workforce was made up of 6.3 million employed people. By May 2014 the figure was 11.5 million people (ABS 2014a). This more than doubling of the actively employed workforce reflects more than a rising population; it also reflects changes in the way we work and who is working. The labour-force participation rate, that is the proportion of those aged fifteen to sixty-four years who is either working or actively looking for work has risen from around 61 per cent in 1983 to nearly 66 per cent in 2010 (ABS 2014a). Yet, while more Australians are participating in the labour market than ever before, the labour market in which they participate is very different to that which existed in 1980. This transformation encompasses major deregulation, shifts in employment among sectors as well as in occupational structure and large-scale alteration in the gender and age composition of Australian workers.

It is important to remember that the labour market is just that, a market in which labour is bought and sold. This labour is not just physical; it also refers to knowledge and expertise labour as undertaken by tradespeople such as plumbers and hairdressers or professionals such as doctors, teachers and engineers. In this market, buyers (employers) and sellers (workers) negotiate labour prices and conditions. In some periods (high unemployment or oversupply of some skills) there are more sellers than buyers and the sellers are pitted against each other to secure employment. Those with more attractive labour-market attributes obtain positions over those with lesser attributes. In other times (low unemployment or in areas of skills shortages) it is the buyers who vie for sellers' labour. In this scenario the buyers need to offer the best employment conditions and rewards to attract the labour they need. The capacity to buy or sell labour is significantly shaped by the market.

As well as being a market, the labour market is also a key social and economic institution. This centrality to our society's economic and political systems means that the Australian state is intimately connected with the operation of the labour market. While the workings of the labour market itself are now largely deregulated, the state still exerts considerable control through social and economic policy. It remains the role of the state to set formal rules and conditions under which the labour market operates, such as minimum wages, safety standards and equal opportunity provisions. The state also retains the mandate to further deregulate or reregulate aspects of the labour market. Less obviously, other state policies can also directly impact on the labour market, for example, the provision or non-provision of child-care services, which can dictate whether women with young children are able to take up employment.

Historically, the relationship between the state and the labour market in Australia is one of entrenched state involvement in the setting of labour-market conditions. The unique Australian system, dubbed by Castles (1985:110) as 'the wage-earners' welfare state' (see Chapter 5), effectively put a floor under the labour market and moderated wage inequality during most of the twentieth century. The state–labour-market relationship has now significantly altered. Over the last thirty years the employment protection measures inherent in the old wage-earners' welfare state have largely disappeared. As a major aspect of larger-scale economic restructuring, the operations of the labour market have been heavily influenced by the growing impact of globalisation on financial markets and trade and the related adoption of a neo-liberalist economic policy framework by most developed nations, including Australia.

The transformed Australian labour market of 2014 and beyond can be summarised in nine key changes to the structures that underpin it:

1   Employment in service industries, retail, hospitality, and health and community sectors have grown, while manufacturing and utilities employment have decreased.
2   There are significant changes in the skills mix of occupations, with increases at the higher and lower levels and a reduction in intermediate skills jobs.
3   The proportion of women participating in the labour market, especially women with children, has grown dramatically.
4   The proportion of part-time, casual jobs and lower-paid jobs has increased dramatically, especially in the services sector.
5   High unemployment rates were common from the 1970s to the mid-1990s but have reduced to almost unprecedented low levels in the late 1990s and early 2000s.

6   Major skills shortages have emerged in the 2000s to the extent that workers are being bought to Australia from overseas on temporary working visas to fill positions.

7   Earnings inequality has increased, especially among males.

8   A growing polarisation of households into work-rich, dual-income households and those who are work poor, with little or no access to work.

9   The workforce is older, and this group is affected by changes to pension eligibility ages.

8.3   Theorising labour and work

A restructured labour market results in a restructured world of work, not just in Australia but across Western industrialised nations. In analysing this phenomenon, social theorists agree that it reflects a new reality of working life rather than a transitory phase. The inherently less secure world of work is theoretically linked to Australia's move to a consuming rather than a producing society (Bauman 1998) and the economic and political globalisation associated with the technological success of advanced capitalism (Beck 2000; Beck & Beck-Gernsheim 2002).

Beck (2000) argues that we have to rethink and redefine work, especially how we deal with the risks of fragile work. Increased employment-based risk is an outcome of attempts to rationalise and restructure work and employment. The tradition of lifelong, full-time employment and the generous, standardised and state-controlled conditions of employment that characterised the norm, at least for male workers, in the post-Second World War period has now been replaced by less secure, individualised employment contracts. Yet individualisation, the attitude of late modernity in which individuals must develop and act on their own perspective of life, is also closely associated with the labour market. Sociologists Beck and Beck-Gernsheim (2002:32) argue that, in late modernity 'individualisation is a product of the labour market and manifests itself in the acquisition, proffering and application of a variety of work skills'. The labour market acts as the key vehicle for social mobility and the driving force in the individualisation of people's lives. As soon as an individual enters the labour market they leave behind other patterns and arrangements and are forced to take charge of their own life. Such personal control makes possible the experience of a personal destiny.

Such changes have obvious inequality implications. The increasing uncertainties now permeating the labour market do not hold the same consequences for all. Bauman (1998:33–5), for example, argues that the flexible labour market has led to a deep divide in the types of work available. In our consumer society, he argues, gratifying, rewarding and self-fulfilling work that is regarded as a vocation is becoming a privilege of the few. This occupational elite have access to the 'elevated professions', high-reward jobs that require the same qualities demanded for the appreciation of art—good taste, sophistication, discernment, disinterested dedication and a lot of schooling—in Bourdieu's terms, high cultural and academic capital. For the rest of the workforce Bauman predicts jobs that are uniformly abject and worthless, and which are likely to be performed only out of necessity and only if the worker is denied access to any other means of survival. These jobs will also be increasingly short-term, 'available until further notice'-type employment where the risk of being downsized or the workplace rationalised is an everyday reality.

In Beck and Beck-Gernsheim's view (2002) it is the competition in the labour market between individuals that leads to unequal outcomes. For those with fewer credentials and therefore fewer career opportunities, the precarious nature of contemporary employment will, over time, blur the boundary between employment and unemployment. Those with lower, unequal skills will tend to move in and out of different forms of paid employment over their working lives. For those with in-demand or scarce skills, the more open and flexible aspects of employment may open up significant new opportunities, thereby enhancing their life options.

While the future of work may not be quite as bleak as portrayed by Bauman, this new terrain has resonance in Australia. As Borland, Gregory and Sheehan (2001) point out, under the market-economy criteria associated with labour-market restructuring, the old Australian labour market was deemed as unduly rigid. As a consequence, economic policy since the mid-1980s has progressively deregulated the wages and working conditions of Australian workers. The desired result—a flexible labour market—has produced substantial changes in employment options and opportunities for many Australians. For those from lower socioeconomic social groups especially, these changes have been largely unfavourable, with many full-time permanent jobs in manufacturing and other industries replaced by part-time, casual, insecure work, probably in a service industry.

Contemporary Australia

ABS DEFINITIONS OF EMPLOYMENT AND UNEMPLOYMENT

Unemployed: people aged fifteen and over who were not employed during the survey reference week but who had actively looked for work in the four weeks up to the reference week and were available to start work in the reference week.

Underemployed: people aged fifteen years and over working less than thirty-five hours a week who wanted to work additional hours and were available to start work with more hours.

Unemployment rate: the number of employed persons in any group expressed as a percentage of the labour force in the same group.

Labour force participation rate: the labour force expressed as a percentage of the working age (fifteen to sixty-four years) population. This is done by taking the number of employed people and dividing it by the population of people who could potentially be employed.

Discouraged job seekers: people with marginal attachment to the labour force who want to work and are available to start work within four weeks, and whose main reason for not looking for work was that they believed they would not find a job for labour-market-related reasons (e.g. too young, too old, in ill-health or disabled, poorly skilled, language, ethnicity, no jobs in locality or line of work, no jobs with suitable hours or no jobs at all).

Full-time employed: people who usually worked thirty-five hours or more a week (in all jobs) and others who, although usually working less than thirty-five hours a week, worked thirty-five hours or more during the survey reference week.

Part-time employed: people who usually worked less than thirty-five hours a week (in all jobs) and who did so during the survey reference week or were not at work during the reference week.

Sources: ABS 2014a

8.4   Patterns of inequality

The differential impact of labour-market transformation in Australia means that there are clear winners and losers. Economic geographers Sally Weller and Michael Webber (2001) argue that, as market forces have increasingly driven the labour market, advantage and disadvantage have built incrementally, generating an ever-increasing divergence in individual labour-market outcomes and social inequality. The risk of only being able to access part-time or casual work is much higher among those with lower educational and skills levels. Being Indigenous, female or a recent immigrant also significantly raises the risk of unemployment or insecure employment. Similarly, geographic location is important in those states or territories, or in regional or rural areas, experiencing significantly more of the negative effects of labour-market restructuring and significantly less of the positive outcomes. Conversely, while lower-level positions have been in contraction, significant growth has been experienced in the professional sector. Changes to age pension eligibility as a response to the looming retirement of a large section of the workforce mean that the different groups among the baby boomer generation will experience differential effects of these changes. The differing and unequal impacts of labour-market change on different segments of the population are discussed throughout this section.

8.4.1   Labour force status

A graphic consequence of labour market restructuring has been the rise in part-time, casual and short-term contract work. For low-skilled workers especially, stable and easily accessible employment has largely been replaced by casual, flexible, short-term, part-time work and high rates of unemployment. Between 1971 and 2014 the proportion of workers employed full-time has declined from 89 per cent to 65 per cent. More than a third of working Australians are now in part-time and/or casual work. This decline in full-time employment is influenced but not entirely driven by a rise of female labour-force participation. Female workers are almost three times as likely as male workers to be employed part-time, with nearly half of all female employees employed part-time (47.7 per cent in 2012; AIHW 2013). Australian women's rates of part-time work is mostly driven by the need to balance child-care responsibilities. The current pattern in Australia is for women to reduce their working hours while their children are young rather than leaving the labour market completely, as was more likely in earlier years. This patterning, of part-time rather than full-time work, is one of the reasons that the labour-force participation for Australian women aged thirty to thirty-four years (average childbearing age), is lower than it is in many other Western nations. Australia ranks twenty-fifth out of thirty-five OECD countries in the level of labour-force participation of women in this age group (ABS 2013g).

Although women make up around three-quarters of part-time workers, more Australian men are now working part-time. ABS data indicate that, rather than being related to child care, for men the pattern of part-time work is U-shaped, with men more likely to work part-time at the start and the end of their working lives. This pattern is explained by the premise that younger men experience difficulty in entering the full-time labour market and also that they combine work with study. Those who are older may transition into retirement by moving from full-time to part-time work. Walter and Jackson (2007) found that more than 80 per cent of older Australians would prefer to retire gradually, to reduce their hours in their current occupation over time, rather than retire all at once. More recent data from the ABS (2012c) finds that of those workers currently working full-time and intending to retire, approximately 40 per cent intended to take up part-time work before retirement. Of these, nearly two-thirds planned to remain with their current employer; a quarter intended to work for a different employer. Of those intending to change their employer, just over half were looking to move to a different line of work, while a third planned to work on a contract basis and the remaining group intended to work more hours from home (ABS 2013f).

While those at the end of their working lives may look to part-time work as a way to ease into retirement, most part-time workers face a different scenario. For the majority of part-time workers, part-time work also means casual work. While the ABS defines a casual worker as one without leave provisions, from an inequality perspective, casual workers are usually distinguished in the Australian labour market by the differing and lesser conditions of their employment. In comparison to permanent workers, casual workers typically work under the following conditions:

- less job security
- less likely to have set working hours
- less say in start and finishing times
- fewer work hours per week
- more likely to be on call
- less likely to receive training, particularly formal training
- more likely to be paid by a labour-hire firm
- considerably lower pay than permanent employees
- likely to have no guarantee of the hours they work
- more likely to have variable earnings.

Pocock 2005; Watson 2003

The trend away from full-time permanent work to part-time casual positions is also predicated on the major sectoral shift in jobs from manufacturing to the service sector. In 1966, the highest employment industries in Australia were manufacturing (26 per cent) and wholesale and retail trade (21 per cent). In 2012 (ABS 2013g) manufacturing accounted for just 8 per cent of employed Australians, and it was the health care and social assistance industry that was the highest proportional employer (12 per cent), followed by retail trade (11 per cent) and construction (9 per cent). Mining accounted for only 2 per cent of employment, despite the Australian mining boom. While service sector jobs are increasing in number, more of these jobs are casual, part-time positions and predominantly based in lower-skilled occupations and seasonal industries than jobs in other sectors. In accommodation, cafes and restaurants, and in the agriculture, forestry and fishing sectors, more than half of all jobs are now casual positions. Employment options in the retail sector follow a similar pattern. The shift from production to service industries has reduced the opportunities for blue-collar workers and increased the opportunities for more skilled workers. Professionals are now the most common occupational group, followed by clerical and administrative workers and technicians and trades workers. The growth in some service industries also reflects other labour-market changes. The higher proportion of women in the labour market, for example, means that the number of people employed in the child-care sector rose nearly 80 per cent between 2002 and 2012 (ABS 2012e).

The gendered and occupational trends of part-time work are clearly demonstrated in Table 8.1 and Table 8.2, which compare male and female part-time worker status by the industry of their employment in 1996 and 2012 respectively. (These data are presented in two tables because the changing nature of the Australian labour force necessitated a change in how the ABS classified occupations from 2008 onwards.) As can be seen, male workers are far less likely than female workers, in both 1996 and 2012, to be part-time. However, the proportion of part-time workers has risen for male and female workers during this period, with male part-time rates rising from just under 12 per cent in 1996 to over 16 per cent in 2012. For female workers part-time rates have risen to 47 per cent, but this increase is explained more by higher female labour-force participation in 2012 than it is by a greater proportion of women choosing to work part-time.

The pattern of part-time work across occupational groups is distinctive, but different for each gender. For men, across 1996 and 2012, sales and service workers and labourers account for nearly half of all part-time workers. This suggests that, for men, such part-time work might be all they can find. For women, those in sales occupations also make up a relatively large proportion of part-time workers. The other large group (in both 1996 and 2012) is advanced and intermediate clerical workers. This group, heavily represented within the public service, may have more active choice in whether they are full-time or part-time. They are also much less likely to be casual workers, and likely able to return to full-time work when their children are older. The same circumstances are likely to apply for male and female part-time workers who are managers or professionals.

Table 8.1   Part-time work status by gender and occupation, 1996

Occupation	Men (%)	Women (%)
Managers and administrators	3.1	2.6
Professionals	10.8	14.5
Associate professionals	5.3	4.6
Tradespersons and related workers	9.3	2.2
Advanced clerical and service workers	1.0	10.2
Intermediate clerical, sales and service workers	10.2	27.2
Intermediate production and transport workers	13.3	2.4
Elementary clerical, sales and service workers	20.5	23.9
Labourers and related workers	26.5	12.4
Part-time workers of total employed	11.7	42.9

Table 8.2   Part-time work status by gender and occupation, 2012

Occupation	Men (%)	Women (%)
Managers	6.2	4.8
Professionals	14.7	19.1
Technicians and trades workers	12.5	4.4
Community and personal service workers	12.4	19.9
Clerical and administrative workers	5.9	21.7
Sales workers	15.8	18.9
Machinery operators and drivers	7.8	0.9
Labourers	24.7	10.4
Part-time workers of total employed	16.5	47.0

Source: ABS 2013i

The question of whether part-time or casual workers are such by choice or situation is vexed. Proponents argue that the flexibility of part-time or casual work suits many workers and point to the generally high levels of job satisfaction recorded by part-time workers. For older workers coming to the end of working life, easing into retirement via part-time work may be a preferred option. For others, such as women with family responsibilities, the choice to work part-time is complicated by a lack of flexibility or of family-friendly options at work and a lack of social supports to allow them to fulfil their family obligations. In 2012, two-thirds of those outside of the labour market or not looking for more hours of work were women for whom 'caring for children' was the most commonly reported reason

(ABS 2013g). The downside of part-time and casual work over full-time permanent work is also obvious in terms of job security, income levels and employment conditions. Estimates of the average weekly total cash earnings of part-time workers are below the national average. And surveys of people who were unemployed or looking for more hours of work have found that a lack of alternative work options is the most common reason given for why they are working the hours they are (ABS 2013g).

Critics of the casualisation trend argue that, regardless of job satisfaction, casualisation undermines workers' position in the labour market, which leads to a proliferation of poor-quality, low-security, low-paying jobs (Pocock 2005; Watson 2005). This critique is borne out by Watson's analysis, which finds that even taking into account the loadings paid to casuals, casual workers are between 12 and 17 per cent worse off than if they performed the same work in a permanent position. Social researcher Jenny Chalmers (2007), in analysing four waves of HILDA data, found that 40 per cent of casual workers in 2001 had not transitioned to permanent work by 2004. This mixed result, she suggests, indicates definite elements of a trap of casual employment, as well as some evidence of a bridge to ongoing work.

8.4.2   Unemployment

The Australian labour market is experiencing a period of record high employment. Despite the global financial crisis, unemployment in Australia is at lows unprecedented in the last thirty years. In March 2014, for example, the national unemployment rate was 5.8 per cent (ABC 2014b). But within this picture of high employment there is debate about the validity of official measures of unemployment. The key question here is at what point should an individual with access to only limited, insecure and unpredictable hours of employment be categorised as unemployed rather than as a casual worker? Officially, the answer is that a person is counted as employed if they worked one hour or more in the previous week, a very broad definition that means that many officially 'employed' people are still unemployed enough to receive the full rate of the Newstart payment. Critics such as ACOSS and the Centre for Full Employment and Equity at the University of Newcastle posit that if a more realistic definition of 'employed' were used—working at least one day per week, for example—then the unemployment rate would likely double (Senate 2004; Nicholson 2004).

Australians of working age (fifteen to sixty-four years) classified by the ABS as 'not in the labour force' are also not included in official unemployment figures. The ABS notes that around one-quarter of these people are actually marginally attached to the workforce, that is, they want to work and are either looking for work or are available to start work but do not satisfy all the criteria of being either employed or unemployed. ABS data also indicates that the 'not in the labour force' group includes a substantial group of discouraged job seekers—people who want to work but are not actively looking as they do not believe they will find a job. In 2013 the ABS reported that there were 117,200 discouraged job seekers aged fifteen years and over, and that, in a shift from historical patterns where females dominated this group, the proportion of male discouraged job seekers now make up 53 per cent of this total (ABS 2014a).

underemployment Refers to individuals in employment who are seeking to increase their hours of paid labour.

A key inequality-related question in looking at unemployment and **underemployment** is whether there is an unemployment problem or a jobs problem. Both sort of problems can, of course, co-exist, but the patterns inherent in unemployment data suggest it is more likely to be a social issue around a lack of suitable jobs for a significant proportion of the population than it is an employment-related deficit among job seekers. First, the likelihood of not being employed in the restructured Australian labour market has a strong educational bias. Australian and international research continuously link lower levels of education to labour-market disadvantage and marginalisation through such factors as unemployment, low labour-force participation and part-time and casual work with lesser conditions or pay (Borooah & Mangan 2002; ACOSS 2005; AMP.NATSEM 2005; Babb 2005; ABS 2006d). Leaving school before completing Year 12 is a high risk factor for unemployment or marginal attachment to the labour market, and Australians with lower levels of qualifications are twice as likely to be unemployed as those with higher-level qualifications. For example, in 2012, 18 per cent of those who did not complete Year 12 were unemployed compared to an unemployment rate of 11 per cent of those who did. As outlined in Chapter 7 there is a linear relationship between level of education and unemployment. There is also a locational aspect to unemployment, with rates varying considerably across regions and across states. In March 2014, unemployment in the ACT was 3.4 per cent, versus 7.4 per cent in Tasmania (ABC 2014b).

In 2012–13 the ABS asked unemployed people for the first time about factors that would assist them in obtaining a job (Table 8.3). As can be seen, for both male and female workers, getting a job that matched their skills and experience was a key factor.

Table 8.3   Factors rated as very important for getting a job

Factors	Male (%)	Female (%)
Getting a job that matches skills and experience	61	68
Ability to work a set number of hours on set days	48	51
Getting support for training/studying to improve skills	48	53
Getting help with job search activities	41	46

Source: ABS 2013g:14

The decline of lower skilled occupations is also related to an increase in job retrenchment and redundancies. While no longer at the 1991 peak of 6.5 per cent of all employees, retrenchment remains a significant part of the labour market in the 2000s. In 2012 more than 400,000 people were retrenched, made redundant, had their employer go out of business, were dismissed or had an employer with no available work (ABS 2014a). Again, the distribution of redundancy or retrenchment is not random but patterned by industry type and geographic location—manufacturing industries located in what had previously been the heavy industrial areas of states such as Tasmania, Victoria and South Australia were especially vulnerable.

The likely labour-market fate of retrenched workers is not rosy. Weller and Webber (2001), in one of the few examinations of retrenched Australian workers, found that most experienced increasingly precarious forms of employment, high rates of exclusion from the labour market and corresponding high rates of ongoing welfare dependence. The researchers followed the employment outcomes of a group of workers displaced by the restructuring of the textile, clothing and footwear industries in the early 1990s, from 1993 to March 1997. While a lucky few improved their labour-market position post-retrenchment, most exchanged what had been secure full-time, semi-skilled employment for a sequence of insecure, low-paid, low-skill jobs, punctuated by periods of unemployment. The research concludes that 'the economic restructuring that did away with these workers' medium- and low-skill manufacturing jobs did not generate new jobs that most of these workers could realistically access, even after extensive retraining' (Weller & Webber 2001:161). After the recent large-scale retrenchments of workers in the automotive industry in Australia, it is likely that there will be another group of workers facing the same experiences.

8.4.3   Life stage and retirement

The likelihood of being unemployed can be related to an individual's lifecycle stage. Young people in particular tend to have a higher unemployment rate, and older workers are also particularly vulnerable to underemployment or unemployment. This latter group, especially those retrenched from their jobs, tend to disappear from the labour market, often relabelled as 'retired'. But though people who are classed as retired are not counted as unemployed, evidence suggests that for many retirement is to some extent involuntary and they would have preferred to stay employed. Data from the HILDA longitudinal study (2005) found that around half of the 24 per cent of forty-five-to-sixty-four-year-olds who reported that they are retired also reported that there had been an element of workplace pressure for them to take their retirement.

Retirement, or the prospect of retirement from the labour market, brings with it a number of concerns that affect different groups of working people in different ways. For example, ABS data found that the most common factors given by older workers affecting their decision about when to retire were financial security, personal health and physical abilities, and reaching the age where they were eligible to access an age or a service pension (ABS 2013f). Older low- or non-skilled men and women are particularly vulnerable to reaching an older working age (fifty years and older) with little financial security, reduced physical capacity to continue in what are often jobs with high physical demands and little prospect of other employment options compared to higher-skilled workers. As such, older less-skilled workers are not only more likely to have fewer positive options about how and when to retire, but are twice as likely as those with formal qualifications to be no longer participating in the workforce between the ages of forty-four and sixty-four years

(AMP.NATSEM 2005). Recent changes in the age of eligibility of age pensions (see below) exacerbate the risk for older, low-skilled workers.

Demographic change is also now interacting with economic change, exacerbating the restructuring effects and creating its own labour market impacts. As in other Western industrialised countries, the proportion of the Australian population over fifty years of age is rising alongside a corresponding decrease in the proportion of younger Australians entering the workforce. The changing age profile has significant labour market implications, with the most immediate and most dramatic effect being labour market shortages. While youth unemployment remains a problem in Australia, there is a concurrent concern about what will happen to the ratio of employed to non-employed persons within our society as the baby boomer generation retires. These concerns are behind the frequent public debates about the cost of the age pension and encouragement from government for older workers to remain in the labour force for longer.

This policy push appears to be working, at least to some extent: since 2002 the labour-force participation of older Australians has risen considerably. In 2012, 34 per cent of men and 20 per cent of women aged sixty-five to sixty-nine years were in the labour force (ABS 2013g). Of course, not all of this additional labour-force participation among older people is voluntary: O'Loughlin et al. (2010, cited in Chomik & Piggott 2012) report that negative effects of the global financial crisis on the superannuation and savings of older workers had led to over 40 per cent of women and 30 per cent of men to postpone their retirement. But most older workers still intend to retire in their mid-60s—recent data found that the average age at which people intended to retire was 63.8 years for men and 63 years for women (ABS 2013f).

Concern about the ageing of the Australian labour force is also behind recent increases in the age of eligibility for the age pension. In 2009 the Labor Government raised the age of eligibility from sixty-five years, where it had been since the age pension was introduced in the early twentieth century, to sixty-seven years (for those born after 1 January 1957) (Department of Social Services 2013). Under 2014 Abbott Government budget measures, the qualifying age for any Australian born after 1 January 1966—a group now aged close to fifty years—will rise to seventy years.

8.4.4   Employment polarisation: Work-rich and work-poor

The rise in low-wage work and the occupation polarisation of employment has led to the creation of two groups, the work-rich and the work-poor. The phenomenon of being work-poor is mostly discussed in terms of families, with the term 'jobless families' used to describe households where no adult is engaged in the labour market. Nearly two-thirds of workless families are also sole-parent families. In June 2011, nearly 40 per cent of sole-parent families with a child under fifteen were 'jobless' compared to only 5 per cent of couple families. This proportion, although high, is a reduction from the 2005 figure of 46 per cent of sole-parent families with no adult engaged in the labour market (AIHW 2013).

Additionally, although women in sole-parent households are gaining employment at a faster rate than the average worker, they are failing to keep up with women in couple families in workplace entry. Higher rates of unemployment among sole parents also largely reflect the lower educational levels among this group compared to partnered mothers and the higher burden of child care for families where there is only one resident adult (Walter 2002). The proportion of children living in jobless families in Australia is nearly double the OECD average (15 per cent compared with 9 per cent), with Australia having the fourth-highest proportion among OECD countries of children aged under fourteen living in jobless families (AIHW 2013:73).

Those who are work-rich tend to be in higher-skilled occupations. For the work-rich, the outcomes are not necessarily all positive: work-rich usually means time-poor. At the higher end of the employment spectrum the average number of hours worked by full-time workers and the proportion of employees who work long hours has increased in recent decades. The Australia at Work Study (2013), a national five-year longitudinal survey of working age being conducted by the University of Sydney Business School has found that half of all full-time employees report working more hours per week than the standard of thirty-five to forty hours. The study established that, despite the global financial crisis, the practice of full-time workers working longer hours increased between 2006 and 2010. In 2010, just over one-quarter of full-time workers reported that they were usually working between forty and forty-nine hours per week. Another quarter reported that they were usually working fifty or more hours per week. The study found that for many of these workers, these extra hours were not compensated by overtime or other wage supplements. The results showed that in 2010, 22 per cent of full-time workers worked up to five unpaid hours per week, 14 per cent reported six to ten unpaid hours per week and 15 per cent reported working eleven or more unpaid hours per week. Within these figures, male workers were much more likely to be working long or very long hours than female workers. Occupationally, managers and administrators, paraprofessional and intermediate production workers (both men and women) were more likely to be working longer hours than other occupations. Research (Wooden & Drago 2007) on working-hours preferences has found that a significant proportion of workers expressed a preference for different hours. This trend is strongest among those working longer hours. Around 54 per cent of men and 64 per cent of women working more than fifty hours per week would prefer fewer hours. In contrast, only 3 per cent of men and less than 1 per cent of women working such hours preferred more hours.

Two very different social phenomena can be associated with the rising demands that work is placing on some groups. First is the strain that many professional and other workers increasingly feel as a result of trying to manage their work obligations with family and other life activities. One response is the trend referred to by demographers as 'downshifting' or the 'sea-change syndrome', where overworked, overbusy, city-based, mostly professional workers actively choose to live with less money in order to reduce the hours and consequent pressure of work, so they can have a greater and more personally satisfying work–life balance. Such a choice is restricted to those workers with the means to fund a more leisurely life. Second, and opposite, are those for whom increasing hours and demands of work are embraced as a complete and exciting lifestyle. The title of a book by authors Helen Trinca and Catherine Fox (2004), *Better than Sex: How a Whole Generation Got Hooked on Work*, sums up this phenomenon. Rather than decrying the incessant demands of work, work is celebrated as a key part of many people's identities that provides excitement, inspiration and empowerment. The mobile office, where laptops and mobile phones are carried on the person, mean that being anywhere can also be 'being at work' (Elliot 2004). It is hard, though, to imagine a casual service-industry worker feeling the same way about their work.

Another key division in the work-rich/work-poor divide is location and stage in the life and work cycle. Job growth is locationally uneven in Australia. Tasmania has consistently had the highest unemployment rate over the years, an unenviable position that can be linked to a number of factors, including the state's older population, lower levels of education and its previous heavy-industry economic base, which was decimated through the decline of manufacturing that occurred over the last two decades. In March 2014, Tasmania retained its position with an unemployment rate of 7.6 per cent, compared to South Australia with an unemployment rate of 7.1 per cent, Victoria with 6.4 per cent, Queensland with 6.1 per cent, New South Wales with 5.3 per cent, Western Australia with 4.9 per cent, Northern Territory with 3.8 per cent and ACT with 3.4 per cent (ABC 2014b). As can be seen from these figures, the current resources boom in Western Australia and Queensland is reflected in these states' low levels of unemployment, which are unprecedented.

8.4.5   Indigenous people and the labour market

While labour-force participation among Indigenous people is rising, a broader examination of the data indicates that Indigenous people remain heavily disadvantaged on labour-market indicators and experience a different relationship to the labour market than do non-Indigenous Australians. On the night of the 2011 census, Indigenous unemployment across the nation stood at just over 17 per cent. The Indigenous unemployment situation at the national level has worsened since then—the ABS reports it at 21 per cent for the period 2012–13 (for those aged fifteen to sixty-four years). This rate is more than four times higher than the national unemployment rate of all Australians during the same period (ABS 2013h).

Indigenous unemployment and labour-market participation varies by region and location, with those in remote and regional areas experiencing higher rates of unemployment than those residing in major cities. Figure 8.1 compares unemployment rates across locations and between Indigenous and non-Indigenous populations, using data from the 2011 census of population and housing. As shown, the unemployment rate in the metropolitan city of Perth was lower, at 18 per cent, than that in Dubbo, where Indigenous unemployment was 21 per cent. And the unemployment rate in the remote Northern Territory township of Maningrida was as high as 24 per cent (a comparison for the non-Indigenous population of Maningrida is not included as this group is usually made up of temporary workers rather than permanent residents of the town).

Figure 8.1 Indigenous and non-Indigenous unemployment rates, 2011

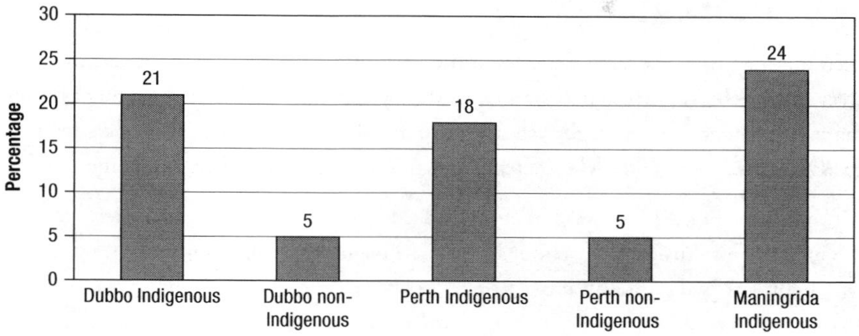

Source: ABS 2012a

What is more remarkable is the similarity of the Indigenous unemployment positions across these three locations. In both Perth and Dubbo, the Indigenous unemployment rate was more than three times that of the non-Indigenous unemployment rate. These comparison rates of Indigenous to non-Indigenous unemployment are repeated around the nation. Regardless of where Aboriginal and Torres Strait Islanders live in Australia, the Indigenous unemployment rate is still likely to be about four times that of their non-Indigenous co-residents. Indigenous people also experience lower rates of labour-market participation because of child-rearing responsibilities and higher levels of ill health and mobility, adding up to startling statistics: in 2012–13 just under half (47.5 per cent) of Aboriginal and Torres Strait Islander people aged fifteen to sixty-four years were employed (ABS 2013h).

As Walter has argued, the parallels of place are central to understanding that being an Indigenous person in Australia is correlated directly with a common position on the lowest rung of society's socioeconomic hierarchy: 'There is an Indigenous specific location fundamentally related to poverty and exclusion' (2008:35). This position is also correlated with lower levels of education. As discussed in Chapter 7, Aboriginal and Torres Strait Islander people, regardless of location, are disadvantaged in terms of educational achievement: in 2012–13, only 46 per cent of Aboriginal and Torres Strait Islander people aged twenty years and over had completed Year 12 or a Certificate III or above. This rate, when age-standardised, equates to Aboriginal and Torres Strait Islander people, nationally, being only around half as likely as non-Indigenous people to have achieved this level of education (ABS 2013h).

Despite the grimness of the figures there is also some reason for optimism. Between 1996 and 2011 the employment rate of Indigenous women rose from 26 to 39 per cent. While this rate is still much lower than the 56 per cent employment rate of other Australian women, in 2011, the rate of increase was higher, indicating a partial closing of the gap. For Indigenous men the picture is similar, with the employment rate rising from 31 per cent to 45 per cent between 1996 and 2011 (compared to the employment rate rise of other Australian men of 65 to 68 per cent during the same period; Gray et al. 2013).

8.5   Women, children and the labour market

As noted in Chapter 3, the achievements of the Australian wage-earners' welfare state were effectively only achieved for male workers. In this system female dependence was assumed and materially ensured by a wage system that paid women at a lower rate than men. As Justice Higgins stated in 1907 when setting out his core principles of a living wage:

> The principle of the living wage has been applied to women, but with a difference, as women are not usually legally responsible for the maintenance of a family. A women's minimum is based on the average cost of her own living to one who supports herself by her own exertions. A woman or girl with a comfortable home cannot be left to underbid in wages other women or girls who are less fortunate.
>
> Source: Jones 1983:17

The predictable result of wage discrimination and social norms that regarded women's primary role as a homemaker and mother were extremely low levels of female labour-market participation. With the passage in the 1970s of equal wage legislation, this entrenched pattern began to change and has not paused since: over the past three decades, workforce participation among Australian women increased by more than 50 per cent. Most of this rise is related to increases in the proportion of women with children in the labour market. Women are also returning to work at progressively earlier stages of their children's lives. Yet while the workforce participation rates of mothers now approach those of women without children, their pattern of employment is very different. For the majority of Australian mothers of dependent children, employment is part-time or casual in order to facilitate both their family and their work obligations.

Contemporary Australia

WORKING WOMEN AND WORK-LIFE OUTCOMES

Research by Skinner et al. (2012) found that the work-life outcomes for women working full-time are worsening. Full-time-working women, they report, face continuing and increasing strains in their capacity to combine paid work and care. This a problem for a country that aims to increase women's workforce participation, sustain fertility and respond to the needs of an ageing population. The wish to sustain fertility rates and support the ageing population are both likely to intensify care responsibilities and sit at odds with policy aims of raising the level of women's participation in the labour force. They also sit at odds with current inflexible work arrangements, work intensification and unsupportive workplaces. Skinner et al.

identify the following indicators as contributing to declining work-life outcomes for full-time women workers:

- Work-life interference has increased from 2007 to 2012.
- Full-time-working women's dissatisfaction with their work-life balance has risen (from 15.9 per cent in 2008 to 27.5 per cent in 2012) while men's has showed no change.
- Full-time-working women's experience of chronic time pressure has increased, with 68.6 per cent often or almost always feeling rushed and pressed for time, up from 63.4 per cent in 2008 (with no change amongst full-time-working men).
- In 2012 the gap between full-time-working women's actual and preferred work hours is the largest since 2007; they prefer, on average, to work 8.7 fewer hours a week than they do.
- Nearly 42 per cent of mothers in full-time employment would prefer to work part-time—the largest proportion since 2007.

8.5.1   Women's wages

Despite the existence of equal wage legislation for over thirty years now, women's wages still do not equal those of men. Even when the higher proportion of part-time work among women is taken into account, women still do not earn income at the same level as Australian men. Some, though certainly not all, of this discrepancy can be explained by the tendency of men and women to cluster in different industries and occupations—women tend to be employed in industries that have lower wages, such as the services sector. For example, in 2012, employees in the accommodation and food services industry, which is dominated by female workers, had the lowest average weekly total cash earnings (ABS 2013j). In contrast, average weekly total cash earnings were highest for employees in the mining industry, an industry dominated by male workers. However, the lower level of earnings for women is consistent across industry sectors.

The gender pay gap is defined as the difference between women's and men's average weekly full-time equivalent earnings and is expressed as a percentage of men's earnings (Workplace Gender Equality Agency 2014). In 2013 the gender pay gap in Australia was 17.1 per cent (that is, women's wages, on average, were 17.1 per cent lower than men's wages). While there have been minor fluctuations over the last twenty years, essentially the gap has stayed the same. The Workplace Gender Equality Agency (2014) identified a number of factors that contribute to the wage gap. These include:

- the segregation of women and men in different industry sectors
- a lack of women in more senior (and more highly paid) positions
- women's higher unpaid caring responsibilities
- differences in education, work experience and seniority
- discrimination, both direct and indirect.

In world rankings, Australia's gender pay gap is relatively low—in a recent comparison of G20 countries, only Canada, the United Kingdom and Indonesia reported comparable levels of inequality. The same report notes, however, that none of the G20 countries report wage parity between women and men and that women also do an average of two to five more hours a day of unpaid work than men (Millman 2014).

8.5.2   Women's employment: Individual choice or socially embedded?

Australian women, then, despite three decades of rising labour-market participation, retain different and unequal patterns of employment, by occupation and industry sector. For women with children, such patterns are usually attributed to choices about the primacy of their mothering and family roles. Women's choices about paid and unpaid work are not made in a social vacuum, though; rather, they occur within a social and economic system in which such choices are directly influenced by social and economic policies and their outcomes. The over-representation of mothers in part-time jobs, for example, is generally attributed to family choices about integrating labour-market work and household obligations, but the rising workforce participation of Australian mothers also coincides with market-economy demand for labour-market flexibility and the growth of part-time and casual jobs. So it is not the labour market fitting into women's job demands, rather it is women fitting into the part-time, temporary and casual nature of the restructured Australian labour market.

These patterns have significant inequality dimensions. Women may make a pragmatic decision to take on part-time and casual work to enable them to meet their family and parenting responsibilities, but the evidence suggests they do so at considerable labour-market risk. Such decisions operate to marginalise women with children into the lower-status, less-secure, lower-skilled and lower-paid sector of the labour market. Chalmers' (2007) longitudinal analysis of mothers in part-time and casual positions found that having young children tended to decrease these women's durations of casual work. Combined with the finding that part-time work is associated with longer periods of casual work, Chalmers suggests 'the possibility that part-time casual employment might be trapping mothers in jobs they cannot escape when, and if, they want to return to more career-enhancing work as their children gain independence' (2007:19).

Social policy also directly impacts on family labour choices and arrangements. Australia has a 'poorly configured "work and care" regime" where paid work increasingly encroaches upon care' (Pocock 2005:123). Women's labour-market trends, therefore, rather than being about mothers' choices, may instead reflect 'the inadequacies of social arrangements for women's proper career, pay and job security, notably the restricted provision of childcare' (Silva 1996:25). A major example of the impact of social policy change are the Welfare to Work policy measures. Introduced in 2006, and tightened further in 2013, these measures predominantly impact sole parents (of whom more than 80 per cent are female) on the Parenting Payment Single (PPS) benefit. Under current guidelines, sole parents lose their entitlement to PPS once their youngest child turns eight (Department of Human Services 2014c), and are transferred to Newstart Allowance, which has lower rates of benefit and high levels of interaction with Centrelink and job-seeking requirements. The changes have equality ramifications for all Australian women with children, regardless of their current partnered status: nearly 90 per cent of Australian sole mothers were previously partnered or married mothers (Walter 2002). All women with dependent children are potentially sole parents, and policy redefinitions of a sole mother as a worker-mother who must participate in the labour market have not led to other changes in the framework of policy logic.

While welfare policies now obligate market activity for Australian sole mothers, child-care services remain expensive and difficult to access. How the parenting work needs of sole-mother households can be reconciled with the growing imperative for-labour market work are unexplained within dominant policy discourses. While sole-mother households certainly require income to meet family needs in lieu of that from a partner, the parental obligations and duties of sole mothers also remain constant. Maternal employment may generate household income but the performance of labour-market activity necessitates a trade-off in family time. This dual need for family income plus parenting and household time creates an income–time conundrum (Walter 2002), but within the Welfare to Work policy framework, the limited definition of work as paid work skews the perspective. While the importance of the family is a regular topic of political rhetoric, the validity of unpaid work is restricted to that performed in two-parent families. The work that is required to make and maintain a sole-parent family does not receive the same public recognition.

8.6   The labour market and social mobility

The question of how open a nation is in terms of movement between occupational groups is important in the study of social inequality. It raises questions about whether inequality per se is of concern or whether only inequality that is entrenched, that passes from one generation to the next, is the issue. The legitimation of democracy is based on the premise of the equality of its citizens: although circumstances may differ, the opportunity exists for equality of outcomes, especially in the economic arena. From this perspective, intragenerational inequality is of less concern than intergenerational inequality. In fact, a high level of **intragenerational mobility** would suggest that meritocratic principles are operating, since the position an individual is born into is not a prediction of where they will end up. A high degree of intergenerational stability would suggest that rather than a being a meritocracy the society is characterised by the inheritance of disadvantage and that processes of social closure are operating to exclude some groups from access to societal resources.

intragenerational mobility
Movement up or down a social stratification system within an individual's lifetime.

An examination of the relationship between occupational change and social mobility involves more than an analysis of positioning within the labour market. Goldthorpe (cited in Glass 1954) argued that in interpreting such changes it is necessary to distinguish between structural and circulation mobility. Structural mobility is where the major changes are due to a changing occupational structure. This phenomenon was prominent in most Western nations in the period following the Second World War as part of the transition from a manufacturing to a service economy. This meant that the reduction in the proportion of manual jobs was directly related to the increase in the proportion of non-manual, and therefore middle-class, jobs. Circulation mobility, on the other hand, results from an open class structure and is independent of structural changes in the occupational hierarchy. Goldthorpe reported on studies that found that the relatively high level of mobility that occurred in Britain in the second half of the twentieth century was, in fact, structural mobility. While people believed they lived in a meritocratic society because they or their family had experienced upward mobility, in reality this mobility resulted from changes in the occupational structure. This suggests that perceptions of living in a highly fluid social world without firm boundaries between classes is to some degree an illusion. The changes that have occurred may have resulted not from the recognition and reward of individual qualities but from structural changes to the economy.

While research on social mobility in Australia is limited, a similar phenomenon appears to have occurred here. Leigh (2007) calculated that there is little evidence of any significant

intergenerational mobility
Movement up or down a social stratification system across two or more generations.

intergenerational mobility in Australia, up or down, for the last forty years. Moreover, the evidence on social mobility in Australia suggests that while there is considerable movement between occupational categories, most mobility is generated by changes in the occupational structure. Present-day young Australians are as likely to reproduce the class position of their parents as they are to change it and the social mobility direction of contemporary Australian youth is not necessarily up. In attempting to make a judgment on Australia's level of social mobility, Argy (2005) pointed to patterns in the USA, where, despite high levels of economic liberalisation and a well-developed market economy, intergenerational mobility is either static or declining. He contends that Australia's move towards similar free-market conditions, in the labour force and elsewhere, predicts the same trend, with a consequent reduction in equality of opportunity as well as equality of outcome. The patterns of mobility for men and women also differs. Women are more likely to breach the manual/non-manual barrier but only to enter clerical jobs that offer little more reward than manual positions. In this regard, much female occupationally based social mobility is structural rather than circulatory, a response to the rise in service work available rather than a step up the occupational ladder. This conclusion fits well with Hayes' (1990) research on intergenerational mobility among employed and non-employed women. She found that daughters tend to inherit the class positions of their mothers and that there has been little change in the strength of this association during the postwar era.

Gilding's (2005) interviews with wealthy Australians also identified the significance of social capital within the family. In his study, family relationships were central to the accumulation of capital and succession planning between generations. Prominent families drew on their social networks to access promising employment positions. They also established family business institutions that assisted family members to maximise and manage their inheritance. Conversely, there is evidence that just as advantage is inherited, so is disadvantage. Numerous studies in Australia and overseas have demonstrated a pattern of intergenerational poverty and social exclusion that, while not complete, is nonetheless significant (Vinson 2007; d'Addio 2007). Inheritance patterns work so that those who have the least economic need also have the greatest chance of inheriting significant wealth (Kelly & Harding 2007), while those at the bottom of the ladder are lucky if they do not inherit debts.

8.7   Emerging labour-force trends

Despite the huge change in the structure and shape of the Australian labour market over the last three decades, such change is likely to be only the harbinger of further restructuring, and most likely further inequality. As stated at the beginning of this chapter, the major factors behind current trends and patterns in the Australian labour market are the structural changes linked to the increasingly dominant market economy and the effects of population ageing. These two factors also appear as the key to emerging trends.

The ageing of the population and reduction of new entrants into the labour market underpin the skills shortages currently being experienced. While most prominent in areas of highly skilled labour, skills shortages are apparent in many sectors of the labour market. Changes linked to skills shortages are wage increases for those with the skills and labour that are in demand, and a change in the patterning of the where, when and how of employment for many workers. For example, miners from all over the country are working in Western Australia during the mining boom. Many do not live in the area in which they work; rather, they fly in to work for a set of shifts and return to their home states in between.

Globalisation and the demands of the market economy are the primary forces behind the continuing outsourcing of jobs to cheaper overseas locations as well as an increasing demand for imported labour via guest worker visas. The result is a seemingly contradictory situation: jobs move out of Australia at the same time as workers are being imported. The interaction between the state and the labour market is all-important in how these trends play out in inequality terms. Sociologist Paul Henman (2001a) maintains that the decline of full-time jobs and the rise of part-time casual employment results in an increase in people combining part-time wages with part-rate benefits to survive economically. Thus, labour-market flexibility must also mean an increase in welfare dependency, with substantial movement between receipt of welfare payments and low-wage work. Rather than providing avenues for people to move off benefits, increasing the availability of part-time work has instead exacerbated welfare-recipient numbers and entrenched labour-market inequality. This pattern is confirmed by data that show that while unemployment rates are coming down, the number of Australians reliant on income-support payments is not declining at the same rate.

8.8 Conclusion

Employment is a socially created resource and the labour market is the vehicle by which this resource is distributed. Across the Western world, economic restructuring and its attendant social and labour market restructuring has substantially altered the world of work for Australian workers. The result is increased inequality within the workforce. While for some the restructured labour market has created opportunities and access to greater material and social benefits, there has also been an emergence of groups that are particularly vulnerable to inequality in the distribution of the employment resource.

So, who are the winners and who are the losers in the reformed Australian labour market? The overall result has been a net transfer of jobs to high-skilled or middle-class households at the cost of low-skilled, working-class households.

High-skilled workers, especially high-skilled women and those living in metropolitan areas, are the major beneficiaries from labour-market restructuring. Low-skilled men and working-class households, especially in regional areas, along with Indigenous men and female workers, have been the major losers. More critically, the rising rate of part-time and casual employment, particularly among male employees, indicates a major shift in the structure of the Australian workforce. Although the number of jobs in the Australian labour market has increased overall, the quality of these jobs varies significantly: neither the quality nor the quantity distribution of work has been shared evenly throughout the population.

The patterns of winners and losers in the reformed Australian labour market highlight the clustering of labour-market risk borne by different groups. Although the labour market has changed across a range of dimensions, including the conditions of employment, life-course trajectory, its security and rewards, to name just a few, in the main it is the same groups that are at risk in all these areas. In relation to employment conditions, highly skilled and educated male workers occupy the most secure positions with the greatest prospects for career advancement and the highest-level reward in terms of job satisfaction, remuneration, status and superannuation. For this group, the labour market can indeed be the bridge to greater social mobility and social and economic success. For higher skilled and educated women, while greater career opportunities and rewards exist than ever before, partnering and parenting are significant labour-market liabilities that reduce opportunities and options across the life course. Caring responsibilities are not restricted to children, but also include caring for grandchildren, elderly parents, or ill or disabled partners. For low-skilled men and women, working life is increasingly less secure, more likely to be poorly paid, with fewer opportunities for advancement or development and reducing quality of employment conditions. Their social and economic outcomes range from low status, inability to obtain loans and other social goods because of labour force uncertainty, and a likely ongoing relationship, throughout their life-course, with Centrelink and the stigmatisation of benefit receipt. The labour-market position for Indigenous Australians is even more dire, with little to suggest any tangible improvement in the foreseeable future. As outlined in Chapter 7, education is the plank by which workers gain access to higher paid, more secure and more rewarding employment. The education route, however, is not equally accessible to all. Those who shoulder the burden of inequality within the labour market are also significantly more likely to have unequal access to educational resources.

Discussion questions

1 Identify the key changes associated with the influence of globalisation and neoliberalism on the Australian labour market over the last thirty years.
2 In your own words, outline Beck and Beck-Gernsheim's argument that the key source of individualisation in contemporary society is the labour market. What effect does this have on inequality today?
3 Bauman argues that the flexible labour market has led to a deep divide in the types of work available. What are the types of work Bauman is referring to?
4 Who are the clear winners and losers of labour market transformation in Australia?

9

○

THE FAMILY

○

9.1   Introduction

Most Australians live their lives within a family structure and the family occupies a central position within Australian society. Yet the social position of the family is multifaceted and contradictory. It is at the same time a bedrock social institution and an intensely private realm. The family is variously positioned as something that requires support and exhorted to provide more support, to be the purveyor of family values and to be the centre of care, nurture and moral guidance. This incongruity of differing social notions of the family is demonstrated in the contrast between Beck's (2002) argument that the family is a **zombie category** of social institution, dead but still alive, and portrayals of the family as the lynchpin of society's social and moral fabric. These contradictory conceptions of the family highlight that the family, in conceptual and actual form, is an entity that incorporates moral, political, cultural and economic dimensions.

zombie category
A description for changing family formations, such as rising cohabitation and out-of-wedlock birth rates—the family here is a zombie because it represents ideas that seem to be alive but are really dead.

The family is also a site of social difference and, the evidence suggests, a site of significant social inequality. The rapid social change evidenced in the increasing diversity of Australian families, especially over the last three decades, is a vital element of that inequality. The family is a site of differential distribution of social, political, economic and symbolic resources. Both within the family and at the institutional level, gender is the key determinant of the risk of inequality, although this operates in different ways at each level. This chapter is relevant to the third of this study's guiding questions (how is the distribution of Australia's social, political, economic and cultural resources reproduced across different social groups?) and the fourth question because it examines how subjectivities are implicated in the creation of social inequality through the way the family is constructed and perceived by different social groups. The ideological and moral discourses surrounding the family, and their related interaction with the state and consequent policy, are strongly connected to the experience of family-related inequality.

9.2   Family as a site of diversity

The complexity of the Australian Bureau of Statistics' definition of a family as 'two or more persons, one of whom is at least fifteen years of age, who are related by blood, marriage (registered or de facto), adoption, step or fostering and who are usually resident in the same household' highlights the difficulty of trying to determine exactly what a family is. Using this definition, 90 per cent of Australians live in a family and in 2009–10 there were around 6,345,000 Australian families. Of these, 84 per cent (5.4 million) were couple families, 14 per cent (879,000) were one-parent families and 2 per cent (98,000) were other families (ABS 2010a).

Australian family formation patterns and living arrangements, however, have altered and continue to do so. There is a new terrain of family emerging. Examining the formation patterns, shapes and trajectories of Australian families since the 1970s demonstrates the dramatic nature of this ongoing change. The landscape of family formation and a core societal role of the family—the parenting of children—have changed substantially. Critically, this restructuring has had significant effects on the family as both a site of diversity and inequality.

9.2.1   Marrying less and later, cohabiting more

With Australians now less likely than ever to marry, marriage is no longer a key marker of adulthood. Marriage rates in Australia steadily decreased from the 1980s to the early 2000s, with the crude marriage rate (the annual number of marriages per 1000 people) declining from 6.6 to 5.3 between 1992 and 2002. Since 2002, the crude marriage rate has remained steady, with 123,244 marriages registered in 2012. Most of these marriages (72 per cent) were between people who have not been previously married. Also, those who do marry do so at substantially older ages. The median age at first marriage 1982 to 2012 has risen from twenty-five years in 1982 to thirty years in 2012 for men and from twenty-two years to twenty-eight years for women. The reduction in marriage rates have been partly, but not fully, compensated for by a rise in rates of cohabitation. More than three-quarters (78 per cent) of couples marrying in 2012 had cohabited prior to marriage and these rates are still rising (ABS 2012d).

9.2.2   Separating and divorcing more frequently

Marrying Australians are also more likely to divorce or separate than previously. In 2012, 49,917 divorces were granted and Australia's crude divorce rate per married population stands at 2.2 divorces per 1000 estimated resident population (ABS 2012d). From these trends, it is estimated that one in three Australian marriages will end in divorce (ABS 2010b). Divorce rates appear to have plateaued during the 2000s although, as the rate of marriage itself is declining, a stabilisation of the divorce rate does not necessarily reflect greater relationship stability. We do not know how many cohabiting relationships end in separation, and given that not all cohabiting relationships can be classified as similar in commitment to a marriage, even knowing this figure would not allow a true estimate of the breakdown of marriage or marriage-like relationships to be calculated.

Around half of all Australian divorces involve children under the age of eighteen years; in 2011 there were 24,144 divorces involving children under eighteen (ABS 2012d). Just over half of all marital separations occur in the first decade of marriage but the median duration of marriage is rising, increasing from 10.5 years in 1992 to 12.2 years 2012. This figure is slightly misleading as there is often a significant time lag between marital separation and divorce—a divorce cannot be granted within one year of formal separation. This time gap is demonstrated via the median duration of marriage to separation, which in 2012 was 8.6 years, nearly four years lower than the median duration of marriage to divorce. Over the last twenty years the proportion of joint applications for divorce has increased: in 2010 the number of joint applications outnumbered individual male and female applications for the first time, and in 2012, 40 per cent of all divorce applications were joint applications (ABS 2012d).

9.2.3   Separating marriage and childbearing

In the contemporary Australian family, marriage and childbearing are no longer automatically linked. This change is manifested across two areas: first, the rate of childlessness is rising. Using the proportion of women aged forty-five to forty-nine years who have not had children as an indicator of the level of childlessness, this rate was 14 per cent in 2006, up from 9 per cent in 1986 (ABS 2010a).

Second, the proportion of children born to women not in a registered marriage is rising. In 2012, of the nearly 310,000 births in Australia, around 65 per cent were to mothers in a registered marriage (nuptial birth) and the remainder were to mothers who were not legally married (ex-nuptial birth) (ABS 2012e). As shown in Figure 9.1, the proportion of

Figure 9.1   Births outside marriage as percentage of all births

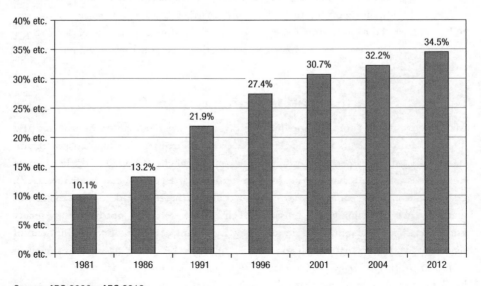

Source: ABS 2006e; ABS 2012e

ex-nuptial births has been rising over the last thirty years from just 10 per cent in the early 1980s to more than one-third of all Australian births in 2012. However, while the mothers of these latter babies may not be legally married to the father of the child, in over 90 per cent of these births the fathers formally acknowledged paternity. This finding correlates with research that has found that over 80 per cent of ex-nuptial births are to women in cohabiting relationships (Walter 2002). So, in contrast to common public perceptions, an ex-nuptial birth is not the same as being born into a sole-parent family; most of these children are being born into couple families.

Another common belief about ex-nuptial births is that many are to teenagers. Again the evidence suggests otherwise, although the picture is mixed. Ex-nuptial births to Australian women aged under nineteen years make up only around 17 per cent of the total number of ex-nuptial births. However, of the 11,000-plus births to teenagers in 2012, only around 600, or 6 per cent, were to teenagers in a registered marriage. And ex-nuptial babies to teenage mothers are slightly less likely to have paternity acknowledged (ABS 2012e). Most ex-nuptial births were to women aged between twenty and twenty-nine years. The median age of all mothers for births registered in 2012 was 30.7 years and the median age of first-time mothers was 29.1 years. The younger age of most ex-nuptial mothers indicates that mothers giving birth outside of a registered marriage tend to be younger than the average age of mothers as a group (ABS 2012e).

9.2.4   Increase in parenting apart

One consequence of these changing family patterns is a rise of parenting apart (Natalier et al. 2007). After dramatic changes to family patterns in the 1970s and 1980s, especially in the rise of sole parents, however, family forms in contemporary Australia are now relatively stable. As shown in Table 9.1, couple families with children are still the dominant family form in Australia. The proportion of one-parent families has also remained relatively stable since the 1990s and this trend is likely to continue. The ABS (2013k) projects that the proportion of one-parent families will increase only 1 percentage point as the proportion of all family types by 2031. The gender breakdown of sole-parent families, with 83 per cent of sole parents being women, is also not projected to change between now and 2031. The result is that more than one million Australian children have a parent living elsewhere. These children experience various living and parenting arrangements, with most living in sole-parent (particularly sole-mother) families and a minority living in blended or step-families. The changes in parenting patterns are also significant, with research finding that nearly 30 per cent of parents of children aged under eighteen years parent apart, as either resident or non-resident parents (Natalier et al. 2007). Being a sole parent, parenting largely apart from a child's other parent, is more than just another family type. Research from the Brotherhood of St Laurence indicates that nearly 40 per cent of sole-parent households experience social exclusion (Brotherhood of St Laurence 2013a).

Table 9.1   Patterns of Australian families, 1995–2011

Families with children aged under 15	1995 %	1999 %	2001 %	2006 %	2011 %
Couple families	81	79	78	79	79
Sole-father families	2	2	2	3	3
Sole-mother families	17	19	19	18	18

Note: Figures have been rounded to the nearest whole number.

Source: ABS 2006b; ABS 2013k

9.3   Theorising the changing family

Family-related change is intertwined with the changing social and economic terrain inhabited by Australian families. But the nature of this connection is not clear-cut. Are the trends, especially those relating to family breakdown and separation, culturally driven choices made at the individual level or are they another aspect of the wider social, economic and political transformation occurring within Australian society? The answer is that the two are inextricably interwoven and to attempt to unpick individual personal choice from structural and societal factors is probably a futile task. A determination to categorise the cause of family change as one or the other is also not necessarily sociologically productive. As Beck (2002:xxii) poignantly comments, the risks and contradictions of our lives continue to be socially produced but the duty and necessity of coping with those risks and contradictions are increasingly individualised.

Politically, the discourse is heavily weighted in favour of individual and culturally linked explanations. Certainly, the day-to-day impact of family change is experienced at the personal level. The data show that the social and individual bonds of partnering and kin relationships have become less permanent over the last few decades and family life events are no longer as rigidly sequenced. Giddens (1992) argues that society is experiencing a period of great social upheaval in the arena of personal relationships, with the majority of this upheaval situated in the site of our most personal relationships, the family. Emerging from under the pressure of female sexual emancipation and autonomy, contemporary Western societies such as Australia are experiencing a transformation of intimacy. All the old rules are now redundant. In their place the conduct of partner, parent-and-child and wider kin relationships must be constantly negotiated and renegotiated throughout life, or at least throughout the life of the relationship. The result is a democratisation of personal relationships. These 'pure relationships', as Giddens terms them, are now entered into for their own sake, 'for what can be derived by each person from a sustained association with another; and by both parties to deliver enough satisfactions for each individual to stay within it' (1992:58). Built on personal choice, the intimate partner relationship is also dissolved by personal choice if the relationship fails to deliver sufficient personal rewards. Separation and divorce trends in society, Giddens argues, are the result of the emergence of personal choice as the predominant guiding forces of intimate relationships as opposed to the social conventions and mores of the past.

Beck and Beck-Gernsheim (2002:8–12 & 83) similarly argue that individualisation increasingly characterises relations among family members. Using the social history of marriage to illustrate the newness of social individualisation processes, they show how the interpretation of marriage has moved from something beyond the individual to an exclusively individual one. In the premodern era, marriage, as a socially binding and prescribed way of life largely removed from individual choice, was a direct component of a stable social and hierarchical order. The prescribed nature of marital and other kin relations loosened with modernity and the separation of the family from the economic sphere. The contemporary outcome, according to Beck and Beck-Gernsheim (2002), is that marriage or partnership are now chosen and lived at one's personal risk. Family separation, breakdown and reformation at the personal level, along with increased diversity at the societal level, are integral to that choice and risk.

This outcome for individuals, families and households cannot be viewed in isolation from wider societal change. Contemporary relationships might be personally chosen and personally experienced but they remain firmly bound by social institutions. Beginning or ending an intimate relationship involves the legal system and the state. Legal processes distribute the partnership's assets and formalise, even decide, how children are supported and parented after relationship breakdown. Partner and family status, while intimate aspects of personal identity, are also of intense importance in an individual's relationship to the state. Access to social support, such as parenting payments after separation or a student loan, are directly impacted by family and relationship status. The process of leading independently chosen lives, say Beck and Beck-Gernsheim (2002:11), is heavily bound by the guidelines and rules of the state, the labour market and the bureaucracy. Increasingly, in liberal Western democracies such as Australia, it is also governed by the rules of the market.

It is here that the rapidly changing landscape of the Australian family is inextricably connected to wider social, economic and political change. Yet the contradictions in women's heightened expectations of equality and the reality of inequality are key factors (Giddens 1992; Beck & Beck-Gernsheim 2002). But women's changing expectations do not arise on their own. They are fundamentally connected to wider change, such as the rising participation of women, especially women with children, in the labour market. In turn the changing labour market is linked with the rise of the global market economy and the decline of the welfare state. In relation to family diversity, for example, while the major life events leading to sole parenthood occur at all levels of Australian society, relationship breakdown is more prevalent among Australians from the lower end of the socioeconomic spectrum. Related to this, it is women without postschool qualifications who are increasingly likely to have children outside marriage and the fathers of ex-nuptial children who are more likely to be unemployed than the fathers of nuptial children (Birrell 2000; Walter 2002).

9.4   Family as the site of social inequality

This dimensional complexity of the family is evident in the way the family is classified in its variation in form, the multiple pathways to its formation and in its interaction with the state at a range of levels. The social responses to the question 'What is a family?' also underpin and shape the diversity of the family as well as its role in creating and maintaining inequality.

Although family is such a central societal concept, just what is meant by the term in contemporary Australia is not straightforward. While few would argue that a married couple and their dependent children form a family unit, other family forms receive less uniform social acceptance. Do a couple without children constitute a family? If so, does this also apply to gay couples? Or, more puzzlingly, do people remain a family after the breakdown of relationships or do they split into multiple families? The term 'family' inevitably raises questions about where the boundaries of family start and end and whether such boundaries are fixed or whether they vary according to time, circumstances and context.

The contentious and perennial nature of these questions is linked to the fact that a 'family' only exists through its social recognition; the social acceptance that this particular group of individuals constitute a family unit. Though some may consider themselves to be a family, unless this understanding is broadly shared in the society in which they live, their family status will remain ambiguous at best (Walter 2004). The socially constructed nature of family is evidenced by its changing form and definitions throughout time and across cultures. In times of rapid family change, the social consensus of 'what a family is' becomes even more fragmented. As demonstrated by Figures 9.2 and 9.3, while agreement about the social standing of a married couple with children is uniform, attitudes towards the family status of sole parents and same-sex couples depends on the presence of children. Also, Australian men are less likely than women to regard any variation from the traditional married couple with children as a family.

Figure 9.2   Attitudes towards status of family forms with children, by gender

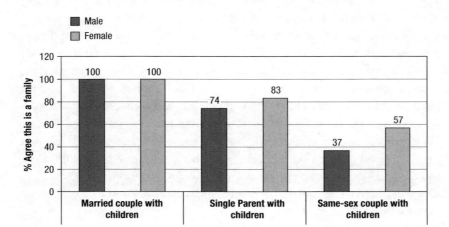

*Respondents who nominated the 'Can't choose' response omitted from analysis

Source: Australian Survey of Social Attitudes Dataset 2003

Figure 9.3   Attitudes towards status of family forms without children, by gender

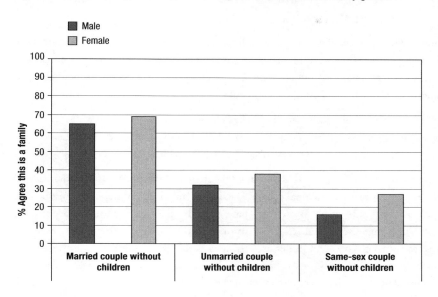

*Respondents who nominated the 'Can't choose' response omitted from analysis
Source: Australian Survey of Social Attitudes Dataset 2003

We might expect that attitudes towards which groups of people can be considered a family will have changed since 2003, but perhaps not as much as we would think. And these attitudes remain important because the question of what is a family has social-diversity and social-inequality implications. The title 'family' is not just a benign categorisation, it also brings with it access to a range of privileges. Apart from the positive social returns, elements of our legal system and welfare state legislation and policy contain core understandings of the rights and needs of the family. Within such systems, some forms of family are more equal than others. While some, such as gay couples, may be refused the title altogether, others, such as sole-parent families, will be regarded as a family but have a lesser status within the social hierarchy than do couple families (Walter 2004). Therefore, when social policy, the media or broader public debate talk about 'the family', the question of just what is meant by the term is important.

The interests and concerns of all family forms are not necessarily parallel. Defining family within certain parameters necessarily privileges some family forms and excludes, demotes or delegitimates the needs of others. Indeed, with the status of family linked so firmly to social benefits, the potential for a clash of interests between family types is high. Legislation that supports, say, married-couple families with a benefit such as income splitting for tax purposes, potentially entrenches the economic disadvantage of sole-parent families. Or in the case of separated parents, the interests of the non-residential and resident parents around issues of child-support payments, family payments and child-residency arrangements are often in direct competition (Walter 2004). Limited definitions of family or hierarchies of social privilege around family type have a very real effect on the way family is lived.

9.4.1　Family as a site of diversity and inequality: The micro level

The family, while perceived as an entity, is, by all definitions, constituted by two or more individual members. The individual level of family, while largely ignored in political and social commentary, is increasingly evident in any analysis of diversity and inequality. As Beck and Beck-Gernsheim (2002:90) comment:

> While the family used to occupy the whole field of vision, now men and women are becoming visible as separate individuals, each linked to the family through different expectations and interests, each experiencing different opportunities and burdens.

Children should also be included as individual members of families. This recognition of the family as comprising individual members is important from an inequality perspective given that there is substantial but clearly patterned diversity in the roles and duties of different family members. Gender is the primary determining factor in such patterns. The patterns of these roles and duties are reflected in the gender-differentiated social and economic circumstances of those members and also in the way they interact with the state. The likelihood of inequality of outcomes for the family's different members is also gendered. Research (Hewitt et al. 2006) suggests that marriage has larger health and wealth benefits for men than for women. Nor are family resources evenly or equally distributed within the family. Men continue to receive a greater share of such resources and have a greater capacity to have their wishes and needs prioritised.

9.4.1.1　Division of family labour

We don't just 'be' a family, we 'do' family. As sociologist David Morgan (1999) suggests: 'family' is a doing word. Doing family involves work, and the labour that must be invested in it is not shared equally—unpaid family work is still mostly women's work. Although Australian women are now in the labour market in unprecedented numbers, they still do a disproportionate amount of family work. Baxter (2002:13) found that the gendered division of family labour 'shows remarkable resilience in the face of dramatic changes in women's level of participation in paid employment'. Improved household technology and conveniences such as takeaway food have altered the shape but not the level of unpaid family work. Overall time spent on housework has fallen by about three hours per week in the last two decades but this has been more than replaced by a rise in the time devoted to caring for children by men and women (Bittman 1995; Baxter 2002; Craig 2002). Family work, especially when there are children in the family, is also much more than housework. Being a parent encompasses a set of tasks that go beyond cleaning and cooking, many of which are not easily measured. Delivering and collecting children to and from school and sporting events; responding to school notices; monitoring and supervision of homework, television programs, bed times and bathing; and spending quality time together, while integral aspects of family life, are also tasks. They involve substantial managerial and organisational skills and, again, it is women who primarily hold this administrative role, coordinating the life of the family and its individual members (Daly 2000; Beck & Beck-Gernsheim 2002).

The discrepancy between men's and women's household labour is obvious even if we only take direct hours of housework into account. Research indicates that full-time-working Australian women with children spend fifteen hours per week cooking and cleaning compared to six hours per week for men. The imbalance is greater if the woman is a part-time worker, with the same research indicating that women who work fewer than thirty-five hours per week) spend on average twenty hours per week on household tasks (AMP. NATSEM 2009).

Are things improving? Evidence suggests change but not necessarily more equality. While the incidence of men taking on the primary household role has certainly increased, in all Western countries, including Australia, the gendered division of labour remains fundamentally intact. Baxter (2002) found a convergence in the amount of time Australian men and women spend in unpaid domestic work over the last twenty years, a change that is not due to men taking on a greater share of domestic duties but to a reduction in the time spent on housework by women. Baxter concludes that a combination of increasing levels of labour-market participation by Australian women and changing household consumption patterns have led to changes in the way domestic labour is distributed, but have not changed its core inequality.

Beck and Beck-Gernsheim (2002:102) argue that the seeming intransigence of women's family workload in the face of a rapidly changing social order is more comprehensible if we consider how the allocation of private sphere tasks are 'closely bound up with the self-image and the life projects of men and women'. While a job, career and personal autonomy are now part of a woman's life project, for men, the change remains mostly 'conceptual'. Thus the question of who does what, while seemingly trivial at the individual task level (such as who cleans the bathroom), actually represents the split between the myth and reality of modernity for families at the macro level. Women, especially, are compromised when the promise of equality hits the reality of the daily experience of inequality within the family.

This conclusion is borne out by recent data showing the continuation of gendered inequality in the household division of labour. Hewitt et al. (2013), investigating Australian men's engagement in shared care and domestic work, found that Australian men continue to do fewer hours of unpaid domestic work, and that what they do is far more likely to involve outdoor tasks such as lawn mowing, car maintenance and taking out rubbish. Women, on the other hand, are more likely to do the laundry, household cleaning and shopping. The overwhelming majority of men involved in this study (95 per cent) reported that they were satisfied or very satisfied with their current domestic labour-sharing arrangements. Money was one factor that makes a difference. Baxter and Hewitt (2013) found that as women's earnings relative to their partner's earnings rise, they are likely to spend less time on domestic work. This may seem like a good arrangement, whereby those earning the least do the most household tasks. However, given that Australian women generally earn less than men, they are automatically in a weaker position from which to bargain on the level of household duties they undertake (Baxter & Hewitt 2013).

9.4.1.2   Financial and social costs

Unequal family task allocation incorporates significant costs and risks to the primary bearers of that unpaid labour. These costs are not just the result of inequalities within the family, but of those embedded in the wider social sphere. The rhetoric of equality, especially for women with family responsibilities, has not been accompanied by a change in structural social practices. Greater labour-market flexibility necessarily means less family flexibility and the scarcity and expense of social supports such as child care exacerbates the squeeze on those primarily responsible for family work. The result is significant inequality within the private and the public spheres. These costs and risks have moral and social dimensions as well as economic ones and reverberate throughout the life course.

In financial terms, the primary caring and domestic responsibility roles held by women come at a considerable cost. Economists Mathew Gray and Bruce Chapman (2001) conservatively estimate that a woman's lifetime earnings are reduced by around 34 per cent if she has one child by the age of twenty-five, and more for subsequent children. These costs are magnified by the less easily quantifiable wage penalties associated with reduced hours of paid work or absence from the workforce during the prime career-building years. Women can also find it difficult to re-enter the workforce, especially to a job of similar status and prospects to that occupied before having children. Economic research (Miller 1993) found that a history of part-time work limits a woman's consequent ability to obtain full-time employment.

Family work obligations also negatively impact on women's financial security in later life. Research evidence suggests that female employees have superannuation savings of less than half that of male employees (Gallagher 2001, cited in Olsberg 2005). This low level of savings is essentially attributable to women's role in rearing children, which normally requires years outside the paid workforce and/or high rates of part-time, casual and low-paid work during the childrearing years. The impact of these costs are summed up by journalist Ann Crittendon (2001:8) who posits that the huge gift of unreimbursed time and labour involved in family work 'explains in a nutshell why adult women are so much poorer than men'.

These inequities are magnified for women in the event of relationship breakdown. In the two-parent model, the costs incurred by the primary carer are informally remunerated through the financial and social support of the other parent—in essence, women swap their unpaid caring work for ongoing interfamilial support and access to the man's higher income now and over the life course. At separation, such arrangements become null and void and the financial risks of marital separation are heavily weighted against the spouse who was the primary carer. Property settlements, superannuation splitting and child support payments may assist, but the wealth of data on the highly disadvantaged position of many Australian women after divorce when compared to men indicate that these ameliorations are severely inadequate (Weston 1993).

9.4.1.3   Gendered division of labour: Winners and losers

The result of inequality is winners and losers, and while the losers of the gendered division of the labour are mostly women, the winners are more widespread. There is the direct benefit gained by other family members, but the state and the public sphere also benefit from an inequitable division of family labour. For the state, the clearest benefit is in the value to the economy of unpaid work performed, in the main, by women. The value of unpaid work in the Australian economy is calculated as equivalent to between 48 and 64 per cent of the gross domestic product (GDP), yet these tasks do not count in terms of GDP or national accounts. In economic terms, family work is deemed as private activity (undertaken privately, in the private sphere) and as such remains economically invisible. Questions about the value to society of child raising or who benefits from women's investment in family are not answered. More critically, the classification of family work as economic non-work allows the public-good benefits of children to be freely accessed by those who have not contributed to the costs. The state and the public sphere directly utilise the end product of such work, the next generation. In economic terms they are effectively free riding on the unpaid work performed in the family (Folbre 1994; Donath 1995; England & Folbre 1999).

The gendered division of labour is explained within economic theory as an earnings function. Becker (1981), in his household production model, contends that as women generally earn less than men it makes sense for the unpaid caring role in the household to be largely undertaken by mothers. The fact that in the vast majority of families it is the woman who holds the major domestic responsibilities and takes time out of the workforce to provide the unpaid caring work is viewed as merely indicating that this is the most sensible family choice. In such explanations, the wider issue of why women's earning functions are lower than men's is not addressed. Such reasoning disregards the inequitable financial, labour and opportunity outcomes of the unpaid family worker, who is still disproportionately an Australian woman.

9.4.2   Family as a site of diversity and inequality: The macro level

Clear patterns of inequality can also be seen between Australian families along socioeconomic and life-chances lines. Some types of families, such as sole-parent or Indigenous families, are much more likely to be poor, with a resultant diminution of life chances for their members. The relatively large number of sole-parent and Indigenous families reliant on welfare payments as their primary source of income means that many fall into the range below which most poverty lines are drawn.

The evidence on the trends in household inequality in Australia is mixed. Incomes are rising for poorer Australian families but the inequality gap between poorer and richer families is not decreasing. National data confirm that the economic pressure on Australian families, including low-income families, has eased over recent boom-time years. Real incomes rose between 1997–98 and 2004–05 for families with children who were situated in the bottom income quintile (McNamara et al. 2004). At the same time, the inequality gap between families from the bottom quartile and those higher up the income scale did not reduce. The National Centre for Social and Economic Modelling reports that most of the income increases for the low income group in recent years were the result of increasing transfer payments (such as family payments) rather than rises in employment or other non-government income. The research concludes that income increases for the bottom quintile of families do not necessarily translate into better standards of living given the higher impact of increased household expenditure on lower-income families (including the impact of the GST) that has occurred in this period.

9.4.2.1   Sole-parent families

Sole-parent families are an increasingly common phenomenon in Australian family life. Sole parenthood in Australia is mostly related to marriage breakdown, with around two-thirds of sole parents having been previously married to their child's other parent. As discussed earlier, the proportion of sole-parent families with children appears to have stabilised at around 20 per cent of all families. While these levels are estimated to stay the same over the next few decades, the current proportions are more than double the rate of 1975 (9 per cent; ABS 2006f). The change in the law to allow no-fault divorce in 1976 at least partly explains this rise—more couples who were in unhappy relationships were able to end those relationships. Regardless, on present indications, up to half of all Australian children will live in a sole-parent family at some point in their childhood.

Sole parenthood and poverty are firmly linked. Sole-parent families are heavily over-represented in low-income households and numerous studies demonstrate that they are consistently far more likely to live in poverty than other family types. More than 21 per cent of sole-parent families were classified as living in poverty in 2010 compared to 7 per cent of couple-with-children families (AIHW 2011a). It is important to distinguish between the experiences of persistent and transient poverty; the latter, while distressing, is ameliorated by a move away from poverty. The Australian Institute of Health and Welfare estimates that more than half of all sole-parent families with children experienced poverty for one or more years over the period of the study. However, only about 10 per cent of these families were in poverty for five or more years, suggesting that for many sole-parent families, poverty is temporary. The same study found that only 4 per cent of couple-with-children families were likely to experience poverty over the medium term (AIHW 2011a). Experience of poverty, even if temporary, has longer term consequences in that it prevents families from building net worth.

The relative poverty of Australian sole-parent families is a longstanding issue. The high incidence of sole-parent poverty was one of the most alarming findings of the 1972–73 Henderson inquiry into poverty, and the continuing high poverty levels of Australian sole parents are confirmed by recent data. A NATSEM study commissioned by the Smith Family (Harding & Greenwell 2001) found that while child poverty declined in the first half of the 1990s, it rose sharply in the second half. Sole parents were identified as the group most at risk of being in poverty.

The poverty of sole parents extends past monetary income into other areas of socioeconomic disadvantage such as housing, employment and social participation (ABS 2007a). Sole parents are far less likely to own or have a mortgage for their own home than couple parents and are far more likely to be in public or private rental accommodation: less than half (44 per cent) of sole parents own or are buying their own home, compared to more than three-quarters of couple parents. In contrast, more than 50 per cent of sole parents rent their accommodation compared to only 20 per cent of couple parents. Additionally, among parents who rent, sole parents are far more likely to be in public housing (Natalier et al. 2007). In 2009–10 the proportion of sole-parent families in social housing was three times that of other households, at 13 per cent. This figure is down from 16 per cent in 2000–01 (AIHW 2011a), but likely indicates a reduction in availability of public housing rather than a reduction in demand.

9.4.2.2   Gender and sole-parent poverty

Poverty among sole parents mostly refers to poverty among sole mothers. Sole fathers make up around 13 per cent of all sole parents with dependent children but are less likely than female sole parents to be in receipt of income support. Sole fathers are consequently likely to be financially better off than sole mothers, recording significantly higher average weekly incomes. This differential is explained to some extent by the greater labour-market participation of sole fathers, which in itself is linked to the tendency of sole fathers to be caring for older, often adolescent, children. Around three-quarters of sole fathers are in the labour force, compared to over 90 per cent of partnered fathers (ABS 2007a).

Yet this link between gender and poverty may not be as clear cut as it first appears. Sociologist Sheila Shaver (1998) argues that while gender is clearly central to continuing high levels of sole-parent poverty, such poverty stems as much from these parents' situation as sole carers of dependent children as from their sex. This claim is validated, she maintains, by poverty data that indicate that sole fathers are also more than usually likely to be poor. Shaver's claim is further borne out by a survey of 650 divorced Australians that showed that younger sole fathers emerged as the most disadvantaged group of men and, more importantly, the economic circumstances of these sole fathers reflected those of younger sole mothers (Weston & Smyth 2000). It appears, then, that in circumstances in which younger fathers' experience of sole parenthood resembles that of younger mothers (that is, having the sole care of younger children without the economic advantage of longer-term labour-market experience) then their levels of poverty are similar. This finding suggests it is the experience of sole parenthood itself, rather than gender, that leads to economic disadvantage: in other words, the sole responsibility for the care of young children rather than the gender of the sole parent is what negatively affects income-earning capacity. As Shaver (1998) notes, the sole parent who commits to full-time parenthood will by definition be poor unless they are able to call upon substantial non-income support resources.

Contemporary Australia

ONE IN SIX CHILDREN LIVE IN POVERTY

A recent report by the Australian Council of Social Services (ACOSS 2013) found that in 2010 one in six children were living at or below the poverty line in Australia (the figure for all ages in one in eight). These data correlate with a report by the Brotherhood of St Laurence (2006) that found that families from poorer suburbs are having more children than those from higher-income suburbs.

9.4.2.3   Indigenous families

Indigenous families sit at the base of the hierarchy of socioeconomic inequality. Making up less than 3 per cent of the Australian population, Indigenous people stand out for their sociodemographic differences and their broad experience of multilevel and clustered inequalities. The Indigenous population is young, with almost 40 per cent aged below fifteen—the median age is twenty-one years compared to thirty-seven years for the non-Indigenous population.

The reason for these demographic differences are twofold. The first is that Aboriginal and Torres Strait Islander people still have much lower life expectancy than non-Indigenous Australians. In Queensland, Western Australia, South Australia and the Northern Territory combined, where the records are best, nearly three-quarters of Indigenous men and nearly two-thirds of Indigenous women die before they reached the age of sixty-five years. In contrast, only around one-quarter of non-Indigenous men and 16 per cent of non-Indigenous women die before they reach this age (ABS 2010e). The result is that only 3 per cent of the Indigenous population is aged sixty-five years or over compared to 13 per cent of the non-Indigenous population. The ABS (2010c) estimates that Indigenous men and women aged thirty-five to fifty-four years die from diabetes at twenty-three and thirty-seven times, respectively, the rates of non-Indigenous people of the same ages.

The other reason for the young Indigenous population is higher fertility rates at younger ages. Indigenous women tend to have more children and at a younger age than non-Indigenous women: the current total Indigenous fertility rate is 2.7 births per woman compared to the national total fertility rate of around 1.9 (AIHW 2011b).

Among Indigenous families, 44 per cent are sole-parent families, nearly double the rate of the general Australian population, and Indigenous families are more likely to be multifamily households (6 per cent compared to 2 per cent), and more than twice as likely to have both parents unemployed.

Contemporary Australia

CLOSING THE GAP

In 2009 the Rudd Government launched the Closing the Gap Indigenous Policy Agenda. The policy set six goals to be achieved within one Indigenous generation and was committed to by all states and territories, with the prime minister to provide an annual report to parliament on progress. Following is how the goals were described in the first 2009 report:

> For the first time, the Australian Government, together with the states and territories through COAG, has set specific and ambitious targets to address

Indigenous disadvantage. The six key targets that form the Closing the Gap objective are to:

1   close the life expectancy gap within a generation
2   halve the gap in mortality rates for Indigenous children under five within a decade
3   ensure access to early childhood education for all Indigenous four-year-olds in remote communities within five years
4   halve the gap in reading, writing and numeracy achievements for children within a decade
5   halve the gap for Indigenous students in Year 12 attainment or equivalent attainment rates by 2020, and
6   halve the gap in employment outcomes between Indigenous and non-Indigenous Australians within a decade.

These agreed measures will form the baseline for measuring progress and reforms each year.

Source: Australian Government 2009a

The prime minister's 2013 report noted an increase in remote Indigenous pre-school enrolments, a reduction in the mortality rate for children under five years and higher levels of Grade 12 completion, but little change in reading, writing and numeracy, employment or life expectancy (Commonwealth of Australia 2013).

Socioeconomically and health-wise the differences between Indigenous and non-Indigenous families are grim. In contemporary Australia, for example, an Aboriginal and Torres Strait Islander child is still nearly three times as likely to die between the ages of one and four years as a non-Indigenous child (ABS 2010d). Indigenous children's physical, social and economic circumstances are also replete with hazards, resulting in disadvantage across every socioeconomic indicator. As outlined in earlier chapters, Indigenous households nationally are likely to be poor: over-represented in the lowest income brackets and under-represented in the top bracket. Most Indigenous families also live in rental housing (68 per cent) and 25 per cent live in what the ABS classifies as overcrowded conditions. This varies by location, with 58 per cent of very remote households overcrowded and 13 per cent of major city households overcrowded, a rate still three times the non-Indigenous equivalent (AIHW 2011b). Educationally, achievement disparity starts early. NAPLAN Grade 3 reading results (Australian Curriculum, Assessment and Reporting Authority 2012) show Indigenous children heavily over-represented in Band 1 (below national minimum standard) in every state and territory. Nationally, Indigenous children's reading results are nearly eight times as likely to be in this band as non-Indigenous children. Retention rates to Year 12 are rising (to 47 per cent in 2010) but remain well below retention rates for non-Indigenous youth (79 per cent) (AIHW 2011b).

Figures from the Australian Institute of Health and Welfare (AIHW 2011b) confirm that Australian Indigenous families endure:

- rates of infant mortality 2.5 times the national average
- twice the national rate of low-birth-weight babies
- youth suicide rates of up to five times the national rate
- higher rates of hospitalisation overall
- high rates of infection of communicable diseases.

Despite improvements, the infant mortality rate for Indigenous Australians is still three times the rate for non-Indigenous Australians and the perinatal death rate for Indigenous babies was 1.5 times that of other Australian babies (ABS 2010d). Indigenous infants are hospitalised at twice the rate of other infants and the maternal mortality rate for Indigenous women is also much higher—in 2008 it was five times the corresponding rate for non-Indigenous women.

It is not surprising, then, that Aboriginal people were more likely to report poorer self-assessed health than non-Indigenous Australians. In fact the ABS estimates that the burden of disease suffered by Indigenous Australians is two and a half times greater than the burden of disease in the total Australian population. Higher mortality is, therefore, matched by higher morbidity, especially relating to common diseases. Not only do Indigenous people experience health issues such circulatory diseases, diabetes, respiratory diseases, musculoskeletal conditions, kidney disease and eye and ear problems at a much higher rate than other Australians, they also tend to experience an earlier onset of disease than other Australians (ABS 2010c). The poor life outcomes from this high disease burn is exacerbated and linked to very high rates of self-harm. Self-harm is the highest cause of death from external causes for Indigenous males and the male suicide rate was almost three times that of non-Indigenous males, with the major differences occurring in younger age groups. The suicide rates for young Indigenous women are five times the corresponding age-specific rates for non-Indigenous females (ABS 2010c).

These grim life circumstances do not just, or even mostly, apply to Indigenous families living in remote communities. As noted, nearly 75 per cent of the Indigenous population is urban, with a full 30 per cent residing in Australia's major cities. Urban Indigenous lives are also predominantly lived in circumstances of all-encompassing poverty—looking at measures of financial stress, for example, around half of all urban Indigenous people are unable to raise $2000 within a week for something important, compared to 14 per cent of non-Indigenous people (Walter 2008).

The comparative disparity between urban Aboriginal and non-Aboriginal populations living in the same locations is demonstrated in Figure 9.4, which compares the Aboriginal and non-Aboriginal populations in Perth across housing indicators. As can be seen, vastly fewer Aboriginal people own their own home and much larger proportions reside in public housing. What is also evident from this figure is the smallness of the change in these housing indicators between 2006 and 2011. The other side of the table compares levels of overcrowding, the proportion of sole-parent families and multiple-family households. Again, Aboriginal families are nearly three times as likely to live in a house with six or more residents and around twice as likely to be a sole-parent family. The proportion of Aboriginal multiple-household families is higher than for the non-Aboriginal population, but by 2011 multiple-family households only made up about 6 per cent of Aboriginal households in Perth.

Figure 9.4   Aboriginal and non-Indigenous housing conditions in Perth, 2006 and 2011

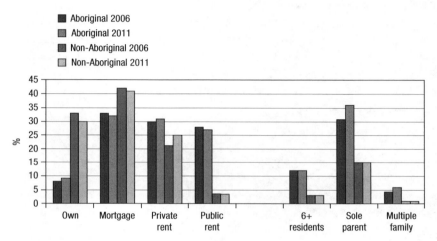

Source: Calculated from 2006 and 2011 census data

Contemporary Australia

○ ○ ○

CHANGING POLICY FOR FAMILIES WITH NEW CHILDREN

The baby bonus

In 2004 the federal government introduced the Maternity Payment ('baby bonus'), a lump sum paid to every mother on the birth of a child, which was widely perceived as an initiative to increase Australia's fertility rate. But, as the following media excerpts show, while all new mothers were eligible, public, media and political debate make it clear that the effect of some babies on the fertility rate ranked higher than others. The babies of teenage mothers, single mothers and Indigenous mothers were more likely to be defined as a social problem than a positive population outcome. A Queensland MP reported anecdotal evidence that the baby bonus scheme has resulted in a population explosion in Cape York Indigenous communities: 'More babies mean more classrooms, [it] means … larger health clinics and I'm not convinced that it is working. I just think that what we're doing is creating more problems for ourselves down the track', the MP was

(continued)

reported as saying (ABC 2007b). In 2006, under public pressure, the Coalition Government announced changes to the Maternity Payment scheme which meant that teenage mothers would no longer be paid the benefit in a lump sum; instead the funds would be paid in fortnightly instalments (ABC 2006b).

In 2013, the Gillard Labor Government replaced the baby bonus with a one-off increase in Family Tax Benefit Part A. Under these arrangements, the payment was reduced from $5000 to $2000 on the birth or adoption of a first child and from $3000 to $1000 for each subsequent child. The income threshold to qualify for these payments was also reduced from $150,000 to $101,000 for household income. This change was deemed to be more than compensated for by the introduction of the Paid Parental Leave scheme (Wade 2013; Department of Human Services 2014d).

Paid Parental Leave

In January 2011, the Paid Parental Leave (PPL) scheme was introduced. The scheme, which is funded through the federal government, was the first ever national parental leave scheme in Australia—it provided a period of paid leave from the workforce for the primary carer after the birth of a child. The PPL was established with three key aims: to enhance the health of babies and mothers by enabling working mothers to spend longer at home with their newborns; to facilitate women's labour-force participation; and to encourage gender equity and improve the work balance of family life. Before the PPL was introduced, just over half of Australian working mothers were entitled to some paid leave after the birth of their child, with around three-quarters eligible for unpaid leave from their employer. To be eligible for leave a person must:

- be the primary carer of a newborn or recently adopted child
- meet the Paid Parental Leave work test
- meet the Paid Parental Leave income test
- be on leave or not working.

The work test is that the claimant must have worked at least ten of the thirteen months before the birth or adoption, with the minimum number of hours worked in that period set at 333 (just over one day per week). The income test is that the claimant must have received income of $150,000 or less in the year before the birth or adoption. Under the PPL eligible parents are paid the equivalent of the national minimum wage, which in mid-2014 was $641.05 per week, for a maximum of eighteen weeks.

The incoming Abbott Government promised to introduce a more generous scheme, to be funded by a levy of 1.5 per cent on large companies (those with a taxable income in excess of $5 million). The plan was that this scheme would keep the same eligibility as the PPL scheme, but be paid over twenty-six weeks and would pay eligible claimants at the rate of their actual pre-birth wage or the national minimum wage, whichever was greater, plus superannuation (Coalition 2013).

9.5   Social exclusion and intergenerational disadvantage

Insufficient income is not a complete measure, nor the most accurate, of household inequality. Rather, cash income operates as a relatively diffuse and inaccurate proxy (see Chapter 4); in recent years the concept of social exclusion has been understood as encompassing broader dimensions of disadvantage. Social exclusion basically refers to the tendency of social and economic disadvantages—unemployment, discrimination, low work and other skills, low income, poor housing, high crime rates, ill health and family breakdown—to cluster and impact on the same families, households and neighbourhoods. Measuring social exclusion rather than just income poverty is particularly useful as it takes into account the multidimensional aspects of inequality and also reflects the tendency of disadvantage and inequalities to cluster (as do privilege and advantage) around subgroups within populations.

The research on the level of social exclusion in Australia is relatively limited to date. One study (Daly et al. 2006) developed a social exclusion index based on the attributes of statistical local areas (SLAs) from the 2001 census. The index incorporates indicators such as family type, parental level of education, occupation and labour force status, housing tenure, household personal computer usage and access to a motor vehicle. The analysis revealed that children residing in rural and regional Australia are at a higher risk of social exclusion. State of residence was also important: one-third of children aged under fifteen in Tasmania and one-quarter in Queensland living in SLAs fell into the bottom decile of the social exclusion index. Within these groupings, living in a sole-parent household where the parent was not in the labour force was the most significantly affecting factor. Families where no member had completed Year 12 and where no one had used a personal computer in the last week were also more vulnerable to social exclusion (AIHW 2005).

Contemporary Australia

FAMILIES AND SOCIAL EXCLUSION

Item 1

The social exclusion monitor, developed by the Brotherhood of St Laurence and the Melbourne Institute of Applied Economic and Social Research, uses data from the annual Household, Income and Labour Dynamics in Australia (HILDA) survey. The 2011 results found that more than one million Australians deal with deep social exclusion. Deep social exclusion is defined as experiencing at least four different sorts of disadvantage, including being on a low income, having little work experience, not being involved in community clubs or associations and not being

(continued)

socially active. Deep exclusion varies across the population; the 2011 analysis found the following characteristics:

- women are more likely to be excluded than men
- half of people over sixty-five experience exclusion
- exclusion is more common among immigrants than native-born Australians
- half of Indigenous Australians experience social exclusion
- more than half of the Australians who have a disability or long-term health condition experience social exclusion
- early school leavers are much more likely to experience exclusion than those with a diploma or degree
- around 40 per cent of single people and sole parents experience social exclusion
- public housing tenants experience social exclusion at more than twice the rate of people living elsewhere.

Source: Brotherhood of St Laurence 2013b

Item 2

Another Australian study (Saunders et al. 2007) found that deprivation, defined as an enforced lack of socially perceived essentials, was highest among sole-parent families. Over half this group was unable to afford dental check-ups for themselves or their children, nearly 40 per cent reported being unable to buy prescribed medication or to fund a hobby or leisure activity for children, and 28 per cent were unable to fund school or school activities for children. Similar to the Brotherhood of St Laurence study, this study found that it was sole parents, along with Indigenous Australians, who rated high levels of social exclusion. Nearly two-thirds of sole parents reported being unable to afford child care, and nearly half reported having less than $500 in emergency funds.

The degree of intergenerational disadvantage reproduced among children growing up in poorer families is of significant interest to policy makers and social commentators. The neoliberal discourse around welfare dependency (see Chapter 5) posits the likelihood of intergenerational transmission of a culture of poverty and dependency as a central concern. In analysing intergenerational disadvantage, it is the extent to which families continue to experience poverty over time rather than the proportions at any given time that is the key indicator. In other words, what is the level of persistent poverty among families as opposed to the proportions of families experiencing temporary or episodic poverty? The relatively late commissioning of longitudinal surveys in Australia makes the answer to this question tentative. Research indicates that while household poverty in one year is not necessarily indicative of continuing household poverty, a significant number of Australian families experience persistent poverty.

As discussed in Chapter 8, the most significant factor for predicting persistent poverty is the labour-force status of the parent(s). Parental movement into or out of the labour force is associated with movements of families into or out of poverty in any one year. Similarly, Marks (2007), in analysing several waves of the longitudinal HILDA data, found that the proportion of households in income poverty in successive years is much lower than the proportion in poverty in a single year. While this suggests that much family poverty is temporary rather than permanent, data from a much longer period of time are needed to ascertain how many households that move out of poverty stay out of poverty in subsequent years.

A lack of regular parental employment is a key factor in explaining family poverty. Political concern about 'workless families', as they are dubbed in the political discourse, is a topical and relatively recent issue; the ABS began to collect data and to use this term only from 1997. Associated social policies around welfare-to-work legislation reflect the broad political concern that children growing up in workless families will be without an employment role model. The feared consequence is that they will be more likely to be without work and to be welfare dependent themselves in adult life.

9.6   The policy context of family inequality

The connection between the political realm and the social reality of family is an essential element in the link between family diversity and inequality, a link that can be seen at two levels: inequality within the family and inequality between families. Political imperatives and consequent policy are overlaid with the ideological and moral discourses around family.

9.6.1   Inequality within families

As discussed, the gendered division of labour is central to inequality within the family. The performance of the majority of unpaid labour within the home penalises women financially and careerwise. The impact that dominant discourses on family and their policy extensions have on this inequality is evident in the effects on the labour-market participation of Australian mothers. A decision to re-enter or remain in the labour market after having a child is not purely about an individual woman's decision; rather, such decisions and the ability to make them are directly impacted by both family-related policy and its underpinning discourses. Most directly, the social provision of tangible supports such as child care is critical. Without access to affordable and suitable child care, a woman's options for returning to the workforce after the birth of a child are greatly reduced. Similarly, the level of access to maternity payment or maternity leave can make a decision to return to employment a supported option or a virtual impossibility.

Less direct in their effect, but equally important, are the dominant social beliefs around the acceptability of combining family obligations and paid work. Australian social attitudes towards maternal labour-force participation tend to be conservative in contrast to other industrialised nations. Evans (2000) reports that Australia ranks twentieth out of twenty-four industrialised nations in social approval of workforce participation of mothers with dependent children. Such beliefs are not equally distributed within the social strata. A woman or family's social milieu is important here, with professional and middle-class women more likely to consider employment and motherhood to be compatible. In a circular relationship, political support for maternal workforce participation in arenas such as provision of maternity leave or child care is influenced by family discourses, and in the last decade the dominant political attitude has been socially conservative.

preference theory Posits that most women in modern societies have a real choice to favour either the private or the public sphere.

The work of British sociologist Catherine Hakim has been particularly influential in Australia. According to Hakim's **preference theory** (2000), most married women now reject the 'egalitarian idealism' of the same roles for husbands and wives, with the majority taking less demanding jobs than their partners so that they can concentrate on child rearing. Hakim argues that the vast majority of women in modern countries now have real choices 'between a life centred on private, family work and a life centred on market work or other activities in the public sphere' (2000:2). Under preference theory women are categorised into three main types:

- work-centred women, who have no children or want to return to work quickly once they have had children
- home-centred women, who regard child rearing as their most important job and who tend to stay out of the labour market after they have children
- adaptive women (the majority of women), who try to balance the two roles by dipping in and out of the workforce.

Public policy, which favours home-centred women, will expand this group to 'its maximum size, will persuade most adaptive women to give priority to family life over other activities, and will probably reduce the size of the work centred group to its smallest size' (Hakim 2000:10).

Hakim's theories were prominent in policy developed in the early 2000s that explicitly privileged couple families with a primary, predominantly home-based carer over other family types. Many types of families, including single-parent and dual-earner families, were eligible for social support, but payments such as the Family Tax Benefit B gave markedly higher benefits to couples qualifying on the basis of a single income. Family Tax Benefit B and the new maternity allowance are paid regardless of the father's income. In contrast, Child Care Benefit is severely income tested against the income of both parents. These types of policies formally encourage partnered mothers to move out of the labour market to concentrate on mothering duties. The introduction of the Paid Parental Leave scheme, by refocusing policy on working mothers, has altered this policy landscape to a situation where families in which both parents work (even if the mother is more likely to be working part-time) are now privileged in social policy.

9.6.2   Inequality between families: Sole- and couple-parent families

Much policy support disappears if partnered women become single parents. Social support of Australian families at the material and attitudinal level is highly reliant on the social and partnered category that the family fits within. Under policy moves over the last fifteen years, sole parents have been reclassified from being parents first to workers first. Mutual obligation principles have been increasingly applied to mandate labour-market participation. Paradoxically, despite the increasingly widespread nature of sole parenthood, in the shifting political and public discourse, it is increasingly defined as problematic. With women heading more than 80 per cent of sole parent families, the problem of sole parenthood mostly means the problem of sole motherhood.

Contemporary Australia

○ ○ ○

MUTUAL OBLIGATION AND SOLE PARENTS

In July 2006 the federal government's welfare-to-work policy measures came into effect. Under this legislation, sole parents whose youngest child is aged eight years or over were no longer eligible to apply for an income-support payment linked to their sole-parent status. Instead, they had to apply for Newstart Allowance and be obliged to seek at least fifteen hours of part-time work per week. Further changes in January 2013 saw these eligibility requirements applied to those who had had their status grandfathered on the pre-2006 eligibility. The result was that a further 100,000 sole parents moved from Parenting Payment Single to Newstart Allowance; a move that reduced payments, had a harsher means test and reduced income tax concessions. The mutual obligations of the new payments were backed up by breaching sanctions for those on welfare payments. In a survey of 500 sole parents affected by the changes in 2013, they reported being between $60 and $160 worse off per week and that they were struggling to raise their children. Half of respondents reported being unable to afford fresh food, while a third struggled with medical costs (ABC 2014c).

The changes in the dominant discourse surrounding sole mothers over the last thirty years is mirrored in changing policy responses. The introduction of no-fault divorce and sole mothers' payments in Australia in the 1970s made it possible for mothers to be independent. From this perspective, it was the poverty of sole-parent families, rather than sole motherhood itself, that constituted the major social policy problem. In retrospect this period was brief. From the late 1980s onwards, the dominant discourse surrounding sole mothers became increasingly negative. Poverty concerns were eclipsed by alarm over the rising number of sole mothers, the level of public expenditure, their lack of involvement in the labour market and perceived links between cycles of low education achievement, criminality and single parenthood.

The changing discourse and associated policy places sole mothers in a contradictory and difficult position. While neoliberalist economics advocate reversing the growth of the welfare state and self-reliance through market work, a reassertion of the caring responsibilities of the family are also prescribed (O'Connor, Orloff & Shaver 1999). Sole mothers stand outside this dominant paradigm. Their reliance on the state, as opposed to the 'legitimate' spousal dependence of partnered mothers, places them at odds with family policy, while their ongoing mothering obligations clash with a reform agenda that reinforces the supremacy of the market. In the division between work and welfare, raising a child alone is no longer deemed work. The changing social policy framework impacts on women according to motherhood and partnered status (Bryson 1992). The position of partnered women under family policies increasingly encourages the primacy of motherhood for this group; for unpartnered women, welfare policy is the dominant framework.

9.6.3   Inequality between families: Indigenous families

Indigenous families have also been singled out in policy terms. The federal government's wide-ranging intervention into Indigenous communities in the Northern Territory was claimed to be needed because of the territory government's apparent lack of response to the ninety-seven recommendations in the Patricia Anderson and Rex Wild *Little Children Are Sacred* (2007) report into child sexual abuse in Aboriginal communities. The intervention (or, as it is now renamed, 'Stronger Futures') is still in place in more than seventy-three communities in the Northern Territory and includes widespread alcohol restrictions, quarantining of welfare payments, health checks for children, involuntary five-year leases on townships, increased policing in particular townships and the scrapping of the permit system for Aboriginal land. Despite the common concern about Indigenous child abuse, none of these specific measures were recommended by the Anderson and Wild report (Anderson & Wild 2007). The intervention, cast as a national emergency, was led by the military and paid no heed to the history of reports, submissions and urgent pleas for action on child sexual abuse, mostly by Aboriginal people, that had been politically and publicly ignored in the thirty years prior. The question is not whether intervention is needed; the question is why this intervention involved the elements it did and why Aboriginal families were subject to punitive unilateral policy such as the quarantining of half of their social welfare payments on the basis of race, rather than on their parenting abilities.

The national emergency rhetoric provided a justification for such unilateral action and, as anthropologist Melinda Hinkson (2007) points out, grounded the crisis in the present, thereby precluding examination of past inaction and chronic lack of infrastructure and support services. Attempts to question the discourse or the policy were labelled as supporting either child abuse or a regime of failed policy. The intervention, which took place in the context of comparable child sexual abuse elsewhere, also represents an implicit ideological statement that Indigenous families are different to non-Indigenous families and can therefore be treated differently—that is, treated less well. Such difference and 'Othering' justifies such radical actions as the suspension of the *Racial Discrimination Act 1975* (Cth) to allow the Northern Territory intervention and the introduction of specifically race-based policies.

The evaluation report of the intervention states that there were eleven convictions for child sexual assault committed in the seventy-three NTER communities in 2011, a rate very similar to the eleven recorded in 2007, the eleven recorded in 2008 and the twelve recorded in 2010. That adds up to forty-four convictions during the four postintervention years, compared to twenty-five in the four years prior (Northern Territory Emergency Response 2011:277). Thus, while the number of convictions have increased in the seventy-three communities under the NTER, most communities record no convictions in any given year. What has changed dramatically is the number of child protection substantiations for Indigenous children, which grew by nearly 140 per cent in the years after 2007 (Northern Territory Emergency Response 2011:27).

9.7   Conclusion

Australian families are experiencing unprecedented levels of change in shape, patterns of formation and parenting arrangements. The result is a terrain of family that is more diverse but, as the evidence in this chapter indicates, still retains its traditional (and perhaps has added new) divisions of social inequality. The link between increasing diversity within and without families and inequality is intertwined with the dominant discourses of family and the consequent relationships between different members of the family and different types of family with the state. Not all family members or all families are equal within these discourses and their consequent positions in social status and within social policy reflects this inequality.

Critically, while patterns of family inequality can be linked to increasing family diversity, especially the rising number of sole-parent families, these material outcomes are not automatic. Rather, they are the result of how such families are perceived and the level of social privilege or disapprobation attached to them. Dominant discourses and their moral and ideological underpinnings play out in views on the legitimacy of different family types and the consequent perceptions about the legitimacy or illegitimacy of their access to social resources. And despite—or perhaps because of—the massive social changes experienced around family, those most at risk of poor access to social resources, and of being deemed less legitimate in their claims, remain the same traditionally unequal groups: women within families, sole-parent families and Indigenous families.

The combination of neoliberal economic policy and social conservatism means that the sociopolitical response to changing family demographics has seen a resurgence in support for the traditional two-parent family organised along defined and gender-related caring and labour-market lines. This dominant discourse of the traditional family, which places the family at the centre of social support, makes little acknowledgment of the mutual interaction between family and labour-market status. The social and political emphasis on family as the centre of care and nurture is in direct conflict with policies such as the welfare-to-work legislation and the thrust of the *Intergenerational Report* (2002), which envisaged married women entering the labour market in ever-increasing numbers to help redress the worker–retiree imbalance that is now emerging. Increasing the role of women in the labour market is also at odds with the neoliberal-related retreat from state provision of services in areas such as child care.

This means that Australian women in families are under increasing pressure. Women are exhorted to participate in the labour market and contribute to their family economically, to raise the Australian fertility rate by having more babies and to prioritise their family care-giving and unpaid labour. The result is an inequitable squeeze on families, particularly on women, with consequent economic inequalities that ripple through the life course in terms of career options, superannuation and the less measurable aspects such as limiting of life course options and choices. The beneficiaries of these inequalities are not just other individual members of families but also the state and the private sector, who directly reap the public good benefits of women's unpaid labour.

There has also been a hardening of the dichotomy between partnered and unpartnered mothers, despite the majority of sole parents in Australia having been previously married. This changing discourse correlates with the rising dominance of the ideologies and political forces of neoliberalism. With need and deservingness now defined in market terms of economic independence and self-reliance, sole mothers form a highly visible group. High levels of income support are taken as evidence of sole mothers' position in the socially and morally damaging culture of welfare dependence, for which increased labour-market activity is proposed as the remediation. For Indigenous families, deprivation is taken as evidence of moral and family failure. In the Northern Territory such representation has seen the suspension of the *Racial Discrimination Act* to allow for the introduction of race-based social policy.

While Australia has undergone large-scale political and economic restructuring, a lot of the factors currently feeding family inequality appear to be related to lack of change. Dominant discourses and social responses to aspects of family do not appear to be changing, or at least not at the same pace as other economic and social arrangements. The gendered division of family work, and social and political attitudes around family status and their associated privileges and deprivations, remain firmly in place.

Discussion questions

1   In your words, define the term 'family'? Identify three reasons why the family is a site of significant social inequality.

2   How have Australian family formation patterns and living arrangements altered over time? Give examples of how family formation patterns are continuing to change.

3   Baxter found that the gendered division of family labour showed 'remarkable resilience in the face of dramatic changes in women's level of participation in paid employment'. What does she mean by this and how can you explain it?

4   What are the main dimensions of inequality between Australian families? To what extent are these clustered around particular families? Why is this occurring?

10

○

PLACE AND SPACE: LOCATIONAL INEQUALITY

○

10.1 Introduction

The places and spaces Australians occupy define and shape identity and life choices. Spaces and places are also vital factors in defining and shaping life chances and trajectories. Where people live, in which house, region or suburb and in which state, and their relationship to their locale and dwelling are core components in understanding the patterning and distribution of social inequality. City and country are not equal in relation to employment and educational opportunities, and spatial inequality is clearly visible between different suburbs of the same city. Similarly, renting and home ownership are not equal forms of housing tenure.

This chapter examines how inequality is manifested across spatial dimensions. It directly addresses the first, third and fourth organising questions of this book, identifying the inequalities related to the geographies of where and how Australians live. Social, political, economic and symbolic resources are spatially distributed, and spatially patterned divisions can be observed across an array of fields. Overlaying these patterned divisions is the observable impact of globalisation. Manifesting in diverse areas, such as rising housing prices and the impact of the postindustrial society in determining divisions of disadvantage and privilege between urban and rural areas and within cities and towns, globalisation is sharply aligned with spatial and geographic inequality. Location and place are also essentially connected with the subjectivities of inequality. The specific spaces and places that people occupy are central to how they view themselves and how others perceive and treat them. Such subjectivities also contribute to feelings of belonging and community. These three elements all have strong connections and at times overlap, but discrete and specific patterns of inequality are evident in each dimension.

10.2   Geographies

The identifiable spatial aspects of inequality are directly observable in the way an individual's or a social group's spatial location influences the level of resources they are able to access. The economic and social circumstances and options of Australians vary significantly by region and geographic location. These locational inequality facets operate at two different, but related, levels. Locational inequality can be linked directly to the place. Some locations have a set of characteristics—remoteness, poor transport and communications services, lack of or decline of local industries and services—that are disadvantageous to all who reside there. Other areas, advantaged by high-quality services and transport, plentiful employment and educational options and their populations, endow their residents with advantages.

Locational inequality can also be a reflection of broader entrenched inequality within a society. Suburbs such as Mosman in Sydney and Toorak in Melbourne are advantaged not just because they are well-placed suburbs with all the attributes such a location brings, but also because they are selected as preferred areas of residence of the economic and social elite. Similarly, areas of high public housing in the south-western suburbs of Sydney, such as Macquarie Fields, are disadvantaged not just because of their location but also because they reflect the high level of social and economic disadvantage of the residents who are housed there. Spatial inequality also displays strong clustering tendencies in its distribution.

10.2.1   Between communities: The rural–city divide

One key dimension of geographical inequality can be found in comparative material well-being. In 2012, 70 per cent of the Australian population lived in major cities, 18 per cent in inner regional areas, 9 per cent in outer regional areas, and just over 2 per cent in remote or very remote areas in Australia (ABS 2013l). Research indicates a growing income disparity between the majority of Australians living in capital cities and those in the rural and regional areas, with incomes on average about 20 per cent higher in capital cities than in non-metropolitan regions. ACOSS (2013) reports that only a third of Australians live outside metropolitan areas yet eighteen of the twenty electorates in Australia with the lowest household incomes are outside the capital cities. The largest differences were in New South Wales and Victoria, where the capital city incomes were around 25 per cent higher than mean incomes across the rest of each state (ABS 2013l). Income disparity is not just about lower incomes overall, but also about a disparity in the proportion of low-income households in city versus regional and rural areas. Around one in six people living in capital cities in 2009–10 lived in lower income households, compared with one in four people living in non-metro areas (AIHW 2013). A key explanation of the income differentials between city and country is the concentration of education, employment and other opportunities in cities, meaning that younger people, especially those with better education and job prospects, are likely to move from regional to urban areas.

Within this broad city-rural divide there is considerable diversity; regional areas are not uniformly disadvantaged. Different levels of inequality are experienced by different areas in different states and territories; patterns of inequality can also be distinguished among communities and regions. A tool the ABS uses to assess summary patterns of spatial inequality is the Socio-Economic Indexes for Areas (SEIFA), which ranks areas according to relative socioeconomic advantage and disadvantage. Socioeconomic data from the 2011 census found Peppermint Grove, a suburb of Perth, Western Australia, was Australia's most advantaged followed by Ku-ring-gai in New South Wales. Australia's most disadvantaged local government areas were Yarrabah and Cherbourg in Queensland (ABS 2013m), both which have predominantly Indigenous populations. It is also not coincidental that both of these areas were until relatively recently government-run reserves for Indigenous people. SEIFA scores allow analyses of other inequality measures by region; for example, Doughney (2002) established that poker machines are disproportionately located in more disadvantaged areas.

Reasons for the disparity in income levels and levels of social dependency between cities and regions are multiple but relate fundamentally (for non-Indigenous areas at least) to changes in the economy. Economically, small towns, regional centres and remote locations suffer from a lack of government and non-government services, most obviously manifested in education, health and transport facilities, as well as banking and other community services. The 1980s and 1990s in particular were periods of labour-market restructuring that resulted in a significant decline in the level and quality of jobs in regional areas. It was also a period of rationalisation of government and private services that saw the demise of many services in these areas, such as banks, schools and hospitals. In other locations, such as the outskirts of the major cities, service infrastructure has not kept pace with rapidly rising populations (Lloyd et al. 2000). Lack of accessible services in an area and inadequate social and economic infrastructure operate to exacerbate the inequality outcomes of low income and low socioeconomic status.

Demographic influences are also important. Australians are relatively mobile, especially after they retire from the labour market. One survey (Jackson & Walter 2007) found that more than one-third of older workers in Australia intend to move to a new location on retirement. Population ageing in Australia has been accompanied by significant shifts in the areas in which older people reside. Coastal towns, in particular, are often seen as desirable and more affordable locations for retirees and others seeking a different lifestyle. The result can be a significant influx of fixed-income and/or welfare-dependent residents. The Queensland coastal town of Hervey Bay, for example, while having one of the fastest growing regional net populations in Australia, also has relatively few people aged between twenty and twenty-nine, but relatively more in the fifty-to-eighty-year age group. Most of this older group are no longer in the workforce and have migrated to the region in recent years. As a consequence the region has a significantly higher welfare-dependency ratio than other areas of the state.

Health also has a locational dimension. Research has established that low socioeconomic status is a relatively strong predictor of early mortality (Turrell & Mathers 2000). Those living in areas with lower SEIFA scores have considerably lower ratings of excellent or very good health and considerably higher ratings of poor or fair health. The reverse is true for those living in higher scoring areas.

10.2.2   Between communities: The state divide

The inequality gap between regional/rural and metro areas can also be observed between states. The different population density of different states is important here because lower populations can equal access to fewer services and, conversely, high populations can attract more services as well as more business and other investment.

Not only do the states and territories vary significantly by size of population (see Figure 10.1), there is also wide divergence between households' incomes. The national average equivalised disposable household income in 2011–12 was $918 per week. State-by-state, the highest average equivalised income households are in the Australian Capital Territory ($1144), followed by Western Australia ($1017) and the non-remote areas of the Northern Territory ($1012). In contrast, households in Victoria have equivalised disposable household incomes 4 per cent below the national average; in South Australia they are 8 per cent below the national average; and in Tasmania household incomes are 15 per cent below the average (ABS 2013l).

Figure 10.1   Australian population by state, 2012

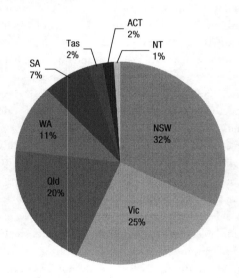

Source: AIHW 2013

Contemporary Australia

TASMANIA: LOW INCOME, HIGH WELFARE

In analyses of household income and income distribution in Australia, Tasmania has long held the lowest ranked position. The latest analysis (ABS 2013l) places

Tasmania at the bottom of the states and territories across a range of wealth and income indicators. The gross mean weekly household income in Tasmania is only around 61 per cent that of the ACT, and around 78 per cent of the national figure. Similarly, Tasmania has the second lowest mean household net worth of all states (just behind Queensland and South Australia).

There are a number of related reasons why Tasmania holds this unenviable position. First, the population in Tasmania is relatively older than the national population. Its median age is forty years compared to thirty-seven years at the national level. This older population is a result of fewer migrants moving to Tasmania and the movement of younger, often more skilled, people out of Tasmania for employment opportunities. The Tasmanian population also has low (by national standards) education levels. Tasmania's apparent retention rate to Year 12 is around 64 per cent compared to around 76 per cent for all Australian youth.

These factors, combined with the downturn in heavy industry, led to nearly a third of Tasmanian households being reliant on welfare payments as their primary source of income. In contrast, just over half of Tasmanian households rely on wages and salaries as their primary source of income, the lowest proportion in the nation.

10.2.3   Within communities: Geographies of division

An aspect of emerging location divisions is the decreasing level of sociospatial contact between different groups within society; that is, there is a growing spatial mismatch in the areas where the rich and the poor reside in our cities. Gentrification of inner cities in combination with nearby traditionally higher status suburbs means that the rich now increasingly live in enclaved wealthy areas. Conversely, the poor can no longer afford to live close to central business districts and are increasingly marginalised in the periphery. As a consequence, most cities now contain very few areas where the rich and the poor brush up against each other. One outcome, Atkinson (2006) argues, is a mutual invisibility of affluence and poverty and a magnification of inequality and division within our cities. Similarly, Baum et al. (2005) refer to mosaics of socioeconomic advantage and disadvantage within our cities that are punctuated by sharp faultlines. They conclude that advantaged and disadvantaged localities tend to be differentiated by how they have been affected by the changing structure of the Australian economy. Some have benefited from the changing nature of work and the new economic mix, whereas others have suffered from the loss of jobs, especially in the manufacturing industries, and a lack of resources or skills to access the new opportunities.

The most obvious manifestation of the growing spatial divide between rich and poor residents is the rising use of insulating devices by the wealthy; these include private streets and gated communities, residential areas that use physical mechanisms to exclude outsiders. Typically, a gated community has a single controlled point of entry, walls, fences or other dividers such as water in canals to delineate the area from the outside environment, and usually incorporates private security services to ensure residents have privacy and security.

Gated communities are becoming increasingly common around the world, including, in more recent times, in Australia. Sanctuary Cove, which opened around twenty five years ago on the Gold Coast, was Australia's first gated community, but many others have since been built, most of them in Queensland.

The spatial boundaries of a gated community are enforced by more than physical barriers. Social distinctions are also used to maintain distance between the wealthy inhabitants and others. Rofe examines the gated community of Sovereign Islands in Queensland and proposes that in this island-based enclave sociospatial exclusion is established not just by the single entry point and visible security personnel, but also by the more 'subtle creation of landscapes of wealth. These landscapes so imbued with a sense of prestige and wealth' that they 'arguably initiate a process of "self-othering" among those beyond their margins' (2006:309). Non-residents, by their lack of observable comparable wealth, are made to feel that they have no right to be there.

Contemporary Australia

MANAGING RESIDENTIAL RISK

Here is an advertisement for land at Long Island, a gated community being built at the northern end of the Gold Coast. The advertisement stresses the security and safety of the new gated community as being central to its lifestyle advantages. Though not explicitly stated, security and safety in this context is about the strict control of who can and cannot enter the suburb. Only those who belong, either as residents or approved visitors, can expect to be granted entry. As can be gleaned from the advertisement, the size, design and construction materials of the housing on the estate are also tightly controlled.

LONG ISLAND

Looking for a new address? Then look no further. Long Island is the last gated community in the prestigious estate of Windaroo. With golf course frontage sites, this estate offers an excellent lifestyle.

Long Island will be distinctive through its characteristics of liveability, security, safety, privacy, and a unique and controlled style in building and landscape design. Long Island has developed a covenant/design guide to ensure investment protection and enhancement of your investment. Design is central to the vision and its capacity to respond to these needs. Key principles that will ensure excellence for Long Island are:

- a high level of security has been incorporated into the design in order to provide maximum peace of mind for residents
- delivery of building, landscape and lifestyle features that emphasise and deliver quality results

- development of a relaxed environment where outdoor living is paramount
- construction of distinctive buildings using materials that blend naturally and gracefully into the local landscape
- provision to allow for a reflection of individual tastes, needs and lifestyles.

Although safety and security are given as major positives of a gated community such as Long Island, studies to date do not indicate that gated communities have lower rates of crime than surrounding areas. Rather, the benefits seem to be more about perception, with people feeling safer behind the gates (O'Sullivan 2005).

10.2.4   Indigenous communities: Inequality within and without

Geographically, the majority of Australia's Indigenous population is regional or urban. Although Indigenous people remain significantly more likely than other Australians to live in remote areas, this is not where the majority of Aboriginal and Torres Strait Islander people live. Nearly one-third of the population is located in the large urban areas and more than 40 per cent reside in regional areas. Indeed, population trends indicate an ongoing Indigenous drift to the larger urban areas (Saunders 2002) and many Indigenous Australians have been resident in urban areas for many generations. Sydney has the largest Indigenous population in Australia, and the areas currently experiencing the highest rates of Indigenous population increase are Brisbane, Broome and Coffs Harbour. But within these cities and towns, the Indigenous community is still economically, spatially and socially separated. Hunter (1996) established that, within regional and urban areas, Indigenous people are concentrated in the suburbs that have fared badly from structural economic change. The situation for those 25 per cent of Indigenous Australians in Australia's remote and very remote areas, where Aboriginal and Torres Strait Islander people make up the majority of the population, the situation is even more dire. Such areas and communities have little economy to change.

The locational inequality of urban Indigenous people is rendered less visible by current statistical reporting, which tends to present aggregate national or state figures. Yet, there is substantial diversity in life circumstances of Indigenous peoples in Australia. Taylor (2006), for example, researching the spatial underpinning of Indigenous disadvantage, argues for greater recognition of the variability of environments in which contemporary Indigenous children are being raised. Aggregate data also underplays the similarity of disadvantaged life circumstances regardless of location. Walter (2008), for example, found that diversity between Indigenous populations in urban, regional and remote locations was dwarfed by a shared socioeconomic positioning and Biddle (2013) found the Indigenous population more socioeconomically disadvantaged in each of the 368 locations examined. Regardless of location, Indigenous people remain clearly unequal across all major socioeconomic indicators.

Even data that indicate an Indigenous presence in wealthier areas cannot be taken as a proxy for the relative advantage of these residents. While SEIFA indexes, for example, can identify the level of disadvantage in areas with high Indigenous populations, they can also lead to false impressions of Indigenous well-being. SEIFA data take information at the collection district level on the presumption that the households of a small area are relatively similar in their level of socioeconomic disadvantage or advantage, a presumption that has led, in turn, to a presumption that urban Indigenous populations living in areas of higher SEIFA rankings are similarly advantaged. A 2004 study (Kennedy & Firman 2006) found such an assumption to be highly misplaced. Indigenous populations in each area suffered a higher level of socioeconomic disadvantage than the non-Indigenous population of the same area. As an example, although around 35,000 Indigenous people in Queensland live in areas that might be classified as middle class using SEIFA rankings, on individual scores only 2000 (around 6 per cent) of this group had scores that matched the score of their area of residence, indicating that the vast majority of those Indigenous people living in middle-class suburbs do not enjoy the same attributes of income, education and employment as their neighbours. The locational inequality among remote, predominantly Indigenous communities is even more clear cut.

Contemporary Australia

LOCATIONAL INEQUALITY

The township of Wadeye in the Northern Territory provides a graphic illustration of just how disadvantaged a location can be.

Wadeye is 320 kilometres south-west of Darwin, via a road that is not drivable for significant parts of the year due to wet season flooding, and has a population of more than 2000. The rapidly growing population is young; almost half of this population is aged under fifteen. Yet even though there is such a large school-age population, there is no high school in Wadeye, only a primary school at which only half the children are enrolled. Despite this gap in educational services, the Northern Territory government spends 47 cents per child in this community for every dollar spent on the average Northern Territory child of school age (Taylor & Stanley 2005). Employment options are also limited. Although most of the population is on low incomes, the cost of food in Wadeye is about 40 per cent higher than in Darwin (Ivory 2005).

To make their case for locational inequality, John Taylor and Owen Stanley (2005) compared the services in Wadeye with those of Longreach in Queensland, a similarly sized and similarly remote community that is not predominantly Aboriginal. In comparison, Wadeye had access to only about half the services that Longreach had. Unlike Longreach, Wadeye has no sealed access road, no hospital, no pharmacy, no mobile phone reception, no magistrate, no fire service, no sporting or social clubs, no TAFE, no high school and no cinema.

10.3   Place and identity

If inequality is connected to location, why do people stay in locations that are clearly disadvantaged and that diminish their life chances? Perhaps people should just move from less prosperous areas to more prosperous ones. While many Australians do move in order to increase their employment, educational and housing options, leaving one place for another is not as simple as just packing and going. Often the very disadvantage that is inherent in a location also operates to trap residents within its confines. Lack of skills, education or resources can tie an individual or family to an area, even if that area offers few prospects for improvement. In relation to Indigenous people Hunter (1996) suggests that despite the additional social and economic disadvantages of Indigenous locations within Australian cities and towns, it is not just a matter of Indigenous people choosing to live elsewhere; there are major Indigenous-specific impediments to such choices that do not apply to other poor Australians.

Additionally, the homes and places in which people live are more than just a house on a street, or a town or a suburb. Place and space often form an integral part of an individual's identity. The subjective elements of place are important. Place and places mean something more than physical spaces with or without services, amenities or opportunities. They form an integral aspect of our sense of community, belonging and identity. This quote from an Australian-based author describing how she feels when she returns to Tahiti, her birthplace and home until she was twenty-two years old, colourfully sums up the essentially subjective but vitally important aspect of place

> My reaction is always the same. As the plane commences its descent, you get to see the Beachcomber Hotel and the beautiful palm trees and my heart goes 'boom'. The plane lands at the international airport at Faa'a and my heart goes 'boom boom!' And then as it passes the row of banana trees, my heart goes 'BOOM BOOM BOOM!' because behind those banana trees is where I'm from, is where I grew up in a fibro shack
>
> Source: Hoffmann 2006

For many people, a particular place, often the place where they were brought up, arouses an emotional response. This attachment to a place is both intensely real and ultimately highly subjective. Such attachments of belonging operate at a number of levels, simultaneously. An individual may feel incredibly Australian, a Queenslander, a rural person, attached to their own town or suburb, even to their street, all at the same or at different times.

But this variability of attachment does not diminish its overall importance. Identity of place is about a person's perceptions of their place in the social and physical landscape. It complements and adds to our sense of individuality and to our sense of social belonging. Somewhat contradictorily, a sense of place can be linked to identity at both an individual and a community level. Bornholt et al. (2006) argue that an identity of place entails related yet discrete local, regional and national identities as a part of personal and social identity. An identity of place characterises the context and locates everyday personal and social experiences. Intense feelings of belonging and loyalty to a place or space are not restricted to areas of privilege. As sociologist Ken Dempsey's 1990 study of a small Victorian town revealed (discussed Chapter 6), despite the inequality or disadvantage present in a particular community, many residents still feel a strong sense of local identity and attachment to their community.

Contemporary Australia

○ ○ ○

TASMANIA: HIGH IDENTITY, HIGH PRIDE

Tasmania's population is on the cusp of decline, driven primarily by population ageing and net interstate migration losses, particularly in the young working- and reproducing-age groups.

As a demographer I research quantitatively the impact of population change on a population, an economy and the workforce. While we know the numbers and ages of the inward and outward movements of the interstate migrants, we know very little about who they are, where they are, why they left and if they would ever come back. But what we do know anecdotally is that there is a strong affinity to Tasmania that remains once Tasmanians leave the state. In order to understand this Tasmanian expat community better I set up the Tasmanian Diaspora Network (www.tasmaniandiaspora.com.au), designed to increase the engagement with people who call Tasmanian home but no longer live there.

While policy-makers and the business community acknowledge the potential resource an engaged expat network can provide an economy and wider population, unless we understand the diaspora and what interests and drives them regarding Tasmania, their potential cannot be fully harnessed.

I am currently undertaking a survey of expat Tasmanians to better understand who they are and their attachment to the state. Initial findings are fascinating. In less than one week, more than 450 expat Tasmanians completed the survey and provided a real insight into the connection to their 'home' state. The majority of expats identify as Tasmanian because they were born there (65 per cent). When expats are asked where they are from, 76 per cent claim to be from Tasmanian first, before being Australian or from where they may currently reside. Over half the expats left Tasmania when they were aged between twenty and twenty-nine, and most of them left to find employment opportunities elsewhere (37 per cent). Interestingly, regardless of how long ago the expats left the state, 81 per cent have a strong, ongoing interest in Tasmania and 65 per cent visit Tasmania at least once a year.

In terms of returning to Tasmania permanently, 45 per cent of expats would like to move back, while 25 per cent do not want to. The most important factors influencing the decision to move back to Tasmania are employment opportunities, lifestyle opportunities and to be close to family. Most expats maintain their connection with Tasmania through their family and friends and increasingly through social media, particularly Facebook.

> Most interesting are the responses to the question "Why do you think you have such a strong connection to Tasmania?" Embedded in these responses is a sense of unbridled pride, ownership and love, combined with a hint of despair that the state hasn't achieved what expats believe is its true potential, preventing them from growing as people in the state they call home.
>
> Lisa Denny (www.lisadenny.com.au)

10.4   Place and environmental risk

Locational inequality is also manifested in the unequal environmental risks faced by different locations and communities. While cities, towns and rural areas are often seen as single locations, different areas within these larger locational spaces face different exposure to environmental dangers. There is research, mostly from the USA, that indicates a spatial relationship between the distribution of environmentally hazardous facilities and dimensions of inequality, such as race and socioeconomic status. Those living in poorer areas face a significantly higher chance of their location containing environmental risks, and socioeconomic disadvantage increases with proximity to and density of environmentally hazardous facilities. In relation to race, research has focused on the institutional rules, regulations and policies that target some communities, resulting in the disproportionate exposure of toxic and hazardous waste by communities with high black populations. Mapping of environmental risk, as indicated by hazardous facility location, has found a clear spatial coincidence between concentrations of environmentally risky facilities and areas of poor, black or other minority populations (Daniels & Friedman 1999; Mennis 2002).

In Australia the different levels of environmental risk faced by different communities and locations are highlighted by the case of towns such as Esperance, a small, relatively remote town on the southern coast of Western Australia. In early 2007 the deaths of more than 4000 birds around the town alerted Esperance residents to an environmental problem. The cause was lead and nickel dust blowing from the port where ore concentrate was being loaded onto ships. Follow-up checks revealed contamination of rainwater tanks and soil in the region. More worryingly, a significant number of Esperance children had elevated lead levels in their blood, which can lead to problems with mental and physical growth. A report by Perth's *Sunday Times* claimed that attendance to environmental conditions in the town and follow-up of the initial problem were highly inadequate (Flint 2007).

A parliamentary enquiry was instigated, with a final report tabled in September 2007. The chairperson's foreword to that report said, in part:

> Firstly, it amazes me that, in this day and age of modern methods of mining, transport, monitoring and assessment, it takes the death of native birds, like the canaries of old, to alert the people of the town of Esperance to the poisoning of their community. Secondly, it amazes me that a Government department, the local prize winning port and a mining

company could so badly let down the families, and especially the children, of Esperance who had placed their trust in those who should have ensured their protection.

Parliament of Western Australia 2007:xi

10.5   Housing

Housing, while providing the basic living requirement of shelter, is far more than just a roof over our heads. It is also a financial asset, a wealth generator and the primary symbol of our social and economic status (Winter 1994). As such it is a key indicator of disadvantage and inequality within Australian society. From a spatial inequality perspective, the type and standard of house, the tenure of occupation, the location of the house and its value all reflect different aspects of locational inequality.

10.5.1   Home ownership in Australia

The Australian housing system is predominantly owner-occupier. In 2011 around 67 per cent of Australians either owned their own home outright or were paying it off via a mortgage. Australia has one of the highest levels of home ownership in the Western world, although the proportion who fully own their home has fallen in recent times. As shown in Table 10.1, there has been a consistent trend of a reduction in outright home ownership over the last two decades, dropping from around 42 per cent in 1994 to around 31 per cent in 2011. What is driving this trend is not completely clear. With an ageing population, we would expect the proportion of the population who own their home without a mortgage to be increasing. The dramatic prices rises in Australia over the last fifteen or so years are implicated, and the rise in the number of investment properties is probably reflected in these figures, as might be the proportion of older homeowners (such as the baby boomer generation) who trade up in housing rather than settling for keeping their older home without a mortgage. Between 1994 and 2011 the proportion of households in private rental accommodation rose from 19 per cent to 25 per cent, while the proportion of the population in public housing fell. These trends reflect larger social and economic trends, but have had a big impact on inequality and how it is manifested as housing inequality.

Table 10.1   Housing tenure in Australia

Tenure type	1994 %	1997 %	2000 %	2003 %	2006 %	2011 %
Owner without a mortgage	41.8	41.3	38.6	36.4	32.6	30.9
Owner with a mortgage	28.3	28.3	32.1	33.1	32.2	36.6
Renter—state housing authority	6.2	5.6	5.8	4.9	4.0	3.9
Renter—private landlord	19.0	20.4	19.9	22.0	22.3	25.1
Other (not stated)	4.7	4.4	6.6	4.4	7.9	4.6

Sources: ABS 2006g; ABS 2013k; ABS 2013n

Most people purchase a home more than once in their lifetime, but the first home purchase is a major financial commitment as well as often marking a move into a different life stage. Of the nearly one million homes purchases in the three years prior to 2012, just over one-third were to first-homebuyers. Most first-homebuyers were young households and couple families with dependent children, and couple-only households made up two-thirds of first-homebuyers with a mortgage (ABS 2013n).

Home ownership, the pre-eminent housing tenure in Australia, provides positive outcomes for homeowners across a range of dimensions. Economically, home ownership delivers security from rental obligations and potential capital gains through rising house prices. Politically, homeowners have private property rights and security of control far in excess of renters. From a cultural perspective, home ownership endows status benefits: not only do homeowners tend to be viewed as stable, respectable members of a society, but an individual or a family's home is also seen as a frame for and a container of the material trappings of their status (Winter 1994).

While high levels of home ownership in Australia are now viewed as normal, this is a relatively recent phenomenon. In 1947 only 53 per cent of Australians were homeowners but strong state support for home building and home ownership in the postwar period saw that proportion rise to a high of 71 per cent in 1966. Badcock and Beer (2000) estimate that for households formed between 1950 and 1970, home ownership might have been has high as 90 per cent. The encouragement of home ownership by the state during the 1950s also led to another unique feature of Australian housing, the suburban sprawl of our major cities. Unlike housing in many other major global cities, where many, including families, live in apartments, over 80 per cent of Australian dwellings are separate houses (Paris 1993).

10.5.2   Housing, home ownership and the state

Home ownership in Australia is regarded almost as a right of social citizenship. But although it confers benefits not accrued by rental or other housing tenure, such benefits are not an automatic aspect of home ownership. The benefits and wealth associated with home ownership are ultimately connected to the dominant ideological position that that particular form of housing tenure has within a society, and to the way this discourse is put into practice by the state via the policies and institutions relating to housing provision.

In what is termed the 'state sponsorship of tenure' thesis, home ownership is accorded a privileged social and economic status (Badcock & Beer 2000). In Australia such privilege is supported by favourable financial and taxation treatment of home ownership; there is little state support for private renters and a minimal public housing sector. Since the 1940s, governments of all persuasions have consistently offered significant policy incentives to encourage more of the population into home ownership. The First Home Owner Grant (FHOG), introduced by the Commonwealth government in July 2000, provides new entrants into the housing market with a one-off payment towards the purchase price of their first home, but it is not unique. Similar subsidy incentives were offered by other governments at different times over the last forty years.

High state support alongside high rates of home ownership also position home ownership as a cornerstone of the Australian welfare state. The interaction between the state and home ownership in this regard is most clearly seen in an examination of welfare provisions for older Australians. The Australian Age Pension scheme, paid at a flat rate, subject to strict income and assets tests and pegged at 25 per cent of average weekly earnings, is relatively meagre compared to that of many other countries. Additional state support for older Australians is delivered via the provision of ancillary benefits such as the health care system, heavily reduced pharmaceutical costs, subsidised aged care places and a range of concessions on items such as travel that are offered by state and local governments. Underpinning this support system, however, are very high rates of home ownership, mostly outright ownership, among older Australians. Housing costs for a significant number of older Australians are thus reduced to only having to pay council rates, which are usually state subsidised, and maintenance costs. Importantly, the Age Pension asset test does not apply to the pensioner's primary residence, no matter how much it is worth. As housing researchers Ian Winter and Wendy Stone (1998) note, state support of home ownership allows for a horizontal redistribution of income from working years to the retirement years. From the perspective of the state, lower levels of welfare provision and related services can be provided for the aged because of their high rates of home ownership. The losers on both sides of the equation are, of course, those who remain renters, the approximately 20 per cent of over 65-year-olds who do not own their own home.

And while an individual's home is considered a totally private asset, the state sponsorship of private home ownership comes at a cost to the state and to taxpayers. The public subsidies flowing to homeowners (although generally invisible) are substantial. Unlike public housing grants, first-homebuyers' schemes and private rental subsidies, subsidies to homeowners and purchasers do not appear in federal or state budgets. Flood (1993, cited in Badcock & Beer 2000) estimates that the benefits to homeowners actually exceed those made to public or private renters. The major area of subsidy for homeowners is capital gains tax exemption for the primary residence, reductions in capital gains tax (50 per cent) for secondary residences and the non-existence in Australia of a tax on imputed rent or significant property taxes on primary residences.

10.5.3   Changing patterns of home ownership and inequality

Housing is a central facet of social exclusion. Without adequate, secure housing other issues relating to economic vulnerability, such as education or work, cannot be addressed. Housing is also the greatest cost facing most households; for low-income households it can also be a significant contributor to levels of poverty. Housing tenure is closely linked to socioeconomic status, with a strong bias of home ownership towards those with greatest economic wealth. With patterns of income correlating with patterns of housing tenure, housing inequality increasingly reflects and reinforces labour-market inequalities. Increasing social and economic divisions around ownership of key means of consumption such as housing, represent a major inequality faultline. Data on the labour-market characteristics of current first-homebuyers in Australia, for example, show that most have higher incomes, with over two-thirds having incomes in the third, fourth and fifth income quintiles, and that over 90 per cent are in full-time employment (Rodrigues 2003).

Housing costs also impose a separate, poverty-related dimension. The proportion of Australians viewed as poor rises significantly once housing costs are taken into account. The changing distribution of housing within Australia, especially the ongoing decrease in low-rent dwellings, exacerbates the impact of housing costs on household poverty. Housing researchers Maryann Wulff, Judith Yates and Terry Burke (2001) found that between 1986 and 1996 the number of Australian households in the private rental market grew by 34 per cent. At the same time, the stock of low rent dwellings in the private rental market declined by 28 per cent: in 1996 there were nearly 70,000 fewer low rent dwellings than there were a decade before, although there were 100,000 more low-income households. The result is a significant decline in the housing stock available to low- and even moderate-income households.

The evidence related to housing polarisation is mixed and is complicated by demographic changes. The delay in marriage and childbearing for many Australian couples, the ageing of the population and the decreased affordability of housing in recent years all affect housing patterns. Winter and Stone (1998) found a pattern of socialtenurial marginalisation rather than sociotenurial polarisation; that is, low-skilled, low-paid Australian households are clustered at the bottom of the tenure hierarchy but there is little evidence of clustering at the top end of the social scale. Sociospatial inequality in Australia is increasing, with rising concentrations of unemployed, low-income households and recent immigrants into the poorer areas of Australian cities, typically, the outer suburbs. A study by sociologists Bob Birrell and Byung-Soo Seol (2004), using recent Korean immigrants as a case study, found that Sydney, as the richest Australian city, is attracting a disproportionate share of immigrants from non-English-speaking countries, many of whom have limited English skills and low levels of labour-market skills. The result is a concentration of such immigrants earning low incomes in Sydney's south-western suburbs.

10.5.4   Housing stress

The combined result of rising costs for housing is manifested in increasing levels of what is termed 'housing stress'. Housing stress is generally defined as a household spending 30 per cent of more of its income on housing costs, with severe housing stress defined as spending more than 50 per cent of a household's income on housing costs. Housing stress is experienced both by those who pay mortgage and those who pay rent. It is estimated that nearly 1.6 million Australian households are experiencing housing stress (AIHW 2013) and this rate has increased over the last twenty years. The proportion of those in severe housing stress has also risen significantly. Housing stress is not limited to low income earners— 58 per cent of households experiencing housing stress are not low-income households. However, low-income mortgagees are estimated to be 1.7 times as likely as all mortgagees to be classified as being in housing stress (AIHW 2013). An AMP.NATSEM study (2004) found that the majority (two-thirds) of those in housing stress are private renters, with up to one in five families in the private rental market experiencing housing stress. There is also a spatial dimension to housing stress; residents of Queensland and Tasmania are the most at risk and those in Canberra the least. While Tasmania in particular has cheaper housing, that state's high rates of low-income households means housing costs, even though they are lower than in other states, remain unaffordable. Housing stress is also more prevalent in the capital cities and the fast-growing urban regions on the eastern seaboard (Phillips, Chin & Harding 2006). Family type is also a significant risk indicator. Being a sole parent family significantly increases the chances of experiencing housing stress, while couple households without children have the lowest risk.

10.5.5   The state and rental housing tenure

The rising influence of neoliberal social and economic policies have impacted on the housing market. In policy terms the responsibility for determining housing outcomes for Australian citizens is now increasingly being relegated to the market. This fundamental change can be seen by the moves in government funding away from public housing provision. While state support for home ownership was previously supplemented by the development of large public housing estates, state support for low-income housing has, since the 1980s, increasingly gravitated towards subsidies for private rental. Winter and Stone (1998), for example, found that between 1985 and 1995 there was a sevenfold increase in government budget outlays on private rent assistance. Most of these funds are expended through the rent assistance payment made through Centrelink.

The corollary of rising subsidies for private rent is that state investment in public housing has been wound back. But the demand for public housing has not fallen in line with the reduction in properties. In mid-2012, more than 200,000 Australia households were on public housing or state-owned and -managed Indigenous housing waiting lists (AIHW 2013:viii). These demands for public housing are much greater than the supply, and many of those needing to access public housing have been discouraged from applying because of the long waiting lists.

The reduction in public housing stock has increasingly seen public housing become welfare housing. The majority of public housing tenants are also in receipt of Centrelink payments (Winter & Stone 1998). Only those deemed to be in the greatest need are likely to be successful in achieving public housing tenancy, a trend that is confirmed by a study by Bryson and Winter (1999) that was a follow-up to Bryson and Thompson's (1972) groundbreaking study, *An Australian Newtown*, about a mostly public-housing suburb on the fringes of Melbourne. Comparing the situations of 1966 and 1996, the authors found that much of the previous public housing stock in the suburb had moved into private ownership, and that the proportion of public renters had dwindled from 39 to 16 per cent. What public housing remained was focused upon the very poor and had become a marginalised and residualised form of tenure. In 1996, there was a clear divide in the community between the private owners and the remaining public tenants, with the public tenants living in the poorest-quality housing stock, much of which had been poorly maintained and was located in the least desirable part of the suburb.

10.5.6   Changing housing careers and inequality

Housing careers is the set of housing cultural norms and practices associated with an individual's position in the life course. The housing careers of Australians have, until recently at least, followed a fairly predictable pattern. Young, single adulthood is traditionally associated with entry to private renting, typically in inner-city locations. As young adults move on to partnering and childbearing they are likely to enter home ownership, typically in outer-suburban locations. Once established, families tend to remain in their family home; they pay off the mortgage and perhaps, as their children grow, upgrade to a better house in a better suburb. Older age, accompanied by the death of a spouse or ill health, may force a move into smaller, easier-to-maintain accommodation, and perhaps eventually to supported accommodation such as living with adult children, in an aged-care hostel or a nursing home.

Recent evidence suggests that the links between forms of housing consumption and stages of the life course have changed. Life course may no longer be the predominant driver of housing careers. The plurality of life-course options—delays in leaving the parental home, later and reduced levels of family formation, the rise of the single-parent family, separation and divorce of couples, remarriage and repartnering, blended families, early and late retirement and so on—all operate to make the relationship between life course and type and level of housing consumption significantly more complex and far less linear than they once were.

10.5.7   Housing affordability: Generational inequality?

The burgeoning real estate market in most parts of Australia has been a major feature of the late 1990s and early 2000s. Causes and consequences associated with this housing boom include the rise in the popularity of housing as an investment vehicle for cashed-up baby boomers and the rapid construction of large numbers of investment unit blocks in all major capital cities. Table 10.2 illustrates the still rising cost of housing in our major cities.

Table 10.2   Median price of established house transfers, 2003–13

	December 2002 $000	December 2006 $000	September 2013 $000
Sydney	444.0	500.0	670.0
Melbourne	280.0	359.9	520.0
Brisbane	208.0	340.0	446.0
Perth	205.0	456.0	520.0
Adelaide	195.0	295.0	395.0
Hobart	128.0	275.3	325.3
Darwin	195.0	380.0	570.0

Source: ABS 2005; ABS 2007b; ABS 2014b

The mortgages households need to obtain are increasing at a faster rate than wages. The ABS (2013n) reports that median monthly mortgage repayments rose by nearly 40 per cent from 2006 to 2011 while median weekly household income only increased by 20 per cent during the same period. Renters are also faced with higher housing costs, with median weekly household rent increasing by nearly 50 per cent in the 2006–11 period. Housing affordability is now calculated to be at its lowest level in 25 years and is still declining. While housing costs for all Australians have increased over the last decade, location obviously makes a difference. Housing is certainly not cheap in Hobart, but with a median price in 2013 of less than half of the median price of housing in Sydney, it is certainly more affordable.

One result is an increasing housing affordability gap for young and new homebuyers, and the emergence of a wealth divide between the baby boomer generation and generations X and Y based on property ownership. In what might be termed 'generational inequality', home ownership rates among younger Australians are gradually falling. The reasons for this drop are not entirely clear. Although rising house prices certainly are a factor, researchers found that a delay rather than a move away from home ownership is the better explanation of changing patterns of home ownership among the young (McDonald & Merlo 2002; Baxter & McDonald 2004). Later marriage and family formation patterns among the young reduced any differences in home ownership rates across the age cohorts.

10.5.8　Are all homeowners winners?

While home ownership obviously operates to reduce the likelihood of poverty, does home ownership automatically lead to wealth accumulation? Do all homeowners benefit equally? While home ownership is a social equaliser in that it provides tangible benefits for all, in other respects the benefits of home ownership reflect class divisions in society. Those at the higher levels are more highly privileged by home ownership than the less well off. For working or lower middle class groups, home ownership, while providing benefits, can also mean financial entrapment in high debt and housing stress. Housing wealth accumulation from this perspective, rather than reducing inequality, reinforces the existing concentration of private wealth into the hands of the economic elite. Badcock and Beer (2000) found that housing wealth within Australia is unequally distributed and reinforces existing inequality. In short, housing wealth for the majority tended to directly reflect occupational and income inequities.

10.6　Homelessness

There is a sizeable group of Australians who have no secure home, location or place. The ABS (2003) reported that on census night in 2001, there were 99,000 Australians who were homeless. On census night in 2011 (AIHW 2013) there were 105,200 people homeless. Of these, around 6 per cent were experiencing primary homelessness, sleeping rough or in improvised dwellings; the remainder were split between those experiencing secondary homelessness, staying temporarily with friends, acquaintances and relatives, and those staying in short-term and emergency accommodation such as boarding houses or Supported Accommodation Assistance Program (SAAP) accommodation, a category of homelessness generally referred to as tertiary homelessness (Parker et al. 2002). The majority of those who were homeless were male (56 per cent), three-quarters were aged under forty-five years, and around 17 per cent were aged twelve years, indicating that a significant number of those who were homeless were homeless as a family. Tasmania and Western Australia had the highest proportions of people who were experiencing primary homelessness. Tasmania, however, had the lowest rate of homelessness per population. The highest rate of homelessness was in the Northern Territory with a rate of 731 per 10,000 population; this statistic includes a large Indigenous component (AIHW 2013).

Homelessness is neither evenly nor randomly distributed in Australian society. Some individuals and groups are far more likely to experience homelessness than others. The young, those with a mental illness and Indigenous people are all heavily represented in the homelessness figures. For example, although the majority of people who were homeless were younger men, homeless women and younger people (especially those aged under eighteen years) were more likely to be in receipt of support from homelessness agencies (AIHW 2013).

The pathway to homelessness tends to be a financial crisis and such crises are more likely experienced by families on low incomes and with high levels of housing stress or an inability to obtain affordable housing (Chamberlain & Johnson 2013; Johnson et al. 2008 cited in AIHW 2013:297). Most of the children who were homeless on census night were most commonly living in severely crowded dwellings. Such early homelessness can have an intergenerational effect: children who experience homelessness are more likely to become homeless adults (Chamberlain & Mackenzie 2008; d'Addio 2007; Mackenzie & Chamberlain 2003, cited in AIHW 2013:283).

10.6.1   Homelessness and youth

The conventional picture of homelessness is one of a young person unable to return home, and to a certain extent this is accurate. Young people are disproportionately represented among those who are homeless. Youth homelessness is manifested differently across social and temporal characteristics. Young homeless people tend to be under-represented among those experiencing tertiary homelessness (for example, people living in boarding houses) but are over-represented among those experiencing secondary homelessness—they stay temporarily with friends and other family, such as a sibling, rather than parents, and form about 20 per cent of those living in improvised dwellings and tents and who sleep out. The major reasons young people give for being homeless are relationship or family breakdown and eviction, or the ending of their previous accommodation arrangements.

Rural youth face specific risks around homelessness. Research has found that most rural youth experience secondary or tertiary homelessness rather than primary homelessness, which makes their homelessness less visible. Homelessness for rural youth is compounded by tighter labour opportunities and limited rental housing markets in many rural areas (Beer & Randolph 2006). This research also found that children and youth who had been previously wards of the state or in the state care system were very likely to experience homelessness and that young people from low-income families were also more likely to become homeless (Beer & Randolph 2006).

10.6.2   Homelessness and mental illness

The Australian studies of Susan Parker, Lucy Limbers and Emma McKeon (2002) suggest that the proportion of homeless people who have diagnosable mental disorders is as high as 80 per cent and growing. This estimate is supported by research from the Human Rights and Equal Opportunities Commission (HREOC 1993), which found that people affected by mental illness face a critical shortage of appropriate affordable housing. This shortage is exacerbated by the exclusion of many people with mental illness from housing options by government housing programs and the private sector either because they were too expensive (private rental) or because of inflexible criteria (public housing). The HREOC report noted that many people with serious mental illness experience a process of geographical drift. Socioeconomic decline associated with the illness, weakened family and social support networks and repeated changes of geographic location result in residence in disadvantaged areas, poverty and homelessness. Since poor housing, poor neighbourhoods and poor communities are also associated with mental health complications, a destructive cycle of increasing difficulties is generated for people with mental health problems. Although most individuals recover from an acute episode of illness, complications such as homelessness and social isolation may occur (HREOC 1993:4). Current high rental prices and scarcity of cheaper accommodation exacerbate problems of housing accessibility for those with a mental illness.

10.6.3   Indigenous homelessness

Indigenous people and families are particularly at risk of homelessness and have a comparative rate of homelessness over ten times that of non-Indigenous Australians (ABS 2012a). On census night in 2011, around 30,000 Indigenous Australians were homeless, or about 28 per cent of all those counted as homeless. Nearly three-quarters of Aboriginal and Torres Strait Islanders classified as homeless were living in severely crowded dwellings compared to less than a third of non-Indigenous homeless people. These data should only be considered estimates. The difficulty with data for Indigenous people, and for all those who are homeless, is that it can be very hard to identify who is homeless on the night of each five-yearly census of population and housing. By definition, those who are homeless do not have a stable address.

Indigenous people are also the primary occupants of another group of the homeless: public place dwellers. Public place dwellers are those who live in public or semi-public settings, such as parks, in the grounds of churches, on beaches and riverbanks, in vacant lots or dilapidated buildings. Social researchers Paul Memmot et al. (2004) report that although these public place dwellers are categorised as homeless, some consider themselves to be both placed and homed and prefer to think of themselves as 'parkies', 'long grassers' or 'river campers' rather than homeless. Such distinctions should be tempered by the recognition that the alternative accommodation options for such people are largely non-existent. Indigenous people from all locations—remote, regional and metropolitan areas—suffer from a lack of access to accommodation options that is related to either poverty, discrimination or a combination of both. Indigenous youth are especially at risk of homelessness. A Tasmanian study (Jacobs & Walter 2003) found that Indigenous youth were twice as likely as non-Indigenous youth to be in receipt of the homeless rate of Youth Allowance. In their accommodation options the young Aboriginal people revealed incidences of discrimination and very limited choice, often related to lack of income. Within this group, those recently released from youth detention or prison were particularly vulnerable to homelessness.

10.6.4   Homelessness and older people

Another group who are increasingly represented in homelessness statistics are older Australians. Results of the 2011 census indicate that about twenty-six per 1000 people aged between sixty-five and seventy-four were homeless. This rate of homelessness is lower than that for younger groups but is still a sizable number (more than 6200 homeless people were aged at least sixty-five on census night 2011) for a group who most would imagine have stable housing. The majority of older homeless people are men (64 per cent) and most are staying in boarding houses (32 per cent) or staying temporarily with other households (25 per cent); about 10 per cent experience primary homelessness (AIHW 2013). The causes of homelessness among this group are varied but include isolation from family, alcohol and other drug issues and mental health issues as well as poverty and low income.

10.7   Conclusion

Locational inequality is manifested along a number of dimensions. Low incomes, high unemployment and poor social resources tend to be clustered in the same locations, as do their opposites, and for those in marginalised areas the combination can create a vicious circle of multiple disadvantage and inequality. Where Australians live as individuals and as groups directly impacts on life chances and life options. Conditions of postindustrialisation exacerbate the divisions between privileged and disadvantaged spaces. Private and public infrastructure, employment opportunities, educational, medical and other social resources are increasingly concentrated within major metropolitan centres, which privileges those able to afford, or lucky enough to already be placed, within the circle of these resources, but creates even higher barriers to access and options to those outside.

But locational inequality is determined by more than economic factors. The subjective alignment of identity with community and location and the implication of subjectivities in the creation of social inequality is complicated by the identified dimensions of spatial inequality. While individuals and groups may identify with a particular area, this alignment also tends to magnify the social privilege and disadvantage connected to different locations.

Not only do some locational ties bind lives to unequal spaces, but access to more privileged spaces and places are also increasingly monitored and policed. The wealthier are able to, and increasingly do, create enclaves of their own space, such as in gated communities, and in the process engineer a secure spatial and social distance from the lives of the poor.

Global trends in neoliberal economic policy and in the commodity pricing of housing also operate to entrench traditional spatial inequality and open up new areas of inequality. Discourses of policy preferences that place private over public underpin the state's response to locational inequalities and needs. The housing sector is where such responses are most observable. Australians have historically manifested a cultural preference for home ownership, but the spiralling costs of housing increasingly see the young and poorer members of Australian society excluded from entry. Home ownership is in danger of becoming the preserve of economically secure, two-income households. State support for private over public housing solutions, manifested in moves away from public housing provision and towards private rental subsidies for low-income earners, are further entrenching housing inequality. Not only it is home purchasers who are (increasingly) experiencing housing stress but, for many, rental costs have also escalated to unaffordable levels.

Discussion questions

1   How does spatial location impact on the patterning and distribution of social inequality?
2   What are some of the reasons that people stay in places that are disadvantaged? How is identity implicated in the explanation?
3   What is the relationship between housing and inequality? How does the state influence this?
4   What is a housing career and how are housing careers changing?
5   Which groups are most vulnerable to homelessness? How are housing markets implicated in this?

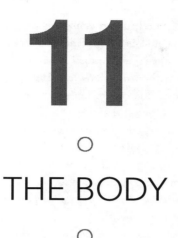

THE BODY

11.1   Introduction

This chapter is most closely concerned with the second and fourth of the book's guiding questions. It considers how the dimensions of inequality are changing in the context of a postindustrial society and the role of ideological and moral discourses in its creation and sustainment. The ideas of Bourdieu and Foucault are used to draw attention to politico-cultural aspects of inequality through an examination of how cultural practices and techniques of power influence bodily practice.

Biomedical constructions of the body as part of nature prevented sustained sociological analysis of it until relatively recently. Yet bodies are as much social as biological products. The sociology of the body has been mainly developed within cultural studies utilising poststructural frameworks, but it has also considered how dominant discourses have been used to scrutinise and regulate whole populations. Three distinct conceptualisations of the body have been identified: the body of individual actors, the social body of collectives and the body politic. The latter refers to the social regulation, surveillance and control of groups of people or populations and is especially relevant to Foucauldian analysis (Scheper-Hughes & Lock, in Lupton 2005:196–7).

Bourdieu's work has been extensively used within the field of cultural studies and, in combination with other theorists, by poststructural feminists examining the role of consumption in gendered performance. Foucault examined how the body has been regulated through the disciplinary practices established by medicine and the 'psy' disciplines such as psychology and psychiatry. Modernity brought with it scrutiny and regulation of bodies and an emphasis on self-regulation. Through the establishment of binaries such as healthy/sick, clean/dirty and regulated/unregulated some groups are stigmatised as morally weak or problematic and therefore deserving of social exclusion. These ideas are examined in this chapter in relation to mental health, gender and Indigeneity, focusing especially on themes of regulation and control.

Although Foucault and Bourdieu were not alone in offering a social understanding of the body, it was not until the mid-1980s that the sociology of the body was established as a subdisciplinary field. A key figure in its establishment was sociologist Bryan Turner who, in his ground-breaking study, *The Body and Society* (1996 [1984]), pointed to the failure of social theory to address the question of the body because of the dominance of biomedical understandings of it. Turner observes that the existence of the body is a taken-for-granted fact, yet sociological theory has avoided its study, instead treating humans as bodiless entities who engage in strategies and are subject to forces separated from any corporeal reality. The body is heavily implicated in the organisation and construction of society yet until recently these physical dimensions of social interaction were ignored.

This antipathy to a social understanding of corporeality lies in the origin of the disciplines. At the time of the Enlightenment, when the social sciences first appeared, the French philosopher Descartes was influential. Descartes argued that creation could be divided into two fundamental forms: physical and mental. This established a dualistic understanding of creation in which the world of nature was distinct from the world of humans. Cartesian dualism was fundamental to Western thought in the modern era and academic disciplines of today were founded on it. The distinction between human and nature was matched by the distinction between art and science, with the human sciences opposing biological ones. As an object of study the body was allocated to the natural sphere, examined as an external object uncontaminated by the social. The absence of the social from an understanding of the body is well described by feminist researcher Elisabeth Grosz (1994:x):

> [The body] has generally remained mired in presumptions regarding its naturalness, its fundamentally biological and precultural status, its immunity to cultural, social and historical factors, its brute status as given, unchangeable, inert, and passive, manipulable under scientifically regulated conditions.

Sociologists feared to enter this space because of the risk of biological reductionism, which explains human behaviour in terms of biological imperatives rather than human social arrangements. Anything that does not belong to nature cannot be studied scientifically. Since the body is a creation of nature it cannot be the legitimate object of study by sociology, which emerged as a way of challenging assumptions about nature as an explanation of social life. In arguing for a sociology of the body Turner is not seeking to develop a sociobiological approach to corporeality, but to do the reverse. Sociobiology applies scientific understandings to social phenomena, privileging biological explanations over social. The sociology of the body reverses this, seeking to debunk biological explanations and instead to demonstrate the sociality that underlies them.

Turner links this new attention to the body with its prominent display in contemporary culture where it has become detached from social and political aspects of society. The body has become a primary site of consumption and is central to the construction of identity. As such it is deeply implicated in cultural aspects of inequality and difference.

11.2   Bourdieu and consuming bodies

Bourdieu's analysis of the embodied dimensions of hierarchy arose from his concern with consumption. He recognised that the body is a site of differentiation expressed through patterns of taste. He wrote that 'the sign-bearing, sign-wearing body is also a producer of signs which are physically marked by the relationship to the body' (2007 [1979]:192). He used the example of tastes in food to illustrate this, noting that different taste patterns lead to different body shapes and so what appears to be natural actually reveals deep social dispositions. Taste as 'class culture turned into nature that is, *embodied*, helps to shape the class body' (2007 [1979]:190; italics in the original).

It is through our daily practices of consumption that our habitus is inscribed on the body: through the way we walk, our accent and 'our uses of the body in work and leisure ... that the class distribution of bodily properties is determined' (2007 [1979]:190). Class is not the only influence on the body; gender profoundly shapes bodily practice. Bourdieu takes the example of eating fish to illustrate this, pointing out that men dislike fish because it is fiddly and not sufficiently filling. It involves 'nibbling and picking' rather than 'whole-hearted male gulps and mouthfuls' and so violates masculine notions of identity (2007 [1979]:190–1). We signal our identity through our mannerisms and these are enacted through bodily practices.

Bourdieu develops the idea of physical capital to capture the embodied aspects of power. Physical capital is an aspect of cultural capital that is expressed in postures and preferences that position us in relation to social categories, such as masculinity or femininity. Like economic and social capital, physical capital is a resource that is unequally distributed and can be converted to other forms of capital. The most obvious forms of physical capital are beauty, strength and sporting prowess. A beautiful person attracts attention, which can be used to advantage and converted to a career, such as modelling or acting. Research shows that those others perceive to be physically beautiful are disproportionately represented in well-paid jobs. Athleticism also carries social honour as well as career opportunities. Sportspeople do not have to be highly intelligent or born into wealth to become national heroes and earn big money. But the relationship between taste and the body also magnifies social inequalities because of differences in opportunities for the conversion of physical capital into other forms of capital (Shilling 1991:656). Sport, for example, offers a pathway to wealth but the high risks associated with it are much greater for working-class people whose choices are formed within a much narrower opportunity range than the middle and upper classes. Engaging in sport has, therefore, different meanings for different social groups. For upper-class groups the networking opportunities it offers may be more important than the prospects of a lucrative career (Shilling 1991:656).

Mannerisms are also an important aspect of physical capital and literally embody cultural capital. The way we speak, our accent and the words we use, our comportment and habits are cultural attributes that form part of everyday bodily practice. Writing about gender, Bourdieu observes how differences in posture signal gender identity:

> The opposition between male and female is realised in posture, in the gestures and
> movements of the body, in the form of opposition between the straight and the bent,

between firmness, uprightness and directness ... and restraint, reserve and flexibility (1990:70).

To greet someone with a high five signifies a certain type of cultural knowledge as well as identification with it. Mediated by other factors such as skin colour, age and the vocabulary and accent that accompany this gesture, it signals who we are. Our physical practices and appearance are aspects of power because they are judged by those around us and used as cues to locate us in social space. The big man in a suit, with a loud voice and firm gestures sitting at a boardroom desk, carries connotations of wealth and power. The Urban Dictionary (urbandictionary.com) defines a 'Westy' as 'Someone who lives in the western suburbs ... usually angry people with pale, crappy skin, a testament to the amount of junk food and soft drink they usually consume'. The site goes on to link this group to low intelligence and dropping out of school early. Here social and geographic location are linked to a moral judgment of taste preferences which are perceived to be embodied in physical appearance. Such judgments lead to discriminatory practices that work in both directions, assisting those who conform to social expectations of moral worthiness and impeding those who violate them.

Bourdieu argues that our physical appearance and behaviour are shaped by practices that are embodied aspects of the habitus. They express our social location and identity. They are aspects of collective experience that are, Bourdieu argues, socially learnt from a young age and therefore expressed unconsciously. They are so deeply ingrained in our sense of self that they become habitual practices that we do not think about as we enact them. In this sense, the habitus is a collection of socially situated habits inscribed on bodies that communicate our social location and form the basis of judgments by others that work to reproduce it. It represents an external social order that is internalised in the body and represented in practices that reproduce hierarchy. This is not to suggest a straightforward correspondence between bodily activities and class. Bourdieu's social relational approach recognises that as social groups draw on cultural practices to position themselves, so their association with different groups will change over time. Practices formally associated with elite classes may, for example, become democratised over time. This can be seen in relation to sport, where a practice such as rugby, for example, was once associated with upper-class men but is now popular across all social groups.

Bourdieu's ideas about the body have been widely used by feminists and cultural theorists to illustrate how cultural practices are embodied and how they establish hierarchical relationships. Shilling points out that bodily practices are essential to the project of the self that is described by Giddens (1991). The refashioning of the body through activities of taste represents an important site for the expression of self-identity. This has been greatly assisted by contemporary technologies that make the body malleable in ways unavailable to previous generations; it contributes to the plasticity of the self that is one of the features of postindustrialisation. Dieting, exercise, reproductive technologies and surgery make it possible to reshape the body in ways that challenge modernist assumptions about its naturalness. The self-determined construction and reconstruction of the body is an expression of the individualisation that characterises contemporary society.

11.3   Foucault and the disciplined body

Foucault's analysis of the body forms part of his genealogical approach to the historical study of knowledge and power. He was one of the first theorists to point out that the materiality of human existence had been overlooked by social theory, which instead treated humans as entirely cerebral. His work counters this with an examination of how knowledge has been used to inscribe power on bodies. In *Discipline and Punish: The Birth of the Prison* (1995 [1975]) Foucault examines how forms of knowledge are implicated in the exercise of power and imprinted on bodies. Foucault uses the term 'body' in a literal and a symbolic sense to refer to the corporeal body of agents and the collective body of human groupings, as in the 'body politic'.

In charting the transformation of forms of punishment in a hundred-year period in France between the eighteenth and nineteenth centuries, Foucault develops a theory of power in which sovereign power is transformed into disciplinary power. Sovereign power is individual and arbitrary, applied externally to the body of the subject in a public setting as the visible exercise of the authority of the sovereign. Foucault argues that in the eighteenth century the infliction of pain on the body of the criminal provided physical as well as symbolic retribution for the harm done by the criminal to the king. But this form of punishment was not without its problems. It satisfied the need for vengeance but its effectiveness as a deterrent was diminished because the agonies of the criminal engendered sympathy in the crowd and sometimes led to riots. At a more profound social level, the arbitrary exercise of the king's power offended the principle of routine and order that was emerging as a defining feature of modernity at this time.

Foucault argues that over the course of the next hundred years disciplinary power replaced sovereign power as the primary mechanism for the governing of populations. Disciplinary power is based on disciplinary knowledge, which regulates the body through the establishment of minute regimes, such as keeping to a strict timetable and controlling what enters the body. Its expression is most visible in the establishment of the prison, where the lives of prisoners are regulated according to a strict timetable. The system is apparently rational and egalitarian in its application because it applies to all offenders and is based on bureaucratic-technical principles. This establishes a new governmental regime, the aim of which is to produce bodies that can be subjected to the processes of observation and recording required of modern capitalism. The production of docile bodies involves a new form of surveillance, which, while being imposed externally, is ultimately established through internal self-regulation. Foucault uses the example of the prison to illustrate the external imposition of surveillance through the panopticon, an architectural form designed by Jeremy Bentham and popular in the nineteenth century. The panopticon comprises a complex of buildings in which surveillance personnel located in a central observation tower can see into each of the cells that radiate from it. The arrangement, involving the unequal gaze of the guards over the prisoners, engenders an internal form of self-regulation among the inmates that creates compliant bodies because the inmates never know whether they are being watched.

Foucault argues that this type of regulatory institution is central to the apparatus of social control in modernity because it produces the disciplined, self-regulatory bodies required by industrial systems. It has its parallel in institutions such as the school and the hospital where disciplinary knowledge is employed to monitor and regulate the body and so control the population in the ways required for the operation of complex industrial economies. By disciplinary knowledge, Foucault is referring to the new forms of intellectual knowledge found in medicine and many of the psy professions, including psychology, psychiatry and social work. These employ the clinical gaze to carefully observe, record and monitor the population for the purpose of its control and regulation. Bodies are also encouraged to be self-regulating through the imposition of disciplinary practices involving internally imposed regimes of control. The surveillance of the self through, for example, fitness, dieting, hygiene or time-management regimes, makes each individual their own overseer with the effect that power is exercised continually and with minimal cost (Foucault 1980:155).

11.4   Regulating mental illness: From the asylum to community care

Foucault's ideas about the role of disciplinary knowledge in the regulation of bodies provide a useful way of understanding the treatment of people experiencing mental illness and the inequalities that arise from this. Mental illness is inseparable from the fact that it relates to behaviours that are judged to be abnormal. To be mentally ill is to be defined as violating the standards of normality that operate within specific cultures. In the case of physical illness, the norm is the structural and functional integrity of the human body. Radical psychiatrist Thomas Szasz points out that:

> Although the desirability of physical health, as such, is an ethical value, what health is can be stated in anatomical and physiological terms. What is the norm, deviation from which is regarded as mental illness? This question cannot be easily answered. But whatever this norm may be, we can be certain of only one thing: namely, that it must be stated in terms of psychosocial, ethical and legal concepts (1970:15).

There is a close relationship between mental illness and the abuse of human rights in the name of moral regulation and state security. In the former Soviet Union political dissidents were repressed by being diagnosed as insane and incarcerated in isolated locations (Smith 1996). Similar claims have been made about the abuse of psychiatric labels in China (Munro 2000). In Australia, as in other Western nations, there is a long history of institutional abuse. In the 1970s at Chelmsford Private Hospital in Sydney, twenty-four people died as a result of deep sleep therapy and another twenty-four patients committed suicide within twelve months of undergoing treatment (Anderson 1991). In the 1970s and 1980s in the psychiatric ward of Townsville General Hospital, patients were subjected to a systematic regime of abuse, including the administration of psychiatric drugs at thirty times the recommended doses.

The potential for institutional and social abuse of the mentally ill has been recognised by the United Nations, which has laid down principles for the protection and treatment of people suffering from a mental disorder (United Nations 1991). At the same time, governments everywhere have legislation that denies fundamental human rights to the mentally ill. In Australia, mental health legislation in every state and territory provides for the forced incarceration and treatment of those judged to be suffering from a diagnosable mental illness and who are assessed as a danger to the safety of others or whose own health and safety is assessed to be at risk. If a person is deemed to have a mental incapacity they can be placed under a guardianship or administration order, which removes rights from them such as financial control and where they live. Such legislation walks a tightrope between the abuse of the rights of the individual to self-determination, and abuse through denial of access to needed services. This is especially the case with psychiatric disorders involving psychoses in which the question of self-determination is compromised by features of the illness. While radical psychiatry and some feminists question the need for psychiatric treatment, especially if it is forced, clinicians argue that to deny it represents an equally damaging violation of the right to appropriate care.

The social construction of mental illness is apparent in the way different cultures interpret symptoms differently. All cultures have notions of normal and abnormal behaviour but the way in which they define and explain them differs. Some Indigenous people, for example, regard experiencing the presence of recently dead relatives as normal, whereas in Western culture this is likely to be understood as an indication of psychosis. The higher recovery rate from psychotic symptoms has been explained as being due to more positive interpretations of aspects of the illness, rather than the pathologising explanations that prevail in Western culture (Cheetham & Cheetham 1976).

The history of the treatment of mental illness was used by Foucault to illustrate how changing forms of knowledge affected the treatment of the body. In *Madness and Civilization* (1965) he showed how the treatment of mental illness had changed with the development of new technologies of power. In medieval Europe there was no distinction between madness and other constructions of 'dangerousness' such as being a criminal or leper. But in the centuries that followed, new forms of knowledge led to the separation of the mentally ill from other forms of 'badness'. Foucault argues that in the seventeenth and eighteenth centuries the mentally ill were segregated from society, eventually being locked up in asylums, where they were subjected to the clinical gaze of the medical profession, which treated them as an object of scientific, rather than moral, enquiry. This transition was justified on the grounds of being more humane, but Foucault argues that it was characterised by many abuses of power.

11.4.1   Deinstitutionalisation

Foucault's arguments formed part of a broader critique of the asylum, which contributed to the process of deinstitutionalisation of the mentally ill from the 1950s onwards. As with earlier changes to the treatment of the mentally ill this transition was accompanied by claims that it was a more progressive form of care. The incarceration of the mentally ill in lunatic asylums had initially been designed as a form of refuge for populations who could not survive in the harsh conditions of normal society (Cade, in Savy 2005:206). Here inmates would be given the appropriate therapeutic and moral treatment that would enable their return to civilisation; however, by the second half of the twentieth century the asylums were synonymous with human rights abuses. Overcrowding, understaffing, underfunding and bureaucratic ineptitude combined to create an atmosphere that tolerated the often severe maltreatment of inmates. Beating, shackling and the use of seclusion were routine practices, as were dubious, often harmful, medical experimentation. These abuses were documented in numerous reports that appeared throughout the nineteenth and twentieth centuries (Lewis, in Savy 2005:207).

Concern at these abuses, combined with other factors, including the availability of a new breed of psychotropic drugs (Shadish, Lurigio & Lewis 1989:2) and, in some countries, a demand for labour in a period of economic expansion (Warner 1989) led to a process of deinstitutionalisation in English-speaking countries, in which mental inpatients were released for treatment in the community. This movement received further impetus from the view that community treatment would be far less costly than institutional care.

Community treatment was welcomed by human service professionals because it was widely perceived to offer an enhanced quality of life for people with psychiatric disorders through the reduction of stigma and social isolation, the improvement of interpersonal relationships and a decline in the dependence and mental deterioration associated with hospitalisation (Wing 1967:219–38; Gallagher 1980:313). But by the 1970s, it had become apparent that community treatment had failed to achieve many of these goals and had created new problems, including the revolving door the mentally ill individual experiences being based in the community but repeatedly returning for short spells in hospital. Mental illness was also characterised by high levels of homelessness, poor and inadequate access to treatment, increased stress on relatives and stigmatisation within the community (Miles 1981:117–28; Doll & Thompson 1979:262–7; Smoyak 2004:25). A report into the Third National Mental Health Strategy (2003–08) identified a system in crisis, with difficulties including inadequate access to acute and emergency care, patchy service provision with under-resourcing of rural and regional areas, inadequate provision of community services, insufficient focus on early intervention and the continued failure to achieve core human rights goals of social, economic and political participation (Mental Health Council of Australia 2005:62).

Since then, mental health policy has emphasised principles of recovery, social inclusion, consumer participation and the minimisation of involuntary treatment such as seclusion. These principles are evident in the Fourth National Mental Health Plan, which aimed to address problems through the identification of priority areas including social inclusion and recovery, prevention and early intervention, service access and coordination and continuity of care (Australian Government 2009b). As well as improving housing, employment, income and overall health outcomes, goals include reducing stigma within the community, improving access to care and continuity of care, and an emphasis on recovery and social inclusion. These policies place Australia at the forefront of mental health policy internationally—yet achievements lag behind these ambitious goals. There remains widespread dissatisfaction with the quality and availability of services, and tensions between care and control and hospital versus community treatment (Department of Health 2013).

The demands of neoliberalism have also changed the discourses associated with community treatment, shifting from therapy towards risk management. Sawyer describes how the new public management within which crisis assessment teams now operate in Victoria has created an obsession with documentation that requires team members to tick the right boxes while treatment services go into decline (Sawyer 2005). A focus on indicators, targets, inputs and outputs is replacing the concern with care. For clinicians, the role of administrator is overtaking their therapeutic role, creating a demoralised and dehumanised workforce. The rhetoric of care remains at the level of policy, but is at odds with the requirements of risk management and the avoidance of litigation. Rather than improving the quality of service delivery, increased regulation has diminished professional discretion and autonomy, increased administrative monitoring and supervision and reshaped professional identities around managerial rather than therapeutic skills. This has resulted in high levels of stress and frustration and has contributed to deskilling within the mental health profession (Sawyer 2011).

A similar disjunction between discourse and reality is identified by sociologist Michael Hazelton (2004) in his argument about the contradiction between the emergence of a human rights agenda in psychiatric care and the tightening of security practices in many health facilities (Hazelton 2004:55). The previously mentioned 2013 report on the progress of mental health reform found that the use of seclusion rooms remains widespread and facilities are still characterised by high levels of security and surveillance (Department of Health 2013).

11.4.2   Mental illness and social exclusion

The data on the social distribution of mental illness suggest a close correlation with social exclusion, especially for those experiencing low prevalence disorders such as schizophrenia. Mental illness is the largest single cause of disability in Australia, amounting to 24 per cent of the burden of non-fatal disease. Compared with other serious health conditions, including cancer and cardiovascular disease, people with mental illness have the lowest likelihood of being in the labour force. There is also a close association between mental illness and both criminalisation and homelessness. Estimates suggest that up to 75 per cent of homeless adults, and around 40 per cent of prisoners, have a mental illness (Department of Health 2013).

It seems that low socioeconomic status is both a cause and an effect of mental illness. Mental illness, especially schizophrenia, is associated with reduced social functioning, which can impact on capacity to obtain and hold down a job and to maintain personal relationships. People with a mental illness may also experience discrimination and stigma, which can lead to social isolation and poor self-esteem. Employers may be reluctant to employ people with a mental illness who also have great difficulty accessing suitable affordable housing partly because of their low income but also because of prejudice from real estate agents and landlords. Relationships with friends and relatives may also be strained or non-existent.

While the removal of stigma and discrimination is a federal government priority (Department of Health 2013), the failure of community treatment and the continued social exclusion of people experiencing mental illness can be linked to neoliberal policies that construct mentally ill people as individuals, responsible for their own health through the expectation that they make 'sensible choices'. Community treatment was introduced in the expectation that carers and consumers would establish a new relationship with the state, a relationship based on mutual respect and recognition of expertise. Instead, treatment services today use families as a resource, while simultaneously offering fewer opportunities for consultation on the planning and delivery of mental health services (Henderson 2005).

Although it is important to acknowledge the failings of community treatment, people experiencing mental illness are no longer hidden from view and the public gaze is tied to a human rights agenda in which the vulnerability of people with mental health needs is acknowledged. The problems associated with community treatment are also recognised as being caused by a lack of funding and poor policy development rather than the principle of community treatment itself. The expense of the asylums, the potential for abuse behind closed doors and the stigmatised status of inmates are too well documented to abandon community treatment to return to that model. Deinstitutionalisation may be unfinished business, but the critical issue is not whether we should return to the asylums, but how we can make community treatment work. The consumer movement associated with a recovery model of treatment emphasises empowerment and social inclusion of mental health consumers and provides an important check on governments in the delivery of mental health services.

11.5   Gendered bodies

Feminist writers have written prolifically on the embodied aspects of gender and much of their work has implications for social inequality. Shilling (1991) divides feminist approaches into naturalistic, poststructuralist and dialectical. While their epistemological position differs, each of these ways of understanding gendered bodily practices starts with an understanding that the way the body is managed is an expression of unequal social relations. The gendered body is ineluctably associated with characteristics of strength and weakness central to relations of inferiority and superiority.

The naturalistic approach to embodied aspects of gender inequality argues that patriarchal forces distort natural differences of bodily shape. Psychoanalyst Susie Orbach, for example, argues that the demand for the thin female body distorts unconscious desires to eat, thereby creating destructive emotional urges linked with compulsive eating patterns (Shilling 1991:659). Author Kim Chenin writes of a 'tyranny of slenderness' (1983, in Shilling 1991:659) imposed by men on women as a result of their fears of female power. Men's position of social power enables them to convert this into beliefs about female inferiority that are accepted by women and converted into restrictive and obsessive practices on their bodies. Unlike men, who are socialised to take pride in their bodies, women are under constant pressure to improve their physical appearance and to regard this as vital for their relationships with men, especially in relation to partnering. Their hypercritical approach to their bodies leads to unnecessary, sometimes dangerous, practices such as cosmetic surgery and liposuction as well as serious illnesses such as anorexia.

Contemporary Australia

○ ○ ○

GOVERNING GIRLS' BODIES

When pre-publicity about a new book by US author Paul Kramer was released in 2011, it generated some controversy. *Maggie Goes on a Diet* is about a 14-year-old girl who is insecure, feels unattractive and thinks she might be bullied because of her weight. She goes on a diet, loses weight and as a result her life is transformed and she becomes the school's star soccer player. The book is aimed at children aged six to twelve years and, according to the author, is designed to encourage children to understand that other children can be mean and that they should learn to take things into their own hands and change things, including developing a healthy lifestyle and looking better. Critics included parents, health gurus and eating-disorder specialists, who argued that the book sent the wrong message to children about body image and that the real risk was the pressure on children to conform to unrealistic expectations about their appearance. They argued that there is an association between demands for thinness and the rise in eating disorders among young children, particularly girls under twelve years.

For feminist activist Jocelynne Scutt the book is also problematic because it equates slimness and femininity with being loved. She writes:

> Maggie is depicted on the book's front cover, red-haired, pig-tailed and wearing all-enveloping sweatshirt and jeans – with a more than chubby appearance. She gazes into a full-length mirror, holding a skimpy pink gown up to her chest: it appears to be a ball-dress, though it could be a negligee or undergarment, sleeveless, vee-necked and definitely too slinky and 'skinny' for her ample frame. The reflection in the mirror is of a slim, hollow-cheeked red-head whose body would have no difficulty slipping into the rose-pale petticoat-like frock that—in parody of 'Maggie'—she, too, holds before her. The mirror image represents what 'Maggie' will become, if only she reads Mr Kramer's book … The message is 'diet to become slim' *and* 'diet to be loved' … Maggie, fat on the field (as the book describes and pictures), is the target of laughter, taunts and (implied) ribald comment. A six-month diet, and she not only becomes sleek and slender, she is surrounded by adoring (young) male eyes.

Source: Scutt 2011

(continued)

Scutt notes how the sexualisation of young girls is becoming accepted in Australia, with children as young as two years old featuring in beauty pageants. In the USA there are reports of a four-year-old child who won the competition in a Dolly Parton outfit in which she wore a padded bottom and fake breasts. While their supporters claim that child beauty pageants are just for fun and encourage bonding between mothers and daughters, from Scutt's perspective the risk is that children will be robbed of their childhood and that their future health and safety will be jeopardised through a lifetime of dieting and compromised self-identity.

Poststructuralist approaches reverse the body–society relationship proposed by writers such as Orbach by employing a Foucauldian perspective, which regards the body as accessible only through language. In this approach the body does not exist in nature but is instead socially constructed. Like naturalists, poststructuralists pay attention to the bodily practices of dieting and exercise but understand them as self-disciplining regimes resulting from discourses of beauty and health (Turner, in Shilling 1991:662). Historical approaches trace the disciplining of the female body through discourses of female beauty, which require women to engage in restrictive practices such as wearing corsets (Vertinsky, in Shilling 1991:662). The regulation of women's bodies has literally and symbolically restricted women's movement through practices such as the wearing of garments that restrain activity and confine them to the private sphere. Bodily practices are also implicated in moral discourses about good and bad women through, for example, acceptable and unacceptable dress codes or bodily postures.

The dialectical approach attempts to combine the insights of poststructuralist and naturalistic approaches. Unlike poststructuralism, it acknowledges the material existence of the body but also sees it as subject to social change. The approach is dialectical because it sees the body as constitutive of social relations yet also restrained by its materiality. The dialectical approach therefore avoids the weakness of poststructuralist accounts, which imply that bodies are passive recipients of social arrangements, and the difficulties of naturalist accounts, which see them as formed by nature (Shilling 1991). Connell's work on gender and masculinities fits within this framework (1995, 2005). It emphasises performative aspects of gender while situating this within an understanding of sources of social power. In recognising the multiple forms in which masculinities are practised, he accounts for the role of masculinity in relations of domination and subordination, which apply within and across the genders.

11.6   The governance of black bodies

Foucault's arguments about the regulation of populations through disciplinary practices is a helpful way of understanding the construction of Indigeneity in Australia. The idea of governance has been developed by sociologist Nikolas Rose to describe how political power is used to control conduct for the purpose of public policy (1996). He applies these ideas to contemporary neoliberal regimes, which use the discourse of rights and duties to construct subjects as self-disciplining and self-governing. Those who fail to conform are constructed as morally bankrupt individuals who do not deserve the support of the state.

These ideas are especially relevant to Indigenous populations, whose black bodies, different culture, and history of resistance to white authority make them especially susceptible to stigmatisation. Contemporary discourses about welfare dependence represents precisely the kind of critique and moral blaming that Rose identifies as part of neoliberal forms of governmentality. The idea of governance can also be applied to the history of the relationship between Indigenous populations and the Australian state as far back as settlement. From the beginning, science was enlisted to document, analyse and control Indigenous people in ways that denied their cultural and personal autonomy and constructed Indigenous culture as inferior and destined for extinction. The documentation of Indigenous lives is vividly and tragically described in the report produced by the Royal Commission into Aboriginal Deaths in Custody:

> Through the files, Commissioners could trace the familiar pattern of state intervention into, and control of, Aboriginal lives. The files start from birth; perhaps recording a child adopted out, perhaps its birth merely being noted as a costly additional burden; through childhood, perhaps forcibly removed from parents after having been categorised as having mixed racial origins and therefore being denied an upbringing by parents and family; through encounters at school, probably to be described as truant, intractable and unteachable; to juvenile courts, magistrates courts, possibly Supreme Court; through the dismissive entries in medical records ('drunk again'), and in the standard entries in the note books of police investigating death in a cell ('no suspicious circumstances').

> The official record keepers saw all, recorded all, and rarely knew well or at all the people they wrote about (1991:12).

11.6.1   State control

This precise accounting of Indigenous populations was situated within a discourse that constructed them as a social problem to be resolved through state regulation and control. It began in the early to mid-1800s, once the major dispossession of Indigenous people from the valuable land in the eastern states had been accomplished, when the question of what to do with the remnant Indigenous population—those not struck down by disease or frontier violence—emerged. Destitute Indigenous people were living a marginal existence on the fringes of European towns or trying to eke out an existence in the small patches of as yet unused pastoral land, usually poor country around colonial settlements. Their presence was seen as a social problem for a number of reasons. Not only were they an unpleasant reminder that the term 'settlement' was really a euphemism for dispossession, but as the 'Other' they were also considered to be criminal, dirty and disease-ridden and, as such, a threat to colonial society. The dominant assumption in the colonial state, which prevailed until the 1930s, was that these remnant populations would soon die out, but there were concerns that they should be seen to be cared for in a humanitarian way—to smooth the pillow of a dying race, as it was described. But the colonial powers were also anxious that this inevitable end should be achieved as soon as possible because of the threat that Indigenous people presented to white civilisation. Indigenous populations living close to towns increased the risk of miscegenation—the birth of more hybrids or half-castes. The public policy answer to this discourse, which constructed Indigenous people as a social problem (rather than a military or police problem as earlier), was the various protective legislations that provided the framework for the surveillance and control of Indigenous lives.

In Victoria, the *Act to Provide for the Protection and Management of the Aboriginal Natives of Victoria 1869* gave the state the power to prescribe where Indigenous people could live and allowed the state to forcibly remove all Indigenous people living in Victoria to reserves or missions and regulate Indigenous employment conditions. As a consequence, Indigenous people were rounded up and moved to reserves such as Framlingham or Corranderk. As the process of dispossession extended, so Queensland, Western Australia and the Northern Territory introduced their own versions of protective legislation. The most notorious of these was the *Queensland Act*, which came into being in 1897 and provided extensive control over the problematic Indigenous populations by relocating them to specific areas. This restricted their freedom of movement, where they could live, the employment they took up, their freedom to marry and raise children, their reading material, leisure activities and almost all other areas of personal autonomy. These restrictions were enforced by penalties and imprisonment on the reserves for up to fourteen days for infringements. Colin Tatz (1982) lists some of the crimes Indigenous people were imprisoned for under this system:

- absconding from a dormitory
- gambling, playing cards
- calling the hygiene officer a big-eyed bastard
- being untidy at a public function
- failing to produce a sample of faeces for the hygiene officer
- wilfully destroying the bottle provided for the purpose.

Tatz insists that these are not dramatic cases, but just a few among reams and reams of similar crimes, and that they occurred well into the twentieth century because these Acts were not repealed in most states until the 1960s; in Queensland some were still in force until the early 1980s.

By the late nineteenth century it had started to become obvious that Indigenous people were not dying out as predicted but were mixing with white people, creating a growing number of half-castes who were now seen to be a new variant of the Indigenous problem. The state's response was to redraft protective legislation and redefine Indigenous people of mixed descent as non-Aboriginal, and to remove them from the influence of their black families, who usually lived on missions and reserves. This excerpt of a letter to a family at Framlingham shows the punitive approach with which this new policy was applied:

> In accordance with the Act of Parliament for the merging of Half-Caste children with
> the white people of the colony ... your children over the age of 14 [are to] be at once

placed out to service among white people ... Under no circumstances can rations be
granted to you, if you do not carry out the established law of the land.

Source: Chesterman & Galligan 1997:25

By 1900 the Victorian Board for the Protection of Aborigines had regulations that
required all half-caste children on stations to be sent to industrial schools once they reached
twelve years of age. From these policies came others that removed fairer skinned Indigenous
children from their Aboriginal mothers with the aim of assimilating them into white society,
thereby solving the Aboriginal problem. Some of these policies that were introduced in the
early 1900s were still in existence in the early 1980s.

11.6.2   The Indigenous 'problem' and the market

The 1967 referendum finally removed the parts of the Constitution that disallowed
Indigenous people from being counted in the census and that allowed the Commonwealth
to make laws that specifically related to Indigenous people. Although this represented a
new era for Indigenous people in Australia, their construction as a social problem remained
but became reconstructed in terms of socioeconomic disadvantage. Policy solutions in
response included those relating to education and employment, and self-determination
rather than assimilation—all designed to redress some of the results of marginalisation and
exclusion from the previous 150 years. Affirmative action programs of various sorts were
constructed, which were usually piecemeal and scattered in their application, consultation
and Indigenous involvement.

By the mid-1990s, Indigenous people were again recategorised in relation to yet another
form of social problem. The 'problem' was constructed in the language of the market, in
terms of the individual rather than community, and as responsibilities rather than rights. In
a similar vein, self-determination was deemed to have failed and was now viewed as part of
the problem, not the solution.

The 'failure' of Indigenous people to achieve equality once the previous artificial
barriers (being confined to reserves and not allowed to vote) were removed, and after they
had access to targeted assistance, is deemed to be proof of their true inferior nature. These
constructions of Indigenous people invert the conventional economic and moral values
of the dominant society and lay the blame not on the biological inferiority of Indigenous
bodies but on cultural inferiority. Beliefs that Indigenous people are 'culturally incapable' of
managing money, as suggested in 2003 by the then federal Minister for Regional Services,
Territories and Local Government Wilson Tuckey (Haebich 2004), justify discriminatory
and paternalistic practices. Yet when public companies such as the insurer HIH and the
telecommunications company One.Tel collapse as a result of corrupt or incompetent
practices by their wealthy owners and managers, there is no suggestion that these failures
result from rich white men's cultural inability to handle money.

This differential labelling of behaviour reveals how language problematises certain groups
according to collective attributes of cultural identity. Policy debate about the role of what is
referred to as welfare dependency in the creation of dysfunctional Indigenous communities
illustrates this. The view that 'negative welfare' is 'poisonous and socially corruptive' has

become a prominent policy discourse, and is supported by some black social commentators, including Indigenous activist and lawyer Noel Pearson in relation to Indigenous communities in the Cape York Peninsula (1999), and Bess Price (Sky News 2014). Negative welfare is the provision of welfare without expectation of responsibilities, which, it is argued, creates dependence and disempowers the recipients. The discourse of welfare dependence has long been used to individualise social issues whose roots are deeply embedded in social arrangements. Familiar targets include sole parents, the unemployed and, more recently, disability groups. But the nature of the discourse in relation to Indigenous people is distinct in that the pejorative term is directly linked to a moral judgment about the cultural attributes of Indigeneity itself and is directly correlated with laziness, drunkenness, violence and immorality. Indigenous welfare dependents are constructed as doubly deviant, for being outside the labour market and for being Indigenous. In this account, the extreme nature of Indigenous disadvantage is linked less to the trauma of dispossession than to the moral consequences of being denied economic opportunity.

This view overlooks the breakup of families and generations of criminalisation, economic exploitation and social and juridical exclusion. The extreme over-representation of Indigenous people in the criminal justice system, for example, can only be understood in the context of the disciplinary practices related to colonisation. From the earliest days of settlement, the coercive arm of the state, initially the army and then later the police, was involved in controlling and regulating Indigenous people. Their roles have included hunting them down in order to relocate them on missions and reserves in the eighteenth and nineteenth centuries, assisting with the removal of children in the twentieth century, and arresting and incarcerating them in the twentieth and twenty-first centuries.

Imprisonment rates for Indigenous people today are fifteen times higher than the rate for non-Indigenous prisoners. The rates vary between states and are highest in Western Australia, where the ratio of Indigenous imprisonment rates is twenty times higher than the non-Indigenous rate. Despite the recommendations of the Royal Commission into Deaths in Custody, rates of imprisonment are increasing: between 2002 and 2012, imprisonment rates increased from 1262 per 100,000 adult Indigenous people to 1914. This compares with an increase of 123 to 129 per 100,000 adult non-Indigenous people (ABS 2013o). The level of over-representation increases as Indigenous people move deeper into the system, so that it is at its most extreme within the prison system. The report of the Royal Commission into Aboriginal Deaths in Custody (1991) argued that this over-representation explained why so many Indigenous people died in custody.

This was a controversial conclusion because it failed to identify the actions of police officers in responsibility for the deaths. The report also argued that the high crime rate among Indigenous people was the result of their history of dispossession, cultural dislocation and disempowerment. One of the most telling findings was that forty-three of the ninety-nine Indigenous deaths investigated by the commission were of people who had been removed from their families as children. Over-policing and racial discrimination were also identified as causes. Cunneen (2001) writes of the 'trifecta' of police charges that are often applied to Indigenous people: offensive language or behaviour, resisting arrest and assault. The visibility of Indigenous bodies, cultural differences and the compounded effects of previous hostile interactions with official agencies create a situation of deviancy amplification that contributes to Indigenous incarceration.

11.7   Conclusion

The material in this chapter has drawn on the sociology of the body to show how inequality is manifested at the level of corporeal forms and through the control of populations. Bourdieu's analysis of the relationship between embodied cultural practices and hierarchy shows how the body is a key site for practices of inequality. For Bourdieu, embodied inequalities are masked because they are integral to our sense of self. For the most part, we bear the physical marks of our class, gender, ethnicity and race unconsciously. Yet the social constructedness of inequality means that these features are also fluid and open to change. This is especially true in conditions of postindustrialisation where the project of the self requires constant review and regeneration. In combination with other theoretical approaches, Bourdieu's has proved especially valuable in the field of gender and sexuality studies where it has deepened understanding of how bodily practices are employed to construct and maintain these distinctions, while also being open to change.

Foucault's work on the body is especially important for understanding technologies of power, which lead to the social exclusion and marginalisation of certain groups. His ideas on the role of language in creating moral discourses that justify the regulation and control of difference provide a powerful perspective on the relationship between the state and disadvantaged groups such as Indigenous Australians and the mentally ill. More generally, Foucault shows how disciplinary knowledge has been used to control the body politic and establish conformity within the population. His analysis of the internalisation of governance through self-discipline is especially relevant to neoliberal regimes for whom the ideology of rights and responsibilities is predicated on the ontological assumption that the good citizen is the self-regulating citizen.

Much of the research on the body has been conducted within a poststructuralist or postmodern framework. From an inequality perspective this has been problematic because denying the existence of hard realities draws attention from the examination of the social determinants underpinning unequal access to resources. Instead it conveys an individualised view of contemporary social arrangements in which division becomes difference and actors are free to choose their position in social space. There is a large body of work within this field that focuses on the cultural expression of difference, which, from the perspective of inequality theorists, is superficial in its concerns and contributes to a more general denial of issues of disadvantage. Yet the material in this chapter has also shown that such a judgment ignores the insights that a focus on the sociology of the body can offer by drawing attention to how cultural and symbolic aspects of inequality are implicated in individualised experience which are nonetheless socially distributed. It therefore contributes to an understanding of how contemporary arrangements for inequality are clustered in ways that are at once individual and collective.

Discussion questions

1   Explain the meaning of the term 'the sociology of the body'. Why is this idea important for understanding social inequality?

2   How did Bourdieu conceptualise the body? Describe his concerns with consumption and the embodied aspects of power.

3   Explain the meaning of Foucault's concepts of sovereign power and disciplinary power. How do these ideas contribute to an understanding of the treatment of mental illness?

4   What do feminists mean when they argue that patterns of food consumption are linked to patriarchy? Do you agree?

5   How has the discourse of welfare dependence been used to construct Indigenous Australians? What is your view on this debate?

PART **4**

CONCLUSION

12

○

TRANSFORMING INEQUALITY

○

12.1   Introduction

The key message from this analysis of the dimensions of inequality in Australia in the first quarter of the twenty-first century is that, despite decades of prosperity, inequality remains a central feature of social life and while it is undergoing significant transformation there remain important continuities. The book also argues that despite the existence of forces pushing towards greater inequality, this is not inevitable and the extent to which it becomes a reality reflects choices that we make as a nation. Policy decisions are a powerful influence on the contours of inequality and, while they are enacted within the economic and other constraints of a globalised world, they are nonetheless formulated on the basis of particular sets of values and beliefs whose effects have different implications for egalitarianism.

As we move towards the end of the second decade of the twenty-first century, Australia is enjoying high levels of prosperity, a robust labour market and growth across most economic sectors. Australia's strong resources sector protected it from the shock of the global financial crisis, and the demand for consumer goods and personal services remains strong and exemplifies Australia's wealth and confidence as a first-world nation. But it is also a nation undergoing rapid social change, which underpins the changes in dimensions of inequality—of which the most significant is a growth in inequality. The impact of globalisation and the social policy responses to these changes have been associated with the individualisation of nearly all facets of social arrangements, including those relating to hierarchy and the provision of welfare support. The traditional coordinates of gender and class, while retaining significant elements of their classic shape, are culturally distinct from their previous manifestations. Yet amid this significant change, some things remain the same. Indigeneity remains firmly embedded in an all-encompassing inequality, and many of the variables associated with poverty and marginalisation remain unchanged from those identified by Henderson over four decades ago (Australian Government 1975).

As the traditional faultlines of social inequality alter, the way we understand them must also shift. Analysing contemporary inequality today requires a multifaceted approach that takes account of multiple variables and subjectivities and locates this approach in the context of the changed global and national terrain.

In this concluding chapter the evidence of the preceding chapters is drawn together and interpreted around the book's five guiding questions:

1   What are the main dimensions of social inequality in contemporary Australian society? How is marginality distributed and what are the causes of this?

2   How are these dimensions changing in the context of globalisation and a postindustrial society?

3   How is the distribution of Australia's social, political, economic and cultural resources reproduced across different social groups? What role does the state play in this?

4   How are subjectivities implicated in the creation of social inequality? What contribution do political and moral discourses make to its sustainment?

5   How does this analysis inform current debates about the kind of society Australia is, and what kind it can or should become?

To answer these questions this chapter begins with an analysis of the implications of the changing terrain of social inequality for theoretical approaches to the field. Second, the effects of globalisation on inequality are summarised. Third, the implications of this for the distribution of the risk of inequality are explored in terms of the patterning, social reproduction and underlying causes of inequality. Fourth, the individualisation of inequality is linked with contemporary discourses of neoliberalism and their effects on broader understandings within public perceptions. Finally, the question of the future of inequality is examined.

12.2   Implications for theorising inequality

This book began with an account of the theoretical challenges that the changing terrain of social inequality represented for social theory, and for social stratification theorists in particular. It argued that while the movement towards 'post' understandings of social division were initially resisted by many theorists, some of the insights of cultural theory were gradually being accommodated alongside the structural approach to social inequality that characterised its analysis throughout most of the twentieth century. The theorist identified as critical to this rapprochement was Bourdieu and this was reflected in our use of his concepts of cultural and social capital. In addition, we signalled that we would approach the field taking an eclectic approach that acknowledged its multidimensionality and relational aspects in order to account for the contrasting and complicated patterning of inequality that characterises its appearance in contemporary Australia.

This approach has been useful in accounting for the divergent social forces now impacting on the creation of social hierarchy and division. It has permitted the use of concepts and ideas that, in the past, would have been seen as opposing but that today enable a full account of how inequality is manifested and experienced. It has also facilitated a cautious approach to any claims being made about the direction and future of inequality since it acknowledges the essentially unpredictable and contingent nature of human social formations.

The postindustrial order and the globalising of Australian society at the economic, political and cultural levels complicate and reduce the explanatory power of traditional theories of inequality, especially those based on class-related structural aspects. Patterns of social stratification based on single variables can no longer be directly used as a proxy for complex hierarchies of inequality.

Yet there remains a gap in current paradigms for understanding the way that hierarchical relationships are manifested today. Cultural explanations, while broadening and enriching understandings of social and cultural diversity at the individual and group level, do not provide wholly satisfactory explanations for inequality. Privileged cultural identities and differences in patterns of consumption have replaced class as visible markers of inequality but the effect of class on life chances remains much the same. The impacts of cultural assumptions on race, while observable in some arenas, are more cosmetic than real. In general, cultural theories still significantly underestimate or fail to address the endurance of inequality across multiple dimensions. While concepts such as habitus enable some bridging of the gap there remain theoretical and empirical disconnects between the two approaches.

One of the ways in which this book has attempted to address this is through the idea of clustering inequalities. Implicit in this concept is an acknowledgment that solid notions such as class and ethnicity need to be understood as intersecting variables that can be separated analytically but are experienced holistically. In the real world, the impact of social attributes such as age and location are neither experienced nor understood as separate factors but as aspects of identity that locate actors in social space. Their effect is layered in complex ways that a straightforward interpretation in terms of individual variables cannot capture. The way that social determinants of inequality intersect is central to its explanation. Inequalities cluster across different dimensions and must, therefore, be examined in terms of their multidimensionality. It is not just socioeconomic disadvantage plus gender, for example, but also the interplay and intersection between the two that produces effects that are at once individual and collective. The social attributes attached to inequality combine in variable and divergent ways, creating interactions that cannot be simply captured. Privilege and disadvantage in one dimension are reinforced by their absence or presence in a second or a third dimension. For example, being from a low socioeconomic background is a strong indicator of negative equality, clustering across the major sites in the labour force, in relation to the acquisition of skills. But its occurrence is deeply intertwined with other variables, such as gender and race, and while these have collective effects they occur in a context of individualised self-direction, so that the experience is one that is personal and understood as self-determined. It is for this reason that contemporary approaches to the analysis of social inequality must employ notions of identity and the body without discarding concepts such as class and gender.

The idea of clustering inequality also signals the spatial aspect of inequality that is one of its features in contemporary Australia. Advantage and disadvantage are increasingly fixed in particular localities. Weak labour-market opportunities, poorly developed services and high levels of crime combine with other factors such as environmental risk and stigmatisation to further concentrate social dislocation. The physical clustering of poverty is paralleled by signs that the wealthy are seeking to insulate themselves from the unpleasant experience of proximity to disadvantage by establishing secure havens, protected by visible and invisible barriers that shield them from the social fall-out that is the other side of their privilege.

Another useful way of conceptualising the kind of arrangements within which inequality is manifested today is the idea of entrenched inequality. This carries with it an association of social arrangements that are solid without implying the reification associated with the idea of social structure. It conveys a sense of the existence of barriers to social mobility that emphasises that these barriers are nonetheless socially constructed and open to change.

12.3   The altered landscape of inequality

The Australia of the 2000s is a different place to the Australia of the 1970s, the era of the first specifically Australian inequality studies. The processes of globalisation are implicitly and explicitly implicated in this change and are directly connected to the current distribution of social hierarchy and the growth in inequality. Globalisation has transformed the economy, creating new demands, opportunities and divisions. The demands of the global economy have raised the value of education and skills, which has facilitated social mobility and the growth of wealth at the top, but also entrenched and magnified the disadvantage of those with limited amounts of education and skills, resulting in an increase in inequality. Globalisation is deeply implicated in the process of detraditionalisation and its corresponding individualising effects, creating a new language of blame, entitlement and privilege. The global economy has elevated consumption to the central axis of social existence, suggesting that identity rather than class should be the key variable of social analysis.

The strength of the global economy has created new opportunities for many Australians. Inflation is now a concern, though it has been fuelled by strong personal and corporate consumption born of economic well-being rather than by recession. The emerging labour-market squeeze has improved employment security and small-business conditions. Unemployment, a major issue of the 1970s, is relatively low and the education, job and career choices, especially for the young, continue to expand.

Politically, globalisation has been associated with huge shifts in welfare provision. The social democracy of the 1970s and 1980s, with its supportive and expanding welfare state, centralised wage fixing, public ownership of key industries such as power and water, and the broad public provision of major services such as health, education and transport, has long gone. The welfare state remains, but under the influence of neoliberalism, support is more individualised, targeted, stigmatised and, for most, benefit receipt is now linked to market-based obligations and increasing demands for behavioural change. A significant proportion of previously publicly owned and operated institutions are now privatised and a rising number of employees work under individual workplace contracts rather than the previous norm of collective agreements.

The trend to individualism and individualised identity is also apparent at the cultural level. It is increasingly influenced by globalisation and other global factors and is linked to underlying social divisions. Aboriginal youths adopt hip-hop as an expression of black identity, and middle-class youths and young adults document their individuality on Facebook. While collective cultural identities still exist—asserting themselves at times of cultural stress, such as the rampant nationalism exhibited during the Cronulla riots—they tend to be secondary, rather than the overt influence on an individual's self-identity. Socioeconomic differences continue to be aligned with cultural differences and varying expressions of cultural identity, but the traditional divisions between the working, middle and upper classes are now more blurred. In postindustrial Australia, for white Australians at least, reflexively organised patterns of consumption, rather than ascribed affiliations, form the medium around which identity is built. For those designated culturally 'Other', cultural rather than racial difference has become the primary identifier of their difference, usually pejoratively.

These transformations are also evident within the private domain. Increasing diversity in family and household living arrangements and partnering and parenting practices have created new pressures and tensions within gender relations and in the nexus between the private and public domains. The conflicting demands of global economic competition and neoliberal social conservatism are experienced by all women and families but impact differentially on different family forms, with sole-parent families most severely affected.

In this restructured Australia, inequality is the same and different. Manifestations of inequality are altering, but the embedded faultlines also remain strongly apparent. The traditional aspects remain visible, but economic inequality is growing and the clustering of inequality in relation to gender and class is more layered and diverse. Altering subjectivities also create barriers to a straightforward analysis and interpretation, further complicated by evidence of emerging new dimensions of inequality.

Overall, there is a growing body of evidence that there are distinct groups of winners and losers. The gains of national prosperity can be observed across large sections of the Australian population, but the distribution has been highly uneven. The biggest winners are those already at the top of the hierarchy. The economic resources of the wealthy have increased at a significantly faster rate than those of other groups. Those with substantial stock market investments and business interests have enjoyed increases in wealth well beyond those below them. Some of the wealth generated by years of economic growth has also flowed—or at least trickled down—to those at the higher levels of the middle sectors whose access to material and cultural resources has enabled them to reap the rewards of the growth in well-paid professional jobs and to invest in and profit from economic growth.

Others have remained outside this circle of advantage. The analysis of winners and losers examined in this study provides clear evidence that disadvantage is not confined to the random few whose unfortunate position is best understood as their lack of individual capacity to access the available opportunities. Rather, the evidence suggests that inequality remains patterned along the familiar lines of economic and social position in which traditional factors such as class, gender and ethnicity are implicated. Those caught in unenviable locations are the usual suspects of Australian inequality, and an important part of the explanation of their situations are objective factors, such as their parenting and partnered status, their location in poorly serviced urban and rural regions, and by the intergenerational effects of inequality on physical and mental well-being. Most tellingly, many of those at the bottom of the social hierarchy have, over time, stayed there. The lived experience of inequality for these Australians is periods, if not lives, of poverty and deprivation, and experiences of exclusion and marginalisation that reduce their life chances, options and outcomes.

The external factors implicated in the reproduction of inequality are matched with internal ones relating to cultural forces and the lived experiences of social marginalisation. Bourdieu's notion of habitus explains how the effects of inequality are internalised, creating social dispositions which interplay with social realities of knowledge and opportunity. Notions of deservingness create social barriers which, while they are invisible, are nonetheless difficult to cross. The subjectivities of inequality are therefore central to its explanation and endurance.

12.4 Analysing the distribution of risk: Change and continuity

How best can the plethora of data on contemporary Australian inequality be analysed and interpreted? Refocusing the evidence across the core sociological variables of ethnicity, class and gender highlights the changes and continuities that have occurred. Answering the questions What is different? How is it different? and What is the same? is a necessarily imperfect exercise but by collating the evidence in this way both the weight and distribution of inequality are brought into sharp relief. Here, the argument is that inequality displays a clustering effect, which is in some aspects manifested in its geographical dispersal and, in others, reflected in its multidimensional and intersectoral character.

12.4.1 The enduring and entrenched (inequalities of race)

Race remains the most consistently palpable dimension of inequality. Those from non-Western countries, especially recently arrived immigrants, refugees and asylum seekers, are disadvantaged and often disenfranchised in Australian society. While the position of recent immigrants appears improved in educational and labour market outcomes compared with the outcomes of those in earlier decades, this improvement turns more on restrictive immigration patterns than any base reduction in inequality. Those arriving now are likely to be already more advantaged in terms of cultural, material and social capital.

The ongoing centrality of race is most marked by the disturbing position of Indigenous Australians across all indicators of disadvantage. Indigeneity remains intractably central to the contemporary practice of inequality. Regardless of family, cultural, country and colonising history or geographic location, Indigenous people's common position on the lowest rung of this society's socioeconomic hierarchy is undisputed. Despite over a decade of economic growth, a major policy effort to improve the health and well-being of Indigenous people, and substantial improvements in areas such as mortality rates, educational attendance and employment, there remain major areas in need of improvement. The comparative data bear witness to the deep-rooted, obdurate and multifaceted nature of Indigenous exclusion—this evidence includes the continuing huge gap in life expectancy, the high suicide rate, continuing high rates of infant mortality and low birth weights, high rates of household overcrowding, low levels of education and educational achievement and high levels of incarceration. Over one-third of Indigenous Australians are on weekly incomes of under $300, school retention rates from Years 10 to 12 are 25 per cent below the national average (Productivity Commission 2014) and the unemployment rate for Indigenous people is more than three times the non-Indigenous rate (ABS 2013p). Extreme levels of overcrowding and low levels of home ownership contribute to the continuing spatial disadvantage of Indigenous people, whether in remote locations with infrastructure deficiencies unheard of in other Australian communities, or in disadvantaged and poorly serviced enclaves within regional towns and urban locations.

Despite the regular descriptions of Indigenous disadvantage in official statistics, explanations remain sparse. The extreme and entrenched position of Indigenous people at standards of living well below the levels accepted as normal by the rest of the population tends to be accepted as a self-evident fact. But Indigenous inequality has a social underpinning that is uniquely Indigenous and therefore needs to be analysed within its present and past social and structural contexts. The unenviable social placement of Indigeneity in Australia is underscored and maintained by the social and political conceptualisations of Aboriginal people as 'different'. This Othering emanates from the unequal power dynamics embedded in Indigenous–settler relations in Australia. These lived social relations create and sustain the discourses that divide Aboriginal peoples in a racially specific and stigmatising way as well as circumscribing Indigenous choices to envisage or enact a different future.

This circumscribed terrain is a domain of Aboriginality that is clustered across multiple dimensions. Indigeneity in Australia is marked by inherited, population-wide, socioeconomic deprivation, which is compounded by visible and invisible exclusions from privilege. Indigenous invisibility is a feature of everyday life, evident in Australia's view of itself and from its arenas of significance. Absent physically and figuratively from spheres of influence at all levels, Indigenous people are spatially and socially separated from non-Indigenous Australia, despite physical proximity in urban and regional areas. For most white Australians, Indigenous people exist only as stereotypes, displayed and kneaded into a parade of judged, but personally remote, dystopias. Alongside these absences sits the burden of disregard, whereby an environment of broadly and commonly expressed disrespect for Indigenous people and culture go unremarked. Dramatically curtailed life chances create a habitus for Indigenous people in which the harsh realities of daily existence have become normalised. For many, the lived experience of the domain of Aboriginality is a dispossession from the possibilities of a different future (Walter 2008).

Although Indigeneity is the area of inequality that manifests the greatest constancy, one area of change is in the way Indigenous inequality is viewed and responded to socially and politically within Australian society. Neoliberal principles now underpin an unrelenting and rising intensity of market solutions to Indigenous issues but, rather than replacing older, racially aligned discourses, the dominant discourses have absorbed them. Cultural understandings of pejorative difference are today merged with neoliberal imperatives.

This hybridised discourse and its incongruity is evident in the contradictory positioning of Indigenous people within the reforming welfare state. In a racially distinct response, Indigenous people as a group are singled out and targeted as so problematically welfare dependent that behavioural conditions have been placed on their access to income support payments. Yet under the atomised individualism of neoliberal discourse, Indigenous people are defined as individual poor Australians, who just happen to be Indigenous and whose poverty must therefore be addressed on an individual basis. Their collective marginalisation from the market economy is framed as an individual problem the solution to which lies in individual reformation. Indigeneity is thus placed in a double bind of disadvantage: on the one hand, state and territory policies detach it from normal discourses of the Australian, while on the other hand, the complex and multidimensional nature of Indigenous disadvantage is obscured by claims that Indigenous people are complicit in their own disadvantage.

Despite the evidence of clearly observable racially based faultlines of social division, individualised discourses have subdued the connection between race and inequality. Indeed, today the term 'race' is eschewed within public, political and academic discourses. Diluted into less confronting words such as 'ethnicity', 'culture' or even 'culturally and linguistically diverse', this obfuscation is justified on the basis of concerns about using race as a marker of difference. But not talking about race does nothing to limit its impact. Nor does such blurring diminish the potency of whiteness as a marker of privilege. The equating of whiteness with normality and individual humanness means that the dominant position of the dominant racial grouping remains unexamined and unchallenged (see Chapter 2). Though filtered through the realities of gender and class, whiteness still brings with it an uncontested priority to be deemed a deserving recipient of Australia's resources. The legitimacy of alternative claims tends to decline in line with their distance from physical and cultural whiteness. From this perspective all non-whites occupy positions of diminished privilege.

12.4.2   The ambiguity of class

Class remains a fundamental determinant of life chances, but the fragmentation of traditional class identities and trajectories have altered its subjectivities, interpretation and, ultimately, its impact. In the simplest analysis, the impact of class on life chances is evident across all the sites and spheres of inequality. Those from the middle and upper groupings and their children retain privileged access to society's resources. Those from lower socioeconomic backgrounds continue to experience higher barriers and a reduced allocation of social, political and cultural resources across the lifespan.

The most evident manifestation of the continuing importance of class is in the labour market and occupational structure. The evidence here shows that disadvantage has been magnified by the processes of globalisation and associated societal change. While new opportunities have certainly been created, the postindustrial labour market has also reinforced labour-market-related dimensions of inequality. Both the quantity and quality of employment for lower-skilled, lower-educated workers have greatly reduced, and while unemployment rates are at historic lows, the risk of unemployment or redundancy remains heavily weighted towards those in lower-skilled, less-secure positions. The tightening labour market has reduced the risk of unemployment but not necessarily the risk of low income and job insecurity. Manual and service workers have been particularly negatively affected by labour-market restructuring. Young people from lower-class backgrounds, especially young men, continue to lack the acquisition of the knowledge and skills required to take advantage of the opportunities of a postindustrial society. This underachievement is reflected in the ongoing under-representation of young people from poorer socioeconomic backgrounds within higher education. Despite the rise in educational places, options and associated rewards, the proportional participation rate of poorer young people has not increased over the last few decades. Socioeconomic disadvantage is compounded by locational disadvantage, as young people from rural and regional areas face reduced access to, and capacity to make use of, educational resources.

One of the ironies of this analysis is that the booming labour market is exacerbating the cultural and academic capital divisions between those from the lower and middle classes. It is white, middle-class young people who are benefiting most from the opportunities for social mobility, which is engendered by their easy access to educational resources. For young, working-class men especially, the plentiful job options reduce the incentives and legitimise the disincentives to participate in the obtaining of credentials. An end to good economic times, however, will bring such divisions into sharper relief.

While the role of credentials in occupational mobility has yet to translate into a social system based on genuinely meritocratic principles, education and skills acquisition can act as reducers of inequality and as platforms to upward social mobility. Enacting education's role as a reducer rather than a reproducer of inequality is the key. Until this role is fulfilled, class will retain its importance as a determinant of social inequality.

12.4.3   Subjectivities of class

Culturally, a diminution of class as a social distinction in Australia is clearly observable. The restructuring of the labour market has seen a rapid decline in jobs tagged as 'blue-collar jobs', such as those in the manufacturing industry. The decline in union membership and the dissolution of what was once the almost automatic class-based political affiliations of previous generations and the rise of new distinctions such as the 'aspirational classes' have also had an impact. The result is a dramatically altered face of class and a belief that we are all now middle class. This perception is aided by prosperous times and the tendency of Australians to be deeply resistant to discussing class or inequality. As a self-proclaimed egalitarian nation, the idea of class divisions within our society seems unAustralian.

Even so, such perceptions are largely surface-deep, rather than reflecting fundamental changes in the organisational lines of Australian society. The diminution of class is more observable in its lack of currency within popular discourse, aided by the blurring and metamorphosing of previous distinctions into new forms, than it is in any reality. The way class is expressed, culturally and structurally, has altered significantly, but it remains a defining social feature. Most social mobility observed in Australia remains structural rather than circulatory, derived from broad occupational changes rather than a reduction in entrenched social arrangements. There has been almost no observable change in the level of circular mobility over the last four decades. The rise of the service sector has meant fewer Australians in traditional working-class jobs, and a huge increase in lower level clerical and service positions. These jobs may not be as dirty or dangerous as those in many primary and secondary industries, or as physically hard, but the divisions between these and higher-level positions remains largely intact. Such jobs tend to have relatively low pay, low job security, are often casual and part-time and come with restrictive work conditions and limited opportunities for advancement. The job held by Brett, Kim's husband in the television series *Kath and Kim*, as a salesperson in an electrical goods and furniture superstore typifies such employment. Labelling such jobs as white collar and, therefore by definition, middle class, is inaccurate. Binary divisions, such as blue and white collar, conflate limited aspects of work conditions with position in the occupational hierarchy. Such categorisation is increasingly anachronistic in a postindustrial society. While the working class no longer live in crowded conditions in the inner suburbs, the sprawling, poorly serviced and remote outer suburbs of major Australian cities have taken their place. The living conditions are certainly better but the social and locational separation from the professional and managerial classes remain. Locational place, especially residential space, is a crucial identifier of how we see ourselves, and its importance has heightened over recent decades. The where and how we live remain essentially a product of socioeconomic background and its embedded options of status and affiliation.

Individualisation and the speed of social and cultural change have exacerbated the perception that class is largely defunct as a means of understanding inequality. The emphasis on cultural facets and lifestyle and a belief in individual capacity to write and determine one's own biography disconnects concepts of class from social identity. But the struggle to create our own life story in this individualised world remains connected to social class, regardless of personal awareness of that link. Identities and the types and purposes of consumption attached to them still stem from our social milieu and the social actors that move within them, even as they adopt and/or reinterpret global trends or schemas. Class is inscribed on identity, and the realities of cultural, social and economic capital enable or circumscribe individual choice.

The perception of social identity and lifestyle as a self-constructed project achieved through consumption and choice may have more resonance among the privileged. Such a belief system allows the reaping of cultural, academic and material privileges while retaining a sense of deserved meritocratic reward, strengthening discourses of elitism and entitlement. Class-related colloquialisms such as 'bogan' and 'pov school' (poor public school) indicate the enduring presence of class distinctions. Crucially, such terms do not just refer to social difference but also relate strongly to perceptions and realities of economic and cultural inequality.

12.4.4   The altering dimensions of gender

Gender also remains an enduring determinant of life chances across the sites of inequality though the form and intensity of gender's influence has significantly altered. No one would seriously argue that Australian women and girls now have life chances that are fully equal to men and boys, but the interpretation of gender-related inequalities is far less straightforward than it was in the past. Divided and layered by aspects of race and class, the current gender dimensions are also caught within influential but sometimes contradictory moral and ideological subjectivities and discourses.

The increased presence of women in the labour force highlights the altered terrain in which Australian women now live their lives. Labour-force participation is the norm and there is emerging evidence that within the professions, at least, new opportunities are available to women, and they are making some, if limited, inroads into areas from which they were previously excluded. The broadening of life options for women is founded on the changing social and political subjectivities about gender roles and, more pragmatically, the translation of these subjectivities into realities via legislation in arenas such as equal pay and anti-discrimination. Demographic changes, especially the ageing of the population and the increasing labour demands of the postindustrial economy for highly skilled employees, of whom women form an increasing number, have also played a part. Underpinning these changes are reduced inequalities in access to education. At all levels Australian girls and women are now excelling educationally; they are achieving higher levels of academic participation and success than are boys and men.

Changes in opportunity have been accompanied by changing subjectivities. Women, especially young women, expect equality of life chances and options in fields such as the labour market and education. They also expect these options to be achievable in combination with their gendered expectations of partnering and raising a family. Australian men, while perhaps not quite so dedicated to altered and equitable gender roles, have, in principle if not fully in action, largely accepted the validity of these expectations. Australian society is still gendered but the sharp divisions associated with that are being whittled down. While women's widened expectations of equality and life options remain in reality somewhat elusive, the fact that such expectations are held and constructed as legitimate is a major transition.

Gender, though central to individual identity and cultural patterns of consumption, is also less prescriptive of how men and women plot out and imagine their life biographies. The way gender is woven into patterns of consumption and lifestyle is, in many ways, now able to be selected. The performance of the masculine or the feminine now has far more scripts, options and levels of intensity that can be chosen, adopted and varied as needed or desired. In the most optimistic reading of these changed subjectivities, gender is increasingly an aspect of personhood, rather than a defining and confining unalterable. Nevertheless, this interpretation is tempered by the overshadowing impact of class and race. While the influence of gender on hierarchical relationships is waning, the racial attribute of not being white and the class attribute of not being middle class diminish the efficacy of this change.

The scripts, options and ways of enacting gender are, to a significant level, defined for Australian women and men by their position in the socioeconomic and racial hierarchy.

Enthusiasm for the view that the influence of gender on inequality is declining is also compromised by its continued relevance in the sites of the labour market and the home. While women may be achieving educationally, the evidence shows that such achievement is confined within relatively narrow areas that do not translate into the most highly paid jobs. Male occupational choice remains wider, better remunerated and less demanding of specific knowledge and skills. More than three decades after equal wage legislation, women in the labour market remain unequally paid, and there is evidence to suggest that in some areas the gap may be widening. Even within industry sectors female workers are not achieving remuneration and opportunities for advancement at the same level as men. Australian female CEOs remain few in number and are remunerated, on average, at two-thirds the level of male CEOs. While this pattern varies across occupations, there remains little indication that for women, wage or career parity with men is likely within the foreseeable future. Similarly, women are over-represented among casual, insecure and poorly paid workers of the postindustrial economy. Low-skilled women remain marginalised in the service sector, with access to few resources with which to improve their position.

12.4.4.1 Gender, family and embedded social arrangements

At the base of these ongoing inequities are women's continuing primary responsibilities for raising and nurturing children and their high contribution of unpaid labour. The unequal division of labour within the private sphere disadvantages women across the lifespan but privileges men and children, as well as the state and employers. The benefits flowing to these latter two largely unspoken beneficiaries perhaps explains the persistent lack of social support for measures that would facilitate women's ability to combine parenting and workforce roles in the same way as men. A reduction in gender inequality requires a similar size reduction in gender privilege. It also requires a broader realignment of economic and social arrangements, and the distribution of benefits built on the presumption of women's unpaid labour as parents, carers, family managers and domestic workers. The lack of support for women's unpaid work, such as suitable child-care and/or maternity leave pay and provisions, are significant barriers to greater social equality. Severe limitation and shaping of the choices made by Australian women is the common, and entirely predictable, consequence.

12.4.4.2 Gender-based discourse incompatibility

A further source of the stable dimensions of gender inequality is the incompatible but paired discourses of market economics and social conservatism. On one side sits the state's support for higher levels of fertility within the context of the two-parent family, defined along the traditional gender-related division between caring and labour-market participation. Directly conflicting with this are the neoliberal imperatives of encouraging more women, especially women with children, into the labour market to raise productivity and meet the demands of the market economy. The retreat from state provision of services in areas such as child care exacerbates women's increasingly pressurised and unequal position in contemporary Australian society.

Such contradictory expectations are incongruent with social and cultural expectations of gender-based equality. Here the reformed subjectivities of gender meet the inflexibilities of social arrangements that have not reformed at the same pace. While gender itself may now be more malleable in its interpretation and lived reality, choices about the way gender is integrated into identity and lifestyle collapse against the hard rock of social reality. Nor have the subjectivities of mothering changed at the same pace as those of gender more generally. The moral and ideological concepts around mothering have tended to remain walled off from the broader changes around gender. The result is that many of the new opportunities and freedoms around gender are largely closed off once a woman becomes a mother. These incongruities also explain, to a significant extent, why social and political expectations of gender equality are so rarely achievable in the lived experience of individual men and women.

Discourses around individualisation are also gendered and carry significant implications for social inequality. The risk of poverty and social exclusion for women is dramatically intensified if they become sole parents. Sole parents remain, and are likely to continue to remain, intractably poor in comparison to couple-parent households across different measures of deprivation and social exclusion. The workforce imperatives for welfare-to-work legislation labels sole parents, alone among mothers, as unemployed workers. While the evidence suggests that disadvantages experienced by sole parents relate to their sole responsibility for parenting rather than to gender per se, women remain the large majority of sole parents and an even larger majority of sole parents with younger dependent children.

These inequalities are sharpened by the moral and ideological discourses of the family. Within and between families, hierarchies of entitlement to individual and social resources linger. Interpretations of the legitimacy or illegitimacy of whose claims are prioritised are structured on traditional patterns of privilege. The current outcome is that within families the claims of women remain subservient, as do sole-parent families when compared with traditional two-parent families.

12.4.4.3 Generational inequalities

Generational inequality is a further area of advantage and disadvantage that is changing. In the past, generational inequality was associated with poverty among older retirees, often men who did not own their own homes, as well as young, unemployed people. Today the shape of generational inequality is more amorphous, with gender, race and class remaining influential, even if in less predictable or linear patterns and varying between sites. Younger generations, for example, those below thirty-five, and who perform well in the educational stakes, are poised to take advantage of benefits and opportunities of a prosperous nation linked to global labour markets. In contrast, older workers across the occupations are less able or capable of capitalising on these options, either through lack of the required knowledge or skills or the lack of flexibility to adapt to the demands of the global labour market.

Despite their advantage in education and occupational opportunities, young people are disproportionately affected by the dramatic reductions in housing affordability.

While poor youth and young adults are most severely affected by housing shortages, it is likely to be the middle class who are feeling the effect most egregiously, given their strong cultural attachment to the notion of home ownership. Housing expectations tend to be linked to socioeconomic position but even the relatively economically privileged no longer ease into home ownership.

This situation is exacerbated, especially for middle-class youth and young adults, by their likely incurrence of HECS debts. The increased educational equity for young women, alongside the continuing trend for partnering within the socioeconomic groups, means that for many young couples a double HECS debt burdens their establishment of post-educational careers, independence and housing. It remains to be seen if generational disadvantage in housing and debt levels is adequately compensated for by generational advantage in occupational and education opportunities.

12.5   Discourses of inequality

Alterations in the distribution of inequality are mirrored in altering perceptions of inequality across the political, cultural and social landscapes. Discourses of social redistribution and social support have been largely replaced by those of market forces and an emphasis on individual achievement and self-responsibility. Neoliberal constructions of individuals as free agents actively shaping their life trajectory, by definition hold no place for social or hierarchical explanations of social position. As a result, debates on inequality in Australia increasingly reflect individualistic explanations. The emergence of new discourses of elitism associated with growing individualisation are creating new barriers that justify the already privileged while diminishing sympathy for those less fortunately placed.

Key policy responses to inequality imported from nations such as the USA and the United Kingdom are also implicated in contemporary directions of social inequality. Just as global trends and forces brought ideologies of neoliberalism into Australia, so too have they brought policy directions in welfare state reform, mutual obligations and the rationale of market principles as a response to social distribution. These trends have redefined the state's relationship with unequal groups. For the disadvantaged the consequence is an increasing exposure to the state's authoritative power. The implementation of more coercive policy based on market principles, such as mutual obligation for sole parents or welfare quarantining in the case of Indigenous people, now typify the tenor of the state's interaction with the poor.

The ideological and moral assumptions and presumptions within these discourses frame how inequality is understood politically and socially in Australia. They translate into understandings of the causes and determinants of inequality, dividing the nation into winners and losers and signalling the appropriate response to the individuals and groups affected. Despite clear signs of horizontal and vertical inequality in life chances, dominant explanations of distributional inequality increasingly focus on individual deficit and agency, suggesting that disadvantage is a lifestyle choice rather than due to embedded arrangements that deny equal access to resources. The causative determinants of inequality, privilege and disadvantage are thus also deemed to be individually based, alongside their proposed cures.

Contemporary understandings of inequality are, therefore, being transformed in their representation within political and economic discourses and social subjectivities. While there are similarities with older ideologies and theoretical understandings of inequality, such as the culture of poverty thesis, the influence of neoliberal ideologies determines market principles, such as private investment, effort and initiative, to be the panacea for inequality. The most visible result of the individualising of the risk of inequality is an entrenching of the stigmatising of the poor observable in the discourses apparent in welfare reform ideologies. But the new discourses of inequality also apply to the winners in the inequality stakes. Though only rarely given unequivocal public voice, the corollary of discourses of individual undeservingness, poor work ethic, personal deficiencies, and poor and deliberately inappropriate lifestyle choices, is a mirror discourse of deservingness, endeavour, personal attributes, and right choices and decisions for the reapers of the rewards of the postindustrial society. Contemporary discourses of inequality position it as essentially the result of meritocratic forces, with the attached social rewards and sanctions based on individual worth.

While meritocracy has always been the dominant discourse justifying unequal reward in Western democracies, its form today is distinct from that of earlier eras. In the period following the Second World War it was closely linked with ideals of egalitarianism, with visions of a nation in which social divisions would be minimised and poverty and entrenched disadvantage would disappear. Today, the strengthening of discourses of egalitarianism in relation to political equality is not matched by a new language of social and economic egalitarianism. Instead, individualisation and the development of a 'me' culture of entitlement carries with it an underbelly of unentitlement for the socially excluded. The language of meritocracy remains, implicit in notions such as deservingness, which helps to shape assumptions about its existence. But its paradoxical effect is to support the normalisation of inequality and a discourse of blame for those who fail to meet the demands of the market economy. In this emerging discourse, the split between the myth of meritocracy and the absence of genuine equality of opportunity, let alone distributional equality, that exists within our communities remains unexamined. While the evidence is there in numerous studies documenting the harsh realities of some people's lives, and the barriers that they face in improving them, there is an absence of a national conversation about what kind of nation we are becoming or should want to be, and the place of egalitarianism within it.

12.6   The future of inequality

Any attempt to predict the future of inequality must commence with an acknowledgment of the poor track record of attempts to predict futures of any kind where humans are involved. The complexity of social arrangements, the push and pull of multiple forces, the risks and uncertainties that characterise most areas of social life require the most cautious approach in the formulation of broad generalisations about the future of inequality. For these reasons this endeavour is concerned not so much to make predictions but to provide an account that captures current tendencies and their implications for the future.

At this particular time in our history, Australian society might be regarded as being at the inequality crossroads. Changes in the dimensions and manifestations of inequality are evident, but so also are its seemingly intractable embedded patterns. While the changes in inequality are neither even nor random, the likelihood of rising or reducing of levels of inequality appears finely balanced. The evidence suggests that in some sites and spheres, traditional dimensions of inequality are receding but, although its form may change, there remain large numbers of people whose lives are precarious and their experience is of social exclusion. The future of inequality is likely to be one in which the boundaries of inequality will remain, but they will vary in their shape, opacity and rigidity.

The capacity and possibility exists for the economic, political and cultural opportunities being delivered by the global economy to be spread more broadly throughout the population. The possibilities inherent in an expanding global economy and the new opportunities presented by emerging technologies and forms of knowledge offer unprecedented prospects for social mobility. But the intersection of social, cultural and economic capital will also ensure that those born into privilege will maintain their privileged positions. While many of the social constraints of earlier decades have loosened, our social systems, especially as they relate to privilege, have not become uniformly open or meritocratic. Unless more effectively balanced by a social justice agenda within government, the application of market principles will continue to enhance the capacity of the wealthy to ensure that their offspring reproduce their advantage. The direction of education policy is critical to this, since it is through the capacity to purchase quality education that the wealthy compensate for lack of natural ability in succeeding generations. An increasingly privatised education system is, then, one of the most important ways that the pendulum can swing further towards increased and more rigid lines of social division and distance.

The decline of class as a central axis of personal and group identity seems likely to continue, thereby enhancing inegalitarian tendencies. The ease of explaining social position in terms of personality traits will become more potent with the absence of a language and culture that acknowledges the power of collective forces. While socioeconomic factors are unlikely to ever disappear from the fabric of inequality, their power as an explanation of social division might be confined to those stuck at the very bottom of the socioeconomic hierarchy. The same trend of declining relevance is also evident in gender, perhaps with greater justification. While the disappearance of class is real in many key dimensions, economic divisions are persistent and, if anything, are actually growing. This is less the case with gender where the separate universes of men and women are increasingly overlapping and becoming more equal. Yet while gender is becoming less prescriptive of life experiences and chances than in the past, this is occurring only slowly and in limited areas. Gender is still a strong determinant of family position and labour-market engagement and reward. The importance of race has certainly not retreated. White privilege is not declining and the clustering of inequalities around Indigeneity in terms of poverty, education, labour-market options, health and life expectancy disparities, and stigmatised position is so overwhelming that these disparities are normalised in the national psyche. While erupting regularly as a 'national tragedy' in the media and the political sphere, the intrusion of Indigenous inequality into the Australian consciousness has until now been largely transient. Racial divisions are also evident in ongoing debates about multiculturalism and the negative portrayals of some migrant groups, especially those from the Arab world, and these show no sign of dissipating. So far, the significance of this aspect of inequality has been more cultural than economic. It remains to be seen whether the kind of ethnic ghettoisation of low-socioeconomic-status migrant groups that has occurred overseas will develop in the Australia of the future.

The failure of existing barriers to soften significantly suggests a limited capacity for increased social, economic and cultural mobility or the reduction of economic and cultural inequality. It seems that the differential impact of global forces are reinforcing the position of the already advantaged through their access to education and social capital and the enhanced opportunities for further accumulation of wealth. Only time will tell if the possibilities for democratisation and a concern with human rights that accompany globalisation will override these inegalitarian trends.

12.7   Conclusion

Does it matter? What harm is there in leaving inequality to take its natural course as global, social, economic and cultural changes dictate? We would argue that it matters a great deal and that with inequality comes considerable social harm. Discourses that present inequality as an inevitable and necessary product of society reify the phenomenon. Under these ideas, inequality is positioned as a natural companion to social and economic change, whose ebbs and flows are largely outside human responsibility, and this is seen as right and how things should remain. Yet this is patently not the case. Social inequality is not natural but is socially constructed, a variable product of our social, economic, cultural and political arrangements.

The patterns of these arrangements are not random but firmly marshalled in the interests of some groups over others. Despite changes in the manifestations of inequality, the gulf between those at the top and bottom of the hierarchy seems no more bridgeable now than in the past. The clustering of patterns of privilege and disadvantage, with inheritance playing a central role in shaping these patterns, challenges the reigning ideologies of meritocracy and deserved reward. The contention that patterns of inequality have societally constructed origins is also supported by the changing discourses around key aspects of inequality as social, economic and political circumstances alter. In recent times these discourses have operated to rationalise privilege and individualise disadvantage. In turn the legitimacy of these discourses has been reinforced by the state's adoption of their central premises in the pattern of its political and policy responses.

Inequality is also not just about poverty. The argument that increasing inequality is unproblematic because it is not necessarily associated with higher levels of poverty is specious. Inequality is not just about differences in material wealth: the economic dimension of inequality is integrally connected with inequality across all the other dimensions. Differential access to economic resources denotes capacity or incapacity to participate meaningfully in society. In turn, this capacity underpins the opportunity to lead a life that is valued by society. Most importantly, it is also deeply implicated in the capacity to lead a self-valued life. While some inequality might be inevitable, the level, form and intensity of inequality in a society reflects the validity of its broader social arrangements. Higher inequality is not socially harmless; rather it hardens the arteries of societal functioning, deepens divisions between groups, eats away at individual and collective community responsibility and inures citizens to injustice and suffering. It is also a waste of human potential. High and entrenched patterns of inequality are necessarily contradictory in a society that claims to be fair and meritocratic.

How then is the future likely to unfold? While the outlook for inequality in Australia is to some extent unpredictable and buffeted in a way not previously experienced by global trends and processes, such uncertainty is not a reason for fatalism. What is certain is that future reductions in inequality across sites and spheres are not inevitable. There is no automatic linear progression or evolution of greater equality in Australia and no pipeline effect. Inequality can increase as easily as, if not more easily than, it can decrease. And, despite seemingly accepting dominant discourses around the inevitability of inequality and its individualistic causes and remedies, a majority of Australians continue to express concern with and discomfort at its current levels. There remains within Australian society a critical social awareness that the burdens and benefits of inequality are unevenly and unjustly distributed. But a reduction in inequality cannot be left to chance, the vagaries of market economics, or the good works of private philanthropists or the community sector. Reducing inequality requires a sustained commitment by the whole of society, with governments playing a leading role.

Discussion questions

1   How do you explain the coexistence of high levels of prosperity, a robust labour market and growth across most economic sectors with the growth in inequality that has occurred in recent years?

2   Identify three factors that are critical to the explanation of the enduring nature of Indigenous inequality. If you were prime minister what would you do to address the disadvantage experienced by Indigenous Australians?

3   What is meant by the term 'the fragmentation of traditional class identities'? How is it evident within Australian society?

4   Using online and print media, provide some examples of neoliberal discourses on inequality. What are the ideological and moral assumptions that underpin them?

5   Do you agree that a reduction in gender inequality requires a similar size reduction in gender privilege?

Glossary

agency and structure

Two key ideas used by sociologists to explain how social phenomena are derived from a combination of choices made by free-acting individuals (agency) and externally imposed social arrangements (structure). Different social theories tend to emphasise one aspect at the expense of the other, although there are theories that attempt the challenging task of combining these two aspects of social life into a single theory.

alienation

At the heart of this concept is the idea of the separation of the inalienable, of something separated that should not be separated. In sociology its use implies a fundamental injustice and source of social ills. Marx argued that in capitalism alienation takes many forms and leads to a pervasive feeling of malaise, which is felt throughout society regardless of social class. Marx's theory of alienation was based on his views that labour was an inherent human quality, that people should have control over their own lives and that property was a common good. Capitalism violates all these principles because, under capitalism, labour is bought and sold like any other commodity, workers have no control over the productive process and do not own the goods they produce. A further source of alienation is the dominance and widespread acceptance of false beliefs that justify and maintain arrangements that are essentially exploitative.

assimilation

The process by which immigrants are expected to surrender their own culture and adopt the lifestyle and culture of the dominant group.

biological essentialism

The belief that biology determines social behaviour.

complex inequalities

The idea of complex inequalities has come into prominence in the last twenty years. Although the term has been applied differently by different scholars, they have in common a view that in advanced industrial economies inequality cannot be understood as a unidimensional phenomenon, but instead is multisectoral, diverse and changing.

conspicuous consumption

The idea of conspicuous consumption was first developed by Veblen who used it to refer to the conspicuous display of wealth by America's aristocracy in the nineteenth century. He argued that they used this display to distinguish themselves from the middle and lower classes. Today the term is used to refer to any form of excessive consumption used by different groups to position themselves in the social hierarchy.

critical theory

Refers to a number of theories, including Marxist conflict theory and the theories of the Frankfurt School, that have in common an attempt to challenge conventional understandings of social phenomena. While many critical theorists are sympathetic to Marx's ideas about the exploitative nature of capitalism, they do not necessarily share his structural approach to the analysis of society.

cultural capital

Suggests that culture operates as a resource that can be possessed, similar to economic goods and wealth, to create hierarchies in society. As used by Bourdieu, cultural capital refers to a form of value associated with consumption patterns, lifestyle choices, social attributes and formal qualifications.

cultural hegemony

A term used by Gramsci to suggest that one of the ways in which the state wields power is by encouraging ideas that reinforce the status quo.

cultural mobility

Emmison uses this term to describe the extent to which different social groups are able to move more or less freely between different cultural realms. His research suggested that the higher levels of cultural competence associated with professionals carries with it higher levels of cultural mobility.

cultural omnivore/univore

Petersen uses the term 'cultural omnivore' to describe the ability of some groups to move between different cultural realms. In contrast, the cultural practices of the cultural univore are more restricted and localised.

cultural turn

The transition within social theory from a concern with the economy as the main sphere of sociological interest towards a concern with culture, understood as an autonomous sphere. This transition began in the late 1970s and can be linked to the transition from a manufacturing to a service economy in Western nations.

culture

In its broadest sense culture refers to the values and ways of life that characterise certain groups. In contemporary sociology the term has taken the specific meaning of cultural production, in contrast to the material, technological and structural.

culture of poverty

A concept based on Oscar Lewis' anthropological account of the life of a poor Mexican family, in which he describes how extreme poverty results in values, attitudes and behaviours among the poor that ultimately condemns them to an intergenerational cycle of poverty.

death of class

Refers to the argument that class is of little relevance today because social collectives such as the working class have today become fragmented. There are no longer clearly defined social groups who share a common experience and who stand in political opposition to other social groups.

discourse

Discourses are particular scientific and specialist languages that comprise certain knowledges and ways of behaving considered appropriate by the majority of people influenced by that discourse. According to Foucault discourses are the main phenomenon of power.

dual labour market

This term refers to the segmentation of the labour market into one highly advantaged sector, the primary labour market, and a secondary, less advantaged, sector. Individuals in the primary labour market possess high-level skills and enjoy full-time, secure work and benefits such as retirement benefits. Individuals in the secondary labour market have lower level skills, are often employed casual or part-time and lack the benefits enjoyed by people working in the primary labour market. Males are typically over-represented in the primary labour market while women and ethnic minorities are over-represented in the secondary labour market.

economic determinism

While especially associated with Marxism, this term refers to any approach that sees economic forces as the decisive determinant of social arrangements.

egalitarianism

This term can be interpreted in many different ways but in the field of social inequality it usually refers to the minimisation of differences of income and wealth between social groups. Implicit in this latter understanding is the idea that people should not be exploited or marginalised. In some usages the term egalitarianism may also refer to the minimisation of differences in social status.

elite theory

A political theory that argues that power is held by one or a number of relatively small groups who owe their position to specific social, political or economic factors.

embourgeoisement thesis

One of the first theories to argue that class distinctions were declining. It appeared in the 1950s when the appearance of mass consumption led to the claim that affluence was eroding working-class consciousness and that working-class people were adopting middle-class attitudes and behaviours.

epistemology

The study of knowledge and how we can know the world.

feminism

A wide range of theories that place women at the centre of analysis. Early feminist theories were concerned with highlighting the invisibility of women as an object of analysis for social research and, more generally, within society. Feminist writers drew attention to women's oppression and sought practical changes that would improve their position. Postmodern feminist theories have pointed out that much of feminist theory has been conducted from the perspective of white, middle-class women. In pointing to the diversity of women's experience, they called into question the existence of gender itself as well as notions such as masculinity and femininity.

field

Field is Bourdieu's explanation of social life as an arena in which actors compete to locate themselves. It refers to domains of social life, such as politics or education, in which struggles for social position are enacted. Fields can be of any size and importance, from large institutions such as the education system to smaller ones such as team sports. Fields are shaped and reshaped through the practices of the players in the field, their relations to each other and the relations of the field to other fields.

functionalism (consensus theory)

Functionalism treats society as a system made up of self-regulating and interacting parts. It asks the question 'How is society possible?' and answers it by examining the contribution each part of society makes to the maintenance of the whole. Traditional functionalism, as developed by Durkheim and Parsons, is based on the organic analogy, which compares society to a living organism that has needs that must be met if it is to survive. Just as a living creature can become sick, so a society that is disordered can be understood to be out of balance and in danger. A well-functioning society is one in which each component contributes to the maintenance of the whole.

gender hierarchy

Developed by Connell, this term is concerned with how the idea of a hegemonic masculinity has become the ideal against which all men measure themselves and are measured by others. Other forms of masculinity, such as complicit masculinity and homosexual masculinity, as well as emphasised femininity, are subordinated to this ideal, yet all marginalised forms of masculinity benefit from its dominant position in the patriarchal order.

Gini coefficient

An inequality measure in which 0 equates to perfect equality and 1 equates to perfect inequality (where one unit owns all the resources and the rest own nothing).

globalisation

The growing interdependence between different peoples, regions and countries, and the disappearance of national boundaries due to technological developments and communication becoming more instantaneous. It is associated with the compression of time and space, as distant events are experienced in real time, and also with the growth of individualisation.

habitus

Bourdieu's concept of the habitus describes a patterned way of thinking about the world, a set of values and orientations that derive from groupings in society. It describes how individuals develop attitudes and dispositions and how they engage in practices.

historical materialism

Marx's theory of social change, which posits that the material conditions of society lay the foundation for everything else. The type of political system, social relations and cultural forms are all dependent on how a society meets its material needs.

homelessness

When a person has no permanent home or place to stay. Primary homelessness refers to those who have no secure home, location or place. Secondary homelessness refers to people who stay temporarily with friends, acquaintances and relatives. Tertiary homelessness includes people living in boarding houses.

identity

The ongoing sense of self and the process of self-development and definition. Giddens uses the concepts of self-identity and social identity to distinguish between the way we subjectively develop a unique sense of ourselves and the characteristics attributed to us by others.

ideology

A concept based on Marx's argument that in any age shared ideas or beliefs are used to justify the interests of the dominant social class. This implied that culture was controlled by the ruling class in its own interest. The failure of the rest of society to recognise this manipulation was due to working-class alienation, which blinded them to the reality of their exploitation.

individualism

The belief in the autonomy of the individual human being in social action so that whatever befalls a person or group is viewed as their individual responsibility.

intergenerational mobility

Movement up or down a social stratification system across two or more generations.

intragenerational mobility

Movement up or down a social stratification system within an individual's lifetime.

knowledge society

The transformation of society away from an economy based on the manufacture of goods, to one based on the production of knowledge.

late modern theory

Used by Beck and Giddens to signal their emphasis on the continuity with modernity rather than a radical break with it as advocated by postmodernists.

life chances

The material advantages or disadvantages and social and cultural opportunities that different social groups can expect within a particular society. Access to health care and education are examples of things that affect an individual's life chances.

lifestyles

Refers to patterns of consumption (goods, services and culture) that are not rooted in collective identities but emerge out of the impact of globalisation on self-identity.

liquid modernity

Bauman uses this term to describe the fluid and swiftly changing nature of contemporary social arrangements.

meritocracy

A society where social position is achieved through ability and effort rather than ascribed on the basis of age or social background.

modernism

Generally refers to the period since the Middle Ages and the Renaissance and is associated with the replacement of traditional society with modern social forms. Modernism is often defined as a belief in rationality and that progress and truth can be achieved through science.

multiculturalism

The acknowledgment and promotion of cultural pluralism in contrast to the cultural unification associated with, for example, assimilation policies.

neoliberalism

Neoliberal ideologies centre on a commitment to minimise the role of the state and maximise that of the market. It imposes the regulatory force of the market on states and believes the market to be the most efficient mechanism for allocating social and political resources.

new capitalism

New capitalism requires a highly mobile, innovative and mutable workforce, able and willing to embrace change, new knowledge and new horizons. This new culture is not bereft of socialites but is associated with a fluidity and openness that runs counter to the collective ideals that pervaded the second half of the twentieth century.

objective poverty

Poverty as determined by external criteria against which the situation of individuals and groups is measured.

old capitalism

Old capitalism was predicated on the image of large, stable bureaucracies that provided predictable benefits and encouraged a life within institutions.

Othering

This term was first popularised by Said who used it to explain the way in which the West turned the land, culture and peoples of the East into objects for study and colonisation. Othering implies a relationship of domination and subordination in which the 'Other' is constructed as inferior and whose inadequacies and moral weakness justify social and economic exclusion.

party

Weber used the term 'party' to refer to the organised expression of class and status groups to support their interests. It is similar to, but broader than, the notion of political party because it includes organisational groupings such as trade unions. Party, together with class and status, were, according to Weber, the primary dimensions of power.

patriarchy

At its most straightforward the idea of patriarchy suggests a society in which men as a social group dominate women as a social group, especially through the role of the father within the family. Beyond this, the concept provides little insight into the existence of different types of male domination or how this situation arises.

petit bourgeoisie

The class of capitalist small-business owners. Marx used this concept to differentiate small- and large-business owners.

postindustrial society

A social order based on a knowledge economy, in which services rather than manufactured goods are the primary products. It implies globalisation, post-Fordist economic arrangements, a high degree of fluidity and rapid social change. It acknowledges the centrality and autonomy of culture as a key sphere of social life.

postmodernism

The belief that society is no longer governed by history or progress and that it is highly individualistic and pluralistic.

poststructuralism

A broad range of ideas that have in common a rejection of structuralist social theories. Rather than seeing social forms as having solid foundations based on such things as economic arrangements, poststructuralist theories argue that they are constantly negotiated and subject to change. A basic tenet of poststructuralism is that language is central to understanding society, as language is the site where meanings are produced and negotiated. Foucault is often referred to as one of the major poststructuralists because of his refusal to commit to an underlying order or power. Instead he locates power within discursive practices which at different times and places exert power over people.

postwelfare state

This idea challenges the ideas of welfare associated with the modern interventionist state, and promotes instead the benefits of allowing the free rein of market forces to allow self-governing individuals to meet their own needs.

poverty

The idea of poverty has been the subject of much debate because whether an individual or group can be said to be poor is always a matter of subjective interpretation. Absolute poverty refers to extreme poverty, a situation in which the requirements necessary for a healthy existence are absent. Relative poverty refers to a condition of poverty relative to the overall standards of living within the broader community. Objective poverty refers to the failure of an individual or group to meet certain identified standards. Subjective poverty refers to subjective perceptions of being poor. Poverty is multidimensional and relative in nature, and has a close association with social exclusion.

poverty line

A measure used to define a certain income level, below which people are said to be living in poverty. Although recent approaches to poverty suggest that multidimensional measures are better, poverty lines remain important because their historical use enables comparisons with previous rates of poverty.

precariat

Individuals who are unable to find permanent jobs and who face a lifelong existence of insecurity. Their lack of rights-based state benefits, such as superannuation, makes them 'denizens' rather than citizens. They live on the economic edge, in a permanent state of debt.

preference theory

Hakim's preference theory posits that most women in modern societies have a real choice to favour either the private or the public sphere. Preference theory categorises women into three groups: work-centred women, who have no children or want to return to the labour market quickly; home-centred women, who regard child rearing as their most important job; and the majority of women, categorised as adaptive women, who try to balance the two roles by dipping in and out of the workforce.

production and consumption

In traditional stratification theory, understanding how people earned their living was regarded as the most revealing social attribute. This position implies the primacy of the economy. But today it is consumption rather than production that is the most striking feature of social life. The liberation of the individual from structural constraints means that social identity is reflexively constructed and this is established through consumption.

proletarianisation

The process by which some sections of the middle class, such as clerical workers, experience changes to their work that make them increasingly comparable to manual workers.

reflexivity

Describes how the knowledge we gain about society can affect the way we act in it. Our everyday practices are not just reflexive but are also constitutive of the situations to which they refer.

relative autonomy

A concept developed by Marxists in the 1970s to counter charges that Marxist theory was economically deterministic. It suggests that although the economy is the main source of power and social change, cultural forces have some independent power of their own.

risk

A term used by Beck to describe how industrial society has created many new dangers and risks unknown in previous ages. What characterises risk in late modernity is that it is generated by human activity, especially the application of scientific knowledge, it is uncalculable and it is global in its reach. Risk is associated with global catastrophes and events such as global warming, genetically modified foods and terrorism.

ruling class

A Marxist term that suggests that those who own and control the means of material production also control the state and the production of ideas.

service economy

The decline of manual labour and the expansion of the service sector.

social capital

A concept that, when used by Bourdieu, refers to the social networks and sources of support that are available to people to draw on as a resource. According to Bourdieu, the nature of one's social capital signals one's social position. He argued that the dominant class deliberately utilises its social networks to, for example, get their children into private schools and prestigious universities.

social class

The concept of social class is used in two senses. It may be used generally to refer to the broad idea of a class grouping or, in its most correct sense, specifically to refer to groups of people whose similar economic position is matched by a shared sense of social identity. In the latter case it implies a common lifestyle associated with a particular occupation or other shared economic characteristic.

social closure

Weber argued that when groups develop a sense of shared identity they use it to control access to scarce resources through strategies of social inclusion and exclusion. This usually involves some claim to monopoly over a particular area of social life so that only those who belong to a specific group can take advantage of it.

social exclusion

The exclusion of groups or individuals from participation in mainstream social and economic life. It is concerned with understanding the processes behind the creation and reproduction of exclusion and the power relationships between social groups when some groups exclude others from access to social resources.

social inequality

Refers to differences between groups of people that are hierarchical in nature. At its most basic it refers to the hierarchical distribution of social, political, economic and cultural resources.

social mobility

The movement of individuals and groups between different socioeconomic positions (see also 'intergenerational mobility' and 'intragenerational mobility').

socioeconomic status

A measure of standing in the community that generally relates to an individual's, family's or group's relative income, occupation, wealth and education.

status

The social honour and prestige accorded to a person or groups by other members of society. Status may be positive or negative. Status groups are usually associated with distinctive lifestyles, such as language, dress or other forms of cultural practice.

stratification

The existence in society of structured inequalities between groups in terms of their access to material and symbolic rewards. The concept refers to a model of social inequality that specifies the relationship between particular variables such as wealth and social standing. Implicit in the term is the idea of a systematic and enduring pattern of inequality that is transmitted across generations, built into institutions and practised in everyday activities.

structural or circulation mobility

Goldthorpe distinguished between structural and circulation mobility in order to differentiate between social mobility that arises from structural changes to the occupational order of society, such as the decline in manual labour since the Second World War, and the social mobility that arises from the free circulation of individuals and groups as a result of their own abilities and efforts, unimpeded by ascribed characteristics such as class or gender.

structuralism

The term structuralism originates from linguistics, especially from Saussure and Chomsky, who saw language as a signifying and structural system. Structuralism generally refers to any form of analysis or theory in which structure takes priority over agency.

structuration theory

Developed by Giddens in an attempt to account for agency and structure, that is, how we shape the social world through our individual actions and how we are reshaped by society.

subjective poverty

Subjective poverty concerns the way that people experience situations of poverty, the dynamics of their daily lives and its impact on their families.

subjectivity

How we see ourselves and our relations with others, based on our immediate and relatively limited understandings and experience of social life.

symbolic capital

A form of value that means nothing in itself but is dependent on whether other people believe someone possesses it.

symbolic violence

Any violence that is exerted upon people in a symbolic rather than physical way. Bourdieu defines symbolic violence as 'every power which manages to impose meanings and to impose them as legitimate by concealing the power relations which are the basis for its force'. One example of symbolic violence is gender relations in the workplace, where many women are treated as inferior and denied the same opportunities as men.

three faces of power

This model was developed by Lukes to explain how power operates directly and indirectly. The one-dimensional view of power refers to power used overtly and deliberately to enforce the preferences or decisions of one group over those of another. The two-dimensional view of power refers to power as the ability to not only make decisions but to also control the political agenda to the extent that potential issues, either as express policy preferences or as grievances, are kept out of the political process. The three-dimensional view of power is the power to shape, influence and determine the wants of others. This most effective and insidious use of power prevents conflict arising in the first place by convincing the less powerful group that the more powerful group's interests are also their interests.

time–space compression

A term used by Harvey to refer to the processes by which time and space are compressed so that distant events, such as conflicts in the Middle East, are experienced in real time across the globe and processes of communication are sped up through new technologies such as mobile phones and the internet.

underemployment

Refers to individuals in employment who are seeking to increase their hours of paid labour.

unemployment

Rates of unemployment measure the proportion of people over the age of fifteen who are available for work and actively looking for it but cannot get a paid job.

welfare state

The mechanism through which social policy is developed and delivered. In capitalist economies its main function is to allocate resources in a climate of conflicting claims.

work rich, work poor

This idea refers to the polarisation of employment between a highly paid, highly skilled group whose excessive work hours mean they have little time for leisure, and a second group of lowly skilled, lowly paid workers whose relationship with the labour market is precarious, intermittent and often involves casual and part-time work.

zombie category

A term used by Beck and Beck-Gernsheim to describe changing family formations, such as rising cohabitation and out-of-wedlock birth rates. The family in this categorisation is a zombie because it represents ideas that seem to be alive but in reality are dead.

Bibliography

ABC (2006b) 'Baby Bonus Split for Teen Mums', *ABC News*, 12 November, www.abc.net.au/news/2006-11-12/baby-bonus-split-for-teen-mums/1307420 (accessed 4 September 2014).

ABC (2007a) 'Draft Citizenship Guidelines Unveiled', *ABC News*, 26 August, www.abc.net.au/news/stories/2007/08/26/2015358.htm (accessed 4 September 2014).

ABC (2007b) 'Baby Bonus by Instalment Ineffective: Single Mothers' Group', *ABC News*, 17 July, www.abc.net.au/news/2007-07-17/baby-bonus-by-instalment-ineffective-single/2504888 (accessed 20 June 2014).

ABC (2014a) 'Dole Changes Not the Answer to High Youth Unemployment, Academic John Spoehr Argues', *ABC News*, 8 May, www.abc.net.au/news/2014-05-08/dole-changes-not-the-answer-to-chronic-high-youth-unemployment-/5438924 (accessed 18 June 2014).

ABC (2014b) 'Surprise Unemployment Drop As 18,000 Jobs Added in March', *ABC News*, 10 April, www.abc.net.au/news/2014-04-10/unemployment-drops-in-march-as-18000-jobs-added/5380672 (accessed 14 August 2014).

ABC (2014c) 'Single Parents on Newstart Allowance Reveal Decline in Nutrition, Mental Health and Large Debts', *ABC News*, 5 February, www.abc.net.au/news/2014-02-05/single-parents-moved-onto-newstart-suffering-poor-nutrition/5239702 (accessed 19 June 2014).

Abercrombie, N., Hill, S. & Turner, B. (1980) *The Dominant Ideology Thesis*, Allen & Unwin, London.

ABS (2003) *Hidden Homelessness in Australia*, media release, www.abs.gov.au/AUSSTATS, 5 October 2007.

ABS (2004) *Measures of Australia's Progress 2004*, catalogue no. 1370.0, Australian Bureau of Statistics: Canberra.

ABS (2005) *Housing Price Indexes: Eight Capital Cities*, catalogue no. 6416.0, Australian Bureau of Statistics: Canberra.

ABS (2006a) *Household Wealth and Wealth Distribution Australia 2003–04*, catalogue no. 6554.0, Australian Bureau of Statistics: Canberra.

ABS (2006b) *Australian Social Trends 2006*, catalogue no. 4102.0, www.abs.gov.au/AUSSTATS/abs@.nsf/DetailsPage/4102.02006?OpenDocument (accessed 4 September 2014).

ABS (2006c) *Information Paper: Census of Population and Housing—Socio-Economic Indexes for Areas, Australia, 2001*, www.abs.gov.au/Ausstats, 8 January 2006.

ABS (2006d) *Labour Force Australia*, catalogue no. 6203.0, Australian Bureau of Statistics: Canberra.

ABS (2006e) *Schools*, catalogue no. 4221.0, Australian Bureau of Statistics: Canberra.

ABS (2006f) *Year Book Australia 2006*, catalogue no. 1301.0, Australian Bureau of Statistics: Canberra.

ABS (2006g) *Housing Occupancy and Costs, Australia 2003–2004*, catalogue no. 4130, Australian Bureau of Statistics: Canberra.

ABS (2007a) *Australian Social Trends 2007*, catalogue no. 4102.0, Australian Bureau of Statistics: Canberra.

ABS (2007b) *Measures of Australia's Progress 2006*, catalogue no. 1370, Australian Bureau of Statistics: Canberra, www.ausstats.abs.gov.au/AUSSTATS/subscriber.nsf/0/47132EE72 AC3581DCA25717F0004ACE8/$File/13700_2006.pdf (accessed 30 December 2007).

ABS (2007c) 'One-Parent Families', *Australian Social Trends, 2007*, Australian Bureau of Statistics: Canberra, www.abs.gov.au/AUSSTATS/abs@.nsf/Latestproducts/ F4B15709EC89CB1ECA25732C002079B2?opendocument (accessed 19 June 2014).

ABS (2010a) *Family Characteristics, Australia, 2009–2010*, catalogue no. 4442.0, Australian Bureau of Statistics: Canberra, www.abs.gov.au/AUSSTATS/abs@.nsf/Latestproducts/ 4442.0Glossary12009-10?opendocument&tabname=Notes&prodno= 4442.0&issue=2009-10&num=&view= (accessed 10 June 2014).

ABS (2010b) 'Parental Divorce or Death during Childhood', *Australian Social Trends 2010*, catalogue no. 4102.0, Australian Bureau of Statistics: Canberra, www.ausstats.abs.gov.au/ AUSSTATS/subscriber.nsf/LookupAttach/4102.0Publication29.09.105/$File/41020_ DeathDivorce.pdf (accessed 19 June 2014).

ABS (2010c) *The Health and Welfare of Australia's Aboriginal and Torres Strait Islander Peoples*, October 2010, catalogue no. 4704.0, Australian Bureau of Statistics: Canberra, www.abs .gov.au/AUSSTATS/abs@.nsf/lookup/4704.0Chapter230Oct+2010#financialstress (accessed 20 June 2014).

ABS (2010d) 'One for the Country: Recent Trends in Fertility', *Australian Social Trends 2010*, catalogue 4102.0, Australian Bureau of Statistics: Canberra, www.ausstats.abs.gov.au/ AUSSTATS/subscriber.nsf/LookupAttach/4102.0Publication14.12.102/$File/41020_ Fertility2010.pdf (accessed 10 June 2014).

ABS (2010e) *Deaths Australia 2009*, catalogue no. 3302.0, Australian Bureau of Statistics: Canberra.

ABS (2011) *Australian Social Trends, September 2011: Are All Schools Uniform?* catalogue no. 4102.0, Australian Bureau of Statistics: Canberra, www.ausstats.abs.gov.au/ AUSSTATS/subscriber.nsf/LookupAttach/4102.0Publication21.09.115/$File/41020_ Schools_Sep2011.pdf (accessed 27 May 2014).

ABS (2012a) *Aboriginal and Torres Strait Islander Peoples (Indigenous) Profile, 2011 Census of Population and Housing*, catalogue no. 2002.0, Australian Bureau of Statistics: Canberra.

ABS (2012b), *Australian Social Trends: Hitting the Books, Characteristics of Higher Education Students*, catalogue no. 4102.0, Australian Bureau of Statistics: Canberra, www .abs.gov.au/AUSSTATS/abs@.nsf/Lookup/4102.0Main+Features20July+2013 (accessed 14 August 2014).

ABS (2012c) *Schools, Australia, 2012*, catalogue no. 4221.0, Australian Bureau of Statistics: Canberra,www.abs.gov.au/AUSSTATS/abs@.nsf/Lookup/4221.0Main+Features202012? OpenDocument (accessed 4 September 2014).

ABS (2012d) *Marriages and Divorces, Australia, 2012*, catalogue no. 3310.0, Australian Bureau of Statistics: Canberra, www.abs.gov.au/AUSSTATS/abs@.nsf/Products/3310.0~2012~ Chapter~Marriages?OpenDocument (accessed 10 June 2014).

ABS (2012e) *Births, Australia 2012*, catalogue no. 3301.0, Australian Bureau of Statistics: Canberra, www.abs.gov.au/AUSSTATS/abs@.nsf/Products/3301.0~2012~Main+Features~Births?OpenDocument (accessed 10 June 2014).

ABS (2013a) *Household Wealth and Income Distribution 2011–12*, catalogue no. 6654.0, Australian Bureau of Statistics: Canberra.

ABS (2013b) *Measures of Australia's Progress, 2013*, catalogue no. 1370.0, www.abs.gov.au/AUSSTATS/abs@.nsf/Lookup/by%20Subject/1370.0~2013~Main%20Features~Learning %20and%20knowledge~29 (accessed 17 June 2014).

ABS (2013c) *Schools, Australia, 2013*, catalogue no. 4221.0, Australian Bureau of Statistics: Canberra www.abs.gov.au/AUSSTATS/abs@.nsf/mf/4221.0 (accessed 4 September 2014).

ABS (2013d) *Education and Work, Australia, May 2013*, catalogue no. 6227.0, Australian Bureau of Statistics: Canberra, www.abs.gov.au/AUSSTATS/abs@.nsf/Products/6227.0~May+2013~Main+Features~Participation?OpenDocument (accessed 17 June 2014).

ABS (2013e) *Household Use of Information Technology, Australia, 2012–13*, Australian Bureau of Statistics: Canberra, catalogue no. 8146.0, www.abs.gov.au/AUSSTATS/abs@.nsf/Latestproducts/8146.0Main%20Features12012-13?opendocument&tabname=Summary&prodno=8146.0&issue=2012-13&num=&view= (accessed 28 May 2014).

ABS (2013f) *Retirement and Retirement Intentions*, catalogue no. 6238.0, Australian Bureau of Statistics: Canberra, www.ausstats.abs.gov.au/AUSSTATS/subscriber.nsf/0/A46D2A800 1FB64B7CA257C39000B6B09/$File/62380_july%202012%20to%20june%202013.pdf (accessed 17 June 2014).

ABS (2013g) *Barriers and Incentives to Labour Force Participation, Australia, July 2012 to June 2013*, catalogue no. 6239.0, Australian Bureau of Statistics: Canberra, www.abs.gov.au/AUSSTATS/abs@.nsf/mf/6239.0 (accessed 18 June 2014).

ABS (2013h) *Australian Aboriginal and Torres Strait Islander Health Survey: Updated Results, 2012–13*, catalogue no. 4727.0.55.006, Australian Bureau of Statistics: Canberra, www.abs .gov.au/AUSSTATS/abs@.nsf/mf/4727.0.55.006 (accessed 4 September 2014).

ABS (2013i) *Australian Labour Market Statistics Data Cube 6105.0*, Australian Bureau of Statistics: Canberra: www.abs.gov.au/AUSSTATS/abs@.nsf/mf/6105.0 (accessed 4 September 2014).

ABS (2013j) *Employee Earnings and Hours, Australia, May 2012*, catalogue no. 6306.0, Australian Bureau of Statistics: Canberra, www.abs.gov.au/AUSSTATS/abs@.nsf/mf/6306.0 (accessed 18 June 2014).

ABS (2013k) *Australian Social Trends, Data Cube: Family and Community, National Summary, 1998–2012*, catalogue no. 4102.0, Australian Bureau of Statistics: Canberra, www.abs.gov .au/AUSSTATS/abs@.nsf/DetailsPage/4102.0Dec%202012 (accessed 10 June 2014).

ABS (2013l) *Household Income and Income Distribution, Australia*, 2011–12, catalogue no. 6523.0, Australian Bureau of Statistics: Canberra, www.abs.gov.au/AUSSTATS/abs@.nsf/Lookup/6523.0Main+Features22011-12 (accessed 13 June 2014).

ABS (2013m) '2011 Census Data Reveals Australia's Most Advantaged and Disadvantaged Areas', *Media Release 41/2013*, 28 March, Australian Bureau of Statistics: Canberra, www.abs.gov .au/AUSSTATS/abs@.nsf/Lookup/by%20Subject/2033.0.55.001~2011~Media%20

Release~2011%20Census%20(SEIFA)%20for%20Australia%20(Media%20Release)~ 10027 (accessed 24 June 2014).

ABS (2013n), *Housing Occupancy and Costs*, catalogue no. 4130.0, Australian Bureau of Statistics: Canberra, www.ausstats.abs.gov.au/AUSSTATS/subscriber.nsf/0/F7B1C824CA185E15 CA257BD40015751E/$File/41300_2011-12.pdf (accessed 23 June 2014).

ABS (2013o) *Local Government and ABS, 2013*, catalogue no: 1376.0, Australian Bureau of Statistics: Canberra, www.abs.gov.au/AUSSTATS/abs@.nsf/Lookup/1376.0main+featu res3002013 (accessed 23 June 2014).

ABS (2013p) *Australian Social Trends, Nov 2013, Aboriginal and Torres Strait Islander Peoples' Labour Force Outcomes*, catalogue number, 4102.0, Australian Bureau of Statistics: Canberra, www.abs.gov.au/AUSSTATS/abs@.nsf/Lookup/4102.0Main+Features20Nov+2013 (accessed 10 June 2014).

ABS (2014a) Labour Force, Australia, May 2014, catalogue no. 6202.0, Australian Bureau of Statistics: Canberra, www.abs.gov.au/AUSSTATS/abs@.nsf/mf/6202.0 (accessed 17 June 2014).

ABS (2014b) *Residential Property Price Indexes—Eight Capital Cities*, catalogue no. 6416.0, Australian Bureau of Statistics: Canberra, www.ausstats.abs.gov.au/AUSSTATS/meisubs .nsf/0/5AAB2ADE37C7F7AFCA257CD60017CCE8/$File/64160_mar%202014.pdf (accessed 23 June 2014).

ACOSS (2005) *Who Cares? Volume 1: A Profile of Care Workers in Australia's Community Services Industries*, paper 140, Australian Council of Social Service: Strawberry Hills, http://acoss .org.au/images/uploads/387__P_140_Carers.pdf (accessed 30 August 2014).

ACOSS (2013) *Poverty in Australia 2012*, paper 194, Australian Council of Social Service: Strawberry Hills, www.acoss.org.au/uploads/ACOSS%20Poverty%20Report%202012_ Final.pdf (accessed 30 August 2014).

Adorno, T. (1973) *Negative Dialectics*, Seabury Press: New York.

AIHW (2005) *A Picture of Australia's Children*, catalogue no. PHE 58, Australian Institute of Health and Welfare: Canberra.

AIHW (2011a) *Australia's Welfare 2011, Australia's welfare no. 10*, catalogue no. AUS 142, Australian Institute of Health and Welfare: Canberra, www.aihw.gov.au/publication-detail/?id=10737420537&tab=2 (accessed 20 June 2014).

AIHW (2011b) *The Health and Welfare of Australia's Aboriginal and Torres Strait Islander People: An Overview*, catalogue no. IHW 42, Australian Institute of Health and Welfare: Canberra.

AIHW (2013) *Australia's Welfare 2013*, Australia's Welfare Series no. 11, catalogue no. AUS 174, Australian Institute of Health and Welfare: Canberra, www.aihw.gov.au/WorkArea/ DownloadAsset.aspx?id=60129544075 (accessed 24 June 2014).

Albrechtsen, J. (2007) 'Don't Get Sniffy at "Affluenza"', *The Australian*, www.theaustralian. com.au/news/dont-get-sniffy-at-affluenza/story-e6frg6n6-1111114080272 (accessed 29 August 2014).

Alexander, M. (1998) 'Big Business and Directorship Networks: The Centralisation of Economic Power in Australia', *Journal of Sociology*, vol. 34, no. 2, pp.107–34.

Alloway N., Gilbert, P., Gilbert. R. & Muspratt, S. (2004) *Factors Impacting on Student Aspirations and Expectations in Regional Australia*, Evaluations and Investigations Programme no. 04/01, Department of Education, Science and Training: Canberra.

Althusser, L. (1971) *Lenin, Philosophy and Other Essays*, Monthly Review Press: New York.

AMP.NATSEM (2004) 'Household Debt in Australia—Walking the Tightrope', *AMP. NATSEM Income and Wealth Report*, issue 9, www.natsem.canberra.edu.au/storage/AMP_NATSEM_09.pdf (accessed 30 August 2014).

AMP.NATSEM (2005) 'Changing Face of the Australian Labour Force 1985–2005', *AMP. NATSEM Income and Wealth Report*, issue 12.

AMP.NATSEM (2007) 'Baby Boomers—Doing It for Themselves', *AMP.NATSEM Income and Wealth Report*, issue 16.

AMP.NATSEM (2009) 'She Works Hard for the Money: Australian Women and the Gender Divide', *AMP-NATSEM Income and Wealth Report*, issue 22, pp. 1–42, www.natsem. canberra.edu.au/storage/AMP_NATSEM_22.pdf (accessed 19 June 2014).

AMP.NATSEM (2012a) *Smart Australians: Education and Innovation in Australia*, issue 32, October 2012, http://media.corporate-ir.net/media_files/IROL/21/219073/AMP.NATSEM_32_Income_and_Wealth_Report_Smart_Australians.pdf (accessed 17 June 2014).

AMP.NATSEM (2012b) *Prices These Days! The Cost of Living in Australia*, http://natsem .canberra.edu.au/publications/?publication=ampnatsem-income-and-wealth-report-31-prices-these-days-the-cost-of-living-in-australia (accessed 17 August 2014).

Anderson, I. (1991) 'Nightmare on Chelmsford, Sydney', *New Scientist*, 1750, January, www .newscientist.com/article/mg12917500.400-nightmare-on-chelmsford-sydney.html (accessed 30 December 2007).

Anderson, K.F. (2013) 'Diagnosing Discrimination: Stress from Perceived Racism and the Mental and Physical Health Effects', *Sociological Inquiry*, vol. 83, no. 1, pp. 55–81.

Anderson, P. & Wild, R. (2007) *Ampe Akelyernemane Meke Mekarle: 'Little Children Are Sacred'*, Northern Territory Government.

Anthias, F. (2001) 'New Hybridities, Old Concepts: The Limits of Culture', *Ethnic and Racial Studies*, vol. 24, pp. 617–41.

Argy, F. (2005) 'Equality of Opportunity—Is It a Factor or an Illusion?', *On Line Opinion*, 7 September, www.onlineopinion.com.au/print.asp?article=228 (accessed 13 February 2006).

Atkinson, A. & Leigh, A. (2006) *The Distribution of Top Incomes in Australia: Using Income Taxation Statistics to Study Income Distribution*, Centre for Economic Policy Research, Australian National University: Canberra.

Atkinson, R. (2006) 'Padding the Bunker: Strategies of Middle-Class Disaffiliation and Colonisation in the City', *Urban Studies*, vol. 43, no. 4, pp. 819–32.

Australia at Work (2013) 'Hours of Work for Full-Time Employees: Usual and Unpaid', fact sheet no. 25, Workplace Research Centre, University of Sydney Business School, www .australiaatwork.org.au/assets/25.%20Unpaid%20hours%20FT.pdf

Australian Curriculum, Assessment and Reporting Authority (2012) *NAPLAN Achievement in Reading, Persuasive Writing, Language Conventions and Numeracy: National Report for 2012*, Australian Curriculum, Assessment and Reporting Authority: Sydney.

Australian Government (1975) *Poverty in Australia: First Main Report, April 1975*, Australian Government Publishing Service: Canberra.

Australian Government (2002) *Intergenerational Report 2002–2003*, budget papers 5.

Australian Government (2009a) *Closing the Gap on Indigenous Disadvantage: The Challenge for Australia*, February, www.dss.gov.au/sites/default/files/documents/05_2012/closing_the_gap.pdf

Australian Government (2009b) *Fourth National Mental Health Plan: An Agenda for Collaborative Government Action in Mental Health 2009–2014*, www.health.gov.au/internet/main/publishing.nsf/Content/mental-pubs-f-plan09 (accessed 16 August 2014).

Australian Government (2013) *Closing the Gap on Indigenous Disadvantage: Prime Minister's Report 2013*, www.dss.gov.au/sites/default/files/documents/02_2013/00313-ctg-report_fa1.pdf

Australian Government (2014) *Budget 2014–15: Higher Education*, 13 May.

Babb, P. (2005) 'A Summary Article of Focus on Social Inequalities', Office for National Statistics UK.

Bacchi, C. L. (1999) *Women, Policy and Politics: The Construction of Policy Problems*, Sage: London

Badcock, B. & Beer, A. (2000) *Home Truths: Property Ownership and Housing Wealth in Australia*, Melbourne University Press: Melbourne.

Barnes, L. L., Mendes de Leon, C. F., Lewis, T. T., Bienias, J. L., Wilson, R. S. & Evans, D. A. (2008) 'Perceived Discrimination and Mortality in a Population-Based Study of Older Adults', *American Journal of Public Health* vol. 98, no. 7, pp. 1241–7.

Baum, S., O'Connor, K. & Stimson, R. (2005) *Suburbs of Advantage and Disadvantage: Fault Lines Exposed*, 1(1): 03.1–03.47, http://books.publishing.monash.edu/apps/bookworm/view/Fault+Lines+Exposed%3A+Advantage+and+Disadvantage+Across+Australia%E2%80%99s+Settlement+System/138/xhtml/cover.xml (accessed 4 September 2014).

Bauman, Z. (1989) *Modernity and the Holocaust*, Polity Press: Cambridge.

Bauman, Z. (1998) *Work, Consumerism and the New Poor*, Open University Press: Buckingham.

Bauman, Z. (2000) *Liquid Modernity*, Polity Press: Cambridge.

Bauman, Z. (2005) *Work, Consumerism and the New Poor* (2nd edn), Open University Press: Maidenhead.

Baxter, J. (2002) 'Patterns of Change and Stability in the Gender Division of Household Labour in Australia, 1986–1997', *Journal of Sociology*, vol. 38, no. 4, pp. 399–424.

Baxter, J. & Hewitt, B. (2013) 'Negotiating Domestic Labor: Women's Earnings and Housework Time in Australia', *Feminist Economic Research Notes*, vol. 19, no. 1.

Baxter, J. & McDonald, P. (2004) *Home Ownership among Young People in Australia, in Decline or Just Delayed?* Australian Housing and Urban Research Institute: Melbourne.

Beck, U. (1992) *Risk Society: Towards a New Modernity*, Sage: London.

Beck, U. (2000) *The Brave New World of Work*, Polity Press: Cambridge.

Beck, U. (2002) 'The Cosmopolitan Society and Its Enemies', *Theory, Culture & Society*, vol. 19, no. 1–2, pp. 17–44.

Beck, U. & Beck-Gernsheim, E. (2002) *Individualization: Institutionalized Individualism and Its Social and Political Consequences*, Sage: London.

Becker, G. S. (1981) *A Treatise on the Family*, Harvard University Press: Cambridge.

Beer, A. & Randolph, B. (2006) *Youth Homelessness in Rural Australia*, Australian Housing and Urban Research Institute: Melbourne.

Bell, D. (1973) *The Coming of Post-Industrial Society*, Basic Books: New York.

Bennett T., Emmison, M. & Frow, J. (1999) *Accounting for Tastes: Australian Everyday Cultures*, Cambridge University Press: Melbourne.

Bernstein, J. (2013) *The Impact of Inequality on Growth*, Center for American Progress.

Biddle, N. (2013) *CAEPR Indigenous Population Project: 2011 Census Papers, Paper 13*, Centre for Aboriginal Economic Policy Research, Australian National University: Canberra.

Biddle, N., Hunter, B. H. & Schwab, R. G. (2004) 'Mapping Indigenous Education Participation', discussion paper no. 276, Centre for Aboriginal Economic Policy Research, Australian National University: Canberra.

Bin-Sallik, M. (ed.) (2000) *Aboriginal Women by Degrees: Their Stories of the Journey towards Academic Achievement*, University of Queensland Press: Brisbane.

Birrell, B. (2000) 'Australian Mothers: Fewer and Poorer', *People and Place*, vol. 8, no. 2, pp. 33–42.

Birrell, B. & Seol, B. (2004) 'Sydney's Ethnic Underclass', *People and Place*, vol. 6, no. 3.

Bittman, M. (1995) *4154.0 Occasional Paper: Recent Changes in Unpaid Work*, www.abs.gov.au/AUSSTATS (accessed 15 February 2001).

Blainey, G. (1984) 'Sadly, Multiculturalism often Means: "Australians Come Second"', *The Age*, 21 September.

Boese, M. & Scutella, R. (2006) *The Brotherhood's Social Barometer: Challenges Facing Australian Youth*, www.bsl.org.au/pdfs/BSL_Social_Barometer_youth_challenges.pdf

Bolt, A. (2009) 'The New Tribe of White Blacks', *Herald Sun* 21 August (accessed 14 June 2014).

Borland, J., Gregory, R. & Sheehan, P. (2001) 'Inequality and Economic Change', in J. Borland, R. Gregory & P. Sheehan (eds), *Work Rich, Work Poor: Inequality and Economic Change in Australia*, CFES: Sydney.

Bornholt, L. J., Piccolo, A. & O'Loughlin, M. (2006) 'Understanding "Identity of Place": Thoughts and Feelings on Local, Regional and National Identity for Adolescents and Young Adults in Urban Contexts', in H. W. Marsh, J. Baumert, G. E. Richards & U. Trautwein (eds), *Proceedings of Third International Biennial SELF Research Conference, 'Self-Concept, Motivation and Identity. Where To from Here?', Berlin, 4–7 July*.

Borooah, V. & Mangan, J. (2002) 'An Analysis of Occupational Outcomes for Indigenous and Asian Employees in Australia', *The Economic Record*, The Economic Society of Australia, vol. 78, no. 240, pp. 31–49

Bottero, W. (2005) *Stratification: Social Division and Inequality*, Routledge: Abingdon.

Bottomore, T. (1993) *Political Sociology* (2nd edn), Pluto Press: London.

Bourdieu, P. (1984) *Distinction: A Social Critique of the Judgement of Taste*, Routledge & Kegan Paul: New York.

Bourdieu, P. (1986) 'The Forms of Capital', in J. G. Richardson (ed.), *Handbook of Theory and Research for the Sociology of Education*, Greenwood Press: New York.

Bourdieu, P. (1990) *The Logic of Practice*, Stanford University Press, Palo Alto.

Bourdieu, P. (2001 [1998]) *Masculine Domination* (trans. R. Nice), Stanford University Press: Stanford.

Bourdieu, P. (2007 [1979]) *Distinction: A Social Critique of the Judgement of Taste*, Harvard University Press: New York.

Bourdieu, P. & Passeron, J. (1990) *Reproduction in Education, Society and Culture*, Sage: London.

Bourdieu, P. & Wacquant, L. (1992) *An Invitation to Reflexive Sociology*, Chicago University Press: Chicago.

Bourke, C., Burden, J. & Moore, S. (1996) *Factors Affecting Performance of Aboriginal and Torres Strait Islander Students at Australian Universities: A Case Study*, Commonwealth of Australia: Canberra.

Bradshaw, J. (2003) *How Has the Notion of Social Exclusion Developed in the European Discourse?* plenary address to the 2003 Australian Social Policy conference, Social Policy Research Centre, University of New South Wales: Sydney.

Brooks, D. (2000) *Bobos in Paradise: The New Upper Class and How They Got There*, Simon & Schuster, New York.

Brotherhood of St Laurence (2006) The Brotherhood's Social Barometer: Challenges Facing Australian Youth, Brotherhood of St Laurence: Brunswick, www.bsl.org.au/pdfs/BSL_Social_Barometer_youth_challenges.pdf (accessed 30 August 2014).

Brotherhood of St Laurence (2013a) 'Household Type', *Social Exclusion Monitor*, Brotherhood of St Laurence and Melbourne Institute, www.bsl.org.au/Social-exclusion-monitor/Who-experiences-social-exclusion/Household-type.aspx (accessed 20 June 2014).

Brotherhood of St Laurence (2013b) 'Who experiences social exclusion?' *Social Exclusion Monitor*, Brotherhood of St Laurence and Melbourne Institute, www.bsl.org.au/Social-exclusion-monitor/Who-experiences-social-exclusion (accessed 20 June 2014).

BRW (2013) 'BRW Rich 200', *Business Review Weekly*, www.brw.com.au/lists/rich-200/2013 (accessed 15 April 2014).

Bryson, L. (1992) *Welfare and the State: Who Benefits?* Macmillan: London.

Bryson, L. & Thompson, F. (1972) *An Australian Newtown: Life and Leadership in a Working Class Suburb*, Penguin: Blackburn.

Bryson, L. & Winter, I. (1999) *Social Change, Suburban Lives: An Australian Newtown, 1960s to 1990s*, Allen & Unwin: Sydney.

Bunda, T. & McConville, G. (2002) 'Indigenous Higher Education, Myths, Cuts and Obvious Decline', *Campus Review*, 29 May–2 June, pp. 13–18.

Burchardt, T., Le Grand, J. & Piachaud, D. (2002) 'Introduction', in T. Burchardt, J. Le Grand & D. Paichaud (eds), *Social Exclusion*, Oxford University Press: Oxford.

Butler, J. (1999) *Gender Trouble: Feminism and the Subversion of Identity* (2nd edn), Routledge: New York.

Castles, F. (1985) *The Working Class and Welfare: Reflections on the Political Development of the Welfare State in Australia and New Zealand, 1890–1980*, Allen & Unwin: Wellington.

Castles, F. (2000) 'Advanced Welfare States', in R. E. Goodin & D. Mitchell (eds), *The Foundations of the Welfare State*, vol. 2, Edward Elgar: Cheltenham.

Castles, S. & Kosack, G. (1973) *Immigrant Workers and Class Structure in Western Europe*, Oxford University Press: Oxford.

Centre for the Study of Higher Education (2008) *Participation and Equity: A Review of the Participation in Higher Education of People from Low Socioeconomic Backgrounds and Indigenous People*, University of Melbourne: Melbourne.

Centrelink (2001) *Budget 2001: Key Facts*, Canberra, www.centrelink.gov.au (accessed 6 June 2001).

Chalmers, J. (2007) 'Is Casual Employment a "Bridge" or a "Trap"?' paper presented at the HILDA Survey Research Conference, 19–20 July, University of Melbourne: Melbourne.

Chamberlain, C. (1983) *Class Consciousness in Australia*, Allen & Unwin: Sydney.

Chamberlain, C. & Johnson, G. (2013) 'Pathways into adult homelessness', *Journal of Sociology*, vol. 49, pp. 60–77.

Chamberlain, C. & MacKenzie, D. (2008) 'Australian Census Analytic Program: Counting the Homeless 2006', catalogue no. 2050.0, Australian Bureau of Statistics: Canberra.

Charlesworth, S. (2000) *A Phenomenology of Working Class Culture*, Cambridge University Press: Cambridge.

Cheetham, W. S. & Cheetham, R. J. (1976) 'Concepts of Mental Illness among the Xhosa People in South Africa', *Australian and New Zealand Journal of Psychiatry*, vol. 10, pp. 39–45.

Chesterman, J. & Galligan, B. (1997) *Citizens without Rights: Aborigines and Australian Citizenship*, Cambridge University Press: Cambridge.

Chomik, R. & Piggott, J. (2012) *Mature-Age Labour Force Participation: Trends, Barriers, Incentives and Future Potential*, http://cepar.edu.au/media/93861/participation_paper.pdf (accessed 16 June 2014).

Coalition (2013) 'The Coalition's Policy for Paid Parental Leave, August', http://lpaweb-static.s3.amazonaws.com/The%20Coalition%E2%80%99s%20Policy%20for%20Paid%20Parental%20Leave.pdf (accessed 19 June 2014).

Colebatch, T. (2013) 'Country's Rich Have Lion's Share of Income Growth', *Sydney Morning Herald* 10 October, www.smh.com.au/federal-politics/political-news/countrys-rich-have-lions-share-of-income-growth-20131009-2v8q2.html

Collins, C., Kenway, J. & McLeod, J. (2000) *Factors Influencing the Educational Performance of Males and Females in School and Their Initial Destinations after Leaving School*, Commonwealth Department of Education, Training and Youth Affairs: Canberra.

Collins, J. (1991) *Migrant Hands in a Distant Land: Australia's Postwar Immigration*, Pluto Press: Sydney.

Collins, J., Noble, G., Poynting, S. & Tabar, P. (2000) *Kebabs, Kids, Cops and Crime*, Pluto Press: Sydney.

Connell, R. W. (1995) *Masculinities*, Allen & Unwin: Sydney.

Connell, R. W. (2005) *Masculinities* (2nd edn), Allen & Unwin: Sydney.

Connell, R. W. (2007) *Southern Theory: The Global Dynamics of Knowledge in Social Science*, Allen & Unwin: Sydney

Connell, R. W. & Irving T. H. (1980) *Class Structure in Australian History*, Longman Cheshire: Melbourne.

Considine, G., Watson, I. & Hall, R. (2005) 'Who's Missing Out? Access and Equity in Vocational Education and Training', Evaluation Program Report, NCVER.

Cowan, J. (2007) '"Thousands" Missing Out on High School in NT', *ABC News*, www.abc .net.au/news/2007-03-21/thousands-missing-out-on-high-school-in-nt/2222112 (accessed 5 September 2014).

Cowlishaw, G. (1999) *Rednecks, Eggheads and Blackfellas: A Study of Racial Power and Intimacy in Australia*, Allen & Unwin: Sydney.

Cowlishaw, G. (2004) 'Racial Positioning, Privilege and Public Debate', in A. Moreton-Robinson (ed.), *Whitening Race: Essays in Social and Cultural Criticism*, Aboriginal Studies Press: Canberra.

Cox, O. (1970) *Caste, Class and Race*, Monthly Review Press: New York.

Craig, L. (2002) *The Time Cost of Parenthood: An Analysis of Daily Workload*, Social Policy Research Centre, University of New South Wales: Sydney.

Creighton, A. (2014) 'Australia's Problem Is Not Poverty but an Addiction to Welfare', *The Australian* 17 January.

Crittendon, A. (2001) *The Price of Motherhood*, Henry Holt & Company: New York.

Crompton, R. (1998) *Class and Stratification: An Introduction to Current Debates* (2nd edn), Polity: Cambridge.

Crompton, R. & Mann, M. (1986) *Gender and Stratification*, Polity Press: Cambridge.

Crook, A. (2011) 'Double-Page "Correction" for Bolt's Racial Discrimination', *Crikey* 19 October, www.crikey.com.au/2011/10/19/double-page-correction-for-bolts-racial-discrimination (accessed 1 June 2014).

Cunneen, C. (2001) *Conflict, Politics and Crime: Aboriginal Communities and the Police*, Allen & Unwin: Sydney.

d'Addio, A. (2007) 'Intergenerational Transmission of Disadvantage: Mobility or Immobility across Generations?' a review of the evidence for OECD countries, http://econpapers .repec.org/paper/oecelsaab/52-en.htm (accessed 23 February 2008).

Dahrendorf, R. (1959) *Class and Class Conflict*, Routledge & Kegan Paul: London.

Daly, A., McNamara, J., Tanton, R., Harding, A. & Yap, M. (2006) 'Indicators of Social Exclusion for Australia's Children: An Analysis by State and Age Group', paper presented at the

University of Queensland Social Research Centre Opening and Conference, 18–19 July, NATSEM, University of Canberra.

Daly, K. (2000) 'Gendered Time in Families: Navigating Uncertainty and Contradiction', paper presented at TASA 2000 Sociological Sites/Sights conference, Australian Sociological Association, 3–6 December, Adelaide.

Daniels, G. & Friedman, S. (1999) 'Spatial Inequality and the Distribution of Industrial Toxic Releases', *Social Science Quarterly*, vol. 80, no. 2, pp. 244–62.

Davis, K. (1937) 'The Sociology of Prostitution', *American Sociology Review*, vol. 2, no. 5 pp. 744–55.

Davis, K. & Moore, W. (1945) 'Some Principles of Stratification', *American Sociological Review*, vol. 10, no. 2, pp. 242–49.

Dean, H. (1992) 'Poverty Discourse and the Disempowerment of the Poor', *Critical Social Policy*, vol. 12, no. 2 (35), pp. 79–88.

Dean, H. & Taylor-Gooby, P. (1992) *Dependency Culture*, Harvester Wheatsheaf: Hemel Hempstead.

Dean, M. & Hindess, B. (1998) *Governing Australia: Studies in Contemporary Rationalities of Government*, Cambridge University Press: Melbourne.

Delphy, C. (1984) *Close to Home: A Materialist Analysis of Women's Exploitation*, Hutchison: London.

Dempsey, K. (1990) *Smalltown: A Study of Social Inequality, Cohesion and Belonging*, Oxford University Press: Melbourne.

Department of Education (2014) *Indigenous Education Review*, Northern Territory Government, www.education.nt.gov.au/parents-community/students-learning/indigenous-education-review-1 (accessed 17 June 2014).

Department of Health (2013) 'National Mental Health Report 2013: Tracking Progress of Mental Health Reform in Australia 1993–2011', www.health.gov.au/internet/publications/publishing.nsf/Content/mental-pubs-n-report13-toc (accessed 16 August 2014).

Department of Human Services (2013) 'Parenting Payment', www.humanservices.gov.au/customer/enablers/centrelink/parenting-payment/changes-to-parenting-payment

Department of Human Services (2014a) 'Assistance for Isolated Children Scheme', www.humanservices.gov.au/customer/services/centrelink/assistance-for-isolated-children

Department of Human Services (2014b) 'Payment Rates for Abstudy', www.humanservices.gov.au/customer/enablers/centrelink/abstudy/payment-rates

Department of Human Services (2014c) 'Choosing between Parental Leave Pay and Baby Bonus', www.humanservices.gov.au/customer/enablers/centrelink/baby-bonus/choosing-between-ppl-and-bb

Department of Human Services (2014d) 'Baby Bonus', www.humanservices.gov.au/customer/enablers/centrelink/newborn-upfront-payment-and-newborn-supplement/eligibility-for-nupns

Department of Immigration and Citizenship (2012) *Migration Trends 2011–12 at a Glance*.

Department of Social Services (2013) *Age Pension*, www.dss.gov.au/our-responsibilities/seniors/benefits-payments/age-pension

Derrida, J. (1991) *A Derrida Reader: Between the Blinds*, Harvester: Hemel Hempstead.

DEST (2003) *Educating Boys: Issues and Information*, Department of Education, Science and Training.

DEST (2005) *Higher Education Report 2005*, Department of Education, Science and Training.

Devine, F. (1997) *Social Class in America and Britain*, Edinburgh University Press: Edinburgh.

Devine, F. (2004) *Class Practices: How Parents Help Their Children Get Good Jobs*, Cambridge University Press: Cambridge.

Devine, F. & Savage, M. (2005) 'The Cultural Turn, Sociology and Class Analysis', in F. Devine, M. Savage, J. Scott & R. Crompton (eds), *Rethinking Class: Culture, Identities and Lifestyle*, Palgrave Macmillan: Basingstoke.

Doll, W. & Thompson, E. H. (1979) 'Family Coping with the Mentally Ill', in J. R. Folta & E. S. Deck, *A Sociological Framework for Patient Care*, John Wiley & Sons: Brisbane.

Donath, S. (1995) 'The Invisible Child: A Feminist Critique of Economic Theory', *Social Security Journal*, June, pp. 98–101.

Doughney, J. (2002) 'Socioeconomic Banditry: Poker Machines and Income Redistribution in Victoria', in T. Eardley & B. Bradbury (eds), *Competing Visions: Refereed Proceedings of the National Social Policy Conference 2001*, SPRC report 1/02, Social Policy Research Centre, University of New South Wales: Sydney.

Doussa, J. von (2004) 'Conflict and Countering Terrorism: Civil and Political Rights and the Rule of Law', speech presented at the Seventh International Conference for National Human Rights Institutions, 14–17 September, Seoul, www.hreoc.gov.au/about/media/speeches/speeches_president/2004/koreaterrorismworkshop.html (accessed 30 January 2008).

Dunn, K., Forrest, J., Babacan, H., Paradies Y. & Pedersen, A. (2011) *Challenging Racism, the Anti-Racism Research Project: National Level Findings*, www.uws.edu.au/__data/assets/pdf_file/0007/173635/NationalLevelFindingsV1.pdf (accessed 1 June 2014).

Durkheim, E. (1962) *Socialism*, Collier Books: New York.

Dusseldorp Skills Forum (2006) *How Young People Are Faring at a Glance*, Dusseldorp Skills Forum: Sydney.

EAG (2013) *Australia: Overview of the Education System*, http://gpseducation.oecd.org/CountryProfile?primaryCountry=AUS&treshold=10&topic=EO (accessed 27 May 2014).

EAPN (2014) *How Is Poverty Measured?* The European Anti-Poverty Network, www.eapn.eu/en/what-is-poverty/how-is-poverty-measured (accessed 14 April 2014).

Elliot, H. (2004) 'The Joy of Work', *Weekend Australian Review*, 19–20 June, p. 15.

Emery, K. (2014) 'More Wage Earners Turn to Foodbank', *The West Australian* 30 January, https://au.news.yahoo.com/a/21168710

Emmison, M. (1991) 'Wright and Goldthorpe: Constructing the Agenda of Class Analysis', in J. Baxter et al., *Class Analysis and Contemporary Australia*, Palgrave Macmillan: Melbourne, pp. 38–65.

Emmison, M. (2003) 'Social Class and Cultural Mobility', *Journal of Sociology*, vol. 39, no. 3, pp. 211–30.

Encel, J. D. (2000) 'Indigenous Participation in Higher Education', occasional paper 00/C, Higher Education Division, DETYA: Canberra.

England, P. & Folbre, N. (1999) 'Who Should Pay for the Kids?' *Annals of the American Academy of Political and Social Science*, vol. 563, pp. 194–207.

Erikson, R. & Goldthorpe, J. (1992) *The Constant Flux: A Study of Class Mobility in Industrial Societies*, University of Oxford Press: Oxford.

Esping-Andersen, G. (1990) *The Three Worlds of Welfare Capitalism*, Princeton University Press: Princeton.

Evans, M. D. R. (2000) 'Women's Participation in the Labour Force: Ideals and Behaviour', *Australian Social Monitor*, vol. 3, no. 2, pp. 49–57.

Ferdinand, A., Paradies, Y. & Kelaher, M. (2013) *Mental Health Impacts of Racial Discrimination in Victorian Aboriginal Communities: The Localities Embracing and Accepting Diversity (LEAD) Experiences of Racism Survey*, Lowitja Institute: Melbourne.

Ferrier, F. (2006) 'A Review of Higher Education Equity Research in Australia: 2000–2005', working paper no. 64, Monash University: Melbourne.

Fincher, R. & Saunders, P. (2001) *Creating Unequal Futures? Rethinking Inequality, Poverty and Disadvantage*, Allen & Unwin: Sydney.

Firestone, S. (1970) *The Dialectic of Sex*, William Morrow: New York.

Fletcher, M. & Guttmann, B. (2013) *Income in Australia, Economic Roundup, Issue 2: The Treasury*, The Treasury, Australian Government: Canberra.

Flint, J. (2007) 'Esperance Lead Pain Ignored', *Sunday Times*, 28 April.

Folbre, N. (1994) *Who Pays for the Kids? Gender and the Structure of Constraint*, Routledge: London.

Foucault, M. (1965) *Madness and Civilization: A History of Insanity in the Age of Reason*, Pantheon Books: New York.

Foucault, M. (1980) 'The Eye of Power', in C. Gordon (ed.), *Power/Knowledge: Selected Interviews and Other Writings: 1972–1977*, Pantheon Books: New York.

Foucault, M. (1995 [1975]) *Discipline and Punish: The Birth of the Prison*, Vintage Books: New York.

Fukuyama, F. (1992) *The End of History and the Last Man*, The Free Press: New York.

Fullarton, S., Walker, M., Ainley, J. & Hillman, K. (2003) 'Patterns of Participation in Year 12', Longitudinal Surveys of Australian Youth Report no. 33, Australian Council for Education Research: Camberwell.

Galbraith, J. (1958) *The Affluent Society*, Hamish Hamilton, London.

Gale, T. & Parker, S. (2013) 'Widening Participation in Australian Higher Education', Report to the Higher Education Funding Council for England and the Office of Fair Access, England, CFE (Research and Consulting) Ltd, Leicester, and Edge Hill University, Lancashire, www.deakin.edu.au/arts-ed/efi/pubs/wp-in-australian-he.pdf (accessed 30 August 2014).

Gallagher, B. J. (1980) *The Sociology of Mental Illness*, Prentice Hall: Englewood Cliffs.

Gans, H. (1976) 'The Uses of Poverty: The Poor Pay All', *Social Policy*, July/August, pp. 20–4.

Gerth, H. H. & Mills, C. W. (1948) *From Max Weber: Essays in Sociology*, Routledge & Kegan: London.

Giddens, A. (1971) *Capitalism and Modern Social Theory*, Cambridge University Press: Cambridge.

Giddens, A. (1991) *Modernity and Self-Identity*, Polity Press: Cambridge.

Giddens, A. (1992) *The Transformation of Intimacy: Sexuality, Love Eroticism and Modern Societies*, Stanford University Press: Stanford.

Giddens, A. (1994) 'Durkheim's Political Sociology', in P. Hamilton, *Emile Durkheim, Critical Assessments*, Routledge: London, pp. 184–219.

Giddens, A. (2001) 'The Question of Inequality', in A. Giddens (ed.), *The Global Third Way Debate*, Polity Press: Cambridge.

Gilding, M. (2004) 'Entrepreneurs, Elites and the Ruling Class: The Changing Structure of Power and Wealth in Australian Society', *Australian Journal of Political Science*, vol. 39, no. 1, pp. 127–43.

Gilding, M. (2005) 'Families and Fortunes: Accumulation, Management Succession and Inheritance in Wealthy Families', *Journal of Sociology*, vol. 41, no. 1, pp. 29–45.

Gibson, R., Wilson, S., Denemark, D., Meagher, G. & Western, M. (2004) The Australian Survey of Social Attitudes 2003 [data file]. Canberra: Australian Social Science Data Archive, Research School of Social Sciences, Australian National University.

Glass, D. (1954) *Social Mobility in Britain*, Routledge & Kegan Paul: London.

Goertzel, T. G. (1976) *Political Society*, Rand McNally Publishing: Chicago.

Goldthorpe, J. (1980) *Social Mobility and Class Structure in Modern Britain*, Oxford University Press: Oxford.

Goldthorpe, J., Llewelyn C. & Payne, C. (1987) *Social Mobility and Class Structure in Modern Britain*, Oxford University Press: Oxford.

Goldthorpe, J. & Lockwood, D. (1969) *The Affluent Worker in the Class Structure*, Cambridge University Press: London.

Gole, N. (1996) *The Forbidden Modern*, University of Michigan Press: Ann Arbor.

Goodin, R. E., Headey, B., Muffels, R. & Dirven, H. (1999) *The Real Worlds of Welfare Capitalism*, Cambridge University Press: Cambridge.

Goot, M. & Watson, I. (2005) 'Immigration, Multiculturalism and National Identity', in S. Wilson, G. Meagher, R. Gibson, D. Denemark & M. Western (eds), *Australian Social Attitudes: The First Report*, UNSW Press: Sydney.

Gordon D., Adelman, L., Ashworth, K., Bradshaw, J., Levitas, R., Middleton, S., Pantazis, C., Patsios, D., Payne, S., Townsend, P. & Williams, J. (2000) *Poverty and Social Exclusion in Britain*, Joseph Rowntree Foundation: York.

Gramsci, A. (1971) *Selections from the Prison Notebooks*, International Publishers: New York.

Gray, M. & Chapman, B. (2001) 'Foregone Earnings From Child Rearing', *Family Matters*, vol. 58, Autumn, pp. 4–9.

Gray, M., Hunter, B. & Howlett, M. (2013) 'Indigenous Employment: A Story of Continuing Growth', CAEPR Topics Issue no. 2/2013, Centre for Aboriginal Economic Policy Research, Australian National University: Canberra.

Greenville, J., Pobke, C. & Rogers, N. (2013) *Trends in the Distribution of Income in Australia*, Productivity Commission Staff Working Paper: Canberra.

Grosz, E. (1994) *Volatile Bodies*, Bloomington: University of Indiana Press.

Gunder Frank, A. (1966) *The Development of Underdevelopment*, Random House: New York.

Haebich, A. (2004) 'Stolen Wages and Consequential Aboriginal Poverty: A National Issue', speech delivered at the Kathleen Fitzpatrick Lecture, 20 May, University of Melbourne.

Hakim, C. (2000) *Work-Lifestyle Choices in the 21st Century: Preference Theory*, Oxford University Press: Oxford.

Hall, S. (1992) 'Our Mongrel Selves', *New Statesman and Society*, 19 June, pp. 6–8.

Hall, S. (1997) *Representation: Cultural Representations and Signifying Practices*, Sage: London.

Hall, S., Critcher, C., Jefferson, T., Clarke, J. & Roberts, B. (1978) *Policing the Crisis*, Macmillan: London.

Harding, A. & Greenwell, H. (2001) 'Trends in Income and Expenditure Inequality in the 1980s and 1990s: A Re-examination and Further Results', discussion paper no. 57, NATSEM: Canberra.

Harding, A. (2005) 'Recent Trends in Income Inequality in Australia', presentation to the Conference on 'Sustaining Prosperity: New Reform Opportunities for Australia', Melbourne, 31 March, NATSEM: Canberra.

Harding, A., Vu, Q. N. & Payne, A. (2007) 'A Rising Tide? Income Inequality, the Social Safety Net and the Labour Market in Australia', paper presented at the Labour Markets in Australia and Japan, Canberra National Centre for Social and Economic Modelling conference, Canberra.

Harris, E., Nutbeam, D. & Sainsbury, P. (2001) 'Does Our Limited Analysis of the Dimensions of Poverty Limit the Way We Seek Solutions?', in R. Eckersley, J. Dixon & B. Douglas (eds), *The Social Origins of Health and Well-Being*, Cambridge University Press: Melbourne.

Hartmann, H. (1981) 'The Unhappy Marriage of Marxism and Feminism', in L. Sargent (ed.), *Women and Revolution*, Pluto Press: London.

Harvey, D. (1990) *The Condition of Post-Modernity: An Enquiry into the Origins of Social Change*, Blackwell: Oxford.

Hayek, F.A. von (1976) *Law, Legislation and Liberty, vol 2: The Mirage of Social Justice*, University of Chicago Press: Chicago.

Hayes, B. (1990) 'Intergenerational Occupational Mobility among Employed and Non-Employed Women: The Australian Case', *Journal of Sociology*, vol. 26, no. 3, pp. 368–89.

Hayward, D. & Esposto, A. (2004) 'An Unfair Go? Government Funding of Government and Non-Government School Education', policy paper no. 1, Institute of Social Research, Swinburne University of Technology: Melbourne.

Hazelton, M. (2004) 'Mental Health Reform, Citizenship and Human Rights in Four Countries', *International Journal of Health Sociology: Policy, Promotion, Equity & Practice*, vol. 14, no. 3, pp. 43–60.

Headey, B. & Wooden, M. (2007) 'Economic Wellbeing and Subjective Wellbeing: The Effects of Income and Wealth', in L. Manderson (ed.), *Rethinking Well-Being: Essays on Health, Disability and Disadvantage*, Australian Public Intellectual Network: Perth, pp. 91–109.

Henderson, J. (2005) 'Neoliberalism, Community Care and Mental Health Policy', *Health Sociology Review*, vol. 14, no. 3, pp. 242–54.

Henman, P. (2001a) 'Deconstructing Welfare Dependency: The Case of Australian Welfare Reform', *Radical Statistics*, no. 79, www.radstats.org.uk/no079/henman.htm (accessed 13 May 2003).

Henman, P. (2001b) 'The Poverty of Welfare Reform Discourse', paper presented at the National Social Policy Conference 'Competing Visions', 4–6 July, University of New South Wales: Sydney.

Hetherington, D. (2013) 'Per Capita Tax Survey 2012: Public Attitudes towards Taxation and Government Expenditure', Per Capita Research Paper, Percapita www.percapita.org.au/_dbase_upl/2012TaxSurveyFinal.pdf (accessed 1 July 2014).

Hewitt, B., Baxter, J. & Western, M. (2006) 'Family, Work and Health: The Impact of Marriage, Parenthood and Employment on Self-Reported Health of Australian Men and Women', *Journal of Sociology*, vol. 42, no. 1, pp. 61–78.

Hewitt, B., Baxter, J., Givans, S., Murphy, M., Myers, P. & Meiklejohn, C. (2013) *Men's Engagement in Shared Care and Domestic Work in Australia*, Office for Women, Department of Families, Housing, Community Services and Indigenous Affairs: Canberra.

Higley, J., Deacon, D. & Smart, D. (1979) *Elites in Australia*, Routledge & Kegan Paul: London.

Hinkson, M. (2007) 'Introduction: In the Name of the Child', in J. Altman & M. Hinkson (eds), *Coercive Reconciliation*, Arena Publications: Melbourne.

Hodge, B. & O'Carroll, J. (2006) *Borderwork in Multicultural Australia*, Allen & Unwin: Sydney.

Hodgson, H. (2014) 'The Super Rich and Tax: Lifters or Leaners?' *The Conversation* 10 June, http://theconversation.com/the-super-rich-and-tax-lifters-or-leaners-27700

Hoffmann, L. (2006) 'Place and Identity', *ABC News*, www.abc.net.au/local/stories/2006/08/06/1707463.htm (accessed 5 September 2014).

Holmes, D. (2014) 'The Great Global Warming Subsidy: The Truth about Australian Corporate Welfare', *The Conversation* 16 February, http://theconversation.com/the-great-global-warming-subsidy-the-truth-about-australian-corporate-welfare-23281 (accessed 1 July 2014).

hooks, b. (1981) *Ain't I a Woman? Black Women and Feminism*, Pluto Press: London.

Hughes, H. (2002) 'The Politics of Envy: An International Phenomenon', *Policy*, Winter (June–August), Centre for Independent Studies: Sydney.

HREOC (1993) *Human Rights and Mental Illness: Report of the National Inquiry into the Human Rights of People with Mental Illness*, Human Rights and Equal Opportunity Commission: Canberra.

HREOC (2006) *A Statistical Overview of Aboriginal and Torres Strait Islander Peoples in Australia*, Human Rights and Equal Opportunity Commission, www.humanrights.gov.au/social_justice/statistics/index.html (accessed 30 December 2006).

Hunter, B. (1996) 'Aboriginal Australians and the Socioeconomic Status of Urban Neighbourhoods', CAEPR, discussion paper 106, Australian National University: Canberra.

Hunter, B. (1999) 'Three Nations Not One: Indigenous and Other Australian Poverty', CAEPR, working paper no. 1, Australian National University: Canberra.

Ivory, B. (2005) 'Indigenous Governance and Leadership: A Case Study from the Thamarrurr (Port Keats) Region in the Northern Territory', paper presented at Indigenous Community Governance Project (ICGP) and WA and Australian Government Partners workshop, 18 October, Perth.

Jabour, B. (2014) 'Young Australians to Face Six-Month Wait for Unemployment Benefits', *The Guardian* 13 May, www.theguardian.com/world/2014/may/13/young-australians-to-face-six-month-wait-for-unemployment-benefits (accessed 18 June 2014).

Jackson, N. & Walter, M. (2007) 'Retirement Motivated Movement Intentions of Australian Baby Boomers', Demographic Analytical Services, research project no. 6, University of Tasmania: Hobart.

Jacobs, K. & Walter, M. (2003) *An Analysis of the Housing Needs of Younger and Older Aboriginal People in Tasmania*, Aboriginal Housing Services, Housing Department: Hobart.

James, R., Wyn, J., Baldwin, G., Hepworth, G., McInnis, C. & Stephanou, A. (1999) *Rural and Isolated Students and Their Higher Education Choices: A Re-examination of Student Location, Socioeconomic Background, and Educational Advantage and Disadvantage*, AGPS: Canberra.

James, R. (2002) *Socioeconomic Background and Higher Education Participation: An Analysis of School Students' Aspirations and Expectations*, AGPS: Canberra.

James, R., Bexley, E., Devlin, M. & Marginson, S. (2007) *Australian University Student Finances 2006: Final Report*, Universities Australia: Canberra.

Jamrozik, A. (2001) *Social Policy in the Post-Welfare State: Australians on the Threshold of the 21st Century*, Longman: Sydney.

Job Services Australia (2104) *Work for the Dole in Selected Areas*, http://docs.employment.gov.au/system/files/doc/other/140508_wfd_general_factsheet.pdf (accessed 28 May 2014).

Jones, M. A. (1983) *The Australian Welfare State: Growth, Crisis and Change*, George Allen & Unwin: Sydney.

Karvelas, P. (2014) 'McClure Report Calls for Tighter Rules for Disability Support Pension', *The Australian* 29 June, www.theaustralian.com.au/national-affairs/mcclure-report-calls-for-tighter-rules-for-disability-support-pension/story-fn59niix-1226970792655 (accessed 1 July 2014).

Kelley, J. & Evans, M. (1995), 'Class and Class Conflict in Six Western Nations', *American Sociological Review*, vol. 60, no. 2, pp. 157–78.

Kelly, S., Bolton, T. & Harding, A. (2005) *NATSEM Income and Wealth Report 2005*, National Centre for Social and Economic Modelling, University of Canberra: Canberra.

Kelly, S. & Harding, A. (2007) *Don't Rely on the Old Folks' Money: Inheritance Patterns in Australia*, National Centre for Social and Economic Modelling: Canberra, http://apo.org.au/research/dont-rely-old-folks-money-inheritance-patterns-australia (accessed 5 September 2014).

Kennedy, B. & Firman, D. (2006) 'Indigenous SEIFA—Revealing the Ecological Fallacy', paper presented at the 12th Biennial Conference of the Australian Population Association, 'Population and Society: Issues, Research, Policy', 15–17 September, Canberra.

Ker, P. (2013) 'Mining Tax Revenue Slumps', *Sydney Morning Herald* 15 May.

Kramer, P. (2011) *Maggie Goes on a Diet*, Aloha Publishers.

Lamb, S., Walstab, A., Teese, R., Vickers, M. & Rumberger, R. (2004), *Staying on at School: Improving Student Retention in Australia*, Centre for Post-Compulsory Education and Lifelong Learning, University of Melbourne: Melbourne.

Lamont, M. (1992) *Money, Morals and Manners*, University of Chicago Press: Chicago.

Lanzarotta, M. (2008) 'Robert Putnam on Immigration and Social Cohesion', www.hks.harvard.edu/news-events/publications/insight/democratic/robert-putnam (accessed 14 February 2014).

Leigh, A. (2007) 'Intergenerational Mobility in Australia', *B. E. Journal of Economic Analysis & Policy*, www.bepress.com/bejeap/vol7/iss2/art6 (accessed 30 December 2007).

Leigh, A. (2013) *Battlers and Billionaires: The Story of Inequality in Australia*, Black Inc: Melbourne.

Lentin, A. & Titley, G. (2011) *The Crises of Multiculturalism: Racism in a Neoliberal Age*, Zed Books: London.

Lerner, G. (1986) *The Creation of Patriarchy*, Oxford University Press: New York.

Lever, R. (2007) 'CEO Pay Sparks Backlash', *Sydney Morning Herald* 13 February.

Lewis, O. (1961) *Children of Sanchez: Autobiography of a Mexican Family*, Random House.

Lewis, T., Everson-Rose, S. A., Powell, L. H., Matthews, K. A., Brown, C., Karavolos, K., Sutton-Tyrell, K., Jacobs, E. & Wesley, D. (2006) 'Chronic Exposure to Everyday Discrimination and Coronary Artery Calcification in African-American Women: The SWAN Heart Study', *Psychosomatic Medicine*, vol. 68, no. 3, pp. 362–8.

Lipset, S. & Bendix, R. (1959) *Social Mobility in an Industrial Society*, University of California Press: Berkeley.

Lister, R. 2004, *Poverty*, Polity Press: Cambridge.

Lloyd, R., Harding, A. & Hellwig, O. (2000) *Regional Divide? A Study of Income Inequality in Australia*, discussion paper no. 51, Sustaining Regions, National Centre for Social and Economic Modelling: Canberra.

Lombroso, C. (1980 [1895]) *The Female Offender*, Rothman: Littleton.

Lukes, S. (1974) *Power: A Radical View*, Palgrave Macmillan: Basingstoke.

Lupton, D. (2005) 'The Body, Medicine & Society', in J. Germov (ed.), *Second Opinion: An Introduction to Health Sociology*, Oxford University Press: Melbourne.

Lyon, D. (1999) *Postmodernity*, Open University Press: Milton Keynes.

Marks, G. N. (2005) 'Issues in the School-to-Work Transition: Evidence from the Longitudinal Surveys of Australian Youth', *Journal of Sociology*, vol. 41, no. 4, pp. 363–85.

Marks, G. N. (2007) 'Income Poverty, Subjective Poverty and Financial Stress', social policy research paper no. 29, Commonwealth Government Department of Families, Community Services and Indigenous Affairs, Commonwealth of Australia: Canberra.

Marshall, T. H. (1950) *Citizenship and Social Class, and Other Essays*, Cambridge University Press: Cambridge.

Marston, G. (2003) 'Rethinking Social Inequality: The Case of "Illegal Refugees"', paper presented at the first annual conference of the Centre for Research on Social Inclusion, 12 November, Macquarie University: Sydney.

Marx, K. & Engels, F. (1998 [1948]) *The Communist Manifesto*, Allen & Unwin: London.

Maslen, G. (2013) 'Degrees of Separation: More Women Enrolling at Universities', *Sydney Morning Herald* 25 November, www.smh.com.au/national/education/degrees-of-separation-more-women-enrolling-at-universities-20131124-2y46e.html#ixzz34xYJx1Hi (accessed 18 June 2014).

May, J. (2014) 'Middle class, hard working and homeless', *The Age* 8 April, www.theage.com.au/victoria/middle-class-hard-working-and-homeless-20140407-368w7.html

McDonald, P. & Merlo, R. (2002) *Housing and Its Association with Other Life Outcomes*, AHURI, Australian National University Research Centre: Canberra.

MCEETYA (2006) *Australian Directions in Indigenous Education 2005–2008*, Ministerial Council on Education, Employment, Training and Youth Affairs: Melbourne.

McIntosh, P. (1990) 'White Privilege: Unpacking the Invisible Knapsack', *Peace and Freedom*, vol. 49, no. 4, pp.10–12.

McNamara, J., Lloyd, R., Toohey, M. & Harding, A. (2004) *Prosperity for All? How Low Income Families Have Fared in Boom Times*, NATSEM, University of Canberra: Canberra.

Melbourne Institute of Applied Economic and Social Research (2013) *Poverty Lines: Australia*, September Quarter 2013, University of Melbourne: Melbourne.

Memmot, P., Long, S., Chambers, C. & Spring, F. (2004) 'Rethinking Indigenous Homelessness', *AHURI Research and Policy Bulletin*, issue 42, Australian Housing and Urban Research Unit: Melbourne.

Mennis, J. (2002) 'Socioeconomic Disadvantage and Environmentally Hazardous Facility Location in Pennsylvania', *Pennsylvania Geographer*, vol. 40, no. 2, pp. 113–24.

Mental Health Council of Australia (2005) *Not for Service: Experiences of Injustice and Despair in Mental Health Care in Australia*, Mental Health Council of Australia and the Brain and Mind Research Institute: Canberra.

Merton, R. (1968) *Anomie Theory: Social Theory and Social Structure*, The Free Press: New York.

Metcalfe, A. (1988) *For Freedom and Dignity: Historical Agency and Class Structures in the Coalfields of NSW*, Allen & Unwin: Sydney.

Middleton-Moz, J. (1999) *Boiling Point: The High Cost of Unhealthy Anger to Individuals and Society*, HCI Publishers: Deerfield.

Miles, A. (1981) *The Mentally Ill in Contemporary Society*, St. Martin's Press: New York.

Miles, R. (1982) *Racism and Migrant Labour*, Routledge, London.

Miller, C. F. (1993) 'Part-Time Participation over the Life Cycle among Married Women Who Work in the Market', *Applied Economics*, vol. 25, pp. 91–9.

Millett, K. (1968) *Sexual Politics*, Doubleday: New York.

Millman, O. (2014) 'Australian Woman Still 75 Years Behind on Pay Equality Says Oxfam', *The Guardian* 14 July, www.theguardian.com/world/2014/jul/14/australian-women-still-75-years-behind-on-pay-equality-says-oxfam

Mills, C. W. (1956) *The Power Elite*, Oxford University Press: New York.

Mitchell, J. (1971) *Women's Estate*, Penguin: Harmondsworth.

Moreton-Robinson, A. (2000) *Talkin' up to the White Woman: Indigenous Women and Feminism*, University of Queensland Press, St Lucia: Queensland.

Moreton-Robinson, A. (2004) 'Whiteness, Epistemology and Indigenous Representation', in A. Moreton-Robinson (ed.), *Whitening Race: Essays in Social and Cultural Criticism*, Aboriginal Studies Press: Canberra.

Morgan, D. H. J. (1999) 'Risk and Family Practices: Accounting for Change and Fluidity in Family Life', in E. B. Silva & C. Smart (eds), *The New Family?* Sage: London.

Morgan, G. & Poynting, S. (2012) *Global Islamophobia: Muslims and Moral Panic in the West*, Ashgate: Melbourne.

Morgan, J. (2014) 'Tuition Fee Caps Removed in Australian Federal Budget', *The Times Higher Education* 13 May.

Mukherjee, D. (1999) *Socio-economic Status and School System Enrolments*, Australian Centre for Equity Through Education, http://www.aeufederal.org.au/Publications/1999/DMukherjeepaper.pdf (accessed 20 April 2007).

Munro, R. (2000) 'Judicial Psychiatry in China and Its Political Abuses', *Columbia Journal of Asian Law*, vol. 14, pp. 1–128.

Murray, C. (2001) *Underclass + 10: Charles Murray and the British Underclass 1990–2000*, Institute for the Study of Civil Society, in association with *Sunday Times*, London, www.civitas.org.uk/pdf/cs10.pdf (accessed 30 December 2007).

Natalier, K., Walter, M., Wulff, M., Reynolds, M., Baxter, J. & Hewitt, B. (2007) *Child Support and Housing Outcomes: Positioning Paper*, AHURI: Melbourne.

National Tertiary Education Union (2014) *A Degree Shouldn't Cost a Mortgage: The Facts*, www.nteu.org.au/degreemortgage/facts

NBEET (1999) *Rural and Isolation Students and their Higher Education Choices: A Re-examination of Student Location, Socio-economic Background and Educational Advantage and Disadvantage*, National Board of Employment, Education and Training, AGPS: Canberra.

Newman, J. (2000) 'The Challenge of Welfare Dependency in the 21st Century', discussion paper presented at the Welfare Reform Reference Group, Department of Family and Community Services: Canberra.

Nicholson, T. (2004) 'Rubbery Figures Hide Real Jobless Figures', *The Age* 17 December.

Nicoll, F. (2004) 'Reconciliation in and out of Perspective: White Knowing, Seeing, Curating and Being at Home in and Against Indigenous Sovereignty', in A. Moreton-Robinson (ed.), *Whitening Race: Essays in Social and Cultural Criticism*, Aboriginal Studies Press: Canberra.

Norman, J. (2013) 'More Single-Parent Households Living in Poverty, HILDA Survey Finds', *ABC News* 12 June, www.abc.net.au/news/2013-06-12/more-single-parent-households-living-in-poverty-hilda-survey/4747710

Northern Territory Department of Education (1999) *Learning Lessons: An Independent Review of Indigenous Education in the Northern Territory*, www.education.nt.gov.au/__data/assets/pdf_file/0005/7475/learning_lessons_review.pdf (accessed 28 August 2014).

Northern Territory Emergency Response (2011) *Northern Territory Emergency Response Evaluation Report*, http://apo.org.au/research/northern-territory-emergency-response-evaluation-report-2011

Norton, A. (2000) 'Nothing to Fear from Reform', *On Line Opinion*, www.onlineopinion.com.au/view.asp?article=1005 (accessed 30 December 2007).

Norton, A. (2012) *Mapping Australian Higher Education*, Grattan Institute.

O'Connor, J., Orloff, A. & Shaver, S. (1999) *States, Markets, Families: Gender, Liberalism and Social Policy in Australia, Canada, Great Britain and the United States*, Cambridge University Press: Cambridge.

OECD (2012) *OECD Country Profiles, Australia: Student Performance (PISA 2012)*, http://gpseducation.oecd.org/CountryProfile?primaryCountry=AUS&treshold=10&topic=PI (accessed 16 June 2014).

OECD (2013a) *Income Distribution and Poverty* http://stats.oecd.org/Index.aspx?DataSetCode=IDD (accessed 16 June 2014).

OECD (2013b) *Education at a Glance, Country Note, Australia*, www.oecd.org/edu/Australia_EAG2013%20Country%20Note.pdf (accessed 27 May 2014).

OECD (2014) *Life Satisfaction*, OECD Better Life Index, www.oecdbetterlifeindex.org/topics/life-satisfaction (accessed 17 August 2014).

Olsberg, D. (2005) 'Women, Superannuation and Retirement: Grim Prospects Despite Policy Changes', *Just Policy*, no. 35, pp. 31–8.

O'Neill, J. (1999) 'Economy, Equality and Recognition', in L. Ray & A. Sayer (eds), *Culture and Economy after the Cultural Turn*, Sage: London.

Orum, A. M. (2001) *Introduction to Political Sociology*, Prentice Hall: Upper Saddle River.

Ostry, J. D., Berg, A. & Tsangarides, C. G. (2014) *Redistribution, Inequality and Growth*, staff discussion note, International Monetary Fund.

O'Sullivan, M. (2005) 'Behind the Urban Curtains', *Sydney Morning Herald* 4 March.

Pakulski, J. (2004) *Globalising Inequalities: New Patterns of Social Privilege and Disadvantage*, Allen & Unwin: Sydney.

Pakulski, J. & Waters, M. (1996) *The Death of Class*, Sage: London.

Paris, C. (1993) *Housing Australia*, Macmillan Education Australia: Melbourne.

Parker, S., Limbers, L. & McKeon, E. (2002) *Homelessness and Mental Illness: Mapping the Way Home*, Mental Health Coordinating Council: Sydney.

Parliament of Western Australia (2007) *Inquiry into the Cause and Extent of Lead Pollution in the Esperance Area*, Education and Health Standing Committee, report no. 8, September 2007, www.parliament.wa.gov.au/Parliament%5Ccommit.nsf/(Report+Lookup+by+Com+ID) /28F900665F5C386048257831003E970C/$file/COMPLETE+REPORT.FINAL.PT1. pdf (accessed 24 June 2014).

Parsons, T. (1954 [1940]) 'An Analytical Approach to the Theory of Social Stratification', in T. Parsons (ed.), *Essays in Sociological Theory* (rev. edn), Macmillan: New York.

Pearson, N. (1999) 'Positive and Negative Welfare and Australia's Indigenous Communities', *Family Matters*, vol. 54, pp. 30–5.

Pegg, J. (2007) 'The Widening Educational Divide', *ABC News*, 3 January.

Phillips, B., Chin, S. F. & Harding, A. (2006) 'Housing Stress Today: Estimates for Statistical Local Areas in 2005', Australian Consortium for Social and Political Research Incorporated Conference, Sydney, 10–13 December 2006, NATSEM: Canberra.

Phillips, T. & Smith, P. (2000) 'What is "Australian"? Knowledge and Attitudes among a Gallery of Contemporary Australians', *Australian Journal of Political Science*, vol. 35, pp. 203–24.

PIAAC (2012) *Australia: Survey of Adult Skills*, http://gpseducation.oecd.org/CountryProfile? primaryCountry=AUS&treshold=10&topic=AS (accessed 27 May 2014).

Piketty, T. (2013) *Capital in the Twenty-First Century*, Harvard University Press: New York.

PISA (2012) *Australia: Student Performance*, http://gpseducation.oecd.org/CountryProfile? primaryCountry=AUS&treshold=10&topic=PI (accessed 27 May 2014).

Pocock, B. (2005) 'Work, Family and the Shy Social Scientist', in P. Saunders & J. Walker, *Ideas and Influence: Social Science and Social Policy in Australia*, UNSW Press: Sydney, pp. 123–40.

Poynting, S., Tabar, P. & Collins, J. (2004) *Bin Laden in the Suburbs: Criminalising the Arab Other*, Institute of Criminology and the Federation Press: Canberra.

Poynting, S. & Mason, V. (2006) 'Tolerance, Freedom, Justice and Peace?: Britain, Australia and Anti-Muslim Racism Since 11th September 2001', *Journal of Intercultural Studies*, vol. 27, no. 4, pp. 365–92.

Poynting, S. (2007) 'The Resistible Rise of Islamophobia: Anti-Muslim Racism in the UK and Australia before September 11 2001', *Journal of Sociology*, vol. 43, no. 1, pp. 61–86.

Probono Australia (2014) 'Welfare System Shake-Up', http://probonoaustralia.com.au/ news/2014/01/welfare-system-shake# (accessed 1 July 2014).

Productivity Commission (2014) *Report on Government Services 2014: Indigenous Compendium*, http://apo.org.au/research/report-government-services-2014 (accessed 17 August 2014).

Pusey, M. (1991) *Economic Rationalism in Canberra: A Nation-Building State Changes Its Mind*, Cambridge University Press: Cambridge.

Pusey, M. (2003) *The Experience of Middle Australia*, Cambridge University Press: Cambridge.

Putnam, R. D. (2007) 'E Pluribus Unum: Diversity and Community in the Twenty-First Century – The 2006 Johan Skytte Prize', *Scandinavian Political Studies*, vol. 30, no. 2.

Redmond, P. (2006) 'First Aid for Female Casualties of the Information Highway', *Australian Educational Computing*, June, vol. 21, no. 1, pp. 26–32.

Reynolds, H. (2005) *Nowhere People*, Viking: Melbourne.

Richardson, D. & Denniss, R. (2014) *Income and Wealth Inequality in Australia*, policy brief no. 64, The Australia Institute.

Robbins, D. (2000) *Pierre Bourdieu*, Sage: London.

Rodgers, J. R. & Rodgers, J. L. (2010) 'Chronic and Transitory Poverty over the Life Cycle', *Australian Journal of Labour Economics* vol. 13, no. 2, pp. 117–36.

Rodrigues, M. (2003) 'First Home Buyers in Australia', Economic Roundup 2003–04, Domestic Economy Division, Australian Treasury: Canberra.

Rofe, M. W. (2006) 'New Landscapes of Gated Communities: Australia's Sovereign Islands', *Landscape Research*, vol. 31, no. 3, pp. 309–17.

Rose, N. (1996) *Inventing Ourselves*, Cambridge University Press: Cambridge.

Roth, L. (2007) 'Multiculturalism', New South Wales Parliamentary Library Research Service briefing paper no. 9/07, New South Wales Parliament: Sydney.

Rowbotham, S. (1977) *Hidden from History*, Pluto Press, London.

Rowntree, B. S. (1901) *Poverty: A Study of Town Life*, Macmillan: London.

Rowse, T. & Groot, M. (2007) *Divided Nation: Indigenous Affairs and the Imagined Public*, Melbourne University Press: Melbourne.

Royal Commission into Aboriginal Deaths in Custody (1991) *National Report*, AGPS: Canberra.

Rubin, G. (1975) 'The Traffic in Women: Notes on the "Political Economy" of Sex', in R. Reiter, *Toward an Anthropology of Women*, Monthly Review Press: New York.

Said, E. (1978) *Orientalism*, Routledge & Kegan Paul, London.

Saunders, M. (2002) 'Blacks in Shift to the Cities', *The Australian* 27 June.

Saunders, P. (ed.) (2000) *Reforming the Australian Welfare State*, Australian Institute of Family Studies: Melbourne.

Saunders, P. (2003) 'Can Social Exclusion Provide a Framework for Measuring Poverty?', SPRC Discussion Paper no. 127, Social Policy Research Centre, University of New South Wales: Sydney.

Saunders, P. (2004a) *Australia's Welfare Habit and How to Kick It*, Duffy & Snellgrove: Sydney, with the Centre for Independent Studies: Sydney.

Saunders, P. (2004b) 'Lies, Damned Lies and the Senate Poverty Inquiry Report', *Issues Analysis*, no. 46, Centre for Independent Studies: Sydney.

Saunders, P., Naidoo, Y. & Griffiths, M. (2007) *Towards New Indicators of Disadvantage: Deprivation and Social Exclusion in Australia*, Social Policy Research Centre, University of New South Wales: Sydney.

Saunders, P. (2007a) 'Elitism Should Not Be a Dirty Word', *The Australian* 13 August, www.theaustralian.com.au/archive/news/elitism-should-not-be-a-dirty-word/story-e6frg73o-1111114166945 (accessed 14 September 2014).

Saunders, P. (2007b) 'They're Not Really That Poor', *On Line Opinion*, www.onlineopinion.com.au/view.asp?article=6576 (accessed 8 April 2008).

Saunders, P. & Naidoo, Y. (2008) *Social Exclusion and Children*, Towards New Indicators of Disadvantage Project, bulletin no. 4, Social Policy Research Centre, University of NSW: Sydney,   www.bsl.org.au/pdfs/SPRC_tow_new_indicators_of_disadv_bulletin_no4.pdf (accessed 20 June 2014).

Saunders, P. & Wong, M. (2009) *Still Doing It Tough: An Update on Deprivation and Social Exclusion among Welfare Service Clients*, Social Policy Research Centre, University of NSW: Sydney.

Savage, M. (2000) *Class Analysis and Social Transformation*, Oxford University Press: Oxford.

Savy, P. (2005) 'Closing Asylums for the Mentally Ill: Social Consequences', *Health Sociology Review*, vol. 14, no. 3.

Sawyer, A. (2005) 'Deinstitutionalisation and the Conceptualisation of Psychiatric "Risk": The Perspective of a Crisis Team Clinician', *Health Sociology Review*, vol. 14, no. 3.

Sawyer, M. (1976) *Income Distribution in OECD Countries*, OECD: Paris.

Sawyer, M. (2011) 'Translating Mental Health Policy into Practice: Ongoing Challenges and Frustrations', *Health Sociology Review*, vol. 20, no. 2, pp. 114–19.

Schultz, J. (ed.) (2007) *Griffith Review 15: Divided Nation*, ABC Books.

Scutt, J. (2011) 'Denying Childhood: Exploitation and the Body Image of Six-Year Olds', *On Line Opinion* 9 September, www.onlineopinion.com.au/view.asp?article=12585&page=0

Senate Community Affairs References Committee (2004) *A Hand Up, Not a Hand Out: Renewing the Fight Against Poverty*, Senate, Parliament House, Commonwealth of Australia: Canberra.

Sennett, R. & Cobb, J. (1993[1972]) *The Hidden Injuries of Class*, Norton: London.

Sennett, R. (2006) *The Culture of the New Capitalism*, Yale University Press: New Haven.

Shadish, W. R., Lurigio, A. J. & Lewis, D. A. (1989) 'After Deinsitutionalisation: The Present and Future of Mental Health Long-Term', *Journal of Social Issues*, vol. 45, no. 3, pp. 1–15.

Shaver, S. (1998) 'Poverty, Gender and Sole Parenthood', in R. Fincher & J. Neiuwenhuysen (eds), *Australian Poverty: Then and Now*, Melbourne University Press: Melbourne.

Shilling, C. (1991) 'Educating the Body: Physical Capital and the Production of Social Inequalities', *Sociology*, vol. 25, pp. 653–72.

Shilling, C. & Mellor, P. (2001) *The Sociological Ambition*, Sage: London.

Silva, E. B. (1996) 'The Transformation of Mothering', in E. B. Silva (ed.), *Good Enough Mothering? Feminist Perspectives on Lone Motherhood*, Routledge: London.

Skeggs, B. (1997) *Formations of Class and Gender*, Sage: London.

Skinner, N., Hutchinson, C. & Pocock, B. (2012) *The Big Squeeze: Work, Home and Care in 2012*, Australian Work and Life Index 2012, University of South Australia, http://w3.unisa.edu. au/hawkeinstitute/cwl/documents/AWALI2012-National.pdf (accessed 19 June 2014).

Sky News (2014) 'NT Minister Says Land Rights Act Should Go', 16 June www.skynews.com. au/news/politics/national/2014/06/16/nt-minister-says-land-rights-act-should-go.html (accessed 17 August 2014).

Smith, B. & Tomazin, F. (2007) 'Parents Shun State Education', *The Age* 27 February, p. 1.

Smith, P. (2001) *Cultural Theory: An Introduction*, Blackwell Publishing: Oxford.

Smith, P. & Phillips, T. (2001) 'Popular Understandings of the "UnAustralian"', *Journal of Sociology*, vol. 37, no. 4, pp. 323–39.

Smith, T. (1996) *No Asylum: State Psychiatric Repression in the Former USSR*, New York University Press: New York.

Smoyak, S. (2004) 'US Mental Health Policy: Progress and Continuing Problems', in G. Morrall & M. Hazelton (eds), *Mental Health: Global Policies and Human Rights*, Whurr: London.

Standing, G. (2011) *The Precariat: The New Dangerous Classes*, Bloomsbury Academic: London.

Standing, G. (2014) *The Precariat Charter: From Denizens to Citizens*, Bloomsbury Academic: London.

Stanford, D. (2013) 'Income Inequality in Australia: Looking behind the Headline Figures', *VCOSS Voice*, 5 August, Victorian Council of Social Service, http://vcoss.org.au/blog/income-inequality-in-australia-looking-behind-the-headline-figures

Sullivan, L. (2000) 'A Sorry Tale: Welfare against the Family', in P. Saunders (ed.), *Reforming the Australian Welfare State*, Australian Institute of Family Studies: Melbourne.

Swartz, D. (1997) *Culture and Power*, Chicago University Press: London.

Szasz, T. (1970) *The Manufacture of Madness: A Comparative Study of the Inquisition and the Mental Health Movement*, Harper & Row: New York.

Tatz, C. (1982) *Aborigines and Uranium and Other Essays*, Heinemann: Melbourne.

Taylor, J. & Stanley, O. (2005) 'The Opportunity Costs of the Status Quo in the Thamarrurr Region', CAEPR working paper 28, Australian National University: Canberra.

Taylor, J. (2006) *Population and Diversity: Policy Implications of Emerging Indigenous Demographic Trends*, CAEPR discussion paper no. 283/2006, Canberra.

Taylor, M. (2014) 'It's All Relative: The Poverty Wars Are Back', *The Drum* 4 February. www.abc.net.au/news/2014-02-04/taylor-poverty-wars/5237878

Teeple, G. (2000) *Globalization and the Decline of Social Reform: Into the Twenty-First Century*, Garamond: Vancouver.

Tillyard, E. (1952) *The Elizabethan World Picture*, Chatto & Windus: London.

Tomlinson, J. (2004) 'Competing Views of the Benefits of Higher Education', *On Line Opinion*, www.onlineopinion.com.au/view.asp?article=2150 (accessed 30 December 2007).

Touraine, A. (1974) *The Post-Industrial Society*, Random House: New York.

Townsend, P. (1993) *The International Analysis of Poverty*, Harvester Wheatsheaf: London.

Travers, P. & Richardson, S. (1993) *Living Decently: Material Well-Being in Australia*, Oxford University Press: Melbourne.

Trent, F. & Slade, M. (2001) *Declining Rates of Achievement and Retention: The Perceptions of Adolescent Males*, Department of Education, Training and Youth Affairs, Commonwealth of Australia: Canberra.

Trigger, D. (2003) 'Does the Way We Measure Poverty Matter?' discussion paper no. 59, NATSEM: Canberra.

Trinca, H. & Fox, C. (2004) *Better than Sex: How a Whole Generation Got Hooked on Work*, Random House, Sydney.

Turner, B. (1996 [1984]) *The Body and Society: Explorations in Social Theory*, Sage: London.

Turrell, G. & Mathers, C. (2000) 'Socioeconomic Status and Health in Australia', *Medical Journal of Australia*, vol. 172, pp. 434–8.

United Nations (1991) *Principles for the Protection of Persons with Mental Illness and the Improvement of Mental Health Care*, www.un.org/documents/ga/res/46/a46r119.htm (accessed 30 August 2014).

United Nations Development Program (2013) *The 2013 Human Development Report—The Rise of the South: Human Progress in a Diverse World*, Human Development Report Office, United Nations Development Program, pp. 144–7.

Veblen, T. (2006 [1899]) *Theory of the Leisure Class*, Allen & Unwin: London.

Vickers, M. (2005) 'In the Common Good: The Need for a New Approach to Funding Australia's Schools', *Australian Journal of Education*, vol. 49, no. 3, pp. 264–77.

Vieira, S. (2012) *Inequality on the Rise? An Assessment of Current Available Data on Income Inequality at Global, International and National Levels*, background document for the WESS 2013, United Nations Department of Economic and Social Affairs.

Vinson, T. (2007) *Dropping Off the Edge: The Distribution of Disadvantage in Australia*, Catholic Social Services Australia and Jesuit Social Services: Canberra, www.australiandisadvantage. org.au/order.html (accessed 30 January 2008).

Wacquant, L. (1999) 'How Penal Common Sense Comes to Europeans: Notes on the Transatlantic Diffusion of Neoliberal Doxa', *European Societies*, vol. 1, no. 3, pp. 319–52.

Wacquant, L. (2004) *Punishing the Poor: The Neoliberal Government of Social Insecurity*, Duke University Press: London.

Wade, M. (2013) 'Howard Baby Bonus Out but $2.4b in Savings Is In' *Sydney Morning Herald* 14 May, www.smh.com.au/business/federal-budget/howard-baby-bonus-out-but-24b-in-savings-is-in-20130514-2jkre.html (accessed 20 June 2014).

Walter, J. & Woerner, J. (2007) *The Well-Being of Australians: Groups with the Highest and Lowest Well-Being in Australia*, Australian Unity Well-Being Index Survey, 16 January, special report, Australian Centre on Quality of Life, Deakin University: Geelong.

Walter, M. (2002) 'Working Their Way out of Poverty: Sole Motherhood, Work, Welfare and Material Well-Being', *Journal of Sociology*, vol. 38, no. 4, pp. 361–80.

Walter, M. (2004) 'Family Is a Doing Word', *On Line Opinion*, www.onlineopinion.com.au/view .asp?article=2819 (accessed 5 September 2014).

Walter, M. (2007) 'Aboriginality, Poverty and Health: Exploring the Connection', in I. Anderson, F. Baum & M. Bentley (eds), *Beyond Bandaids: Exploring the Underlying Social Determinants of Indigenous Health*, Co-operative Research Centre for Aboriginal Health: Darwin.

Walter, M. & Jackson, N. (2007) *Keeping Australia's Baby Boomers in the Labour Force. A Policy Perspective*, Demographic Analytical Services, research project no. 2, retirement research report, University of Tasmania.

Walter, M. & Saggers, S. (2007) 'Poverty and Social Class', in B. Carson, T. Dunbar, R. Chenhall & R. Bailie (eds), *Social Determinants of Indigenous Health*, Allen & Unwin: Sydney.

Walter, M. (2008) 'Lives of Diversity: Indigenous Australians', *Occasional paper 4/2008, Census Series*, no. 2, Australian Academy of the Social Sciences: Canberra.

Warner, R. (1989) 'Deinstitutionalisation: How Did We Get Where We Are?' *Journal of Social Issues*, vol. 45, no. 3.

Watson, I. (2005) 'Contented Workers in Inferior Jobs? Re-assessing Casual Employment in Australia', *Journal of Industrial Relations*, vol. 4, no. 4, pp. 371–92.

Watson, L. (2003) 'Lifelong Learning in Australia', Department of Education, Science and Training, EIP report no. 3, 13 October.

Weber, M. (1946) 'Science As a Vocation', in H. H. Gerth & C. Wright Mills (trans. & eds), *From Max Weber: Essays in Sociology*, Oxford University Press: New York.

Weber, M. (1949) 'Objectivity in Social Science', in E. Shils & H. French (eds), *The Methodology of the Social Sciences*, The Free Press: New York.

Weber, M. (1976 [1904]) *The Protestant Ethic and the Spirit of Capitalism*, Allen & Unwin: London.

Weber, M. (1978 [1922]) *Economy and Society: An Outline of Interpretive Sociology*, G. Roth & C. Wittich (eds), University of California Press: Berkeley.

Weller, S. & Webber, M. (2001) 'Precarious Employment and Occupational Change', in J. Borland, R. Gregory & P. Sheehan (eds), *Work Rich, Work Poor: Inequality and Economic Change in Australia*, CFES: Sydney.

West, A. (2006) *Inside the Lifestyles of the Rich and Tasteful*, Pluto Press: Melbourne.

Western, M. & Baxter, J. (2007) 'Class and Inequality in Australia', in J. Germov & M. Poole (eds), *Public Sociology*, Allen & Unwin: Sydney.

Western Australian Aboriginal Child Health Survey (2007) *Improving the Educational Experiences of Aboriginal Children and Young People: Summary Booklet*, Telethon Institute for Child Health Research: Perth.

Weston, R. (1993) 'Income Circumstances of Parents and Children: A Longitudinal View', in K. Funder, M. Harrison & R. Weston (eds), *Settling Down Pathways of Parents After Divorce*, monograph no. 13, Australian Institute of Family Studies: Melbourne.

Weston, R. & Smyth, B. (2000) 'Financial Living Standards after Divorce', *Family Matters*, vol. 55, pp. 11–15.

White, N. (2000) 'Creativity Is the Name of the Game', in M. Bin-Sallik (ed.), *Aboriginal Women by Degrees: Their Stories of the Journey towards Academic Achievement*, University of Queensland Press: Brisbane, pp. 92–106.

White, R. (1981) *Inventing Australia*, Allen & Unwin: Sydney.

Whiteford, P. (1997) *Pattern of Benefit Receipt among Lone Parent Families: A Comparison of Australia, New Zealand, the United Kingdom and the United States*, Department of Social Security: Canberra.

Wilkinson, R. & Pickett, K. (2009) *The Spirit Level: Why More Equal Societies almost Always Do Better*, Allen Lane: London.

Williams, C. (1981) *Opencut. The Working Class in an Australian Mining Town*, Allen & Unwin: Sydney.

Williams, D. R. & Neighbors, H. (2001) 'Racism, Discrimination and Hypertension: Evidence and Needed Research', *Ethnicity and Disease*, vol. 11, no. 4, pp. 800–16.

Wilmott, P. & Young, D. (1962) *Family and Kinship in East London*, Penguin: Harmondsworth.

Wilson, B. (2014) *A Share in the Future: Review of Indigenous Education in the Northern Territory*, www.education.nt.gov.au/__data/assets/pdf_file/0007/37294/A-Share-in-the-Future-The-Review-of-Indigenous-Education-in-the-Northern-Territory.pdf

Wing, J. K. (1967) 'Institutionalism in Mental Hospitals', in T. J. Scheff (ed.), *Mental Illness and Social Processes*, Harper & Row: New York.

Workplace Gender Equality Agency (2014) *Gender Pay Gap Statistics*, Australian Government, www.wgea.gov.au/sites/default/files/2014-03-04-Gender_Pay_Gap_factsheet_website. pdf

Wing Sue, D. (2003) *What Does It Mean to be White? The Invisible Whiteness of Being* (DVD), Microtraining and Multicultural Development: New York.

Winter, I. (1994) *The Radical Home Owner: Housing Tenure and Social Change*, Gordon & Breach: Basel.

Winter, I. & Stone, W. (1998) 'Social Polarisation and Housing Careers: Exploring the Interrelationship of Labour and Housing Markets in Australia', working paper no. 13, Australian Institute of Family Studies: Melbourne.

Wooden, M. & Drago, R. (2007) 'The Changing Distribution of Working Hours in Australia', Melbourne Institute Working Paper Series, no. 19/07, Melbourne Institute of Applied Economic and Social Research, University of Melbourne: Melbourne.

Workplace Gender Equality Agency (2014) *Gender Pay Gap Statistics*, Australian Government, www.wgea.gov.au/sites/default/files/2014-03-04-Gender_Pay_Gap_factsheet_website.pdf

Wright, E. O. (1997) *Class Counts: Comparative Studies in Class Analysis*, Cambridge University Press: New York.

Wright, E. O. (2005) 'Foundations of a Neo-Marxist Class Analysis', in E. O. Wright (ed.), *Approaches to Class Analysis*, Cambridge University Press: Cambridge.

Wulff, M., Yates, J. & Burke, T. (2001) *Low Rent Housing in Australia, 1986–1996: How Has It Changed, Who Does It Work for and Who Does It Fail?* FaCS: Canberra.

Xavier, A. (2014) 'BRW Executive Rich List 2014: The 100 Wealthiest Bosses in Australia', *Business Review Weekly* 31 March.

Yeatman, A. (1990) *Femocrats, Technocrats, Bureaucrats: Essays on the Contemporary Australian State*, Allen & Unwin: Sydney.

Yeatman, A. (2000) 'Mutual Obligation: What Sort of Contract Is This?', in P. Saunders (ed.), *Reforming the Australian Welfare State*, Australian Institute of Family Studies: Melbourne.

Young, J. (1999) *The Exclusive Society*, Sage, London.

Index

Printed in Australia
17 Aug 2017
643531